STAGECRAFT

A Handbook for Organization, Construction, and Management

STAGECRAFT

A Handbook for Organization, Construction, and Management

David Welker   *Wake Forest University*

Allyn and Bacon, Inc.   Boston, London, Sydney

Library of Congress Cataloging in Publication Data

Welker, David Harold.
    Stagecraft: a handbook for organization, construction, and management.

    Includes index.
    1. Stage management.   I. Title.
PN2085.W4   792'.025   76–25534
ISBN 0–205–05589–3

10 9 8 7 6 5 4 3   85 84 83 82 81 80

In dedicating this book, I wish I could mention the hundreds of people to whom I owe an overwhelming debt, from whom I am sure I have learned far more than I ever taught them, and who have shared with me triumphs and tragedies, crises and achievements during more than a third of a century of work in the scene shop, but I can give only a few names, each of which will have to stand for dozens more. First is my wife,

Dorothy Welker

who has spent hundreds of hours in the scene shop, sawing, nailing, and painting—work which, though uncongenial, she does with great skill; who has always been willing to help in an emergency; who has prepared vast quantities of punch, cake, and cookies to help students through strikes; and whose skill as a photographer has contributed even more to this book than to my previous texts.

And I have a special debt of gratitude to my sister-in-law,

Mrs. Inez Hall

who helped enthusiastically in building the scenery for my first play as a college teacher.

Among my many students, Gay Lynn Reiter and her husband Osborne Allen Brines II are unique in that both served as shop supervisors during my years in Michigan, and then continued their scene shop work as graduate students in North Carolina.

And finally, two of the finest stagecraft workers with whom I have been associated, Whitney Ballantine, who chose a career in stagecraft after graduation from college; and Mrs. Paula Starks Wilson, who stopped in the scene shop one day out of curiosity, spent the next two years working superbly while protesting that she had no interest in the theater, and then married a technical director. I could go on and on—but these will have to do.

Contents

PART
II
CONSTRUCTION

CHAPTER 9   Plastics   203

CHAPTER 10   Paint Mixing   218

CHAPTER 11 Base Painting and Texturing 239

CHAPTER 12 Detail Painting 261

Contents

CHAPTER 13 Set-Up and Strike

CHAPTER 14   Shifting   322

PART
III
SCENE-SHOP MANAGEMENT

CHAPTER 15   Organizing the Scene Shop   337

CHAPTER 16   Purchasing   352

Preface

Stagecraft skills must be learned; no one is born knowing how to build a flat. Such skills are acquired in three different ways. In community theaters, the laboratory method of training is used almost exclusively; apprentice workers are paired with more experienced people, all of whom operate under the supervision of the technical director.

Not infrequently, people without theatrical experience may be thrown into a position where they must construct scenery or direct actors; that is most often the case in high schools without formal drama programs, in which, as one music teacher said, "I've never set foot on stage, and suddenly I've been told I have to build scenery, plan lighting, and direct our fall show." Necessarily, such a situation requires an emergency cram course, including study of a basic text.

The third method of mastering stagecraft is really a combination of the first two; the worker enrolls in a formal course, with theoretical material presented in an orderly fashion, and with out-of-class laboratory work provided, so that he can apply and master the principles which he has studied in class. This text is primarily planned for such a course, on the college level, but an effort has been made to prepare it so that it will be of equal value as a supplement to the experience of working in a community theater, or for the theater worker who must master stagecraft essentially on his own.

The needs of workers in the various situations are of course not in conflict. Even in college classes, perhaps more than half the students will have had little or no experience in stagecraft, and need full information, clearly stated. The book presents the basic techniques; odd problems, methods seldom used, and materials which might be needed only once every fifteen years have been omitted. When a particular project might be done in various equally effective ways, the one which seems simplest and most convenient has generally been described, occasionally with a note that other methods are possible. The discussion is thus not intended to be all-inclusive, and instructors or technical directors should feel free to substitute other techniques if they find them more convenient. A full treatment of each topic would, at a conservative estimate, have required more than a thousand pages.

The text is unusual in three ways. The first has already been mentioned: an attempt has been made to write it so that it will be clear to the student without previous theatrical experience, without at the same time simplifying the techniques or watering down the information.

The second is the assistance given in scene-shop management. Any stagecraft worker who continues in the theater past his first play or his introductory course is almost certain to be given supervisory responsibilities at some level, and a very large percentage of workers will need to make administrative decisions in later years, including choosing and training a staff, organizing space, and making out purchase orders. The last section of the book is intended to assist them in handling those responsibilities, and probably should be turned to first by the inexperienced person who is suddenly thrown into a position in which he must supervise a production or a full season's program.

Finally, more than a hundred special techniques are scattered throughout the book, set off in boxes. A very few of them are standard methods with which experienced stagecraft workers are familiar; most of them are recent discoveries, some of them made by students. It is hoped that they may be of assistance in solving some of the troublesome problems which constantly arise, and for which the established procedures provide no easy solutions.

Even though the work must often be done under less than ideal conditions, set construction is one of the most interesting of the various theater crafts. Every crew member who works with alertness and dedication makes a discovery which is one of the pleasantest of all experiences—that he can develop unsuspected skills, and that he can do well work which he did not realize he could do at all. The inherent interest of the work, the sharing with others in a complex activity directed toward a common goal, the relaxed informality of the scene shop, and the easy camaraderie which develops among the workers, as well as the experience of personal growth, all make stagecraft work something to be remembered with pleasure. It is hoped that this text will contribute to the ease and effectiveness of that work, and to the pleasantness of those memories.

David Welker

PART
I
INTRODUCTION

1

The Production Staff Takes a Bow

The curtain has just fallen on the last performance of Georges Feydeau's hilarious farce, *A Flea in Her Ear*. As the audience applauds, the curtain rises again, and the costume designer trots on from a door in the stage-right wall, followed by the ten-person costume crew; simultaneously the lighting designer appears through a door in the stage-left wall, with the six members of the light and sound crews. They assemble at the front edge of the stage for their bow, and then separate to make way for the stage manager, the production manager, the business and publicity staffs, and the fourteen-member properties crew.

At this point, a cry rings out from the audience, "Set crew! Set crew!", and the set designer, technical director, shop foreman, shop assistants, the ten scene-shifters and the twenty-four members of the set-construction staff burst through the door at the center of the back wall of the set. The staff members already on stage part like the waters of the Red Sea, and the set workers move into the opening and take their bow, and then separate in turn to make way for Jean-Phillipe Christophe Grill, who has spent a month working on the intricate mechanism for a trick revolving platform used in the play. Chris advances to the front of the stage, falls on one knee and holds out his arms in the traditional Waldensian gesture of triumph and thanksgiving toward the audience, who respond by leaping to their feet, rhythmically chanting "Set crew! Set crew!", and wildly throwing wadded-up play programs into the air. By the time the curtain has at last fallen, and the house lights have been brought up, the actors—who for this one time did not take bows—have removed their makeup, and have nearly finished changing into their street clothes.

It is probably obvious that what has just been described is pure fiction; the rest of this text is factual. Rather than occupying center-stage, even for a curtain call, the production staff is hidden from the audience, before, during, and after a performance. Few members of the audience will be more than dimly aware of who the technical workers are or what they have contributed to the production. They are listed on the program, but that is the part of the program no one reads—except parents looking for the names of their sons and daughters. The attention of the audience is—quite properly —on the actors, and on what they say and do; the technical aspects of the production are simply there, taken for granted, seldom noticed focally or consciously.

FIGURE 1.1   Scenery indicates locale. Mrs. Condomine and Madame Arcati have tea in a British living room. (A set for Noel Coward's *Blithe Spirit*.)

THE FUNCTIONS OF SCENERY

The work of the crews is of vital importance to the effectiveness of a play. Lighting not only makes the actors visible, it can indicate the time of day, provide atmospheric effects, and set the tone of the performance, preparing the audience for a bright farce, a romantic drama, or a somber tragedy. Properties establish locale and time, costumes and makeup help the actors in creating and expressing their characters. But of all technical elements in a production, the setting typically bulks largest. In fact, all of the purposes of the other production elements (and only a few have been listed) are also served by scenery, which reinforces them and provides a solid foundation for the total experience of the audience.

FIGURE 1.2   A bachelor apartment. Notice the impersonal, cliché decoration (zebra cloth, beaded curtains, tufted leather), the drink–fixings on the bar, *left*, the general mess. Not shown in this photograph is an op–art painting of a nude, four feet by six feet, hanging over the desk behind the sofa. (Neil Simon's *Come Blow Your Horn*.)

The scenery is the most visible element of production, occupying a larger area of the stage picture than even the actors themselves. It gives the audience information about the period and locale of a play (Figures 1.1, 1.2, 1.3), saying "This is an ancient castle" (*Macbeth*), or "This is the boardwalk at Atlantic City" (*The Skin of Our Teeth*), or "This is a room in the White House" (*Indians*). The scenery expresses the mood of the play (Figures 1.4, 1.5, 1.6) by the use of appropriate and affective colors and shapes, perhaps by employing the varied colors, twisting lines, and asymmetrical shapes of the art nouveau style to support the farcical speed of *A Flea in Her Ear*, or dark masses of rough stone to set the mood for the tragic terror of Euripedes' *Medea.*

Most importantly, however, the scenery assists the actors in creating the intended experience for the audience (Figures 1.7, 1.8, 1.9). In one production of Shakespeare's *The Tempest*, a freely curving ramp was provided. It began at one side of the stage, above the heads of the audience, swung down and around over a broad opening, and

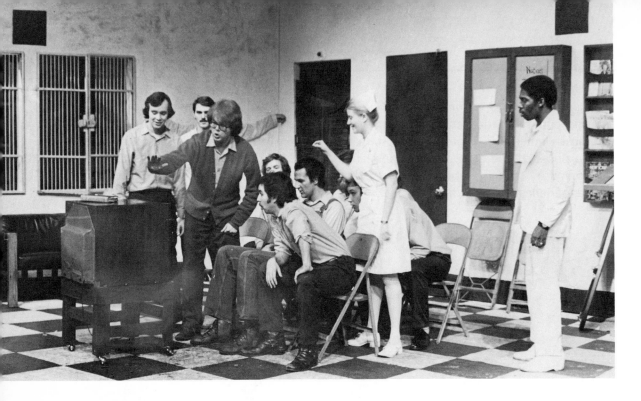

FIGURE 1.3 The lounge of a mental hospital. Notice the institutional decor, the bars on the windows and the signal lights and speakers built into the walls, as well as the spotted walls and the dirt ground permanently into the surface of the floor. (Ken Kesey's *One Flew Over the Cuckoo's Nest*.)

FIGURE 1.4 Scenery expresses the mood of the play. For a play based on fairy tales, the scenery is designed in the spirit of an illustration for a children's book. Painting is used symbolically. The audience is asked to pretend the walls and door of the house are real. Stair treads assume the shape of crescent moons, trees and bushes are shown in silhouette, folded back at an angle like pop-up pictures, and the trunks and branches of the trees writhe as if in motion, each one ending in a clutching three-fingered hand. (Paul Sills, *Story Theater*.)

FIGURE 1.5 The scenery swings in frothy curves suggestive of a Victorian picture frame, backed by lattice copied from summerhouses, to match the high-style burlesque of nineteenth-century attitudes in Oscar Wilde's *The Importance of Being Earnest*. (For another interpretation of this play see Figures 12.2 and 12.3.)

FIGURE 1.6 The stark tragedy of Lorca's *Blood Wedding* is suggested by asymmetric arches, undecorated walls, and bare, black furniture.

FIGURE 1.7   Ariel glides along a fog–covered ramp for a production of Shakespeare's *The Tempest.*

FIGURE 1.8   An apparently random arrangement of platforms, steps, and arches assists the actors in suggesting a trial, with the judges on the highest level, *left*, the prosecutor, *below left*. the accused confronting a witness, and, *between*, the inquisitor supervising the proceedings. (Jean Anouilh and Lillian Hellman, *The Lark*.)

FIGURE 1.9   The scenery, assisted by the imagination of the audience, makes the action of the play clear. While the farmer and his wife eat their supper, a donkey peers in the window, and a hound, a cat, and a rooster wait for his report of what he sees. (*Story Theater*.)

then curved across the stage and down toward the audience. During the performance, the ramp was flooded with a four-inch layer of heavier-than-air fog, which flowed along it and cascaded down over the edge like a waterfall. Appearing out of blackness, a tiny girl playing the part of Ariel glided along the surface, her feet hidden by the fog, apparently floating in a free path curving through the stage space. The assistance provided to the actress in creating the impression of an airy spirit is obvious; it would have been almost impossible to have produced the same effect with equal force and clarity on the bare stage floor, unassisted by scenery.

In another play, *A Thurber Carnival*, one scene requires that an actor pretend to row across the surface of the ocean in a canoe. The play is a comic romp, frankly make-believe. For one production, the set crew built an ingenious silhouette canoe, backed by a supporting structure designed so that the actor could stand inside it, swinging a paddle, with the canoe moving across the stage as he walked along. But the structure was set on eccentric wheels so arranged that as he moved it not only rocked up and down but also from side to side, the two movements being unsynchronized. The result was an effective imitation of the motion of an actual canoe on water; the contrast between the movement and the obvious artificiality of the canoe underlined the comic make-believe quality of the play.

Even more important is the assistance that scenery gives the actors in expressing their interrelationships, and also in controlling the focus of the audience's attention (Figures 1.10, 1.11). When one actor must dominate another, well designed scenery

FIGURE 1.10 In Tom Stoppard's unusual play *Rosencrantz and Guildenstern Are Dead,* the title characters stand at the edge of the action, less often taking part than observing, almost eavesdropping, as they do here.

FIGURE 1.11 The characters in Lanford Watson's *The Rimers of Eldritch* must express varied relationships, in different locales. An apparently random, but in fact carefully planned, series of platforms, with a few symbolic details, assists the actors. A model of the set, *top*; the actual set, *bottom*. *Left*, a cafe with counter and stool (*lower left in model*); *center*, a front porch (*lower right in model*, the railing has been altered to make the actors more visible); *right*, a store counter (*lower center of model*).

will provide the director with positions for both actors that will make it easy for them to express their relationship, perhaps by putting the dominant actor on a platform, and turning the other actor slightly away from the audience.

The exploration of the effect of scenery on theatrical productions is properly part of the study of set design rather than stagecraft, but since the scenery cannot function until it is built, painted, and assembled, an awareness of its importance is significant for the members of the set construction crew. The shape and placement of Ariel's ramp for *The Tempest* were planned by the designer, but if the construction workers had not cut the lumber according to specifications and fastened it together properly, the effect might well have been destroyed, and the entire ramp, instead of being rock-solid, might have collapsed when it was first used.

Especially when he is working on his first play, a set builder may find it difficult to visualize the contribution his project will make to the production. Most of the time he will be guided by what are called working drawings, which give important information about dimensions, joints, methods of fastening, and angles, but which do not indicate very clearly what the structure will look like when finished and set in place on stage. For a production of Anouilh's *The Lark,* one group of people was given the task of constructing an elaborate stained-glass window, six feet wide and twelve feet high, incorporating gothic arches as well as a large rose window (Figure 1.12). It was impossible to visualize the effect of the completed window; the patterns were fragmented and incomprehensible, the crew did most of the work from the back of the structure, and since the appearance depended primarily on the effect of light streaming through the panes, the workers were unable to imagine what it would look like in place, or how

FIGURE 1.12 A stained–glass window for *The Lark.*

important it was to the set as a whole. Furthermore the work was extremely tedious, and it was done in a grubby corner of the scene shop, with crew members sawing and hammering on other projects all around. But when the window was set in place and effectively lit, it not only became the dominant element in the set, but had a brilliance and magnificence which astonished the people who had worked on it. In fact, it was so effective that an engaged couple who attended the play asked if they could use it as the background for their wedding, which was held a few weeks after the end of the show, and which was moved to the theater just to take advantage of the window.

One such experience is enough to demonstrate vividly that even apparently meaningless and tedious scenic projects matter a great deal indeed, and the people who had worked on the window brought ample enthusiasm to their later set construction. For the student who is just starting in stagecraft, it is important to realize that working drawings do not tell the whole story, and that if he works hard and carefully, the result will be important to the play, and something of which he can be proud.

> Gels are an ideal material for representing stained glass, much more effective than the dyed muslin more commonly used. Gels (an inaccurate term) are sheets of colored plastic used to filter stage lights so as to alter their color. The heat of the spotlights tends to fade and wrinkle them, so that they are discarded in considerable quantities. On request, the light crew will save them for scenic use.
>
> The pattern of the leading for a stained glass window is drawn on a sheet of corrugated cardboard or light upson board, and the areas to be filled with glass are cut out with a knife. The cardboard is then fastened to a flat frame or whatever other support the window is to be set into, and painted a dark lead grey. The frame is turned over, and the gels cut to match the pattern (from three-eighths to half an inch larger than the holes), and fastened to the leading with masking tape or glue. If a more realistic effect is desired, the colors can be varied by combining two or more layers of the gel, using the same or different colors. When lit from behind, the effect is breathtaking.

THE PRODUCTION STAFF

The program for the performance of *A Flea in Her Ear,* which was mentioned earlier, lists 101 different people as having been involved in the production (not counting the playwright, the ushers, or the box-office attendants). A multitude of different activities were carried on by these people throughout the six weeks preceding opening night, ranging from the work of the speech consultant, who trained actors in diction, projection, and the use of dialects, to cast and crew members who sewed costumes, collected properties, hung lights, rehearsed the play, and, of course, designed, built, painted, set up, and shifted the scenery. One of the commonest remarks of people who have just begun work in the theater is, "I had no idea all this went on in preparing a play for performance—how in the world do you keep track of everything?"

Over the centuries, but particularly within the last hundred years, methods of organization and operation have been worked out which, if applied effectively, not only do bring order out of the apparent chaos, but make it possible for the work to proceed with at least relative calm, on schedule, efficiently, and with a minimum of friction and confusion. Everyone who works in the theater needs to understand the plan of operation as a whole, and especially his own responsibilities and his place in the pattern.

THE WORK OF THE DIRECTOR

Many different types of theater organization have been tried out in the past. The most significant step, however, in developing the modern system was taken about a hundred years ago, by such great artists as the Duke of Saxe-Meiningen and Constantin Stanislavski, who created a new position, or more sharply defined an old one—that of the director. One of the primary assignments of a director is the administrative job of coordinating the work of the entire staff, including the actors, so that all of the pieces of the production, when finally assembled on stage, fit together precisely to form a harmonious pattern, a unified work of art (Figure 1.13).

FIGURE 1.13   A chart showing the organization of the production staff for a play.

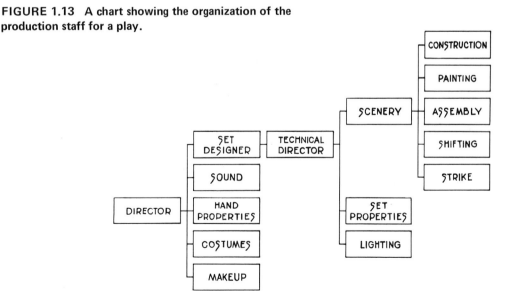

However, no director—no human being—can in one lifetime master all of the aspects of theater production. The director must rely on other artists for the scenery, the lighting, the costumes, and the sound (a representative but not an exhaustive list). While each must be free to be most creative, their work also has to be precisely coordinated. It would be disastrous for the costume designer to prepare a pink dress for the heroine, while the scene designer specified a set decorated with burnt-orange wallpaper, which the lighting designer planned to illuminate in greens and blues.

Chronologically, the director's first task is to analyze the playscript and determine the mood of the production, its basic style, and the specific quality of the experience he intends to create for the audience. This decision will serve as a unifying test for all later planning. Once it has been made, all the designs, so long as they harmonize with it, will probably harmonize with each other.

The next step is to confer with the members of the design staff, occasionally individually but more often as a group. The purpose of this session is to communicate the director's fundamental conception of the play to the staff as clearly as possible. There will be general discussion, requests for clarification, and perhaps mention of special problems. Following the meeting, each artist starts on an exploration of the play in his own area of responsibility, and finally develops a design in harmony with his understanding of the director's approach to it. These designs are then submitted to the director in a series of conferences, which are most often individual although occasionally designers in related areas (lighting and scenery, for example) may be asked to meet together. At these conferences the director will either approve the designs as presented, or more frequently suggest minor changes or point out unsolved problems. It is unusual for designs to be rejected totally. If changes are needed, the designers will continue their work and resubmit revisions. This process is repeated until the designs have been accepted and approved by the director's initialing the plans.

The director may occasionally be consulted following approval of the designs. For example, the costume designer may bring swatches of cloth to him to ask which he prefers for a particular costume. If it becomes necessary to alter the designs in any way, such changes must be submitted to the director for his approval. Usually, however, the director turns to his other responsibilities, the primary one being training the actors, while the production staff operates during the following weeks with little supervision on his part.

The designers have one more responsibility. A painting of a stage set, if it is properly done, will show exactly what the completed set is to look like to the audience, but the construction workers need a great deal more information before they can build, paint, and assemble it. They need dimensions, precise descriptions of shapes, paint samples, information about joinery and bracing, specifications of materials, etc. The designer must therefore record such information. For scenery, such a record takes the form of what are called *working drawings,* in which the different scenic elements are shown clearly in outline form, to scale, with dimensions and materials indicated. Usually additional instructions are printed on the drawings. These drawings form the basis for the work of the stagecraft crew. If they are properly prepared they include all of the information needed to create a set which will precisely match the designer's plan.

THE FUNCTIONS OF THE TECHNICAL DIRECTOR

One person, usually called the *technical director,* is given responsibility for seeing that the set work is carried out effectively, economically, and on schedule. The technical director's relationship to the construction workers is similar to that of the director with regard to the staff as a whole, except that the technical director usually works more closely with his crew, and supervises their work throughout the entire production period. He will analyze the designer's drawings, order any special materials needed, plan the order of work and divide it into a series of projects, prepare a master schedule, and make work assignments to the crew members, either individually or in small groups.

This procedure as it has been described is a kind of theoretical ideal, which is approached in varying degrees in different theaters. Though the organization of a particular theater may differ from this plan, it can most always be best understood in terms of the basic pattern. There are two common deviations. Many excellent theaters do not have quite as large a staff as the discussion suggests, so that one person may handle two or more assignments. For instance, in community and college theaters it is common for the same person not only to design the scenery but also to supervise its construction; very often the set designer may also prepare the lighting design.

The other exception results from the fact that production schedules are often frantically tight, and some steps in the full theoretical procedure may be omitted in order to save time. This occurs most often when staff members are thoroughly acquainted with each others' work and feel that some supervision may be safely dispensed with. For instance, the director may approve a set design at an early stage, when there are still a few problems to be worked out, relying on the designer to correct them satisfactorily without the necessity of an additional conference. Usually, a full set of working drawings would include detailed instructions for building all the necessary flats; however many hours of drafting may be saved by omitting such drawings if the designer is sure that the technical director can supervise the construction of the flats without them. In that case, the designer may simply give him a list of the sizes of flats needed and rely on his proceeding satisfactorily. Even platforms and simple step units may be handled in the same way. The time saved by such shortcuts may mean the difference between an easy work schedule and a frenzied crisis.

THE APPRENTICE SYSTEM

In the New York theater, scenery is built in professional studios, then transported to other studios where it is painted, and finally moved to the specific theater for assembly. In such circumstances, the designer's drawings must be complete and unambiguous. The builders are certified as experienced and skilled, and training them is not part of the procedure. However, in all but fully professional theaters, some training is accepted as an essential activity, and of course in the educational theater it is central to the program. These theaters operate by means of the apprentice system.

Under the apprentice system a completely inexperienced crew member, working on his first show, is assigned to work on a project as a member of a small team with at least one fully experienced member. The skilled workers explain and demonstrate what is required, work side by side with the novice, and develop his knowledge and skill as rapidly as possible. The technical director periodically observes the work, and is constantly available for help with difficult problems. The time needed for supervision and training inevitably reduces the efficiency of the more skilled workers to some extent, but developing new workers is so vitally important for almost all theaters that the time is well spent, and, of course, even the novice is able to contribute to the production.

When the new crew member begins work on his second show, he is no longer a novice. He will probably not yet be ready to begin to train others, and he will still need some supervision himself, but his contribution to the work can be expected to increase significantly. With his third show, he will most probably take his position as a seasoned member of the crew, and can be relied on to work with only minimal supervision and to help in training others.

THE SUPERVISORY STAFF

Most college theaters, and many community theaters, have paid assistants who may be called shop foremen, and who assume some official supervisory responsibility. They are selected from the most experienced and skillful of the crew members who have worked on a series of shows. They differ from other workers in that it is presumed that they do not need to be checked on or supervised, and that they will recognize special problems and difficulties and ask the technical director for assistance when they need it. In college, such assistants are typically seniors or graduate students; in community theaters they are experienced people who have demonstrated initiative, skill, and the ability to work smoothly with others. Of course, at the top of the scene shop organization is the technical director, ideally a fully trained professional worker whose primary functions are supervision and administration. In particular, he is responsible for seeing the work as a whole, planning, assigning, scheduling, and checking to make sure that the projects are done acceptably, and that deadlines are met.

The whole of theater organization is somewhat baffling to a nontheater person. Often, the work seems to be proceeding chaotically. In fact, in a well managed theater it is carefully planned. Individual workers seem to be given almost complete freedom, but in fact, their work is precisely coordinated. There seems to be little or no supervision, but supervision is indeed constant, although unobtrusive, and assistance is available to every worker at every moment in any amount he needs.

One policy is vitally important for every staff member to understand. Theater workers are assumed to be responsible and self-directing. When they are given assignments, it is expected that these assignments will be carried out. To check on every worker constantly would require doubling the staff. Instead, it is assumed that each worker will ask for assistance whenever he needs it. If a worker does not ask for help, it is understood that no problems have arisen. If he needs assistance, the organizational chart identifies where he can find it. The novice asks his fellow team workers for help; a more experienced worker confers with one of the shop foremen; a shop foreman goes to the technical director for help with a problem which he cannot solve. The technical director may consult a textbook or he may confer with the designer if that seems more desirable. As a last resort, the technical director may take insoluble problems to the director. (Unfortunately, the director has no one designated by the chart to whom he can officially turn for help with a difficult problem; it is with him that the buck stops.)

2

From Drawings to Set

Ideally, the drawings that the set designer delivers to the technical director contain all of the information needed for the construction, decoration, and assembly of the scenery. If the construction is to be correct, however, it must conform precisely to the designer's specifications, so that being able to interpret accurately the information given in the drawings is essential to the mastery of stagecraft.

It is easy to learn to read working drawings, and yet misreading causes more errors in the scene shop than any other source of difficulty. There are apparently two reasons for that fact. One is that time spent in studying drawings seems to delay the actual work; crew members are anxious to get on with the construction, and taking half an hour to analyze drawings seems a waste of time. Secondly, the novice is likely to place too great a reliance on his own mind. If at first glance a drawing seems to represent a familiar structure, he may not bother to study it in detail, and even if he has read it carefully, he is likely to trust himself to remember dimensions and other information which in fact he cannot carry accurately in his mind.

One student built a flat with an opening in the shape of a gothic arch. Two diagonal braces were designed to fit in the frame at the top of the flat, tangent to the curves of the arch. When set in place, however, they extended well out into the opening, and after struggling unsuccessfully to fit them, the student asked his technical director for assistance. The director immediately picked up the drawing to check it, but was interrupted by the student, who said "You don't have to check the dimensions; I know I cut the boards the right size." In fact, measuring the braces and comparing them with the drawing demonstrated that the student had reversed two figures in one dimension. The specifications called for one brace to be 3'-4" long, and instead it had been cut 4'-3". When it was recut, it fit exactly as it had been designed. Whenever difficulty appears, the first step in attempting to solve the problem should be to restudy the drawing.

ANALYSIS OF THE WORKING DRAWINGS

The first step in any project consists of a careful study of the relevant drawings. This is so important that it is desirable to describe it in detail.

1. The worker should begin by identifying the unit and determining what it should look like when finished, and how it is to be fitted into the set as a whole. Often the working drawings will include a picture of the completed unit. If they do not, the worker should look at the designer's perspective painting of the finished set, and find the unit he has undertaken to build. If he cannot identify it immediately, referring to the floor plan may help him. As a last resort, he should ask the technical director for assistance.

2. The worker should then glance over the various drawings to identify how they are related. There may be two or more drawings of the same part of the structure; several parts may be shown in separate drawings; one drawing may show some of the parts assembled. How the part shown in each drawing fits into the total structure must be identified.

3. He should then study each individual drawing carefully, carrying out the construction in imagination. In particular, he should look for unusual, unexpected, or inexplicable details. Printed instructions should be read with care.

4. Designers make mistakes, like everyone else, and it is unusual to find a set of working drawings that does not contain some error. Perhaps an essential brace will have been omitted, or the designer may have drawn a dimensional arrow indicating the radius of a circle, and then by mistake have labeled it with the length of the diameter. The worker should be alert to possible errors, and whenever he is puzzled by a detail of the drawings he should ask the technical director to check it with him.

5. While watching for mistakes, the worker should also be alert to specifications for which there is no obvious reason. For example, the design for a pillar may include an apparently unnecessary internal brace; or a drawing for a platform may show diag-

onal braces omitted at points where they might be expected. Such items may be mistakes, and if so they should be corrected, but there may be reasons for them which are not immediately apparent, and in that case it is important that the worker learn what those reasons are before he begins construction.

The two examples given are from actual sets. The working drawings for a pillar for *Blithe Spirit* included an internal brace for which the student who built it could see no purpose. Instead of checking with the technical director or designer, he simply omitted it. In fact, it had been provided to form a support for ornamental molding, to be nailed on after the basic structure had been assembled. Since the support was inside the pillar, it was not discovered that it had been omitted until the pillar was fastened in place on stage and the crew undertook to nail the molding in place. It was too late to take the pilliar apart and add the brace. Instead, it was necessary to spend an additional hour and a half devising a substitute method of fastening on the decorative molding.

For a production of another play, the director asked that the actors be provided with an opening under a platform, which could be reached from off stage, and which could be used in one scene for a surprise entrance. As a result, the platform bracing had to be planned to leave a path wide enough for the actors to creep through from behind the set towards the concealed opening. In this case, the construction workers did ask the reason for the unexpected arrangement of braces, and so the platform was built correctly.

Any designer would be grateful to a crew member who caught an error in the drawings, and got it corrected in advance of construction, so that if the worker finds what looks like an error during his preliminary examination of the drawings, he should ask about it immediately, but no worker should ever alter the design given him without such consultation. What looks like a mistake or an accident may have been carefully planned, and may be essential to the functioning of the scenery.

Having analyzed his working drawings carefully, and having developed a clear picture of the total construction process as well as the appearance of the finished structure, the crew member is ready to start building. Construction techniques will be discussed in later chapters, but first we need to consider the interpretation of drawings in more detail.

TYPES OF PROJECTION

One way of classifying drawings is by the types of projection that are used. Almost always, one or more of four different projection systems are used for theatrical drawings. This discussion will be limited to those four.

1. *Orthographic projection* (The vast majority of set drawings are of this type.)
2. *Oblique projection* (This is used very rarely, but it is the best method of representing one particular kind of scenic unit.)
3. *Isometric projection* (Second in frequency of use.)
4. *Perspective projection* (Every complete group of drawings for a stage set includes one perspective drawing or painting, but seldom more than one.)

The order in which the projections have been listed is significant. Perspective drawings show the set as it would look from the audience. Isometric projection is a compromise between orthographic and perspective (although more closely related to orthographic), and oblique projection is a combination of orthographic and isometric.

ORTHOGRAPHIC PROJECTION

The simplest and perhaps the most familiar projection is orthographic. Technically, it can be defined as the method in which a drawing is created by placing a picture plane (a sheet of cardboard) parallel with a plane surface of an object, extending imaginary lines from the object to the picture plane at right angles to each, and marking their positions on the cardboard so as to form a picture.[1]

If such a definition is puzzling, it can be clarified by referring to ordinary experience. Orthographic drawings appear constantly in daily life, and are the simplest to make. A child drawing a house will most often show it as an orthographic view. City maps are essentially orthographic. Anyone making sketches to use as a guide in building a set of shelves or other furniture is most likely to use orthographic projection. It is the fastest, simplest, and often the clearest method of representing an object, and the easiest to use as a guide in construction—which is why it is more often used in theatrical working drawings than any other type of projection.

Its most striking characteristic is that objects are shown in their true shapes, without distortion. An orthographic drawing of a square object shows it as a square, a circle is shown as a circle, an irregular curve is represented by a line of identical shape.

SCALES

It is possible to make orthographic drawings full scale, that is, the same size as the object represented, and that is the preferred treatment for small scenic elements. For instance, an ornamental shield to be fastened above a fireplace might be shown full scale, or a small picture frame, or a single motif for a wallpaper pattern. Most scenic elements, however, are much larger than the designer's sheets of cardboard, so that he must use a smaller scale. Shapes will remain true, but dimensions will be reduced. The relation between the size of the drawing and the size of the actual object will be indicated on the drawing by an equation:

$$\text{Scale:} \quad 1/2'' = 1'\text{-}0''$$
$$3/4'' = 1'\text{-}0''$$
$$1\ 1/2'' = 1'\text{-}0''$$

In such an equation, the first figure indicates the size of the drawing, and the second the size of the matching space on the actual object.

The use of scales is also part of familiar experience, and should cause little trouble. The major source of error is that different drawings may use different scales. In fact, on a single sheet two or three different scales may be used, with smaller scales to show the object as a whole, and details shown in separate drawings to a larger scale. In that case, the correct scale will be indicated for each drawing, but the worker must remember in moving from drawing to drawing that he must adjust his thinking and measurement each time a new scale is shown.

In using scaled drawings, a special ruler called an architect's scale is invaluable, and every scene shop should have one, although most do not. Probably the scale of $1/2'' = 1'\text{-}0''$ is the most commonly used in set drawings. It is easy enough to measure even feet to such a scale with an ordinary ruler, but if the ruler is divided into sixteenths of an inch, as most are, each division represents not an inch on the drawing but $1\ 1/3''$, and if the scale of $1'' = 1'\text{-}0''$ is used, each division on the ruler represents $2/3''$. The architect's scale shows a half-inch divided into twelve equal parts, so that each one represents an inch on the drawing; other scales are given, twelve altogether on the ordinary triangular architect's ruler, including those most often used in set drawings.

An ordinary ruler can be used conveniently for a particular group of scales, $3/4'' = 1'\text{-}0''$ and its multiples. At the $3/4''$ scale, $1/16''$ on the ruler equals $1''$ on the drawing; at double this scale ($1\ 1/2'' = 1'\text{-}0''$), $1/8''$ on the ruler equals $1''$ on the drawing. Even halving the scale ($3/8'' = 1'\text{-}0''$) results in $1/16''$ on the ruler equaling $2''$ on the drawing, and measurements can still be made with acceptable accuracy. Designers prefer the $1/2''$ or $1''$ scales, for no particular reason. If they can be persuaded to use the more convenient scales in their drawings, the set construction crew can dispense with the architect's scale and use whatever tapes or rulers are at hand.

1. Theoretically, the picture plane need not be parallel with the surface of the object shown in orthographic projection. In practice, set drawings are never made in orthographic with a principal plane angled, and only very rarely is the projection used for an object in which even minor elements are shown out of parallel with the picture plane.

Given the correct scale, the fact that objects are shown in true shape makes it possible to check dimensions, and to find distances which are not stated directly in the drawings. In well prepared drawings, nearly all the dimensions needed will be clearly stated. Occasionally, however, it is useful to make additional measurements, for instance in selecting boards to be used for diagonal braces, so that the measurability of orthographic drawings is of some practical value.

GROUND PLANS

In submitting his designs for the director's approval, the designer provides two drawings, one of which shows the placement of the scenic elements on the floor of the stage. This drawing is prepared as an orthographic projection. It is called a ground plan (or floor plan), and is fundamental to the entire design. It is used by the stagecraft crew as a guide in assembling the scenery on stage, and it can be used to help locate particular scenic elements in the perspective drawing (Figures 2.1, 2.2, 2.3).

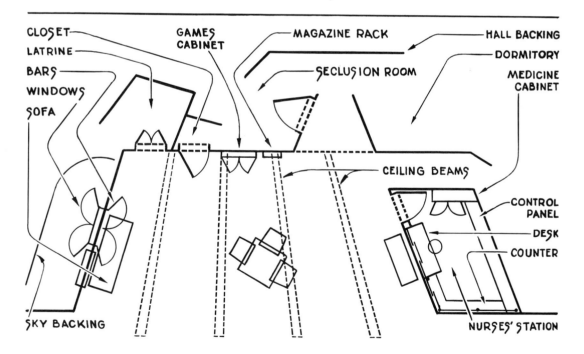

FIGURE 2.1 An interior ground-plan: the lounge in a mental institution, *One Flew Over the Cuckoo's Nest*. (See Figure 1.3 for a photograph of the set.)

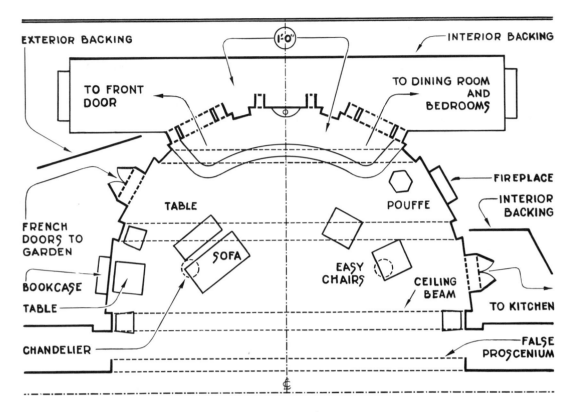

FIGURE 2.2   A living room, *Blithe Spirit*. (See Figure 1.1 for a photograph of the set.)

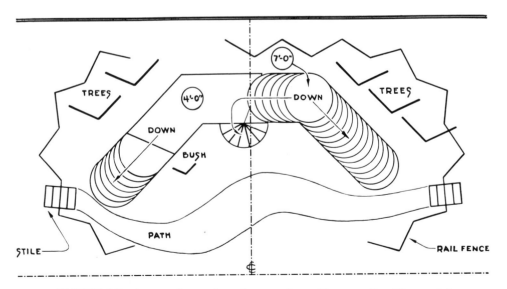

FIGURE 2.3   An exterior set for a fantasy, *Story Theater*. (See Figures 1.4 and 1.9 for photographs of the set.)

Ground plans vary in the amount of information they provide, but all walls will be shown, including door openings; usually three-dimensional decorative units will be included, such as fireplaces or pilasters. Often scenic elements which are not in contact with the stage floor will be shown as if they had been lowered until they touched it— for instance, the position and outline of chandeliers may be indicated, as well as heavy cornices at the top of the walls, although they are sometimes omitted. All platforms and step units will be shown, and usually the outlines of furniture. Often the largest dimensions of pieces of furniture appear at some distance from the floor. For instance, the most significant dimensions of a table are the length and width of the top, although only the tips of the legs rest on the floor. In such cases, the outline of the top is most likely to be shown, as if it were in contact with the floor. If its position is determined by the placement of the legs they may be indicated also.

The ground plan shows true horizontal shapes, but it gives no information about heights, with one exception, and that is the height of platforms, stairs, and ramps. These heights are conventionally represented by printing the dimension figures inside the outline of the unit, and enclosing them in a small circle. If there is not enough space for the figures inside the outline, they will be placed close by, enclosed in a circle, and an arrow run from it to the dimensional unit. For flights of stairs, it is customary to mark the height only of the top step, or of landings; if the steps are irregular in height, each dimension will be given. For ramps, two dimensions are given, indicating the height of the top and bottom edges of the ramp. All heights are shown as measured from the stage floor. Thus a small platform which is actually 1'-6" high, but which stands on a larger platform 3'-0" high, would be dimensioned as 4'-6". If this occasionally causes confusion, it can be corrected by a glance at the working drawings; but to measure heights from varying levels would produce constant difficulty.

The ground plan is of occasional use during construction, but its primary value is as a guide in assembling the scenery on stage. Since this is the last step in the creation of the set, the methods used will be discussed in chapter 13.

The outlines of furniture as shown on the ground plan may be difficult to interpret; the outline of a table may look very much like the outline of a bench, and the outline of a square planter might be identical with that of a square stool. Consequently, the designer will often print identifying labels on the drawing, either inside the units or beside them with arrows pointing to the structures indicated.

CODING

Sets often include many similar but not identical units. For instance, one set might require six platforms, two stair units, and thirty flats. To make it easier to keep track of the drawings and finished structures, many designers assign them code letters or numbers, so that the platforms might be labeled PA, PB, PC, PD, PE, and PF, the stairs SA and SB, and the flats F1, F2, etc. It is convenient to copy such marks on the units as they are completed, in some area which will be invisible to the audience. Often the same labels will be included on the ground plan. For instance, even though the side wall seems continuous to the audience it may be made up of four different flats fastened together. The designer may mark them by drawing short dashes across the line showing where the wall stands on the floor, and then print each code designation behind the flat to which it refers. This kind of coding speeds up assembling the scenery.

FIGURE 2.4 The assembly elevation for *Come Blow Your Horn.* **(See Figure 13.4 for a ground–plan of the set, and Figure 1.2 for a photograph.)**

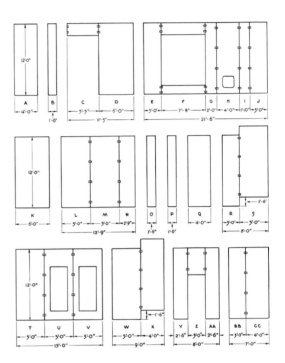

ELEVATIONS

The construction crew needs a great deal of information not given on the floor plan. They need to know the height and shape of flats, the sizes of door and window openings, and the internal structure of platforms. Most of this information will be given in other orthographic drawings.

One of these drawings is called an *elevation* (Figure 2.4). It shows the walls of the set as if they had been laid side by side on the floor, face up. Where they meet at an angle in the set, a space will be left between the sections. In order to get the entire set on a single sheet of cardboard, it is necessary to use a very small scale; the walls may be shown in two rows, so as to make use of a slightly larger scale. At best, it will not be possible to show all details of the walls. For instance, wallpaper patterns or other decorative details may be undrawable. The large elements will be shown, however, including door, window, or arch openings. Fireplaces, pilasters, molding, and cornices may be included, although small details will be omitted. If a wallpaper pattern is to be applied to the walls, the areas in which it appears will probably be indicated; and even draperies and pictures to be hung on the walls may be given in outline.

Dimensions of the different units, including the flats which are combined to make up walls, are given on the construction drawings, and may or may not be indicated in the elevations, but if code letters are used for the flats they will probably be shown. Even if the dimensions of individual elements are not given, the height and overall width of each separate wall will be indicated.

Although elevations may be drawn for any type of scenery, they are most frequently used for sets showing the interior of a room. If one wall of a room were removed, and it were turned toward the audience so they could see inside, the floor, ceiling, and the three remaining walls would have the shape of an open box. Sets of that type, in which the stage space is fully enclosed, are called *box sets*. Of course, numerous deviations from a simple box are introduced—openings are cut for doors and windows, usually the side walls are slanted apart to provide a better view for the audience, and stairs and platforms may be included. The outline of the walls may be varied by bays and extensions, more than three walls may be used, and as an extreme variation the back wall may be omitted and the two side walls swung together until they meet near the back of the stage area, so that the audience is, in effect, looking at the inside corner of a box. Occasionally the ceiling may also be dispensed with. However varied, any set which essentially encloses the acting area is classified as belonging to the box set type.

Since the audience can see some of the areas beyond the set, through the door and window openings, these spaces also constitute part of the stage picture, and must be included in the scenic design and construction. In addition, such scenic units must hide backstage elements which are inharmonious with the setting—the walls of the stage, heat ducts, property tables, stage braces, as well as technicians who work back stage or actors crossing from one side of the stage to the other to reach a far entrance. Since these scenic elements are placed behind openings in the set they are called *backing;* since they are used to hide backstage areas, they are also called *masking.*

Backing may consist of a sky drop (a large unframed sheet of cloth hung at the back of the stage and painted and lit to suggest the sky). More often, the backing consists of flats fastened at a little distance behind the openings. Outside a window, a backing flat may also be painted to represent the sky, perhaps with a few tree branches coming in from the side.

When doors in a set are represented as leading into an adjoining room, they will be backed by flats painted to represent walls. Except for very large openings (a picture window, a wide arch), audiences can usually see very little beyond an opening. Consequently, it is not necessary to build a complete inner room; only the small area visible to the audience need be supplied. Usually the flats are painted simply, with just a spattered base coat (see chapter 11), with perhaps a mopboard or wainscoting suggested by a solid painted area.

The masking flats will be shown in the designer's floor plan. They will also be included in his elevations, most probably at the end of the series, following the flats which make up the major part of the set.

The elevation is helpful in the assembly of the flats in the scene shop, and referring to it at the beginning of a project may make it easier for the crew members to visualize the way their unit fits into the total set. Only the front elevation has been described, showing the side of the flats which will be visible to the audience. Occasionally, a rear elevation will also be provided, especially if there are unusual problems in stiffening the walls or fastening them together.

As guides for actual construction and painting, still more information is needed. Typically, each flat is shown in two additional drawings, one indicating its construction and the other its decoration. Most of the work of building a flat is done from the back, while painting is of course done from the front. Consequently, the construction guide shows the back of the flat, and the painting guide the front. These two drawings are identical with elevations, although that term is never used for them. They differ in that usually only a single flat is shown in one drawing, so that a larger scale can be used.

DIMENSIONING

A basic flat is simply a rectangular frame, covered on one side with cloth. The outlines of the parts of the flat will be drawn in mediumweight lines. Dimensions are indicated by light lines, with an arrowhead at each end. A gap is left in the center of each dimension line, in which figures are printed indicating the distance from the point of one arrowhead to the point of the other.

A few simple variations of this method of indicating dimensions will cause no trouble. If the dimension line showing the width of a flat is placed inside the drawing, the outline of a diagonal brace or some other element might cross it at the center. In that case, the gap for the figures would be moved to one side to promote legibility. An alternative method is to extend the side edges of the flat above or below the drawing for a short distance, using fine lines and leaving a small gap between each extension line and the edge of the flat. The dimension arrow is then placed between the extenders rather than inside the flat.

Sometimes it is desirable to provide two sets of dimensions for the same units. For instance, in his front elevation the designer may choose to indicate the width of each flat individually, and also the total width of each wall section (see Figure 2.4). In that case, the dimensions for the short segments are placed next to the drawing, the extension lines at the ends of the unit are drawn double length, and a single arrow is run across the entire distance, placed at a legible distance below the other figures.

In dimensioning small areas, there may not be space for the shafts of the arrows, the arrowheads, and the necessary figures. The arrowheads may be placed outside the area, pointing toward it, and the figures printed in the space between them; although the arrowheads are pointing in a direction opposite to the usual one, the same rule applies that the dimension figures indicate the distance between their points.

If there is not even enough space to write the figures alone, a solid arrow can be run through it, the dimension written a little distance away, and a directional arrow run to the center of the solid one. With the smallest spaces, the arrowheads can be put outside the space, pointing toward it, and a directional arrow run from the figures to the center of the open space.

Flats are the simplest ordinary scenic elements, but more complicated structures are also usually shown in orthographic drawings, although often in combination with drawings of other types. For instance, supports for platforms, stairs, and ramps are often shown in orthographic. Because of the greater complexity of such units, the dimensioning may be more complicated than for flats, but they should cause little difficulty.

ISOMETRIC PROJECTION

Theoretically, any object can be described accurately by a series of orthographic drawings, but three-dimensional structures may be difficult to visualize. Shaw's *Misalliance* requires the construction of a portable Turkish bath. Orthographic drawings of the side, front, and top would show it accurately, but they would artificially separate the views, and would look very different from the actual structure. A perspective drawing would show the bath as it actually appeared, but it is so difficult—in practice impossible—to work out the dimensions of a structure from a perspective representation.

An ingenious projection has been developed which combines some of the measurability of an orthographic drawing with the impression of three-dimensionality provided by perspective. This is called *isometric projection.* Isometric drawings have little value except to represent units with an essentially boxlike shape. Even an object, like a bench, which deviates from the box shape, is drawn by enclosing it in an imaginary box, and then erasing the base lines after the drawing has been completed.

All isometric drawings are based on one of two three-line grids, which join at one corner of the basic box. Each grid can be interpreted in two ways, as the inside or outside corner of the box. Consequently, four different views are possible: the inside of a box above eye level or below eye level, and the outside of a box above or below eye level. In each case, the box is turned so that the gridded corner points directly at the spectator's eye (Figure 2.5).[1]

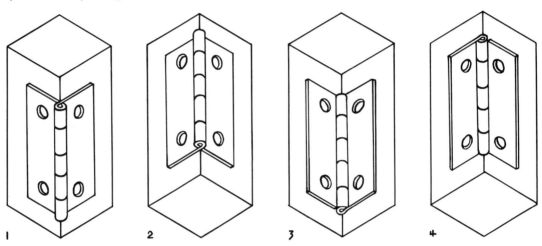

FIGURE 2.5   Isometric positions, illustrated by drawings of hinges fitted against the corners of boxes. *1*, the outside of the box below eye–level; *2*, the outside of the box above eye–level; *3*, the inside of the box above eye–level; *4*, the inside of the box below eye–level. (For the inside views, two sides and one end of each box are omitted.)

Reading isometric drawings requires mastering two principles. (1) A square or rectangle in isometric is distorted, so that two of its corners are opened to larger than 90°, and two are reduced. (2) Accurate measurements (to scale) can be made directly from an isometric drawing so long as the line being measured is parallel to one of the three basic isometric grid lines. Measurements in any other direction will be distorted, and in practice cannot be done. Brief experience in working with isometric drawings will make the use of these principles automatic.

Even with an isometric drawing, essential parts of a structure may be hidden. For example, if it is necessary to show the arrangement of the internal supports of a flight of stairs, they may not be visible, no matter from what angle the finished structure is viewed. A solution to this problem is the *exploded isometric* (Figure 2.6). The parts of the unit which hide the essential elements are lifted up or moved aside, and drawn as if suspended in air. Their actual positions are indicated by running arrows from the corners or other key points to where they were before they were moved. If the parts

1. Theoretically, isometric drawings can be made of any object, which can be placed in any relation to the picture plane. In theatrical practice, views other than those described are almost nonexistent.

removed are simple enough, they may simply be omitted, and a note added such as "platform tops not shown." (It may be instructive to examine all the drawings in the book partly or entirely in isometric: Figures 2.5, 2.6, 3.8, 4.2, 5.1, 6.9, 6.11, 6.13, 6.15, 6.19, 7.1, 7.4, 7.5, 7.8, 7.10, 8.7, 8.8, 8.9, 8.10, 8.11, 8.12, 8.13, 8.14, 12.11, 14.5, and 16.2.)

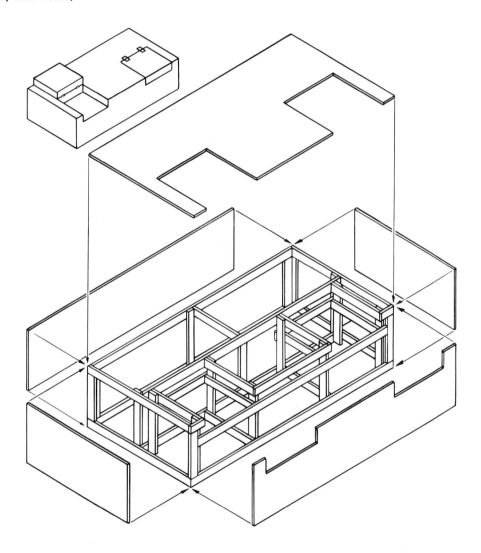

FIGURE 2.6   **Exploded isometric. A platform designed for** *Of Thee I Sing* **is shown. Two sections of the top fold back, leaving areas 1'–6'' high which can be used as seats. An isometric drawing of the assembled platform,** *upper left corner*; **the structure is duplicated to a larger scale in exploded isometric, with the plywood surfacing removed so as to reveal the arrangement of the 1 x 3 framework. Notice that the hinged sections have been omitted from the exploded drawing, as well as the plywood squares forming the seats.**

Marking dimensions of objects shown in isometric is somewhat more difficult than in orthographic drawings. Often matching drawings will be shown in orthographic, with the dimensions given only on the supplementary drawings.

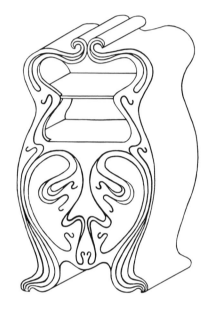

FIGURE 2.7 Oblique projection. A highboy for a production of *A Flea in Her Ear* is shown, with the elaborately shaped front in orthographic projection and the sides shown obliquely so as to indicate thickness. Isometric projection would have so distorted the shape of the front as to make the drawing almost worthless. (See Figure 8.3 for a photograph of the completed highboy.)

OBLIQUE PROJECTION

Occasionally, it is desirable to show three-dimensional objects which have almost no relation to a box shape. This occurs most often in drawing complicated cornices. If a length of cornice with an elaborately curved cross-section were drawn in isometric, the pattern of the curves would be so distorted that it would be almost worthless as a construction guide. Oblique projection, which is a compromise between orthographic and isometric, provides a solution to this problem (Figure 4.1). The most important or complicated view of the object is drawn in orthographic, and consequently shows its true shape and dimensions. From key points in the outline, slanted lines are drawn (at any angle, left or right, and above or below the basic drawing), and the edge of the original drawing is repeated at the ends of the slanted lines, to complete the solid structure (Figure 2.7). Oblique drawings are seldom used, but they should cause the set crew little difficulty. At first glance, they look very much like isometric drawings. The only point to remember is the significant one that one plane is shown in orthographic, and consequently shows true shape and can be measured accurately in any direction.

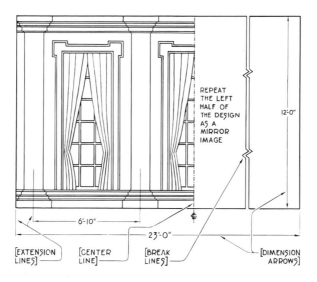

FIGURE 2.8   Drafting conventions. A painting elevation for a set for Richard Brinsley Sheridan's *The Rivals*. (The notes in brackets would not normally be included in the drawing.)

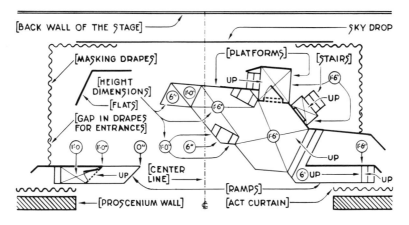

FIGURE 2.9   Drafting conventions illustrated in a ground–plan for Joseph Heller's *We Bombed in New Haven*. (Bracketed explanatory notes added.)

DRAFTING CONVENTIONS

It is desirable that crew members be familiar with a few other drafting conventions (Figure 2.8, 2.9). When it is necessary to show the edge of a piece of scenery which would not actually be visible from the angle at which the unit is drawn, the hidden edge is conventionally represented by a medium-weight line made up of dashes. Center lines are indicated by a light line made up of alternating long and short dashes. Often the letters *C* and *L* are printed on the line, superimposed to form a monogram.

Where only part of an object is shown, the omitted section may be indicated by drawing a straight line across the end of the unit, interrupting it with a zigzag line suggesting a break. If the center section of a unit has no distinctive features, the drawing can often be done to a larger scale by breaking it out and removing it. For instance, if a street lamp were shown complete, it might be necessary to use a very small scale; by omitting the major part of the shaft, the ornamental designs at top and bottom can be shown at a much larger scale. If dimension arrows are shown extending beyond the break, the dimensions given indicate the size of the complete object, with the break filled in. This is the only instance in which dimension arrows differ in length from the actual distance shown.

On the ground plan, a wavy line is conventionally used to indicate the position of the act curtain or of draperies. Doors are shown partly open, and a lightweight arc is drawn marking the path of the door edge as it swings. Platforms are marked by drawing their diagonals with light lines. Usually the circle enclosing the height dimension is placed where the diagonals cross.

When flats must be hinged together, that fact is shown on the elevations by drawing conventional symbols representing hinges across the joints. If the hinges are placed on the front of the flat, each one is shown as a rectangle twice as wide as it is high. If the hinges are to be attached to the back of the flats, the diagonals and the vertical ends of the rectangle are drawn, and the horizontal edges omitted. Sometimes flats to be hinged cannot be shown side by side in the drawing. In that case, a half hinge is placed at the edge of each flat, a square for hinges on the front, and a triangle pointing toward the edge of the flat for hinges to be fastened to the back.

This discussion does not exhaust the subject of using working drawings, but it will be adequate for most projects, and the technical director or designer will be glad to explain the meaning of any symbols which have not been discussed here.

CONSTRUCTION PROCEDURES

Some projects, such as assembling the scenery on stage, require the work of the entire set crew; others can be handled most efficiently by one person working alone. Most units can be built best by small groups of workmen, ranging from two to four or five. Before construction begins, the technical director will have divided the work into individual assignments, and will have decided in what order they should be done. Typically, a group of perhaps three workers will select a project in consultation with the technical director.

Their first step is to study the working drawings for their unit of scenery until they are thoroughly familiar with them. Often the lumber for the entire set will have been precut, and laid out in piles by size. One member of the crew holds the drawings and reads off the number of boards of each size needed, which are collected by the other workers and carried to the construction area. The tools and supplies which will be needed are then taken from the tool room, and the construction begins. When the unit has been finished, it is set aside to clear the work area for other projects, the tools are returned to storage, scraps are disposed of and the work area swept. The members of the team then consult with the technical director, select a new project, and continue their work.

PART

II

CONSTRUCTION

3

Tools and Equipment

Even an experienced carpenter who undertakes to learn set construction is likely to feel baffled when he first walks into the scene shop. Tools that he has come to consider basic may not be available at all, and he may find others which are so strange he cannot guess how they could be used. People who have had no experience in woodworking are likely to feel even more bewildered. With a little experience, however, the tools come to seem comfortable and familiar.

To some extent, what tools are used for a particular job is a matter of personal preference, and tastes vary greatly. Almost every set builder comes to identify a favorite hammer, one that feels right in his hand, and different workers may make quite different choices. One person may use a nail puller frequently; another may use it only as a last resort. One workman may prefer a ratchet screw driver, while another may dislike to use it. One experienced technical director avoids portable circular saws, and uses a saber saw whenever possible—even though he admits that the circular saw is more sensible for many purposes.

Each worker, then, develops his own favorite selection of tools. No textbook list could match more than one such pattern. The descriptions in this chapter must therefore be thought of as a general guide, which will not precisely conform to the practice of any particular scene shop. As he becomes more experienced, each worker will develop his own preferences in the choice of tools, and may omit some of those described here and add others.

SCENIC REQUIREMENTS

The conditions of set building are unlike those of any other type of construction. Ordinary carpenters who build a staircase expect it to last for decades. Stairs for scenery need stand up only during a few weeks' rehearsal and the run of the show. Doors, shelves, corner-cupboards, or fireplaces built for the home can be as heavy as is convenient. On the stage, reducing the weight of similar structures may be a major consideration, even if when finished they look identical to their out-of-theater counterparts. A normal door might cause the walls to shake distractingly every time it was closed; a fireplace mantel may have to be hung on small hooks from a wooden frame covered with cloth; a cupboard may have to be light enough that it can be moved in seconds by two people, during a scene shift. Speed of construction is also an important factor. Only five or six weeks may be available for building and decorating sets representing three rooms, including a dozen pieces of furniture.

The theater, then, has its special requirements, and as might be expected special tools, materials, and techniques have been developed to meet them. One of the most striking of these special considerations is the fact that stage sets are viewed from a much greater distance than similar settings in the outside world. Every set designer knows that to produce a particular effect in a wallpaper pattern, it must be projected—motifs must be enlarged and clarified, contrasts must be sharpened, colors must be brightened. Instead of seeing the pattern from a distance of four or five feet, the nearest viewer may well be as far as twenty feet, and the average viewing distance may be more like thirty or thirty-five feet.

That fact affects scenery in two ways. All elements must be projected to be seen effectively, and defects or mistakes which might be obtrusive in ordinary life may well be invisible to the audience. As a result, construction can be cruder, shaping and fitting can be done with a much larger margin of error than in ordinary life, and by taking advantage of that fact work can often be accelerated.

Tools designed for making fine adjustments, for polishing and finishing, are little used in the theater. Most scene shops have a few such tools, but they are more likely to gather dust in the tool room than they are to be put into constant use. Planes, drawknives, chisels, files, sandpaper, fine-toothed saw blades, and levels are used infrequently. Any tools may be of occasional value, and it would be foolish to throw one away, but those which have been listed are unlikely to be purchased in quantity for the scene shop. Of course, an individual worker may especially prefer one or more of these tools, and may make frequent use of them. One person, for example, may reach automatically for the level to use as a guide in attaching molding, shelf units, a fireplace mantel, or pictures, or for checking the verticality of flats as they are fastened on stage, but more often the placements would be guided by measuring with a tape or judging by eye. The tools which are most commonly used in the scene shop are listed below, in semitabular form.

MEASURING TOOLS

1. Pocket Tapes

Description.   Tapes should be provided at least as long as the height of standard flats (most often 12'-0"). There is some advantage in having tapes as long as the diagonal of a flat (a 16'-0" tape is satisfactory). It should be possible to lock the tape when it has been pulled out, and it should have a spring return.

Use.   The hook at the end of the tape is caught on the corner of a board, the tape is stretched along the board, and the dimension marked with a pencil.

> The hook is convenient for measuring from the end of a board, but it is in the way if the measurement must be started at some distance in, on the surface of a board or flat. It is easier to make the measurement if the tape is set so that the 1' or 2' mark matches the starting point—but remember to adjust the measurement to allow for the end of the tape which extends beyond the area being marked.

Cautions.   For accurate measurement, the tape must be parallel with the edge of the board. Hold the tape back slightly from the edge of the board to provide a space for marking, and be sure to mark the edge which will be closest to the saw blade at the beginning of the cut. In particular, avoid the beginner's mistake of marking the length in the center of the board rather than at the edge. If the cut is to be made with a radial-arm saw, it is a waste of time to draw the entire cut line across the board with a square, but that must be done if the board will be cut with a hand saw, a saber saw, or a portable circular saw.

> If pocket tapes have spring returns, do not allow the blade to snap back into the case at full speed. That will eventually break it. Instead, press the forefinger against the surface of the tape (not the edge—it can cut), to act as a brake and slow down the return, especially for the last foot or so.

Tapes are easily damaged. Retract the tape as soon as measurements have been completed. Do not leave it extended on the work bench or floor. Laying lumber on an extended tape or stepping on it is very likely to damage it, and more than one tape has been destroyed by being sawed through. If the hook at the end is bent, measurements will no longer be accurate. It should be carefully restraightened with two pairs of pliers.

Although short tapes are called pocket tapes, they should not be carried in the pocket. Vast numbers of tapes end up on somebody's chest of drawers because the workers had slipped them in their pockets and forgotten to put them on the tool rack when they left the scene shop.

> In marking two points as a guide to drawing a straight line, always spread them as far apart as possible. If they are placed close together, so that the line extends beyond them, any error will be multiplied.

2. Long Tapes

Description.   The scene shop should have at least one tape long enough to reach from one down-stage corner of the stage to the point where the center line of the stage touches the back wall (that is, the diagonal of half the stage area). A somewhat longer tape is preferable, and the readily available 50-foot length is satisfactory for nearly all theaters. Long tapes do not have a spring return; instead, they are provided with a crank which is used to wind the tape back into its case.

Use.   This tape is used primarily in marking positions on the stage floor when the scenery is assembled.

Cautions.   Long tapes are less likely to be damaged than pocket tapes, but care should be taken that they not be stepped on or left lying on the floor where scenery might be set down or dragged across them.

3. Architect's Scale

(Description and use discussed in chapter 2).

Cautions.   Do not use the scale as a guide for drawing lines; the edge is easily damaged.

4. Yardsticks

Use.   The preferred tool for measuring lengths of cloth to be used in covering flats; of little value for any other purpose.

5. Steel Squares (Carpenter's Squares)

Description.   Cut from a sheet of steel, in an **L** shape, with one leg longer than the other. The commonest dimensions are 2'-0" for one leg and 1'-6" for the other.

Use.   Although the edges of the square are marked in fractions of an inch, the markings may be difficult to see. A square is used primarily to make sure that two boards which are to be fastened together at right angles are placed correctly, most often in building flats but also in assembling supports for platforms and stairs. One leg of the square is placed tight against the edge of one of the two boards, and moved until the other leg touches the second board. If the boards are accurately aligned, they will touch the square all the way along its two edges. If a gap appears, it must be closed by moving the second board, not by shifting the square—a startling but not uncommon error.

> A sheet of plywood makes an excellent square, especially for assembling framing or support units for platforms, stairs, and ramps. The boards are laid on top of the plywood, and aligned with its edges.

6. Try-Square

Description.   A small square made of a steel blade to which is attached a wooden handle thicker than the steel.

Use.   Because of its small size, the try-square is of little value as a guide in placing boards to be joined. It is used primarily for two purposes. One is to check the end of scrap lumber to make sure that it has been cut at a right angle. The other is as a guide for drawing a line across a board which is to be sawed by hand or by a saber or portable circular saw. In marking a board, the inside of the wooden leg of the square is placed tight against the edge of the board, with the steel leg flat against the surface of the board, and a pencil line is drawn along the edge of the steel.

7. Bevel

Description.   Like the try-square, the bevel set or gauge has two blades, one thicker than the other. Provision is made for changing the angle at which they meet, and holding each setting by turning a knurled knob.

Use.   The bevel is used for marking a number of boards at the same angle. For instance, if a platform requires a series of diagonal braces, the ends of which are all cut at identical angles, the bevel can be set at the desired angle and the boards quickly and accurately marked. It is used like the try-square, except that the angles marked will be other than 90°.

8. Pencils

Description.   Some workers prefer carpenter's pencils, which have large flat leads, and which must be sharpened with a knife. Ordinary number 2 pencils are also satisfactory.

9. Pens

Description.   Ordinary ball-point and felt-tipped pens.

Use.   Ball-point pens can be used for marking lumber; they have the advantage that they need not be sharpened. Felt pens are especially convenient for labeling storage boxes and the ends of scrap lumber before it is put on the rack. Occasionally, they may be used to draw lines on flats as a painting guide.

Cautions. Some felt-pen ink bleeds through paint applied over it. If so, they should not be used unless the guide lines are acceptable as part of the design, and they should not be used for permanent flats which will have to be repainted with a different design for a later show.

10. Chalk Lines (Snap Lines)

Description.   The line itself is a string, one end of which is fastened inside a small metal case, with a crank for winding the line into the case. A strip of metal at the side of the case can be slid back, leaving an opening through which three or four spoonfuls of powdered chalk can be inserted. Tapping the case against a wood surface will spread the chalk over the string, which is further coated as it is pulled out by a metal hook fastened to its free end. The chalk line is used to make straight marks across a surface as a guide for cutting or painting.

> The chalk dust sold for use with snap lines is extravagantly overpriced. If the theater uses traditional scene paint (see chapter 10), whiting is entirely satisfactory. It is in fact nothing but powdered chalk, and it costs only about 1/70 as much. Other colors of pigment can be used for marking on a white background.

Use.   Guide points are measured and marked, one close to each end of the line to be drawn. One worker holds the chalk-line case, while another takes hold of the hook at the end of the string and pulls it out to a length slightly greater than the line to be chalked. The handle is then fixed so that no more line can be drawn out, and the string is stretched tightly across the surface to be marked, coinciding with the two points which have been measured. Holding it taut, one of the workers reaches out about two and a half feet and pulls the string straight up in the air off the surface and then lets go. As the line snaps back against the surface, some of the chalk is knocked off it, forming a mark connecting the two measured points.

It is possible, with care, to make a dozen or more visible lines with a single chalking. The first snap of the line is likely to deposit more chalk than is desired; each succeeding snap will leave less and less chalk, until the marks are too faint to see. At that point the line must be rewound into the case, tapped again to distribute the chalk, and pulled out for continued marking. The number of lines which can be printed with a single chalking can be extended if the line is pulled up only a short distance for the first snap, and then tension and height of pull steadily increased as successive lines are marked.

Theoretically, the hook at the end of the string can be caught over the far end of the surface being marked, and the line operated by one person. In fact, especially if long lines are to be printed, it takes many times as long for one person to mark them. Except in emergencies, the chalk line should always be used by two people.

The commercial chalk line which has been described is especially convenient, but it is possible to do the same job with a length of ordinary string, rough enough to pick up the chalk, and a small box of chalkdust or pigment. To deposit chalk on the string, it is put into the box and the chalk and string stirred together, and then taken out for marking.

Cautions.   The chalk line is not completely accurate. Snapping the line two or three times while holding it in the same position is likely to result in lines which do not precisely coincide, demonstrating the range of error involved. In using the line, it is important to make sure that the possible deviations from true position are within the acceptable range of error. It should not, for instance, be used for marking pieces of plywood which must be cut and fitted together with precision. On the other hand, it would nearly always be acceptable for marking the floor of the stage as a guide to painting a tile pattern, or marking flats as a guide for painting mortar lines to simulate a stone or brick wall.

When the string has just been chalked, it is easy to get an unacceptable amount of chalkdust the first two or three times it is snapped. Even if the line is simply allowed to sag on to the surface while setting it in place, a sharp unwanted mark may be left. Especially if the marks are being made on a surface most of which has been given its final coat of paint (as for instance when mortar lines are being marked on a flat which has already been painted to suggest stone), heavy lines snapped in a bright color may soil the painted areas so that they will have to be redone. This can be prevented by shaking some of the chalk off the line before it is first used after rechalking, by snapping it very gently at first, and by using chalk as near the color of the background as possible. The tendency is to provide for maximum contrast, but if the work area is well lit it is possible to use a very faint line as a guide in painting. Using chalk nearly the same color as the background, just slightly darker or lighter, will help greatly in keeping the base coat uncontaminated.

The edge of a sheet of 1/4" plywood makes an excellent guide for drawing straight lines. Often when plywood is cut up for use, a scrap strip will be left running the full eight feet at one edge. This should be saved for use as a straightedge. However, it is important that only the machined edge be used for this purpose. The edge cut in the scene shop is likely to be less accurate. To prevent its being used by mistake, it should be cut irregularly with a saber saw, preferably in an undulating line. Two or three such strips make a useful addition to the scene-shop equipment, and are much more accurate than lengths of 1 X 3 or 1 X 4, which are likely to be warped.

---

11. Compasses

Description. Two types of compasses are useful in the scene shop, small metal compasses about 6″ long, and the large wooden compasses designed to hold chalk for drawing circles on a blackboard. The small compasses sold in dime stores, in which the setting is controlled by friction, with one leg designed to hold an ordinary pencil, are satisfactory, although compasses made for drafting, in which the opening is controlled by turning a knurled knob, are more accurate.

Use. The small compasses will draw circles with diameters up to about 12″; the blackboard compasses can be used for circles up to about 3′ in diameter. The lines made by chalk are seldom accurate enough. Instead, a layer or two of masking tape should be wrapped around a pencil stub, which can then be inserted into the socket of the blackboard compass.

It is sometimes necessary to draw arcs of circles with radii longer than any available compasses. Neither string nor wire can be used effectively—string tends to stretch and wire to kink. Even if the wire does not kink, it is difficult to pull it tight enough to keep it perfectly straight. Two better methods are available.

1. Cut a strip of cardboard a few inches longer than the radius. If necessary, several pieces of cardboard can be lapped at the ends and taped together. Mark a point near one end of the strip, and with a tape measure mark a point at the other end at a distance equal to the radius of the circle needed. Punch a hole at one of these marks just big enough to insert a pencil or the tip of a ball-point pen. Fasten the strip to the plywood or other material on which the circle is to be drawn, using a tack or nail driven through the second point. Set the pencil or pen in the hole and draw the circle, keeping a little tension on the cardboard and watching to make sure it does not catch on slivers of wood and pull crooked.

2. An alternative method is to take a strip of 1/4″ plywood slightly longer than the radius and drill two small holes in it, one to receive a pencil or pen, the other for a nail which is driven into the material to be cut at the center-point of the circle. This is used in the same way as the cardboard compass, except that it is not necessary to keep tension on it to hold it straight.

CUTTING TOOLS

12. Crosscut Hand Saw

Description. A metal blade with a wooden handle. The most convenient length is a little more than two feet. There should be ten teeth to the inch, and the teeth are pointed, as distinguished from the rip saw, which has teeth that end in a straight line, like a chisel.

Use. The crosscut saw is designed for cutting across the wood grain, usually at approximately right angles to the grain. A guide line is first marked across the board to be cut, then the saw is set against the edge of the board, at a point close to the handle. The far edge of the board is grasped with the free hand, and the thumb raised well above the teeth and touching the side of the saw blade. Using the thumb as a guide, the saw is pulled toward the worker, cutting a groove in the corner of the board. The guiding hand is then moved aside, and the saw is pushed backwards and forwards along the marked line until the board has been cut through. The cutting is done by the sharp points of the teeth. Downward pressure is of little value—it interferes with the accuracy of the cut, tires the worker, and may actually retard the cutting. A skilled carpenter saws with fast, easy, controlled strokes.

Cautions. Efficient sawing depends on the sharpness of the teeth. Great care should be taken to prevent their being dulled. They should never be drawn across metal, even a small staple, and used lumber should be inspected for nails, tacks, or staples before it is sawed. Saws should not be laid down on a cement floor or a metal surface, nothing should be piled on top of them, and they should be oiled lightly when stored to prevent their rusting. Saws can be resharpened at moderate expense.

Most cutting in the scene shop is done with power saws, and when boards are cut lengthwise (ripped), power equipment is nearly always used, so that a single crosscut saw is adequate for ordinary construction.

13. Table Saw

Description. The blade of the table saw is disk-shaped, and is powered by a motor which is fastened below the surface of a table, with the blade sticking up through a slot in the table top.

Cautions. For a highly skilled carpenter, the table saw is an indispensable tool; it is cheaper and more flexible than the somewhat similar radial-arm saw. Unfortunately it has a defect which prohibits its use in building scenery, except for the most highly skilled workers, and that is the fact that it is one of the most dangerous of all power tools. The various reasons why it is so hazardous need not be stated in detail. Perhaps the most critical fact is that the easy, natural, automatic way to use the saw is the most dangerous, in contrast with the radial-arm saw, where the natural way to use it is the safe way. More than one worker has lost fingers on the table saw. It is a tool of choice in professional scene shops, but it should not be part of the equipment of an educational or nonprofessional theater, where it might be used by beginning workers.

14. The Radial-Arm Saw (also called the Pull-Over Saw)

Description. The radial-arm saw (Figure 3.1) also makes use of a disk-shaped blade, electrically powered, and has a supporting surface on which the wood is laid while it is being cut. Both the blade and the motor are hung from a metal arm, supported at the back of the table by a shaft. The saw blade can be raised or lowered, and the arm can be swung to various angles, so that cuts can be made at other than 90°. The saw blade can also be swung around at right angles to the arm, and used to rip lumber. As a final adjustment, the blade can be tilted so that it cuts across the lumber at a vertical angle, although this feature is seldom used in set construction.

FIGURE 3.1 Using the radial–arm saw. The worker sights along the blade to make sure it will cut exactly beside the mark on the board. (For this specially posed photograph, she has neglected to put on her safety goggles; they would be required in actual cutting.)

Use. The radial-arm saw is used most often for crosscutting lumber to the lengths needed. It is somewhat less frequently used for cutting plywood; and it is still more rarely used for ripping. It is also valuable in cutting lumber for certain types of joints, but that use will be discussed in chapter 5.

Usually the radial saw is operated with a single disk, but wider cuts can be made by using two or more at the same time. Before removing or adding blades, the saw should always be unplugged. The blade is held in place by a nut fastened to a bolt extending through the center of the blade. This must be unscrewed, the disk removed, the replacement fitted on, and the nut refastened. The disk must be placed so that the teeth at the bottom point away from the operator, toward the back of the table. If the saw turns while the nut is being loosened or tightened, it can be stopped by forcing the end of a piece of scrap wood under it, so that the wood is caught between the teeth and the table. Attempting to hold the saw blade with pliers will damage the teeth; holding it with the hand will damage the fingers—both undesirable effects.

The first time the saw is used, and again whenever the arm has been swung out of 90°, it should be checked to make sure that it will make a true right-angled cut. With the power turned off, pull the blade and motor forward as far as it will go. Lay a carpenter's square on the table to the left of the blade, with the long edge of the square pressed against the guide fence at the back of the table and the short edge of the square placed so that it almost touches the side of the saw blade. Slowly move the blade and motor back toward the supporting pillar. If the radial arm has been set correctly, the teeth will stay at the same distance from the edge of the square; if it has been set too far toward the left, the teeth will move away from the square, and if the arm has been set right of true position, the teeth will move toward the square. If the setting is off, the arm should be adjusted, and when finally moved to true position fastened securely.

Lumber is usually cut by laying it on the saw table with the longer side to the left and the shorter side to the right. It is often convenient to mark it for cutting after it has been set on the table. Push the blade back as far as it will go, and lay the board on the table. Catch the hook of the tape at the left end of the board, forward of the back edge, and stretch it along the board, making sure that it is parallel with the edge of the board, and that the hook stays flat against the end and does not ride up. Keeping slight tension on the tape, mark the dimension on the top surface of the board, at the back edge.

Retract the tape and lay it out of the way. Slide the board along the table, in contact with the guide, until the mark is approximately in line with the blade of the saw. Pull the blade forward until the teeth catch over the corner of the board and check the positioning, if necessary moving the board, so that the left edge of the teeth matches the pencil mark, and the thickness of the blade is set right of the mark. (In the uncommon instances in which the piece needed is placed to the right of the blade, these directions should be reversed. The blade should not be centered on the mark, but should be set so that it will cut entirely out of the waste end of the board.)

Push the blade back well free of the board and turn the motor on. Hold the lumber tight against the guide with the left hand, keeping the hand at an easy distance, well away from the cutting point. Using the hand grip on the saw, pull the blade forward slowly until it nicks the corner of the lumber, then push it back and check to make sure that it is cutting at exactly the right spot. Then pull the blade forward again in a smooth easy motion, entirely through the board, push it back against the supporting pillar, and turn the motor off. The waste piece should be disposed of, and the other piece laid aside.

If more than six boards are to be cut the same length, it is faster to fasten the first board in place. A couple of nails are driven through it into the table, spaced well apart, leaving the heads sticking up to facilitate removal. Both hands are then free, and cutting proceeds as described except that it is no longer necessary to keep hold of the first board to prevent it from shifting. An alternative method is to butt a scrap of lumber against the left end of the first board cut and nail it to the table. The first board is then removed and the second board positioned by sliding it along the guide fence until it strikes the scrap which has been nailed to the table.

It is desirable to mark the length of each board as it is cut, for reasons which are discussed in chapter 17. Only the figures need be written, omitting the conventional inch and foot marks, although the two numbers should be separated by a hyphen to reduce confusion.

Most often, it will be necessary to cut more than one piece of a particular length. It is possible to speed up the cutting by using various shortcuts. If not more than six identical pieces are to be cut, the first should be left in position. Grasp it with the right hand, being careful not to move it, and use the left to slip a second piece of wood against it, setting it so that the left side ends are matched (if it is too long to reach, an assistant can check the alignment). Both boards are then held against the fence with the left hand and the saw blade pulled across the new board and pushed back into place. The left hand slips back to hold the first board, the newly cut board is dropped on the floor or pulled forward out of the way, and a third board put in place for cutting.

Cutting in any quantity can be done more efficiently by two people. One cuts, the other keeps him supplied with lumber, marks the dimensions, and lays the lumber in piles by sizes. If long boards are being cut, he can also check the alignment of the far ends. Although this sounds like an uneven division of labor, both can work at about the same rate, and the cutting will proceed smoothly and at more than double the speed as if it were done by one person unassisted.

Sometimes it is necessary to cut lumber thicker than the ordinary 1 X 3 (which is actually 3/4" thick). The radial saw will cut such lumber, although more slowly than the thinner stock. Rather than attempting to cut through such a piece as a 2 X 4 at a single pass, it is better to raise the saw blade so that it cuts only about a half inch into the 2 X 4. After it has been pulled across and pushed back out of the way, it can be lowered another half inch and the cut made again, repeating this until the board is cut through. Although this sounds complicated, it is actually easy, and at least seems to make the cut faster than a single cut, as well as involving less risk of damage to the saw.

A useful addition to the radial-arm saw is an ordinary yardstick, glued or nailed to the front surface of the fence which serves as a guide in cutting the lumber. Pull the saw blade out half way, and then set the yardstick with the 0 end against the saw-blade, and the 36″ end on the left. This can be used as a guide for cutting lengths of lumber. It does not measure with total accuracy, but it will show approximate lengths, and will often be as accurate as is needed, especially for hidden braces or for corner-blocks. (The numbers will be upside down, but to turn them rightside up would require doing mental subtraction each time the guide was used, and it seems easier to read the dimensions directly, even if reversed.)

The radial-arm saw is used less frequently for cutting plywood. Instead, a saber saw or a portable circular saw are more likely to be preferred. The major defect of the radial saw is that it will cut only a limited distance, shorter than most cuts which must be made in plywood. It is, however, effective in cutting corner-blocks, which most scene shops use in vast quantities.

Corner-blocks are triangles of 1/4″ plywood, of the same shape as half a square cut across through diagonally opposite corners. They are sized by the length of the two sides which meet at right angles. The commonest size is 10″, although the size is not critical, and occasionally odd-sized corner-blocks, smaller or larger than the standard, may be needed. Corner-blocks are usually cut from scrap as it accumulates, maintaining a constant supply. Usually they are cut so that the visible grain of the plywood is parallel to one of the short sides, although sometimes it is more economical to cut them with the hypotenuse of the triangle parallel with the grain.

The radial-arm saw can be used in various ways to cut corner-blocks. Choice of method is a matter of convenience and personal preference. One method involves first cutting the plywood into 10″ squares. One square is then cut carefully diagonally across, and the two halves are nailed to the saw table, one on each side of the saw blade, with the hypotenuses forming a right angle pointing back toward the blade, and their corners meeting on the cut line. These serve as a guide for cutting the other blocks. Each square is fitted between them, held by the left corner, and cut through by pulling the saw forward.

Often scrap plywood is in the form of long strips. If they are seven or eight inches wide, they can be cut into acceptable corner-blocks with the grain parallel to the hypotenuse, and the sizes close enough to the standard for practical use. Measure the width of the strip and draw a line across it at one end, forming a square. Mark one diagonal of this square and cut it carefully with a saber saw. Then place the strip on the radial-saw table so that the diagonal edge fits against the guide fence, and the strip extends at an angle toward the right. Holding the left corner, cut across the strip. Moving the cut piece aside, turn the strip over and replace it in the original position. Continue until the entire strip has been cut. Although this method wastes a small triangle at each end of the strip, the cuts can be made very quickly and with a minimum of measurement.

A third method, which may be preferred by some workers, is to first cut the plywood into squares or strips, and then swing the radial arm to the 45° position and make the diagonal cuts.

It is possible to cut a circle of plywood on a radial-arm saw, for example to use as the wheel of a cart. First draw the circle on the plywood, and mark the center. Roughly trim off the excess plywood. Raise the saw blade so that it just clears the plywood, and pull it out halfway. Set the plywood on the saw table so that it comfortably clears the guide fence and adjust it so that the left edge of the blade cuts exactly at the circumference of the circle. Drive a nail through the center of the circle to hold the plywood in position on the table. Push the sawblade back and lower it to cutting position. Cut across the plywood, then turn it and cut again; repeat until most of the excess wood has been removed. Pull the blade out halfway and lock it so that it will not move. Turn the saw on and slowly revolve the sheet of plywood counterclockwise against the edge of the blade, to form a smooth curve.

Cautions.   The radial saw is an exceptionally safe power tool, largely because the easy, natural way to operate it is the safe way. The left hand is out of the way of the blade, holding the board against the guide, and the right hand is used to pull the blade forward by the hand grip, so it is also out of the way. A worker almost has to try to misuse the saw to handle it dangerously. Nevertheless, a few cautions are worth mentioning.

Always keep the left hand well away from the blade, preferably a foot or more. Usually the waste section of the piece to be cut is placed at the right; if the good section is short, the cut can often be made more safely if the longer waste piece is extended to the left, and the short piece set right of the blade. If it is still necessary to hold the wood too close to the blade, cut it with a different type of saw, hold it down with another piece of wood, or nail it temporarily to the table.

Never under any circumstances hold the right section of the board with the left hand, pulling the saw toward the left wrist with the intention of stopping the blade before it cuts through the wrist! Incredible as that seems, one technical director reports having seen more than one student attempt it. The result, he reported, was loud screams on his part and the physical removal of the offender from the sawing area. Probably anyone who would try such a thoughtless cut (stupid is probably a better word) should be forbidden entry to the scene shop. He could hardly be trusted to use a paint brush safely.

It is important that the blade of the saw not be allowed to catch on the wood and stop turning while the motor continues to run. If this should happen, the worker should train himself to turn off the motor instantly, and then free the blade, rather than attempting to free the blade first. The blade is most likely to catch while cutting plywood, especially if more than one sheet of plywood is being cut at a time; it is better to cut only a single sheet. Remember always to push the saw back after checking the position of the board, before starting the motor.

The radial arm can be safely swung to new angles with the motor plugged in but turned off (but remember to raise the blade before attempting to swing it). The blade can safely be raised or lowered with the motor running. For any other adjustment, particularly removing or replacing a blade, the saw should be unplugged so that it cannot be accidentally switched on while working.

15. The Portable Circular Saw

Description.   Like the radial-arm saw, this has a disk-shaped blade attached to a motor (Figure 3.2); like the saber saw (Figure 3.3), it has a plate which is slid along the surface of the wood when the saw is used.

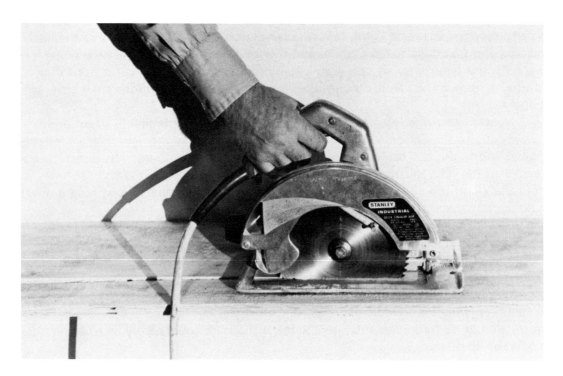

FIGURE 3.2   The portable circular saw in use.

Use. The circular saw can be used only for straight-line cuts, but because it does not have the supporting pillar of the radial-arm saw it can be used to cut anywhere, for example lengthwise through the center of a sheet of plywood, a cut which is impossible with the radial saw. The circular saw is rugged, and will cut much faster than the saber saw. It is especially useful in making long cuts in plywood, but it also can be used for crosscutting or ripping ordinary lumber, and because it is portable it can be used on stage, or for such purposes as shortening the legs of platforms taken from stock.

Cautions. This is a relatively safe power tool. The same precautions against cutting the left hand should be used as with the saber saw, and because it cuts faster such an accident would be much more serious. As with the radial saw, the cord should be disconnected before changing blades, and the blades should be attached so that the teeth at the bottom of the disk point away from the operator when the saw is used.

When a hand power tool is plugged into an extension cord, the ends of the two cords should be tied in a loose knot before they are joined; they will then be much less likely to pull apart as the tool is used.

---

16. The Saber Saw (sometimes called **Portable Jigsaw**)

Description. A small portable electric saw, with a narrow blade which moves up and down with great speed (Figure 3.3).

FIGURE 3.3 **The saber saw in use. Notice that the tip of the blade is visible just below the board; in actual operation, the blade would be moving too fast to register as more than a dim blur.**

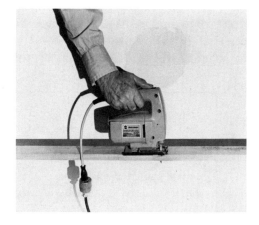

Use. The saber saw has many advantages; it is cheap, light-weight, readily portable, and small enough to be used where there is not space enough to handle other saws. A variety of interchangeable blades are available, it will cut curves of very small radius, it can be used to cut holes in the center of plywood, and it is one of the safest of the power tools. At the same time, it has certain disadvantages. In spite of manufacturers' claims, it will not cut lumber efficiently more than 3/4" thick, it is somewhat more difficult to guide in making straight cuts than other saws, and it has a relatively short life. Although saber saws can be repaired, the cost is likely to be only slightly less than the price of a new saw. In addition, the blades tend to break, although they are cheap enough that replacement is not a major expense. Metal fatigue is a factor in breakage, but misuse is a much more important cause, and only a little care will prevent it. In one scene shop, a crew member broke seven blades in quick succession, not because they were defective but because he was misusing the tool.

The blade moves vertically through a slot in a metal plate. In use, the plate is placed against the surface of the lumber, and the saw slides forward on the bottom of the plate. Girls often find it easier to use the saw if they notice that the movement is like that used in ironing clothes. For some reason, people who use the saber saw for the first time tend to hold it up off the wood, with the result that the entire saw jerks up and down uncontrollably. Instead it should be pressed down firmly but not heavily, and moved smoothly forward.

The operation is controlled by a button at the front of the handle. Most saber saws have a provision for running the saw either with the thumb holding down the button, or with the button locked so that the saw runs continuously. The first method is best if a series of short cuts are to be made, the second is more effective for a long cut.

If the saw is started with the blade in contact with the wood, it is possible for the teeth to lock on the edge of the board and damage the saw. The blade should be held back slightly from the wood before the saw is turned on, and it should be moved into contact only after it has begun to vibrate.

As with the hand saw, the cutting is done by the teeth of the blade. Pushing forward with unnecessary force slows the cutting, makes it more difficult to cut accurately, and may damage the saw. Excessive pressure can be identified by the fact that the sound of the saw drops in pitch as it slows down. The worker should train himself to listen to the saw, and let up on forward pressure whenever he hears a lower pitch.

> The upper half of a saber saw blade tends to get dull first. The blade can still be used even after that section of the blade is too dull to cut effectively. Lay short lengths of 1 X 3 on each side of the cutting line, about an inch apart, and rest the base of the saw on them. This shortens the effective length of the stroke, and the worker should check to make sure that the blade will still cut entirely through the lumber, but this technique will always work for cutting 1/4" plywood.

The ability of the saber saw to cut sharp curves depends on the fact that the blade is something less than a quarter of an inch wide. But if the saw is forced to turn at a radius smaller than its limit, the blade will be weakened, and will either snap immediately or will break the next time it is used.

Set construction often requires cuts which cannot be made with a saber saw in a single forward motion. If the blade must be turned to follow a curve with an extremely small radius, the slot cut by the saw must be enlarged to provide more turning space, by pulling it back and making a series of short cuts side by side in the waste area.

The same method can be used to make a cut which turns at a sharp angle (Figure 3.4). Another method can be illustrated by describing cutting a square hole in the center of a piece of plywood. First a hole is drilled in the middle of the square, slightly larger than the saw blade. The blade is then inserted and a cut made in a curving path which joins one side of the square at a tangent; the cut is continued along the edge of

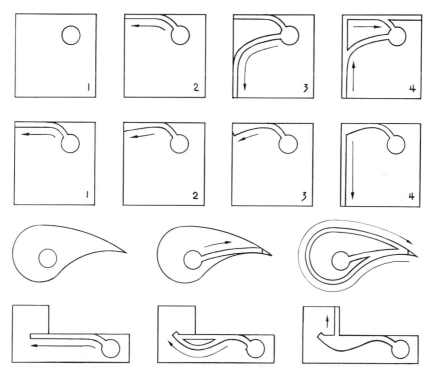

FIGURE 3.4 Making special cuts with the saber saw. In each case, a hole is drilled first to receive the blade. *Top row*, a series of cuts are made with the saw in different directions along the edges of the square to be cut out; *second row*, the end of the initial cut is enlarged by making a series of short cuts until it is possible to turn the blade. *Bottom row*, a crescent-shaped section is cut out to provide space for turning the blade so as to cut an exterior corner. *Third row*, the method of cutting out a leaf-shaped hole. The saw blade is too thick to cut all the way out to the point of the figure; if necessary, the cut can be finished with a knife.

the square to the corner. The blade is then pulled out of the wood, the saw turned around, and the blade reinserted in the slot, pointing in the opposite direction, and the side of the square is cut to the opposite corner. Repeating these cuts for the other sides will remove the center square, leaving a clean, true outline.

Manufacturers sometimes include instructions for starting a saw cut in the center of a sheet of plywood, using the saber saw alone. This method has no advantages, and a number of disadvantages: it is inaccurate, difficult, and likely to damage the blade. Instead, a hole should always be drilled to start the cut.

Heavy or corrugated cardboard can be cut with an ordinary saber saw blade, but knife blades without teeth are also available, and make smoother cuts. They are not suitable for cutting wood or hard pressed boards (like Masonite). The blade fits into a slot in the saw, and is held in place by a set screw. In some saws, the screw runs through a hole in the blade; in others, it simply presses against the side of the blade, holding it by friction. Some set screws are slotted so that they can be turned with a small screwdriver; others require a special wrench, which is supplied along with the saw.

The saw should be disconnected before changing blades. The set screw is loosened, and the blade pulled out with the fingers and replaced; the teeth are placed so that they point away from the operator. The set screw is then retightened, and the saw is ready to use.

If a short piece of the blade is left inside the saw when the blade breaks, it can be removed as follows: loosen the set screw more than usual, hold the saw a few inches above the workbench, base down, plug it in and turn it on; after a few strokes, the short piece will fly out.

Cautions.   The saber saw is one of the safest of power tools. Almost the only way in which the worker can hurt himself with it is in making a cut parallel with the edge of the lumber, and closer to the edge than four inches. He is likely to grasp the edge of the lumber with his free hand, and it is just possible that the blade might run into his fingers, hidden below the wood. Only a little care will prevent that happening.

One other danger is also easily avoided. There is a tendency for people who are using the saber saw for the first time to bend over close to the saw so as to see where it is cutting. Since it throws out sawdust with some force, there is a possibility of getting it in the eyes. The position is quite unnecessary, and in fact makes guiding the saw a little less accurate. The cut can be seen just as clearly if the operator stands erect, leaning slightly forward and to the left, with his eyes far above the spray of sawdust.

Because the blade moves at great speed, if the saw is pulled out of the wood while it is still moving it is likely to bounce unpleasantly on the surface of the wood, with at least a possibility of weakening the blade. The saw should always be turned off and the blade allowed to stop completely before it is removed from the wood.

The blade will resist considerable forward pressure; it can easily be broken if it is twisted (as in cutting too sharp a curve), or pressed sidewise. That is most likely to occur when a cut has been made inaccurately, and the worker attempts to correct it by shaving off a thin layer of the wood. Although that can be done, it is important to resist the tendency to apply sidewise force.

If a saber saw blade breaks off close to the end by which it is fastened, it may still be possible to continue to use it. Turn the set screw well out, remove the small piece of blade still in the saw, push the broken end of the blade well into the socket, and tighten the set screw a little more firmly than usual. This will shorten the cut, so it should be checked to make sure that the blade will still go entirely through the lumber which is being cut.

It may be helpful to summarize these cautions:

1. Never start the saw with the teeth in contact with the wood.
2. Never force the saw to cut curves with a radius smaller than its practical limit.
3. Always wait for the blade to stop moving before removing it from the wood.
4. Keep the plate firmly in contact with the surface of the wood.
5. Train yourself to keep your free hand well out of the way of the blade.
6. When changing blades or making any other adjustment in the saw it should not only be turned off, but the power cord should be disconnected.

17. The Band Saw

Description. The blade of the band saw is in the form of a long, narrow ring (something like the shape of a rubber band). The blade passes over two wheels, one of which is electrically powered. Between them, a working surface is provided on which lumber can be placed, and moved past the saw blade in a straight or curved path. The band saw cuts faster and more smoothly than the saber saw; it is not portable, and is limited in the depth of cut which can be made (it cannot be used, for instance, in cutting in the center of a sheet of plywood, as can the saber saw). Some technical workers prefer the band saw for any cuts which are possible with it; others choose the saber saw as more flexible and less troublesome.

Long straight cuts in a sheet of plywood can be made faster and more accurately with either a saber saw or a portable circular saw if a board is clamped or temporarily nailed to the sheet as a guide. The board must be parallel with the cut, and at a distance from it which will place the saw blade in the right position. The plate of the saw is pressed on the surface of the plywood, and run along with the side edge in contact with the guide.

18. The Brace and Bit

Description. The brace is a **U**-shaped structure, into which a bit can be fitted, one end of which has the shape of a four-sided pyramid; the other end has a pointed tip with screw threads, and larger threads extend about halfway up the shaft.

Bits come in a variety of types and sizes. Each has a number stamped on it indicating in sixteenths of an inch the diameter of the hole which it will cut. Thus, a number 4 bit will drill a hole a quarter of an inch in diameter, a number 6 bit will make a three-eighths inch hole, and a number 8 a half-inch hole.

Use. The brace and bit are held so that the shaft of the bit is at right angles to the surface of the wood, the point is pressed against the wood, the left hand presses down on the wooden pad at the top of the brace, and the right hand grasps the handle at the side and swings it around in horizontal circles. The screw point pulls the bit into and through the wood, and the shaft threads cut a hole.

Sometimes it is necessary to drill a hole where there is not space to turn the brace entirely around, for instance on the underside of a platform, where the legs of the platform may get in the way. By setting a ratchet on the brace, it is possible to swing it through part of the circle, swing back without turning the bit, and then swing forward again.

A nail can be used in a hand brace or a power drill as a bit for boring very small holes, perhaps to run wire through. In order to fit in the chuck, a finishing nail must be used or the shaft of the nail must be clipped off just under the head.

19. The Power Drill

Description. This is a powered version of the brace and bit, with two differences. Since it is electrically powered, it does not have the offset handle of the brace, which is designed to provide greater leverage. Bits for the power drill do not have a screw tip. Because they revolve at much greater speed than the brace and bit, normal pressure will force them through the wood.

Use. Power bits are of various sizes and types, and can easily be fitted in the drill. The power drill requires less effort than the brace-and-bit, and it drills at much greater speed. It is especially useful if a great many holes are to be cut, and it will operate in small spaces without the tedious back-and-forth swing that may be necessary with a brace and bit. Many drills have provision for inserting a special screw-driver blade for setting screws faster than can be done by hand.

Cautions. The drill should be unplugged before changing bits, and care should be taken that when it drills through the wood it does not strike the supporting tables or sawhorses, or, of course, the hand of the operator. To cut effectively, drills must be kept sharp. The bit should not be laid down on a concrete or metal surface, and the worker should check before drilling to make sure that the bit will not run through or against a nail, screw, staple, or other piece of metal.

20. Knives

Description. The most useful knives have a handle made in two parts, held together by a bolt. They are provided with replaceable blades, which are fitted between the two halves of the handle and held firmly in place when the bolt is tightened.

Use. Knives are used most frequently in the scene shop to trim off the edge of canvas after it has been fastened to flats; they can also be used to make short cuts at the edge of the canvas when it is taken from the roll, to make it easier to tear. Their next most frequent use is in cutting cardboard, including corrugated cardboard, light cardboard for patterns, and even upson board.

Cautions. New blades are extremely sharp and should be used with care. Material to be cut may be laid on a wood surface, but not on metal or concrete, which will dull the blades instantly.

21. Rasps

Description. The oldest form of the rasp is similar to a file, except that the surface is covered with pointed teeth, widely spaced, to cut away the surface of a piece of wood quickly.

A relatively new instrument, sold under various brand names, is made of a small perforated metal sheet with similar projecting teeth, the sheet being held in a frame something like a plane, with one handle which serves as a guide, and one used to push it. When the metal plate gets dull, it can be removed and replaced with a new one.

Use. Only fairly rough work can be done with either type of rasp, although for theatrical use the finish is usually acceptable, and it can be further smoothed with sandpaper if necessary. The rasp surface is pressed against the wood and moved back and forth, usually diagonally, to cut it away to the desired shape.

Besides finishing wood, the rasp is also effective in rough shaping of rigid foam plastics, and in shaping units built up from laminated corrugated cardboard (see chapter 9).

22. X-Shaped Tools

Description. Scissors, tinsnips, and pliers are made of two blades, bolted near the center, with handles at one end and cutting edges or gripping surfaces at the other.

Use. Scissors are used most often in cutting canvas for flats, but they have other miscellaneous uses, such as cutting patterns from thin cardboard.

Tinsnips (or tin shears) are used occasionally for cutting sheet metal in the scene shop, more often for cutting wire; wire cutters will do the job better, and pliers less effectively. Pliers are used for turning nuts, bending wire, and other light gripping.

TOOLS FOR JOINING AND SEPARATING

23. Hammers

Description. A hammer is essentially a two-part tool, made up of a head and a wooden handle; some hammers are made of a single piece of steel, so that the handles cannot loosen or break.

Hammers differ in dimension, weight, and shape of head. The three types which are most frequently used in the scene shop are the claw hammer, the rip hammer, and the tack hammer.

The term *claw hammer* is misleading, since rip hammers also have claws. They differ in that the claws of the rip hammer are nearly straight, to make it easier to slip them between boards which must be pried apart, and those of the claw hammer are curved, to make it easier to rock them back when pulling nails. Tack hammers are smaller and lighter, and often are magnetized, so that a tack can be attached to them and swung down and into the wood, rather than being dangerously held with the fingers while it is driven.

Use. Almost everyone can acquire skill in using a hammer, but many people seem more hesitant about its use than with any other tool.

The handle of the hammer produces significant mechanical advantage. It would be possible to drive nails with a hammer head alone, but using the handle provides much greater leverage and force. The longer the handle, or the closer to the end it is held, the greater the advantage. Many beginners tend to hold the handle close to the head, or to "choke it," as carpenters say; they should make a conscious effort to force their hand well away from the head, toward the end of the handle.

However, the greater leverage requires the use of greater muscular power, and a carpenter who uses too heavy a hammer or holds it out too far from the head may quickly become too tired to work efficiently. Each worker should experiment with the hammers available in order to find the weight which is right for him, and should also experiment with holding the handle at different distances. Once he has become accustomed to the most efficient use of the hammer, it will become automatic, but at first a worker who tends to choke the hammer should continually remind himself to push out toward the end of the handle.

In driving a nail, it is held in the left hand, with the point in contact with the wood, and given a light blow or two with the hammer to set it, that is, to drive it into the wood far enough that it will stay in position. The left hand is then removed, and the nail driven in with solid blows all the way. Once the nail is set, there is no longer any advantage in holding it, and it is much safer to get the fingers out of the way.

> When a nail must be driven into a spot where there is not enough space to hold it with the left hand, take a three- or four-inch bolt and screw on the nut a turn or two, so that most of it extends beyond the end of the bolt. Fit the nail head in the hole in the nut, against the end of the bolt, place the point against the wood, and set the nail by tapping the head of the bolt with a hammer. The bolt is then removed and the nail driven all the way with the hammer.

Driving the nail straight, neither knocking it at a slant or bending it, depends on swinging the hammer so that the striking surface is exactly at right angles to the shaft of the nail at the moment of contact. That is easiest to achieve if the work can be placed so that the elbow is about level with the head of the nail. The hammer should be swung firmly and with force. Accuracy is not increased by making weak and timid blows, although beginners often assume so.

The power of the hammer blow depends on the weight of the hammer, the distance between the head and the point where the handle is gripped, the muscular force which is exerted as it is swung down, and the length of the swing. People who hammer ineffectively, besides choking the hammer, often provide little force themselves, relying simply on the weight of the hammer as it falls, and they also often take very short swings, usually on the false assumption that short blows will be more accurate. Forcing the hammer higher on the up-swing and pulling it down sharply on the down-swing will increase efficiency. Occasionally, workers will try to use only the wrist in hammering; lengthening the swing prevents that, and makes use of the more powerful arm muscles.

Some of the force provided by the hammer stroke is reversed, so that the hammer bounces up off the nail. It is efficient to synchronize the hammering with this bounce, so that it provides momentum for the upswing. Each hammer has a rhythm of its own, and if the worker will sense it and make use of it he can drive the nails faster and with less effort. Occasionally a worker displays a rather peculiar pattern in which he strikes one solid blow, lets the hammer bounce up and fall back on the nail, and then raises it for the next productive blow. This not only wastes time, but fails to take advantage of the bounce energy.

One final error is frequent among novice workers. It is a psychological error, and correcting it will often improve efficiency astonishingly. The hammer must of course strike the head of the nail, but if it is to drive the nail into the wood it must continue past that point, pushing the nail down below it. The hammer must therefore be aimed not at the level at which the head of the nail stands, but rather at the surface of the board, where the nail must be driven. Workers who focus on striking the head provide so little energy that driving the nail requires from three to five times as many blows as if they aimed at the point at which it enters the wood.

Skill in nailing is generally thought of as the clearest mark of general ability in carpentry. Careful analysis of nailing techniques will make it possible for the least experienced person to become an effective and economical nailer, and will be a source of justifiable pride for the worker.

Hammers can also be used to pull nails out. If the heads have been driven flush with the surface of the wood, they must be pried up, usually with a screw driver especially designated for that purpose. The claws are then slipped under the head, the handle is grasped close to the end, and it is forced back so that the head rocks on the claws and the nail is pulled out of the wood. As the claws push up against the head of the nail, the hammer must push down against something else. The hammer should be turned so that it is solidly in contact with the wood. Attempting to pull a nail out of the side of a 1 X 3, with the head of the hammer at right angles to the board and pushing only against air, is a frustrating and inefficient experience.

When pulling a nail with a hammer, the greatest leverage is applied at the start of the pull; as the nail comes farther and farther out of the wood, less power is provided by the hammer. If the nail is large and resistant, leverage can be restored by moving the hammer back into the upright position, holding the claws up in contact with the underside of the head of the nail, and slipping a scrap of lumber under the hammer head next to the nail, on the side opposite the claws (Figure 3.5). The thickest piece of lumber should be used which will slip in easily, usually a 1 X 3. For a very resistant nail, additional pieces can be laid on top of the first after the nail has been pulled out still farther.

FIGURE 3.5 Using blocks to pull nails. Four stages of the process: *1*, the nail is started with the hammer alone; *2*, the hammer is rocked forward and a scrap of lumber pushed under it; *3*, the hammer is brought back, pulling the nail out still farther; *4*, a second block has been put on top of the first one, and the nail is pulled out all the way.

Ripsaws and rip hammers sound as if they were intended for the same purpose, but *rip* means different things in the two cases. Rip hammers are used for separating boards which have been fastened together, either to correct mistakes or to take scenery apart after the last performance of a show.

If there is a gap between the boards, the straight claws of the rip hammer can be slipped in, the handle pulled back to widen the gap, and the claws slipped in farther. If the boards are nailed tightly, the claws can be inserted by setting them in place and striking the face of the rip hammer with another hammer, thus driving the claws in between the boards.

It is sometimes easier to separate boards by swinging the handle of the hammer sidewise, in a path parallel with the face of the board, rather than pulling back on it, as would be done in removing a nail.

Occasionally the head of a nail will break off while it is being pulled out, leaving nothing for the claws of the hammer to pull against. Set the claws in place and tap lightly on the face of the hammer with a second hammer, so that it grips the shaft of the nail close to the wood, then swing the hammer sidewise with a rolling motion, rather than rocking it back toward the hammer face. This will bend the nail and pull it out slightly. Swing the hammer in the opposite direction, pushing it down until it touches the face of the lumber. After two or three such swings in alternate directions the nail will pull free.

If the nails fastening the two boards together have been clinched, they should be at least partly straightened before the boards are pried apart. Not only will it be easier to separate them, but there is much less danger of destroying the boards. If the end of the nail has been driven well into the surface of the wood, so that it is not possible to slip the claws of the hammer under it, it should be pried up slightly. As soon as the point is clear of the surface of the wood, the hammer claws should be forced under it, so that the claws are parallel to the horizontal end of the nail, and pointing toward where it is bent. When the hammer has been pushed as far as possible toward the shaft of the nail, it should be rocked forward, pushing the handle toward the claws. This will raise the tip of the nail farther. The hammer should then be slipped out and the nail straightened by striking it from the side.

If the head of a nail breaks off while it is being pulled out, lift the board off the workbench and tap the nail directly down, in other words hammering it back into the board. Then turn the board over and pull it out from the other side.

Cautions. Statistically, more than half the accidents which occur in the scene shop consist of hitting the thumb with a hammer, which may be very painful but which seldom causes serious injury. Such accidents can be almost totally prevented by using sound nailing techniques, but particularly by keeping the left hand out of the way after the nail has been first set into the wood by a few light taps. Beginners tend to continue holding the nail as they strike it harder, and to attempt to force it straight with their fingers if it has begun to go crooked. The fingers will not resist the force of a strong blow, and if the nail goes crooked it is because the face of the hammer was not square with the nail head at the moment of contact. This should be corrected either by pulling out the nail and starting it in a new hole or by striking it once or twice with the face angled in the opposite direction until it has been straightened, and then driving it squarely the rest of the way.

24. Nail Pullers

Description. At first glance, the nail puller looks somewhat like a J-shaped crowbar (Figure 3.6). The top of the long section is shaped to form a handle, and the shaft is surrounded by a cylindrical shield which can be slipped up and down. The curved section at the bottom of the tool is made of a separate piece of steel, pivoted so that it will swing up and down, controlling the space between a pair of short pointed jaws.

FIGURE 3.6   Using the nail puller. *Left*, the nail puller is set at the correct angle so that the jaws bracket the head of the nail, and they are driven into the wood; *right*, the tool is rocked back, pulling up the nail.

Use. The nail puller is the set worker's joy and despair. The only way it can be used is awkwardly, yet it will pull nails effectively when they cannot be removed by any other tool. It tends to be used only when all other methods of pulling nails have failed, but as a tool of last resort it is invaluable.

If the nail puller is placed vertically on a board, with the handle at the top, and then swung at various angles, the pointed jaws at the bottom will open and close. In use, the puller is set over the nail and angled so that the jaws are on opposite sides of the head of the nail to be pulled, close to but not touching it. Holding the handle at the bottom in the left hand, and carefully maintaining the angle of the shaft, the sliding sleeve is grasped with the right hand, pushed up as far as it will go, and then driven down toward the wood with considerable force. Probably a half dozen blows will be necessary; each one forces the pointed jaws into the wood beside the nail. When they are below the nail head, the handle at the top of the shaft is pushed toward the side where the curved end of the J shape rests on the wood. The result is to close the jaws, which move under the nail head and meet on each side of the shaft of the nail. Continuing to push in the same direction with steady force against the handle at the top of the puller will slowly pull the nail out of the wood.

To be used effectively, the nail puller must be placed precisely; when the jaws close, they must be centered on the nail. While they are being driven into the wood, if the angle at which the puller is set shifts, one of the jaws may slip up over the nail, so that it is driven farther into the wood, and will be still more difficult to extricate.

25. Crowbars

Description. The crowbar is made of steel, with a long and a short section forming either the shape of a J or an L.

Use. The strength of the metal, and the leverage provided by the length of the crowbar, make it possible to apply great force in spreading boards apart. Either end of the bar is slipped between boards which have been fastened together, and the other end used to force them apart. The L-shaped bars may be preferable, because the right angle at which the sections are joined makes it easier to use a hammer to drive the end of the bar into the crack between the boards, although they are shorter than the J-shaped bars and so provide less leverage.

26. Screwdrivers

Description. The ordinary screwdriver is a simple metal shaft with a handle at one end and the other end flattened to form a blade ending in a straight line at right angles to the shaft. Ratchet screwdrivers have threaded shafts and moving parts. (Phillips screwdrivers have a pointed end, with ridges which when viewed from the tip form a +; they are seldom used in the scene shop.) Screwdrivers vary in the length of the handle and in the width and thickness of the blade.

Use. The tip of the screwdriver is inserted into the slot in the head of a screw, with the shaft of the screwdriver directly in line with the centerline of the screw. The left thumb and forefinger hold the shaft lightly just above the flattened section, and the right hand grasps the handle at the end of the screwdriver and simultaneously forces it toward the screw and turns it, clockwise to drive the screw into the wood, counterclockwise to remove it. When the right hand has turned the screwdriver as far as is convenient, the fingers of the left hand tighten to hold it firmly, the right hand is slipped back into its original position without turning the screwdriver, the handle is gripped firmly, the grip of the left hand loosened, and the screwdriver is turned again, the shaft slipping between the fingers of the left hand. Although this sounds complicated, a few minutes' practice will make it easy.

> A dime can be used as a makeshift substitute for a screwdriver. This is a very old trick which is useful especially if only a little turning is needed to tighten a screw.

The ratchet screwdriver is placed in the same position with regard to the screw, but the left hand grasps a knurled sleeve just above the blade, and the right hand pushes down on the handle at the end of the driver, alternately letting it slip back to its full length and then pushing down again. The shaft has a button which can be set in three positions; in one, the blade turns clockwise so as to drive the screw into the wood, in another the blade turns so as to remove the screw, and the third setting deactivates the up-and-down movement, so that the screwdriver can be turned manually like an ordinary driver.

Two problems appear in driving screws. The first is that until the screw has begun to bite into the wood it is unstable, and will not stay upright. This can be solved in three ways. (1) The screw can be held lightly in the fingers, and turned with the driver until it is set firmly enough to stay upright; the fingers of the left hand can then be moved up to the shaft, and the driving completed as has been described. (2) A shallow hole considerably smaller than the screw can be drilled in the wood or cut by driving a nail in for a short distance and then pulling it out; the point of the screw can then be forced into the hole either with the fingers or with a few light turns of the screwdriver, and the driving completed by stronger turns. (3) The screw can be held with the fingers and tapped with a hammer until it is set in the wood. However, it must not be driven more than half or two-thirds of the way in. The setting must be completed by using a screwdriver. This third method is the fastest, and the one most frequently used in the scene shop.

> When a screw must be started at a point where there is not room to hold it between the fingers, break out a tooth near the end of a discarded comb, slip the screw into the space where the tooth has been removed, and hold it in place against the board by grasping the end of the comb, until it has been set by a couple of hammer taps. The comb can then be removed and the screw driven in the rest of the way with a screwdriver. A rat-tail comb is the easiest to use for this purpose.

In driving screws, one corner of the blade pushes against one side of the slot in the head of the screw, and the other corner pushes against the other side of the slot. Unless both corners fit squarely in the slot, the blade will slip out. This can result from three causes. (1) When blades are resharpened, the tip is sometimes given the shape of the arc of a circle, rather than a straight line; such screwdrivers should be reground. (2) The slot in the head of the screw may be worn, so that there is not a straight vertical surface for the screwdriver to push against. These screws should be discarded—in the wastebasket, not put back in the screw box. They can never be used, and it is better to get rid of them immediately. (3) The screwdriver may be held at an angle, rather than parallel with the centerline of the screw. This is the commonest source of trouble. It occurs most frequently when the screw has been set at a slight angle. The worker may then hold the screwdriver vertical to the surface of the wood, which would have been correct if the screw itself had been set straight; but the driver must be oriented with the screw, not the surface it is being driven into. Often it may be acceptable to continue driving the screw at an angle. If not, it can be tapped straight with a hammer, and given a tap or two straight down on the head to set it at the correct angle. In any case, it can be turned effectively only if the screwdriver is set into the slot properly. Even a slight error in angle will result in its repeatedly slipping out.

It is best if the blade of the screwdriver exactly matches the slot of the screw, in both width and thickness. Smaller screwdrivers can be used, but if the blade is wider than the screw it will dig out the wood around the head, and if it is thicker than the slot it cannot be used at all.

Most screws used in the scene shop have heads which are flat on top, and which are slightly conical underneath. They are usually driven into the wood until the head is even with the surface, or slightly below it. The last few turns will require greater force, because the head presses against a larger area of the wood. Once they have been firmly set, the worker should resist the temptation to give them just one or two extra turns. These are likely to ream out the hole which the screw has cut in the wood, with a nearly complete loss of holding power. The worker can tell this has happened by the fact that the last turn or two will require less force rather than more. If that happens, the screw should be removed and set in a different hole. If that is not possible, then a longer or wider screw should be driven into the original hole.

> If the same size screw must be reset in a hole which has been accidentally reamed out, slivers of wood should be dipped in glue and forced tightly into the hole until it is nearly filled (wooden matchsticks will do). The pieces which extend above the surface of the board are sliced off with a knife. The screw should be replaced, using only a screwdriver (not setting it first with a hammer), and being careful not to ream out the hole again. The screw will hold firmly after the glue has dried.

Screwdrivers are also frequently used for purposes other than driving screws—opening buckets of paint, digging out the ends of nails which have been driven below the surface of the wood, forcing nail heads up from wood so that the claws of hammers can be slipped under them, prying boards apart, and even as substitutes for chisels, in occasionally chipping out a small section of a board. Purists object to such activities, with greater or less intensity. Undoubtedly they are all to some extent misuses, and some of them may damage the tools. However, quite cheap screwdrivers are available, sometimes for as little as twenty-five cents apiece, and they are so generally useful that it is worth having a few, specially designated for uses other than driving screws. If they are marked, perhaps by painting a colored stripe around the shaft, they are a useful addition to the tool kit. Certainly, screwdrivers which will be used for driving screws should be protected from any misuse which will damage them.

Cautions. It is possible for a worker to produce nasty cuts or blood blisters with a screwdriver. Fortunately, such accidents are almost completely preventable. With an ordinary screwdriver, they are most likely to occur if the worker continues to hold the screw after he has begun to increase pressure with his other hand. The fingers should be moved up on to the shaft of the driver as soon as the screw has been set, so that if the driver slips as the force is increased it will strike the wood rather than the hand.

Injuries from ratchet screwdrivers occur when the operator by mistake grasps the grooved shaft and slams the top of the screwdriver down on his fingers. One such experience will make clear the preferability of holding it by the knurled sleeve just above the blade, but it is better if the proper method can be followed without the painful demonstration.

27. Staplers

Description. Staplers are of varied types, and differ in appearance. All are alike in expelling short lengths of wire, bent in a square U shape. They vary primarily in the size of the staples which they will accommodate, and the amount of force with which they are expelled. The familiar office staplers used to fasten sheets of paper together are nearly useless in the scene shop.

Three types of staplers are of value in building scenery. All three differ from ordinary paper staplers in that the legs of the staples are driven out straight, rather than being bent flat. Two of them are hand powered. The one most commonly found in scene shops is the spring-driven stapler. It has a handle which is automatically returned to its operating position after each staple has been driven.

The second type is called a stapling hammer. It has a fixed handle, and each staple is driven by swinging the entire stapler, and striking the surface to be stapled with a hammer blow.

The third type of stapler is operated, like the spring-driven stapler, by pressing a movable handle, but the force by which the staple is expelled is supplied not by the operator's muscles but by compressed air. Consequently, the stapler must be connected with a hose to an air tank or air pump.

Use.   The hand-powered staplers are used more frequently in attaching canvas to the frames of flats. They are also effective in fastening cardboard of various weights, from very light up through upson board or acoustical tiles. They can be used to fasten upholstery material to furniture, to hold down platform padding, and even to fasten light rugs in place on the stage floor.

Most staplers are designed to take staples with legs of various lengths. Each staple is an individual piece of shaped wire, but they are lightly fastened together to form bars four or five inches long. The stapler is first opened to expose the staple container, a bar of staples is set in, and the stapler shut again. The spring-driven stapler is then set firmly on the material fastened, and a staple is expelled by pressing the handle down. The hand pressure is eased and a spring snaps the handle back into position for driving the next staple.

If the stapler is operating well, the staples will be driven firmly into the wood, with the crossbar of the wire tight against the surface of the material being stapled. Unfortunately staplers often operate less than perfectly; the staples may not be driven in all the way, or one may jam, so that no more staples can be driven out. Staplers are more subject to attacks by gremlins and poltergeists than any other theatrical tools. The closest analysis of the tool itself or the way it is used may fail to reveal why it will drive a thousand staples perfectly, mangle the next two hundred, and then suddenly correct itself and purr along for the rest of the day with no problems. However, a few hints may be helpful.

Staplers tend to jam as they become empty. The staples are pushed forward by a spring, which provides the strongest force when the stapler is fully loaded and weakens as it empties. When staplers begin to function unsatisfactorily, the first step should be to check the supply of staples, and reload if the container is less than half full.

70

If staples are not driven all the way down, the stapler may be riding on an uneven surface, perhaps the edge of the cloth being fastened, so that forcing the handle down rocks the stapler back and lifts the slot where the staples emerge slightly off the surface. The staples can be driven flush with a tap of a hammer. An alternative is to press down at the front of the stapler with the left hand while operating the driving handle with the right. Some staplers have a spot painted on top indicating the best point to press.

If a staple comes out only part way and jams in the slot it must be removed with pliers or by taking the stapler apart; but the next staple is equally likely to jam. First check the supply of staples and reload if it is running low. Second, check the slot; its thickness is usually controlled by a metal plate, which may have loosened, and which can be tightened with a screw driver. Finally, check to make sure that the correct staples are being used. Staples designed for one stapler will seldom fit in another, and each stapler will accept only staples within a certain range of sizes. If the wrong staples have been used, they should be replaced.

If all else fails—and it may—the solution is to switch to a different stapler. By the next day, the malfunctioning stapler may have inexplicably repaired itself.

The most effective use of a spring-driven stapler requires both hands, especially if the stapler is not functioning properly. But in the commonest stapling job, attaching canvas to flats, one hand must be used to keep the cloth tight while it is being stapled. The stapling hammer is the solution to this problem. As it is struck against the material being stapled, the force of the blow triggers the mechanism, and the staple is driven out. Even if the spring-driven stapler is operating perfectly, the stapling hammer is faster. Its only defect is that it is more difficult to place the staples with precision, but for most theatrical purposes, and especially for canvassing flats, the allowable margin of error is large enough that it is not serious.

The compressed air stapler is noisier, more expensive, bulkier, and less portable than the hand staplers, and it requires special equipment. Its great advantage is that it takes less effort, and can drive staples with greater force. These advantages are relatively unimportant for canvassing flats, but they provide a method of assembling flat frames which is much faster than any of the traditional techniques. Instead of using screws or clout nails, the plywood corner-blocks can be attached with the compressed air stapler, easily and with great speed. They do not hold quite as firmly as the other methods, but if the corner-blocks are also glued the joints will be stronger than those made by traditional methods.

Cautions. Staplers are deceptively harmless tools; in fact, if they are unintelligently misused they can be quite dangerous. Usually staples are chosen which have shorter legs than the thickness of the materials being joined. If the legs stick through, they must be bent over and flattened with a hammer. When putting them in, the operator should be careful not to support the materials from underneath with his free hand at the point being stapled, to avoid puncturing the skin.

71

Whenever a stapler is taken from the tool room, the first question is whether it is loaded. The sensible way to find out is to open it, but more than one worker has checked by shooting a staple through the air toward his cupped hand. The staples are expelled with more force than may be suspected, and the cupped-hand technique is very likely to result in serious wounds.

It should not be necessary to warn workers against engaging in stapling duels, in which they shoot staples through the air at each other, but unfortunately such jokers are not totally unknown in the scene shop. Not only can staples inflict flesh wounds, but if one should strike an eye it could easily cause blindness. The level of intelligence demonstrated by such antics matches that of workers who use the crossed-hands technique of operating the radial-arm saw, and the proper response is the same—they should be led firmly out of the scene shop and instructed never to return, restricting their activities to tossing marshmallows through hoops, or some other sport equally free of hazards.

28. Clamps

Description.   In fundamental design, clamps are somewhat like wrenches. They have two jaws, one of which can be moved so as to alter the space between them. The type which is most frequently used in the scene shop is called a **C**-clamp, because the largest of the three pieces of metal from which it is made is shaped something like the letter **C** (Figure 3.7). One tip of the **C** has a flat surface which constitutes one of the two jaws. At the other tip is a threaded hole, through which a special bolt extends, one end of which forms the second jaw of the clamp. The other end of the bolt has a hole in which a metal rod is inserted loosely, which serves as a handle in turning the bolt. **C**-clamps are available in different sizes; the jaw openings can be adjusted from zero up to the distance between the ends of the metal piece forming the **C** shape. In the commonest size, the maximum opening is slightly less than 3".

The second most frequently used instrument is called a *bar clamp*. It operates much like the **C**-clamp, except that instead of one jaw's being fixed, it is a separate piece which can be slid along a metal bar. This bar has notches spaced along one edge, which catch and hold the jaw at particular distances from the end of the clamp. Although it can be moved from notch to notch, once it is in position it becomes fixed, and precise adjustment of the spacing between the jaws is controlled, as with the **C**-clamp, by turning a handle attached to a threaded shaft, thus moving the second jaw. The advantage of the bar clamp is that it provides a wide range of settings, from zero up to just short of the total length of the bar, which may be several feet. When work to be fastened will fit between the jaws of a **C**-clamp, it is to be preferred, as lighter, more convenient, and less awkward than the bar clamp, but for larger projects the bar clamp is invaluable.

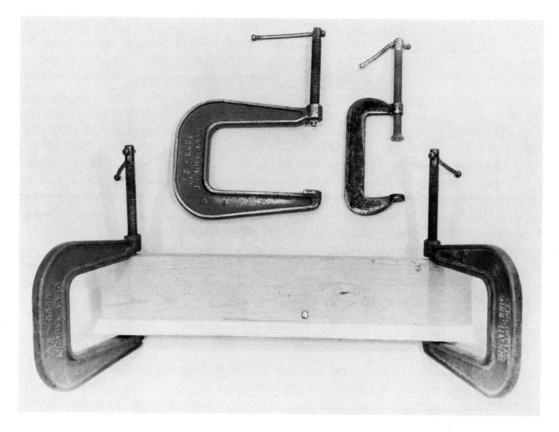

FIGURE 3.7   C–clamps. *Top*, two slightly different shapes. *Below*, clamps
are used to hold two glued boards together while the glue sets (the bottom
board is seen on edge).

A third type of clamp, with wooden jaws, also appears in some scene shops. It
will open wider than a **C**-clamp, but is somewhat clumsy to use.

Use.   Clamps are seldom used except to hold glued joints together while they dry. Few
joints are glued except for furniture, which is subjected to such repeated strain in various directions that the joints are likely to loosen. **C**-clamps can also be used to fasten
the legs of adjacent platforms together on stage. They can then be separated for shifting without having to use tools.

29. Wrenches

Description.   The simplest wrench is a length of steel with a hole or jaws cut at one or
both ends, matching the shape and size of the metal piece to be held or turned. More

complicated wrenches have moving parts which make it possible to alter the distance between the jaws, so that they can be used to hold bolts or pipes of various sizes. Examples of such tools are monkey wrenches, crescent wrenches, and pipe wrenches. Ordinary pliers should also be mentioned, since they do light work of the same type.

Use. Wrenches are most often used in the scene shop to tighten bolts in assembling high platforms. How frequently they are used depends on the preferences and habits of work of the set designer and technical director.

Most jobs require two wrenches. One is set to fit the head of the bolt, and the other slipped over the nut and used to turn it while the bolt is held. The leverage provided by the handle increases the force which can be applied, and holding the wrench near the end of the handle makes maximal use of the leverage.

In most theaters, the light crews make more frequent and varied use of wrenches than do the set crews, and are likely to have a better supply. It is desirable to maintain friendly relations with the light crew, so that the stock of wrenches in the scene shop can be supplemented by borrowing from them.

> An improvised plumb line can be made from a length of thread or light string with a loop tied at one end and a washer fastened to the other.

MISCELLANEOUS EQUIPMENT

31. Sawhorses

Since set construction projects are so varied, it is important to be able to use the work areas as flexibly as possible. Permanent work benches eat up valuable space, so that it is better to support work on sawhorses which can be easily moved, or which can be compactly stored when a large area is needed for activities such as spattering.

A new sawhorse design has been developed which has two advantages as compared to the traditional types: the horses can be extended to any length (even as much as twenty feet or more), and they can be stored more compactly. They have the disadvantage that three separate pieces must be handled each time a sawhorse is set up or moved, which takes a little more time. On the other hand, the individual pieces weigh less than a conventional horse, so that they can be handled by someone for whom the standard type is too heavy to lift.

The new design is shown in Figures 3.8 and 3.9. Each sawhorse consists of two separate leg units, with a slot into which a 2 × 4 is laid. The length of the assembled horse depends on the length of the 2 × 4, so that it can be adjusted to the requirements of the project; for a narrow flat, the 2 × 4s can be three or four feet long; if it is necessary to lay out an entire wall, fifteen- or twenty-foot 2 × 4s can be used. If additional support is needed, a third leg can be set in the middle of the crossbar.

FIGURE 3.8   A new sawhorse design: working drawings.

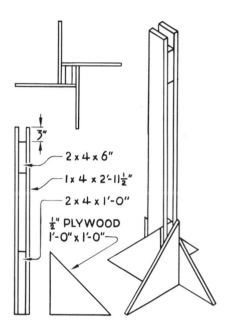

3"

2 x 4 x 6"

1 x 4 x 2'-11½"

2 x 4 x 1'-0"

½" PLYWOOD
1'-0" x 1'-0"

FIGURE 3.9   The new sawhorses in use. Workers fasten hinges on flats laid across three of the sawhorses. *Right,* **a single unused sawhorse is placed to show its construction.**

75

Since the 2 X 4s are neither cut nor nailed, they can be returned to stock when not in use, and the legs will store compactly in a corner or any out-of-the-way space. The experience of a decade seems to demonstrate that the compactness and flexibility of this design makes it better adapted to theater use than the traditional pattern. These horses can be quickly constructed in the scene shop, and ten or twelve of them should be built and kept as permanent equipment.

> Besides supporting flats, the sawhorses can be easily converted into work tables. They should be joined by 2 X 4s seven or eight feet long, placed parallel about three and a half feet apart, and a sheet of 3/4" plywood laid across them. If desired, four nails driven through the plywood into the ends of the 2 X 4s will keep the top from shifting, and when the table is no longer needed the nails can be removed and the plywood and 2 X 4s returned to stock. Such temporary tables are useful not only for construction projects but also for laying out working drawings for analysis and for stacking lumber precut for a set.

32. Other Tools

The experienced worker may be distressed by the fact that some of his favorite tools have been omitted from this list, or that some of the tools described are his last choices rather than his first. Individual workers may make constant use of such tools as a marking gauge, a combination square, a folding rule, a beam compass, a router, a drill press, a push drill, breast drill, or egg-beater drill, a miter box, a draw knife, even a lathe. This discussion is not intended as a criticism of such preferences, or as a restriction on the student's development of the pattern of tools which is most comfortable for him. Rather, it is offered as a point of departure, a description of the tools most commonly used in most scene shops. Certainly, scenery can be effectively constructed with the tools mentioned. As the student becomes experienced, he may want to omit some of those described and add others.

4

Lumber, Cloth, and Hardware

LUMBER

Ideally, lumber for scenery should be straight, light, strong, easily worked, free of defects, cheap, and readily available. In practice it is often necessary to compromise on some or all of those characteristics. Many scene shops have been forced to build major scenery out of lumber to which they would not have given shelf room ten years ago.

The theater has little control over price or availability, and may also have to accept lumber which is somewhat heavier and more difficult to work than is desirable. More serious is the problem of obtaining boards which are straight, strong, and free of defects. Lumber is classified in various grades. There will be considerable variation within a single grade, so that when a load is delivered to the theater many of the boards may be perfectly straight and free of knots or splits; others may be warped in varying degrees, and may have loose knots which seriously weaken them. Formerly, weak and warped lumber would have been sent back to the dealer for replacement. Uniformly good quality lumber can now be obtained only at extravagant cost.

The quality of lumber needed for scenery varies greatly. Even a badly knotted board is likely to have short clear sections which can be used for platform legs; warped lumber will often do for diagonal braces or the interior supports for platforms, and even badly warped boards can often be used to make jacks.

In essence, then, the lumber must be regraded in the scene shop. It may once have been standard procedure to automatically choose the best boards for each project. Workers must now adopt the reverse policy of always choosing the worst which can be used acceptably. In this way, the good lumber can be saved for the most critical parts of the scenery, such as the stiles of flats, which must be strong and straight if the flats are to be usable.

A warped board can often be straightened more than might be expected, provided it can be nailed at a number of points. Suppose, for example, that three platforms standing side by side on stage are to be fastened together by nailing a board across their back legs, and that the board chosen has a good deal of warp. Nail the board to the end leg first, then adjust it so that it matches the desired point on the second leg; pay no attention to the warp beyond that point. Nail to the second leg, then have an assistant force the free end of the board until it matches the correct position on the third leg and nail that. Proceed in this way along the board. When finished it will have been fastened nearly straight. With a straight board, it would be more natural to nail both ends first and then fasten the board to legs between. The method recommended leaves most of the board free to provide leverage for straightening it. Equally important is the fact that the board is set straight only for the point being nailed; to force the entire board straight and hold it while it was being fastened would be impossible.

Strength requirements for scenery are considerably lower than for construction outside the theater, because even semipermanent scenic structures have a much shorter life. A flight of stairs which in a residence might need to hold up for half a century or more, in the theater need last only through the rehearsals and performance of a single show. This is not to suggest that safety can be ignored. Scenery must be as safe to use as any structures outside the theater, but the strength requirements are lower.

Scenery not only needs to last for a shorter period of time, but its use can be calculated more precisely. For the home, stairs must provide support not only for the people who will walk on them but also for carrying unpredictably heavy loads of furniture up them. In the theater, the designer can identify how many actors will use a particular flight of stairs, and also perhaps even the weight of the actors who will use it. The set for The Tempest, which was mentioned in an earlier chapter, included a curving ramp which swung out over a long passageway without visible supports. It was designed to carry not more than two actors at a time, none of whom were of more than average weight. The actors reported that it was rock solid, a fact which was demonstrated to the designer when he glanced at it during a work session and discovered a football player chinning himself on one edge, and observed that there was not the slightest visible sag or sway. Yet the same structure built into a home or an office building would have required two or three times as much support.

TYPES OF LUMBER

The best lumber for building scenery is white pine. In lieu of white pine, lumber must be chosen from whatever types of softwood (evergreen or redwood) are locally available. Ponderosa, cedar, fir, southern pine, and redwood are possibilities. They differ from white pine in being heavier, having more resin, and being more likely to warp and split.

LUMBER DIMENSIONS

Lumber is first roughcut at the sawmill in standard dimensions (for example, in boards an inch thick and three inches wide). It is then planed smooth, with the result that the finished dimensions are smaller. So-called inch lumber is nearly always exactly 3/4" thick, but its width will vary, even among boards delivered by the lumber yard in the same load. For that reason, dimensions which depend on the width of the boards are always stated in such terms as "12'-0" minus 2W" (twelve feet minus two widths), rather than in actual feet and inches. This occurs most often in specifications for flats. Methods of handling such measurements are discussed in chapter 6. Lumber sizes are identified by the original dimensions, but with the term "inches" omitted. Thus, the board described would be called a "1 X 3," and a "2 X 4" was presumably originally cut a full two inches by four inches, although as delivered it will be smaller in both dimensions. The smoothing process does not shorten the boards, so that a board ordered as twelve feet long should be at least that length; often it will be close to an inch longer.

More 1 X 3 lumber is used in the scene shop than all other sizes combined. If it is unobtainable it will be necessary to substitute 1 X 4; 1 X 2 is too light, and larger sizes too heavy and expensive. Most books recommend the use of 1 X 2 for diagonal braces in flats. Although that is entirely acceptable, current supply problems may make it preferable to substitute 1 X 3s. They offer some slight advantages, and the added weight is insignificant. Very heavy 2 X 10 lumber is used by many scene shops to make supports for stairs. The methods of construction recommended in chapter 7 make use of other sizes of lumber, and the 2 X 10s have no other use in ordinary construction.

For platforms higher than 4', and for any weight-bearing structures where there are special support problems, as when large areas must be spanned, 2 X 4s are to be preferred. Experience has demonstrated that it is possible to build broad and high structures out of 1 X 4s or even 1 X 3s without reducing safety or rigidity, but the additional strength of 2 X 4s makes their use much commoner. With one exception (molding), other sizes of lumber can be considered miscellaneous. Sets will occasionally require small quantities of odd-sized lumber, but it is more likely to be specially ordered rather than being carried in stock in quantity. Some of the commoner sizes will be mentioned.

Strips of 1 X 1 lumber (with a square cross section, actually 3/4" X 3/4") are frequently useful, as muntons for windows, as supports for small decorative pieces of other material, and for a variety of unpredictable purposes.

The use of 1 X 2 lumber in making diagonal braces for flats has already been mentioned. 1 X 2s are often needed for furniture construction, as supports for moldings in making cornices and picture frames, and for miscellaneous purposes. Lath (strips of wood 1½" to 2" wide, and thinner than 3/4") can be used for picket fences, lattice work, and various other purposes.

SHAPED LUMBER

Moldings, and the related dowels, are manufactured by taking a standard board and cutting away part of it to form a specially shaped cross-section (Figure 4.1). The price includes the cost not only of the original lumber but also of the work required to re-shape it. A simple quarter-round, 3/4" X 3/4" regularly costs as much as a piece of 1 X 3 of the same length, and more elaborate moldings may cost as much as ten or fifteen times as much as straight lumber. Commercial moldings are designed to be seen from a short distance, and are likely to be ineffective when viewed from the audience. For those reasons it is commoner for scene shops to stock only the simplest and cheapest moldings (quarter-round and cove molding), and to construct larger moldings by combining them with ordinary lumber, plastic shapes, or cardboard. (The construction of cornices and other large molding is discussed in chapter 8.)

Doweling has a circular cross-section. It is made with various diameters, from 1/8" up to 3/4", usually in three-foot lengths. Larger dowels with diameters up to 3" are available in lengths up to 20'. Dowels have miscellaneous uses in the theater, as legs for furniture, as decorations, and in making properties. The larger dowels can be used as rods for draperies.

If a dowel is cut lengthwise through the center line, the result is two pieces of half-round; if one of these is similarly cut, the result is two pieces of quarter-round. Both types are useful in set decoration, and are available from lumber yards.

The final type of molding recommended for stage use is the cove, which is formed by cutting a quarter circle with a half-inch radius into one corner of a 1 X 1 strip. Cove molding is useful in developing larger moldings, and can also be combined to simulate flutings in pilasters and, with somewhat more difficulty, in round columns.

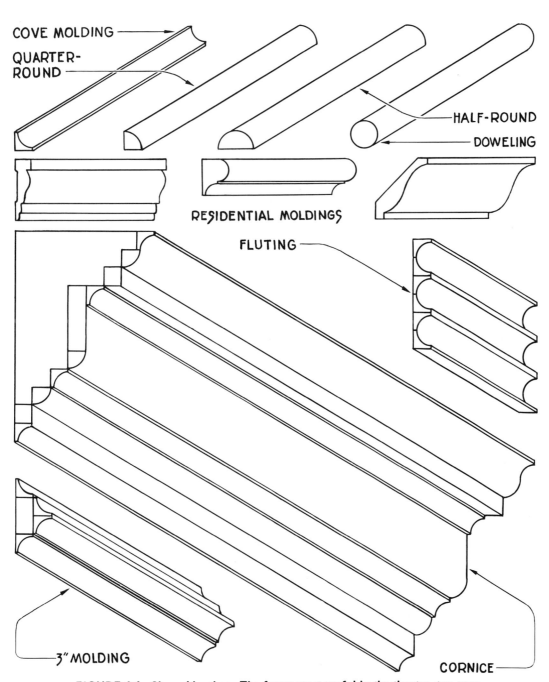

COVE MOLDING

QUARTER-ROUND

HALF-ROUND

DOWELING

RESIDENTIAL MOLDINGS

FLUTING

3" MOLDING

CORNICE

FIGURE 4.1 Shaped lumber. The forms most useful in the theater, *top row;* of these, cove molding and quarter-round are the most frequently used, and half-round the least. Three of many patterns of residential moldings are shown, of occasional but limited value on stage. *Bottom,* typical uses of the commoner moldings, cover molding combined to form fluting for columns, and a bold 3″ molding. *Center,* cove molding and quarter-round combined with standard 1 x 1 and 1 x 3 to form a moderately elaborate cornice.

PLYWOOD

Besides natural lumber, great use is made of plywood in building scenery. Although everyone is familiar with plywood, its most effective use requires some understanding of its characteristics and how it is made.

In cutting ordinary lumber, logs are sawed lengthwise in slabs of the desired thickness. In cutting lumber for plywood, the log is first smoothed to a uniform cylinder, and then revolved against a knife that slices off a thin sheet, which is flattened out as it is cut, like paper towels being unrolled from the cardboard tube in the center. These sheets are then coated with glue, laid on top of each other with the grain of alternate sheets crossed at right angles, and subjected to heavy pressure until the glue dries. Finally the plywood is cut in sheets of uniform size, usually 4' × 8'.

When originally cut, each thin layer is extremely weak, although slightly stronger in one direction than the other. Crossing the grain of successive layers averages the strength, and the glue adds further strength. The result is that the final sheet has great tensile strength, can be easily worked with tools, resists splitting, and can be used to cover large areas quickly.

Because it is built up of thin layers, the thickness can be controlled accurately, and most plywood, unlike ordinary lumber, is very close to true dimension. Thus, a 3/4" sheet can be fastened on top of a platform base 2'-11¼" high with assurance that the finished platform will be precisely 3'-0".

Plywood is readily available in thicknesses of 1/4", 1/2", 5/8", and 3/4", although other dimensions can be obtained by special order. Usually the sheets are made of layers of uniform thickness, although some plywood has thicker center layers. The 1/4" sheets most often have three layers, the 3/4" sheets five layers. The greater the number of layers the more uniform the strength in opposite directions. In three-ply, only the center layer is laid so that the grain runs parallel with the short ends of the sheet; in five-ply two layers run crosswise. The result is that 1/4" sheets are much more flexible in one direction than the other, a fact which can be made use of in building curved units, whereas the thicker plywood provides more uniform rigidity, which is desirable for stair treads or platform tops.

Most of the plywood used in the scene shop is 1/4" or 3/4" thick. The quarter-inch ply is used primarily for making corner-blocks for flats, although it has a wide variety of miscellaneous uses, including facing platforms and curved stairs, providing shaped edges for ground-rows, and making furniture and properties. The 3/4" sheets are used primarily for flooring platforms and as treads for stairs.

Fir plywood is nearly always used for building scenery, with a sanded finish. The heavier plywood is also available more cheaply with a rough surface, which is acceptable for stair treads and platform flooring, since they are padded and covered with canvas. Plywood used for outdoor theaters must be of the exterior type, which will not separate if it is rained on. The cheaper interior plywood is usually purchased for enclosed theaters.

OTHER SHEET MATERIALS

A number of other materials are manufactured in sheet form, each having its own characteristics. Most of them are weaker than plywood of the same thickness, lighter in weight, and more flexible; a few are less flexible and cannot be bent without cracking. One of the most brittle is Masonite, which has a hard, smooth surface and makes an effective floor covering for dance performances. Because it is easily broken, it is better to drill small holes through which nails can be driven. A grey, moderately smooth cardboard is manufactured in large sheets of various thicknesses and sold under the trade name of upson board; the thinner sheets are sometimes called E-Z curve. It has little strength, but is useful for covering the sides of platforms, and the thinnest sheets can be bent to a much smaller radius than plywood. (The Upson company also manufactures other types of sheeting, but they are less frequently used for scenery.) Corrugated cardboard can be bought in large sheets, or salvaged from discarded shipping containers. Its use in furniture construction is discussed in chapter 8.

If cardboard must be bent when attaching it to a frame, it can be shaped more easily if water is applied to the convex side by spraying, spattering, or brushing, and the cardboard fastened in place while it is still damp.

FABRICS

The most frequent use of fabric in the scene shop is as a covering for flats. Many different types of cloth have been used; the commonest are cotton duck and unbleached muslin. All are often loosely referred to as canvas, because linen or cotton canvas was once almost universally used. Muslin is less effective because it is thinner and weaker, but its lower cost has made its use fairly common. Instructions for fastening the cloth on the flat frames are given in chapter 6. Lengths of the same cloth may be sewn together in large sheets called drops, on which a design is painted and which are hung at the back of the stage as an integral part of the scenery.

Platforms and stair steps must be padded to reduce noise, and in most cases the padding is given a protective coating of scenery canvas (chapter 7). Often a large section of canvas is stretched out to cover the entire stage floor before scenery is set in place.

Various types of cloth are used for upholstering furniture and making objects of papier-mâché (see chapter 9). Many kinds of fabric are also used for draperies and window curtains in dressing the set. The stage crew may need to arrange or specially hang masking drapes and a translucent fabric called scrim, as well as a stretched fabric sheet called a cyclorama hung at the back and side edges of the stage to simulate a sky; these units are most likely to be part of the permanent equipment of the theater, so that although the set crew must handle them they need not construct them.

One commercial fabric is especially useful for a variety of purposes in the theater; it is called duvetyn. It is a napped, flannel-like cloth which is available in a range of vivid solid colors, as well as black and white. Because its weave is hidden, it reflects light uniformly in every direction, no matter how it is draped. It is wide and cheap, and can be used for ornamental drapes and upholstery, and in making papier-maché. Unfortunately, it does not stand up well when either washed or drycleaned, but its cost is so low that it can be discarded after it has been used a few times.

HARDWARE

Besides nails, bolts, and screws, a large assortment of metallic devices have been developed for building and joining scenery. Most of them must be ordered from theatrical supply houses; some can be bought at ordinary hardware stores. Of these, some are used in odd ways not intended by their manufacturers. For example, strap hinges make firm but temporary fasteners by which door frames can be locked to flats, and chicken wire is used as a basis for artificial rocks.

NAILS

The basic design of nails seems so simple and obvious that it might be thought impossible to vary it. In fact an amazing variety of nail types have been developed to serve different purposes, many of them applicable to scenic construction (Figure 4.2)

The *common nail* is the basic and most familiar type. It is manufactured in various lengths, which are often identified by an odd system of measurement, the unit of which is a "penny" (abbreviated *d*). A four-penny (or 4d) nail is 1½" long, a 6d nail is 2", and a 10d nail is 3". Either the penny or the inch designation is acceptable. The longer nails also have heads and shafts with larger diameters. Very large nails are sometimes called spikes, and very small nails brads.

The poorer grades of wood which must be used currently often split when common nails are driven into them. *Box nails* are manufactured in the same lengths but with thinner shafts, and are less likely to produce splitting. Reducing the shaft also reduces holding power. Consequently box nails are often given a resinous or synthetic coating which provides more friction so that they will hold more firmly.

Finishing nails also have thinner shafts than common nails of the same length, but their distinctive characteristic is that the heads are much smaller, and are shaped so that they can be driven below the surface of the wood and the hole filled with wood paste. They hold less firmly than common nails because the shafts are thinner and because the head provides little resistance to being pulled through the wood. At theatrical viewing distance, the heads of common or box nails are invisible under paint, so that they are nearly always preferable for scenic use to finishing nails.

Clout nails must be bought from theatrical suppliers. They are softer than other nails, and can be clinched automatically by driving them against a hard surface. They are used almost exclusively in building flats (see chapter 6).

Roofing nails look more like large tacks than like nails. They have unusually broad heads so that they can be used to hold soft material with less chance that it will tear loose. They are most often used in the scene shop to fasten cardboard to frames. The nails are available with either round or square heads, and can also be used decoratively.

Tacks and roofing nails are the most dangerous fasteners when dropped, because they can land point up and cause dangerous and painful wounds if they are stepped on. Whenever one is dropped, work should be stopped immediately and the nail or tack found and picked up.

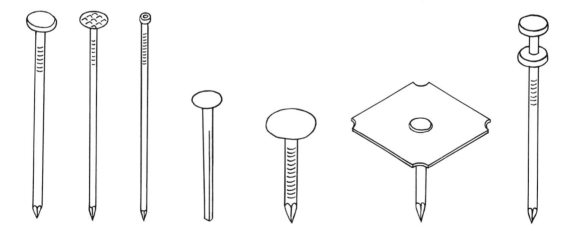

FIGURE 4.2 **The types of nails most useful in the theater.** *Left to right*: **common, box, finishing, clout, round-headed roofing, square-headed roofing, and double-headed.**

Double-headed nails sound like the weird creation of a mad designer. They are in fact very useful, although they are only occasionally needed. They make it possible to fasten two boards together securely and then to take them apart easily. The two heads are set at the same end of the nail with a small gap between them. In use, the nails are driven in until the first head comes in firm contact with the surface of the wood; when they are to be pulled out, the claws of the hammer are slipped between the two heads, the nail is pried out part way, the claws are then slipped under the other head and the nail removed. They are most often used to attach battens to the back of the flats which make up the wall of a set in order to stiffen it. Because they are also used in assembling forms for pouring cement, they are available in ordinary hardware stores.

In an earlier discussion, it was said that a carpenter's skill is often evaluated by his ability to use a hammer effectively; his judgment is often tested by examining the number and arrangement of the nails he has driven. Using more nails than are needed is identified as the mark of an amateur. Knowing how many nails to use, and how to place them, requires some understanding of how nails operate.

When a nail is driven through a board, the point spreads the grain of the wood apart, producing what is in fact a split in the wood. The fibers, forced out of line, pinch the shaft of the nail, and the friction holds it in place. The split may be very small, so short that it is completely hidden by the head of the nail, although in extremely bad lumber it may extend for a foot or more. If the split runs all the way to the end of the board, almost all friction is lost, and the nail will not hold; the fibers must remain firmly joined at each side of the nail. The worker should learn how to assess the behavior of the wood each time a nail is driven, and to take corrective measures whenever the board begins to split unacceptably. One solution is to switch to thinner nails, that is, from common to box nails. Another technique is to turn each nail upside down and strike it with a hammer a couple of times on the point so as to flatten it. It will then tear through the wood rather than push the fibers so far apart. A third solution is to drill a hole with a bit smaller than the shaft of the nail. Often the best solution of all is to get a different board.

> If a long split has developed at the side of a board, and it would be difficult to replace it, spread the sliver out slightly, being careful not to break it off, and work glue into the crack with a small brush or even a strip of cardboard. Press the sliver back into place and drive a few small nails through the edge of the board to hold it together until the glue has set.

The holding power of a nail can be increased enormously by choosing one which is at least a quarter of an inch longer than the combined thickness of the boards being joined, and then turning them over and bending the point sideways. This is called *clinching* the nail.

When clinching nails (other than clout nails), make sure that the head of the nail is resting flat on a solid surface, preferably a clinch plate or a concrete floor, but at least a piece of lumber or heavy plywood. If the nailhead is not firmly supported it is likely to be driven out at least a short distance, leaving some play in the joint.

In order to be effective, clinching must be done properly. First strike the point of the nail sidewise, and then when it has been bent, hammer it straight down. If the first blows are too near the vertical the nail will be driven partly back through the wood, there will be a gap between the head and the surface of the wood, and the joint will not be tight. Bend the nail toward the center of the board. Bending it toward the edge will tend to open the split. Bend the point of the nail at right angles to the grain of the wood. If it is bent parallel with the grain it will lie in the split produced by nailing, and only a little strain on the joint will be required to spread the fibers apart farther and open the joint; if it is driven across several fibers, all of them would have to be broken through before the nail would loosen. Finally, make sure that the point is buried well in the wood, so that it will not catch and tear the hands of people who must move the structure.

If a nail must be clinched when it is not possible to lay the head on a solid surface (for example, if the point must be bent over at the back of a flat already fastened into position on stage), have an assistant hold a scrap of wood or the head of another hammer against the nail head and begin driving almost parallel with the board, hammering only the last few blows at right angles to the lumber after the nail has been bent over as much as possible from the side.

Besides clinching, nails can be made to hold more firmly by driving them at an angle, with the head leaning away from the direction in which the weakening force is likely to be exerted. Driving nails at an angle is, for no discoverable reason, referred to as *toenailing*.

Since each nail pushes the wood fibers apart, if two nails are driven into the same grain, the resulting splits are likely to join, the fibers opening up all the way between both nails, with loss of friction and holding power. A fundamental rule, therefore, is never to drive two nails into the same grain. Obviously, if the nails are ten feet apart the splits will not join, but if possible no two nails should be set in the same grain within the space that a workman can reach while standing in one spot. The result of this rule is that nails often must be staggered in an apparently random pattern, which may offend the worker's esthetic sense, but the suffering involved in having to tear a unit apart and rebuild it because a joint has split open is much less bearable.

Every nail to some extent weakens the wood into which it is driven. The farther apart nails are spread throughout the area of contact between the two boards, the more firmly they will hold, and the fewer nails need be used. Unfortunately, since nails cannot be driven close to the ends of boards without risk of their splitting out, these two considerations must be balanced. The nails must be held back far enough not to split, but otherwise set as far from each other as possible, and in different grains.

The comments which have been made do not apply to plywood. Because the layers are placed with the grain running in different directions, and because the layers are joined firmly by the glue, plywood is almost unsplittable, and nails can be placed wherever convenient. Even with plywood, however, the farther apart they are spread the fewer nails will be needed and the stronger the joint will be.

Some materials are usually tacked rather than nailed, especially padding for stairs and platform tops. Tacks come in various sizes. Since they are likely to be subjected to some strain during the run of a show, it is better to use the larger sizes with broad heads. Tacks can also be used to fasten cardboard.

Staples have even less surface area than nailheads, but because the horizontal wire stretches out for some distance across the material being fastened they will hold even rug padding more firmly than might be thought. The polished wire used to make staples does not provide much friction, but they are satisfactory for fastening padding if it is then covered with canvas, and they will hold glued cardboard in place until it has set. They are most frequently used in attaching canvas to flats.

SCREWS

The holding power of screws depends on two factors. One is that, like nails, they spread the wood fibers apart, producing a tension which helps hold them in place. In addition, the screws are wound with a spiral of sharp threads, which cut grooves in the wood, with solid wood extending into the spaces between the threads. If force is applied so as to pull a screw out directly without turning it, each thread presses against the solid wood just above it, and the screw will not come out until the spiral of wood has been broken loose. Screws consequently provide considerable holding power so long as the wood is intact, but as soon as it is broken they cease to function. If a screw is driven in as far as it will go, and then given one or two last turns with the screwdriver, it will break through the wood, the screw will turn freely, and it will no longer hold. If the screw is replaced with a longer one or one with a thicker shaft, it will cut into new areas of the wood and will hold firmly, although the replacement must be done cautiously, so that the thin new layer of wood is not also reamed out.

A bent screw is unusable. The curved section will swing around, cutting a hole larger than the shaft of the screw and destroying any possibility of friction. As it is turned, the point of the screw bites into the wood and pulls the screw down; a screw with a blunted point is very difficult to drive. A screw with a worn slot will hold once it is set, but is very difficult to turn into the wood. Any screw with one of these defects should be thrown away.

Screws have tapered shafts. The point cuts a small hole, which is steadily enlarged as the thicker shaft above it moves down into the hole. In a sense, the threads cut a series of grooves in the wood which are progressively destroyed and replaced as the screw moves deeper. In other words, only the cuts made by the last few turns of the screw actually serve to hold it tight. That fact makes possible a shortcut in setting screws. It is standard procedure to hold the screw with the point against the wood, as in driving a tack or a nail. It is then given a light blow or two with a hammer to set it, and then, with the fingers out of the way, driven into the wood a half or two-thirds of the way with the hammer—but not more than two-thirds. The final setting must be done with the screwdriver, so that the critical slots will be cut in the wood. Since the hammering can be done faster than turning it with a screwdriver, the time saved when driving even a dozen screws is significant.

Screws are dimensioned by length and by the diameter of the thickest part of the shaft. They are readily obtainable in lengths from 1/4" up to 5", and in diameters from 1/16" to 3/8". The diameters are designated by a system of code numbers; most theatrical hardware is drilled to fit number 9 screws, and 7/8" is the standard length. When used to attach hardware, this just misses going through a 1" board. There may be occasional need for longer or shorter screws, but they are not likely to be stocked in quantity. In addition, head types vary. Some screws have round heads and others oval. Phillips screws have driving slots in the form of a plus-sign, and require special screwdrivers. They are generally avoided in the scene shop.

Wood screws used in the theater have heads which are flat on top and conical on the underside. When driven into wood they should be turned until the top surface is flush with the surface of the wood, or slightly sunken below it. Hinges, cleats, and other hardware which is made to be fastened with screws have dish-shaped holes sized so that when the screws are driven all the way the heads will be level with the upper surface of the metal.

Occasionally it is necessary to fasten hinges or other hardware with holes larger than the heads of the screws in stock. The screws can be prevented from pulling through the holes if small washers can be slipped over the screws before they are driven. If possible, slightly longer screws should be used, since the heads cannot be driven down flush with the surface of the metal.

Screws can easily be removed, and can with care be reset in the same holes, but almost always with some loss of holding power. If any significant reliance is placed on the strength of the joint, they should be replaced with slightly longer or wider screws.

BOLTS

Bolts hold differently from either nails or screws. Like nails, they have heads attached to shafts of uniform diameter—that is, they do not taper, as screws do. Like screws, they are threaded. To fasten two boards together with a bolt, matching holes must be drilled through the boards. They may be of the same diameter as the shaft of the bolt, although they are usually drilled slightly larger. The bolt is then inserted through the holes until the head strikes the surface of the wood. A nut is screwed on the other end where it sticks through the second board, and is turned until it touches the surface of the board. The joint is prevented from separating by the friction between the threads of the bolt and the matching threads of the nut.

> To start a nut on a bolt squarely, the beginning of both sets of threads must be aligned. Set the nut in position, and turn it backwards until a click is heard. The threads are then meshed, and the nut will go on straight if it is turned forward.

Bolts are often used to fasten the supports of high platforms. As the platforms are used by the actors, their movement can easily shift the joints slightly and pull the nut or the head of the bolt into the wood, loosening the joint. For that reason, washers should always be used when the joint is assembled. A washer is first slipped along the shaft of the bolt until it touches the head, the bolt is inserted into the hole, a second washer is slipped over the end of the bolt and against the wood, and the nut is then turned until it touches the washer, and finally tightened with a wrench to make a firm joint. The reason the washers do not pull into the wood is that they provide a larger area of contact than the nut or bolt head. Washers of any size may be used, and if the hole of the size of washer needed is larger than the head or nut, one or more smaller washers can be slipped on to hold it in place.

If the joint is assembled as described, the head of the nut will stick out slightly beyond the surface of the wood, and the nut will stick out on the other side. In the few instances in which that is unacceptable, a hole can be drilled into each of the two surfaces of the wood, wide enough and deep enough that the head and nut (and washers) can be pulled in. The hole for the nut will have to be somewhat larger, since it will be necessary to catch the nut with pliers or a wrench in order to turn it tight.

Bolting is by far the strongest method of fastening commonly available in the theater, and it is used whenever safety depends on a joint's holding. Bolts have the additional characteristic that they do not depend on friction with the wood to hold them tight. They can consequently be removed and replaced without loss of strength, and so are preferred for scenic units which are to be taken apart, stored or transported, and then set up again for reuse.

Stove bolts are relatively light, between 3/16" and 3/8" in diameter, and up to three inches in length. The heads are slotted, and the tops may be flat or rounded. The threads extend for the entire length of the shaft. *Carriage bolts* are larger, both in diameter and the length of the shaft, running up to 10". Only the end of the shaft is threaded, for a distance of between one and two inches, and just below the head is a square-shaped extension, much like a nut but an integral part of the shaft; the heads are not slotted.

Carriage bolts are to be preferred where great strength is required, or where their greater length is needed. Elsewhere, stove bolts have some advantages. The square shank below the head of the carriage bolt is intended to be set in a matching hole in metal, which will prevent its turning, but it is of little value in the soft wood used in scenery, and it makes it more difficult to fit washers under the head. Often the only bolt which is available for a joint is much longer than the thickness of the two pieces of wood, and while it can usually be extended unobtrusively toward the inside of a platform or other structure, the carriage-bolt threads may end at some distance beyond the wood. The unthreaded space can be packed with washers so that they reach into the threaded area and make it possible to tighten the nut against them, but the scene shop may not have enough washers in stock to handle more than a few such joints. It is possible to substitute wooden washers, made from small squares of plywood with holes drilled in them, but the washer closest to the nut must be of metal. Obviously, these problems do not occur with stove bolts. Their only disadvantage is that they provide somewhat less strength, but in the great majority of cases they would be more than adequate.

HINGES

Hinges are used in the theater for their normal purpose of fastening two units together so that one of them will swing. It may seem surprising that they are also regularly used as rigid fasteners. The commonest hinge for theatrical use is made of two approximately square metal plates, 2" on a side, with one edge cut and bent so that the two pieces can be fitted together with a small cylinder running along their common side, through which a pin can be set to hold them joined. The official name of this type of hinge is *2" loose-pin back-flap,* but they are so commonly used that other types of hinges are often ignored, and they are simply referred to as "loose-pin hinges." They are supplied by the manufacturer with pins which fit tightly enough in the socket that they are difficult to pull out with the fingers. It is the nearly universal practice to remove the pins as soon as the hinges are received, and replace them either with common nails or with lengths of wire, of a diameter which will hold them fairly tightly but which permits their being removed more easily. If wire is used, one end is bent to prevent its falling all the way through.

Loose-pin hinges are a versatile all-purpose device, used in many different ways in the scene shop. It is usually necessary to fold walls in order to transport them from the scene shop to the stage, or simply for ease in handling and storing. The individual flats are hinged together on the face, the joints concealed, and the entire wall folded compactly.

Sometimes triangular supporting devices called *jacks* must be attached to the backs of flats (see chapter 8). If the flats are moved during the scene shifts, they will be fastened with hinges, so that they can be folded against the flat. Even if they remain in place throughout the show, they are most likely to be attached with hinges.

When walls made of several flats are unfolded and stood in place on stage, they must be stiffened to keep them in a straight line. One method is to nail boards horizontally along the back of the wall, but such walls cannot be shifted. Another method, which allows disassembly for a scene shift, is to slip metal devices called *S-hooks* over the toggles of the flats; a horizontal board is then set in the free end of the *S*'s and can easily be removed for shift. However, this method sets the face of the board parallel with the surface of the wall, which provides less stiffening than if it were attached on edge. That can be achieved by the use of hinges. The stiffening board is hinged to the frames of the flats, with hinges screwed to the upper face of the board and fastened to alternate vertical framing pieces (*stiles*); other hinges are screwed to the underside of the board, and fastened to the other stiles. The stiffening board is then held horizontal, providing maximum stiffening, and yet it can be removed by pulling the pins out of the hinges.

Flats which meet at the corners of sets are usually fastened by lashing. Occasionally it may be preferable to hinge them. Using loose-pin hinges makes it possible to separate them and rejoin them during shifts.

Platforms which must be shifted during a performance may be fastened to other units of scenery with loose-pin hinges. Folding platforms (*parallels*) must have the leg supports hinged together; and railings for platforms or stairs are often attached by hinges.

It may have been noted that for some of these purposes tight-pin hinges would do as well. The loose-pin hinges are more versatile, since if the pins are not removed they do the work of tight-pin hinges, and yet if it is necessary to separate the units they make that possible.

In one other case having the pins loose is of special advantage. It is often difficult to control the swing of doors in sets. They may tend to ooze open when shut, or to slowly close when it is intended that they be left standing open. The stiffness of opening can be controlled if loose-pin hinges are used, with common nails substituted for the pins. Each nail is laid on a concrete floor or other hard surface and given a sharp blow with a hammer, about a third of the way down from the head of the nail. The point of the bent nail is then inserted into the socket of the hinge, and the nail driven in all the way with the hammer. The bend in the nail provides friction which will make the door less likely to swing when it is not intended to. The stiffness can be adjusted very precisely by straightening the nail slightly, or bending it more.

Long, narrow hinges (3' long and only 1½" wide when open) are useful for special purposes in the theater. They are called *piano hinges* because they were first used to fasten on the tops of grand pianos. In the scene shop they are most often used to join the leaves of screens. They are fastened to the edges of the framing lumber, and since each half-hinge is only 3/4" wide they do not extend out beyond the surface of the lumber. They can be cut into shorter lengths by scoring them crosswise with a hacksaw, and then bending on the line until they break.

Large hinges of decorative shape are sometimes specified by the designer, and intended to be seen by the audience. One other type of hinge is used in a special way. It is called a *strap hinge,* and each leaf is in the shape of a long triangle, the two joined with a tight pin. This type of hinge is used to fasten door frames into flats (see chapter 8).

LASHING

Flats which meet at an angle are most often fastened together by lashing rather than hinging. Three types of cleats are intended to be used in lashing, *lash eyes, lash cleats,* and *tie-off cleats* (Figure 4.3).

A lash eye is fastened just below the corner-block at the top of the right stile of the flat at the worker's left as he faces the backs of the flats. The eye is in the shape of a thick metal strip with a hole for a screw at one end and a larger hole at the other end

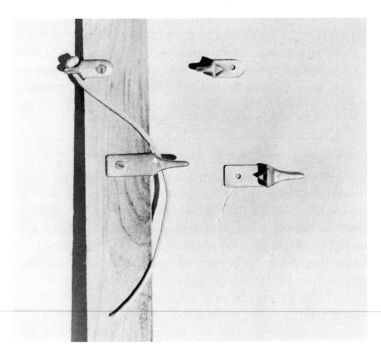

FIGURE 4.3 Lashing hardware. Each piece is shown attached to a 1 x 3, and unattached and turned over to reveal the triangle of metal which is driven into the edge of the wood to hold it firm. *Top*, a lash eye; *bottom*, a lash cleat (a tie-off cleat is not shown).

forming an eye through which the lash rope is threaded; a triangular piece of metal is set below the eye. The cleat is placed horizontally on the stile with the eye extending to the left, and is tapped with a hammer so as to drive the triangular point into the edge of the stile. A screw is then driven into the face of the stile through the small hole.

> As a substitute for a lash eye, a hole can be drilled in the corner-block. A knot is tied in the lash line and the unknotted end is threaded through the hole from the inside and pulled down until it is stopped by the knot. This substitute is as effective as a commercial lash eye. An ordinary screw-eye can also be used, driven into the inside edge of the stile.

Lash cleats are similar in shape, except that the eye is replaced by a finger of metal. A lash cleat is fastened to the adjacent stile of the right flat, a few inches below the lash eye, with the finger pointing away from the joint. A second cleat is fastened to the stile of the left flat, about two and a half feet below the lash eye, a third to the stile of the right flat about two and a half feet farther down, and finally two are set at the same height, about two and a half feet below the third cleat, one in each stile and pointing away from each other. A knot is tied in one end of a rope, which is then threaded through the lash eye and cut about three inches short of the floor, to prevent its being stepped on when the flat is shifted.

> As a substitute for a lash cleat, a nail about 3" long can be driven into the inside edge of the stile. If the head is slanted slightly away from the canvas it will be easier to swing the lash line around it, and if a finishing nail is used the line can be freed more easily. This is not quite so convenient as a commercial lash cleat, but it is perfectly usable, especially in an emergency.

When the flats are in place on stage, the worker takes hold of the rope and swings it right and forward, so it catches behind the top cleat on the right flat, then left and forward to catch it behind the next cleat, on the left flat, then behind the last single cleat on the right flat. It is finally caught behind the left of the bottom pair of cleats, brought right, under, and behind the right cleat, and tied off with a special knot which holds firmly but which can be released by a tug on the end of the rope. At first the worker may find it difficult to swing the rope so as to catch it behind the top cleat; the rope is given a smart swing, so that it slaps against the canvas of the flat, and then is pulled tight at just the right moment. With a little practice, the worker will be able to swing the rope from cleat to cleat and tie it off very quickly (Figure 4.4).

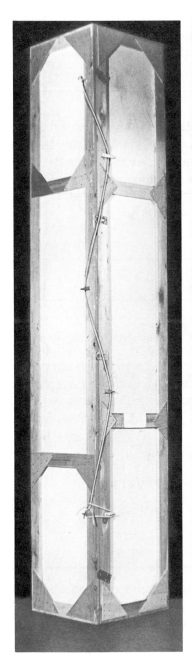

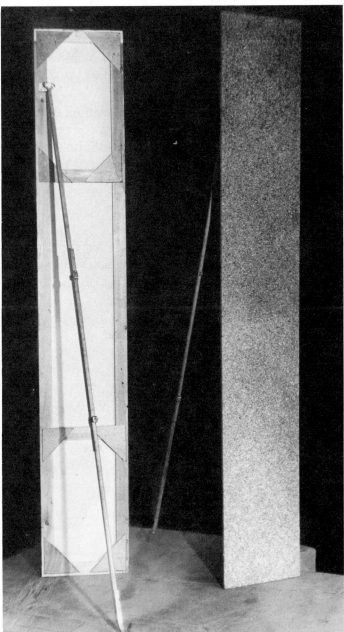

FIGURE 4.4 Two flats lashed together at right angles, shown from back.

FIGURE 4.5 Two flats supported by stage braces, shown from the back and front.

A specially designed tie-off cleat is manufactured to be used in pairs around which lash lines are knotted. The shape makes it slightly easier to tie the knot, but ordinary lash cleats or nail substitutes will do about as well.

Although this is a firm and fast method of joining flats, it is possible for one flat to slide along the face of the other. This is prevented by screwing two or three stop cleats to the flat the edge of which is butted against the face of the other flat. The cleats are placed horizontally on the face of the stile, so that their ends extend about 3/4" beyond the edge of the flat. When the flats are set together and lashed, the edge of the other flat rests against these projections, and is prevented from moving.

Brace cleats make an effective substitute for stop cleats.

It is possible to lash flats together in a single plane, but that is seldom done because the joint between them will be visible. In lashing flats at an angle to each other, the edge of the flat which is nearest to parallel with the center-line of the stage should be butted against the face of the flat which is nearest to parallel with the front edge of the stage. If they are placed in the opposite position, the crack between them will be much more visible to the audience.

STAGE BRACES

Even when walls are stiffened and lashed at the corners, they require additional bracing to hold them vertical and steady. The commonest method of supporting them is by the use of *stage braces* (Figure 4.5). A stage brace is made of two basic parts, lengths of either hardwood or metal tubing, which are held together loosely so that they can be slid along each other, and the total dimension lengthened or shortened. A set-screw is provided for fastening them firmly at any length. Stage braces are available in various sizes, and the range of adjustment extends from slightly longer than the individual sections up to slightly shorter than their combined length. A double hook is fastened to the end of one section, and the opposite end of the other section has a metal extension with one or more holes in it.

The stage brace is caught in a brace cleat, screwed to the stile of one of the flats next to the joint which is to be braced. The brace cleat is a flat sheet of metal with holes cut for screws, and a larger hole for inserting one of the hooks of the brace. It is screwed to the back face of the stile, with the end which has the large hole extending out beyond the edge of the stile toward the center of the flat.

The stage brace is first extended to the approximate length needed and the set-screw finger-tightened so that the sections will not slip while the brace is being handled. The hooked end is lifted up to the level of the cleat and the stage brace turned over, so that the hooks point toward the canvas of the flat. The hook nearest the stile is inserted in the hole in the cleat, and the stage brace turned over by swinging the free hook away from the canvas toward the framing, until it rests flat against the face of the stile. The bottom end of the brace is set against the floor, and a stage screw driven into the floor through the hole which sits most solidly on the floor. Finally, the set-screw is loosened, the sections are slid together or apart until the flat is exactly vertical, the screw is again finger-tightened, and given a turn or two with pliers or by slipping the claws of a hammer around one of the wings.

> A good-sized screw-eye with an opening large enough to insert the hook of a stage brace can be used as a substitute for a brace cleat. It is driven into the inside edge of the stile, with the eye slanted back away from the canvas. This is considerably less convenient than a regular brace cleat, but will serve satisfactorily as an emergency substitute.

Stage braces seem inadequate; they look fragile, and the hooks rattle in the cleat when the brace is shook. In fact, they hold with great firmness, and yet can be removed easily. The effectiveness of the bracing increases with the height of the brace cleat and with the distance between the flat and the point at which the brace is screwed into the floor. Most often the cleats are fastened a foot or two down from the top edge of the flat, and the stage screw driven into the floor three or four feet from the bottom rail. Usually the braces are set directly back from the flats, but they must be placed so that actors are not likely to trip over them if they cross backstage behind the flats, and they must be set so that they cannot be seen by the audience. It may therefore be necessary to angle them to the left or right.

When not enough stage braces are available, simple triangular structures of wood called jacks can be substituted. For certain purposes they are preferable to the commercial braces. Directions for making jacks are given in chapter 8.

Stage screws, which are used to fasten the braces to the floor, are about four inches long. The threaded section is short and heavy, but they have handles attached which make it possible to turn them by hand. They are set by hammering them heavily into the floor; they are then turned by hand as long as that can be done easily. They are then given a few final turns to drive them down tight against the metal end of the brace, using a wrench, a screwdriver stuck through one of the holes in the handle of the screw, or, more commonly, by catching the handle between the claws of a hammer and swinging it so as to force the screw around.

Especially at door openings there may be some tendency for the rails to creep along the floor, so that the flats are no longer vertical. This can be prevented by fastening a *foot-iron* to the back of the flat. Rigid foot-irons are made of a single L-shaped piece of metal, with a hole in the short section large enough to receive a stage screw, and the other section drilled for ordinary screws. Hinged foot-irons are similar, except that the two legs are joined to swing.

> Large strap hinges can be substituted for foot-irons. They should be fastened to the stage floor with the largest screws which will fit in the holes; two screws in each leaf are enough, but they should be spaced as far apart as possible, one close to the pin, the other at the point of the leaf. The primary disadvantage of this substitute is that it takes a little longer to remove the screws than to take out the stage screw used for a regular foot-iron, so if possible this substitute should be used only for units which do not have to be shifted.

The foot-iron is set against the bottom of the flat from behind, with the long leg in contact with the stile and the short leg resting on the floor. It is screwed firmly to the stile, the flat adjusted until it is in exactly the right position, and a stage screw driven into the floor through the hole in the short leg.

> Occasionally there may not be enough space behind a flat to fasten a foot-iron. If the set does not have to be shifted during the performance, the bottom edge can be fastened in place by laying a length of 1 X 3 on the floor behind it, with one edge tight against the back of the rail. The board is nailed to the floor, preferably with double-headed nails, and then a couple of nails are driven through the rail of the flat from the front into the 1 X 3.

MISCELLANEOUS HARDWARE

A few other types of hardware need to be mentioned, less frequently used than those which have been discussed.

Picture hooks-and-eyes are designed to hang units of moderate weight, usually from flats. Either the hook or the eye is fastened to the front of the flat, running screws through the canvas and into a toggle or other part of the frame. The matching eye or hook is then fastened to the back of the object to be hung, and it is set in place by slipping the hook through the eye. This method is used not only to hang pictures, but also to fasten fireplace mantels, cornices, pilasters, mopboards, and bulletin boards. It cannot be used for heavy structures. For instance, picture hooks would not provide adequate support for a shelf filled with actual books.

If a picture or mirror is to be hung on a flat in the area between the toggles, it is possible to fasten it without moving one of the toggles. Attach small screw-eyes to the back of the frame, at least two or three inches down from the top, and fasten wires to them.

Using a brad or a small finishing nail, punch a hole in the canvas just above where each screw-eye will be when the picture is hung, and run the wires through the holes and up the back and fasten them to additional screw-eyes set in the lower edge of the top toggle. If it is necessary to remove the picture during a shift, make small hooks from coathanger wire and fasten the bottom ends of the wires to them; they are then hooked into the screw-eyes on the back of the picture.

This method completely hides the wires. After strike, the tiny holes can be patched from the back, although if they are small enough they will probably be invisible after the flat has been repainted for the next show.

Plates made of strap metal are available in a range of shapes and sizes, drilled to receive screws, and generally used to reinforce wood joints. The commonest shapes resemble the letters **I, L,** and **T.**

T-*plates* can be used for a joint which has the shape of that formed by the toggle and stile of a flat; L-*plates* fit a joint shaped like the stile-rail joint at the corner of a flat. I-*plates* are simply straight strips of metal, and are useful in joining lumber end to end.

One **L**-shaped corner brace is formed from an I-plate bent in the center so that the two sections are at right angles. This is the most commonly used plate, especially for unobtrusively bracing the legs of tables and chairs. The other type of **L**-brace is simply cut from a sheet of metal, and is not bent.

The angle of a 3-dimensional L-brace can be opened beyond 90°, so that it can be fastened to boards set at a wider angle, for example, diagonal braces on furniture or platforms. Set a 1 X 4 on edge and fit the L-brace over it so that the corner points up. Using a glove or holding one leg with several thicknesses of paper toweling to damp the vibration, pound down on the corner with a hammer until it has opened to the correct angle. If the legs bend in the middle, stand the brace so that one leg rests on a flat surface and pound it straight again, then repeat for the other leg.

The advantage of the metal plates is that they are smaller and less visible than plywood fasteners. For example, joining the frame of an ornamental screen with corner-blocks would be likely to destroy the design. L-plates placed on the back would be invisible, and if both sides of the screen must be shown, the wood could be cut back so that the braces were sunk level with the surface.

Sometimes it is necessary to stretch rope or wire very tightly. The *turnbuckle* makes that possible. It has three parts, a central section with a threaded hole at each end, and two bolts fitting the holes, one ending in a hook, the other in an eye.

In using the turnbuckle, the two bolts are first unscrewed as far as can be done without removing them from the center section. A screw-eye is driven into a support back stage in line with the position where the wire is to extend, and the turnbuckle hook is caught in the screw-eye. The wire is tied securely to the eye at the other end of the turnbuckle, run across and passed through another screw-eye set into a support at the opposite end of the path through which the wire is to be stretched. The wire is pulled as tight as can be done easily, and fastened firmly to the screw-eye. The center section of the buckle is then turned with a screwdriver, pliers, or a wrench so as to screw the bolts into it, shortening the overall length and pulling the wire as tight as desired.

Casters are used whenever scenery must be rolled, either as part of the performance or when it is shifted during intermissions. Since they must often bear considerable weight, casters stocked in the scene shop are usually much heavier and more rugged than those used in the home. Rigid casters will move only in two directions; swivel casters will swing into line as the unit is pulled in any direction. When casters are fastened to platforms, solid supports, usually made of 2 X 4 or 2 X 6, must be added, and the casters should be attached with bolts rather than nails or screws. They are most often used for platforms and stair units, and for tip jacks which make it possible to move large wall sections without dismantling or folding them.

Many other types of hardware are used in the theater, but those which have been described are the commonest, and will serve for all but exceptional situations.

5

Wood Joints

Something like a couple of dozen different ways have been devised for fitting two boards together so that they can be joined in a solid structure. The types of joints vary in strength, in appearance, in the length of construction time they require, and in their adaptability to different purposes. Some joints which are common outside the theater are seldom or never used in building scenery. Only those which are most useful in the scene shop will be discussed. All scenic joints must be nailed, bolted, or screwed (or, infrequently, glued). The descriptions which follow assume that nails are to be used, but the choice of other types of fastener would not alter the classification of the joints.

FIGURE 5.1 Lumber terminology: the parts of a board.

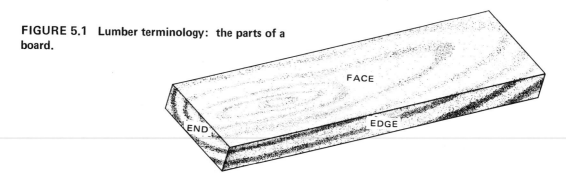

Three terms are used to identify the surfaces of a board (Figure 5.1). As applied to an ordinary 1 × 3, the *faces* are the surfaces with the largest area, the *edges* are the surfaces 3/4" wide running the length of the board, and the *ends* are the smallest surfaces, running across the grain. These terms are not usually used for molding, and of course for lumber with a square cross-section (1 × 1, 2 × 2) the faces and edges would be identical.

LAP JOINTS

The simplest type of joint is the *lap joint* (Figures 5.2, 5.3), which is formed by placing the faces of two boards in contact with each other and nailing through both layers of wood.

The boards lie in different planes, and the joint itself is as thick as the combined thickness of the two boards. This joint is not suitable for flats, because the frame must form a continuous surface to which the canvas can be glued. It is also generally avoided wherever it is visible to the audience, because structures made with it tend to look

FIGURE 5.2 Lap joints. The unit, *left*, has been assembled, with smaller pieces of lumber added to fill the gaps and make all of the surfaces continuous. The worker is laying out a similar structure, *right*. He holds the fourth basic board in his right hand, and one of the fill-in pieces in his left; the three remaining pieces needed to fill the gaps are lying at the bottom of the picture.

crude and unfinished. Nevertheless it may sometimes be specified. For instance, if table legs are set inside the corners of the apron which runs just under the table top, the leg-apron joints would be lap joints.

It is possible to make the framing surfaces level by filling in the gaps on each side with additional boards (Figure 5.2), or, in the case of square or rectangular frames, staggering the placement of the joints, although the weight of the unit will be nearly doubled. However, the lap joint is most frequently used where it will be hidden from the audience, for example to build internal supports for rocks, platforms, or stairs. It is a relatively strong joint and the ease and speed with which it can be constructed make it the first choice wherever its appearance is not objectionable.

FIGURE 5.3 Lap joints in use. Four lap-jointed units have been butted together to form the frame for a stool. Leaning against the stool is a fifth identical unit, illustrating the shape of those making up the frame. (Notice the short dark dashes across the wood, showing where the ends of the nails have been bent over and clinched.)

RUNNING LAP JOINTS

A variation of this type of joint is the *running lap joint,* in which one entire face of each board is in contact with the faces of the boards to which it is fastened. This joint makes it possible to produce a board of any length, so that it is frequently used to stiffen drops which run entirely across the back of the stage, or for beams or false prosceniums, which also run from one side of the stage to the other.

Suppose that a 36'-0" board is needed, and that the longest lumber in stock is 12'-0". Three 12' boards are laid on the floor end to end. Three other 12' boards are taken from stock and one of them cut in halves. A second layer of boards is then laid on top of the three on the floor, with a 6' board at each end and two 12-footers in between. The two layers of boards are fastened together with nails on each side of each joint, and a second set of nails halfway between the joints. This placement of the lumber locates the end of each board at the center of a solid section in the other layer, so that in effect a continuous board is created.

If the running lap joint is used to stiffen the top or bottom of a drop, the edge of the canvas is laid over the first layer of lumber and the second layer is laid on top of the canvas; the nails which hold the boards together then also automatically fasten the canvas in place.

HALVED JOINTS

The lap joint is twice as thick as the individual boards. If each one is cut to half its thickness in the area of contact, the joint will match the board thickness, and the faces of the boards will lie in the same planes. A lap joint altered in this way is called a *halved joint* (or sometimes a half lap) (Figure 5.4).

Suppose that a screen is to be made with rectangular leaves, using halved joints. Imagine the boards for one leaf laid out as if for lap joints; at each corner the side and top boards would meet, with the area of contact forming a square with sides equal to the width of the boards. For a halved joint, each end of each board must be cut to half its thickness in the area of contact.

Take a scrap of board the same width as the framing lumber, lay it across the end of one of the framing boards, and mark the area of contact by drawing a line along the edge of the scrap across the framing board. This is repeated for each end of the four boards. The blade of the radial-arm saw is then raised so that it will cut halfway through the boards. The first board is set in position so that the saw will cut in the waste (the area of contact), with the left edge of the blade cutting precisely at the line which has been marked. The saw blade is then passed over the lumber and pushed back, the board is moved slightly to the left, a second pass made, and so on until the entire square has been cut out to half-thickness. It is possible to speed up the work by

FIGURE 5.4   Halved joints. One unit has been assembled; the worker has
begun to fit together the boards for a second unit. (Compare with Figure 5.2;
here, halving the joints has preserved the continuity of the wood surfaces,
without the necessity of adding fill–in pieces.)

adding one or more blades to the saw, so that a wider cut is made, but even with a single blade the cutting goes fairly quickly, and unless a large number of joints are to be made it may be faster simply to use the blade which is already on the saw.

When both ends of all the boards have been cut in this way, they are placed together and the joints fastened. Especially for a unit such as a screen, which may be moved during the performance, it may be desirable to glue the halved joints as well as nailing them. Since the wood is thinner, splitting may be a problem, so small nails should be used.

Making a neat halved joint requires that the boards be cut exactly halfway through. A scrap of lumber should be used to set the height of the blade. First raise the blade so that it will cut slightly less than halfway through the board, make a single cut across the scrap, and carefully lower the blade and make a second cut at a different point. When the adjustment seems correct, turn the scrap over and make another cut slightly beside the last one. Inspection will indicate whether the setting is correct; the bottoms of the two cuts should line up precisely. If they do not, a final small adjustment can be made.

The advantage of the halved joint is its effect on the appearance of the unit. It is consequently most often used for furniture, including not only screens but chairs and tables. Halved joints take more time than most other joints and are somewhat weaker, so that they are used only when appearance is significant.

NOTCHED JOINTS

The *notched joint* is similar to the halved joint. It differs in that a cut is made in only one of the two boards being joined, and the cut must match the entire thickness of the second board (Figure 5.5). The commonest use of the notched joint is in making

FIGURE 5.5   Notched joints. Various types of notched joints are shown. If the unit is to be used for shelving, surfacing must be fastened to the pairs of boards at top and bottom, to fill in the openings between them.

shelves. The upright supports have grooves cut halfway through them matching the ends of the shelves, which are fitted in and nailed from the outside of the uprights. The result is that the shelves rest on solid lumber, and little strain is put on the nails; the increase in strength is very great. Unless the added strength is significant, shelves would usually be made with the faster and easier butt joints, so that the notched joint is infrequently used in scenery. However, permanent shelves for the scene shop (for instance, for storing paint or hardware) require the additional strength, so that the notched joint would be preferred.

BUTT JOINTS

The *butt joint* is an all-purpose joint, probably used more frequently in the scene shop than all other types of joints combined. In this joint the end, face, or edge of one board is placed flat against one surface of another board, and fastened either by nailing through the two boards or by laying a plywood or metal fastener across the joint and nailing or screwing them together (Figure 5.6).

FIGURE 5.6 Butt joints. *Left,* butt joints used to form a pillar; *right,* an arrangement usable in making shelving. The joint at the bottom often appears on door facings, and is similar to the stile–rail joints used for flats, although there it would always be fastened with triangular plywood corner–blocks rather than with metal L–braces as shown here.

The most frequent use of the butt joint is in building flats. Except for diagonal braces, all the joints of a flat are of this type (see chapter 6). Butt joints are also used for other structures, so varied that it would be difficult to describe them all. Four boards can be fastened together by butt joints arranged edge-to-face to form a square hollow pillar with widths equal to the width of the individual boards plus their thickness. If the boards are narrow, such units can be used as the legs of tables or as banisters. Larger structures can be used for pillars, and if the unit is made of two narrow and one or two wide boards, it can serve as a pilaster. Flats assembled to form a continuous wall are arranged with butt joints (edge-to-edge) hinged on the front. Flats at the corners of a set are lashed, hinged, or nailed together in butt joints (edge-to-face), although usually at an angle larger than 90°.

107

BLOCKED JOINTS

Any type of joint can be strengthened by butting a third piece of wood against the two boards joined, and fastening it to each. Such a joint is said to be *blocked* (Figure 5.7). Technically, the joints of a flat are blocked, since the lumber is held together by triangles of plywood. More often the added block is a length of 1 × 1, or a triangle cut from 1 × 3 or 1 × 4. Triangular blocks are most often used at the top corners of door frames, to supply greater rigidity. Blocking is a fast substitute for notching, as a support for shelves, although it does not supply quite so much strength. Since the added pieces of wood may be unsightly, blocking is usually done only for joints which cannot be seen by the audience. Although any type of joint can be strengthened in this way, probably the commonest use is for blocked butt joints.

FIGURE 5.7   Blocked butt joints. *Top,* small blocks used to reinforce shelving — stronger than straight butt joints, but much weaker than notched joints. *Center,* the corner of a door casing, with triangular blocks reinforcing the joint between the facing and the thickness-piece. *Bottom,* the type of joint used for the corners of flats, held together with a plywood corner-block.

MITERED JOINTS

The *mitered joint* can be thought of as a variation of the butt joint. It differs in that at least one of the boards to be joined is cut at an angle other than 90°. It is most frequently used in the scene shop in fitting diagonal braces into the corners of flats. Both ends of the braces are cut at an angle, usually 45°, so that they will fit tight against the inside edges of the rails and stiles.

The mitered joint has another characteristic which makes it valuable in building decorative elements such as picture frames and paneling. It is the only joint which will carry the pattern of specially shaped lumber around a corner so as to keep the pattern continuous and intact (Figures 5.8, 12.20). Since most frames are rectangular, the commonest miter angle for this purpose is also 45°; other angles produce polygons with varying numbers of sides, depending on the angle.

FIGURE 5.8   Mitered joints. The figure, *lower right*, shows the effect of cutting miters at angles other than 45° cuts, and illustrate the ability of the miter joint to carry a molded shape around a corner without destroying the pattern.

It is easiest to cut 45° miters on the radial-arm saw, which has an automatic setting for that angle. The blade is first raised so that it will swing clear, it is moved to the 45° position and lowered back to cutting height. The lumber is then laid in the ordinary position, flat against the guide fence, and cut by pulling the saw blade across it.

Occasionally it will be necessary to cut angles other than 45°. Suppose for instance that a hexagonal window is set into one wall, which is to be edged with molding. The window is first drawn full size on a sheet of plywood or cardboard. Two pieces of the molding are laid in position on the pattern, extending out beyond the corners and leaving one edge of the hexagon open between them. A third piece of molding is laid on top of the first two, carefully set so that it matches the line of the pattern below it. The edges of this third piece are marked on one of the two bottom pieces, and it is removed. A line is drawn across the marked area connecting the diagonally opposite corners; this is the cutting line for the joint. If the wood is cut on the radial-arm saw, this line is used as a guide in setting the angle of the blade, and all further cuts can be made with the same setting. It may be more convenient to use a saber saw for an odd-angle cut. In that case, the first cut should be made very carefully, and used as a pattern to mark the cutting angle on the remaining pieces of molding.

> It is often difficult to identify the position in which molding must be placed on the saw for a miter cut, even if the angle is 45°. Errors can be avoided by taking a couple of scraps of the molding (from 6″ to a foot long) and cutting the ends in different directions. The scrap is laid on the flat or drawing and turned until the correct cut is in position, and then carried to the saw and set so that the cut fits against the saw blade. The piece to be cut is placed in the same position, and the cut made.

Mitered joints are somewhat tricky to make; baffling errors often appear, and even when a piece of molding has been cut with great care the direction of the cut may prove to be wrong. When the molding is cut in the right direction, a gap may still appear when the boards are fitted together. To make an absolutely tight miter joint requires considerable skill, and more time than can usually be given to it in building scenery. Fortunately even a fair-sized gap is not likely to be visible to the audience, and in any case can be filled with papier-mache or covered with a strip of masking tape before the unit is painted.

LESS FREQUENTLY USED JOINTS

The joints which have been discussed are those most often used in building scenery; they should be adequate for almost any scenic purposes. A few additional types of joints are often mentioned, although seldom used. In the commercial theater, flats are usually built with mortise-and-tenon joints, which are stronger than the butt joints recommended in chapter 6. The butt joints are preferable for noncommercial construction because they can be taken apart so that the flats can be reworked for later productions (something which is forbidden by union rules in the commercial theater), and because they are much easier and faster to make. Mortise-and-tenon joints require an enormous amount of time to make by hand, and even with special power tools are more difficult and slower to construct.

The tongue-and-groove joint is an ingenious invention which makes it possible to fit a series of individual boards together so that when weight is rested on one the stress is spread to the surrounding boards, the entire unit functioning almost like a continuous sheet of lumber. It was formerly standard to use this joint in flooring platforms. Plywood does the same job even more effectively, since it has the actual form of a continuous sheet, and as it has become readily available it has almost entirely replaced tongue-and-grooving. This type of joint is still used in residential and office construction, although even there it is being replaced by plywood.

The running lap joint has been recommended for assembling boards longer than those available in stock. The scarf joint can also be used for the same purpose, and it has the distinction that the thickness of the lumber is not increased. However, the extra thickness is usually needed for stiffening, and the scarf joint is troublesome to make, so that in the great majority of cases the running lap joint would be preferred.

SPEED OF CONSTRUCTION

The following list gives the joints in the order of difficulty and the time required to construct them, starting with the fastest and easiest:

lap joint
running lap joint
butt joint
mitered joint
notched joint
halved joint.

The blocked joint could appear anywhere on the list. Although it is fast to make, it is always added to one of the other joints, so that the total time required would depend on which type of joint it was combined with.

FREQUENCY OF USE

The relative frequency of the various joints depends on the designer's specifications, the preference of the technical director, and the habits of the workers. However, the following list represents fairly typical practice, starting with the most frequently used joint:

butt joint (flats, platforms, etc.)
mitered joint (diagonal braces, molding)
lap joint (hidden structures)
halved joint
notched joint
running lap joint.

Skill in making joints is of the greatest importance in set construction. Fortunately, it is easy to acquire, and the student can expect that after he has made two or three joints of a particular type he will be able to make further ones efficiently and without difficulty.

6

Building Flats

Throughout the last century there has been a steady increase in the use of three-dimensional scenic elements as distinguished from flats. Indeed, many of the most effective of current set designs do not use flats at all. Nevertheless flats must still be considered one of the basic units of scenery. They are combined to form walls, which can be painted to suggest wood, wallpaper, stucco, brick, or stone. Beams, pilasters, false prosceniums, stair plugs, arches, and many other scenic elements may be based on flats. Also, methods similar to those used in building flats are valuable in constructing quite different types of scenery, for instance furniture, platforms, and ramps.

At first thought it would seem that such an apparently simple process as constructing a flat would have been reduced to a single universally used pattern. A study of some dozens of books has revealed the astonishing fact that no two recommend exactly the same techniques. Not only do they differ in details, but methods recommended by some authors are denounced by others as serious errors. To relate in detail all possible variations would require multiplying the length of the discussion many times. Instead, a single pattern of construction will be described, but it should be emphasized that if the literature is representative, each technical director is likely to prefer a somewhat different procedure which may well be as effective as that given here. Any method which results in a smoothly covered rugged structure with square corners and the right dimensions is acceptable.

An experienced worker is likely to find the process specified here somewhat over-detailed. In particular, the instructions call for more frequent checking than most skilled workers need to do. As the student becomes more experienced, he may be able to introduce shortcuts, and to omit steps which have proved unnecessary for him. Nevertheless, it was felt that the beginning student needed detailed guidance, and even as described, the methods are perfectly practical and, once mastered, will make it possible to build flats soundly and efficiently.

The basic flat is essentially a rectangular wooden frame covered with canvas. In order to hold it rigid, two diagonal braces and one or two horizontals are fitted into the frame. Many variations of this basic shape are possible, but almost all of them can be classified in two types—holes may be cut into the flat, and especially shaped edges may be added. These variations will be discussed at the end of the chapter.

THE DIMENSIONS OF FLATS

The height of flats is determined by the architecture of the theater, including the width and height of the stage opening, the dimensions of the acting area, the seating capacity of the theater, and the slant of the auditorium floor, as well as the kinds of plays that are given (opera usually requires taller flats than drawing-room comedy, for example). Every theater has a standard flat height, adjusted to its own conditions, and usually only flats of standard height are kept in stock. If taller or shorter flats are needed for a particular effect they will be specially built. Perhaps the commonest height is 12'-0", but some theaters may choose 14', and small theaters may prefer 10'. Flat heights are usually set at even-numbered feet because lumber is sold in those dimensions.

Flats vary in width, although usually at intervals of a full foot. In the nineteenth century, 5'-9" was set as the maximum width of a flat, for reasons which no longer apply; however, scenery canvas is usually bought in widths of 6'-0", and since it must be trimmed when it is applied, a 6' flat can be covered only with difficulty. Furthermore, flats wider than 5' are difficult to handle and store. In practice, then, flats are likely to be standardized in widths of 1'-0", 2'-0", 3'-0", 4'-0", and 5'-0", with perhaps a few six-footers. The only exception to the full-foot dimension is that several 1'-6" flats should be added to the list. By combining them with other flats, wall sections can be constructed at 6", intervals. For example, a 1'-0" flat and a 1'-6" flat can be joined to make a 2'-6" flat. Solid lumber is often used in place of flats narrower than 1'-0". If a flat of odd width is needed, it is usually constructed by adding a temporary piece to the edge of a standard flat. Thus, a 4'-5½" flat would be built from a standard four-footer, with a 5½" section added so that it could be removed after the show, and the basic flat returned to stock.

In some theaters small flats are called *jogs* because they are often used to produce jogs or bays in the walls of interior sets. However, the dimension used to distinguish between jogs and flats varies from theater to theater, and unless they are stored in well separated areas it seems simpler to use the same term for both.

THE REUSE OF FLATS

In the professional theater, union rules prevent scenery for one show from being saved and used in a later production, so that no provision is made for altering flats. Also, in spite of the discouraging statistics, it is always hoped that each production will have a long run. As a result, professional flats are built as permanent structures, with strong joints which cannot be taken apart. In the noncommercial theater, flats are regularly used over and over again, recombined, altered, cut into, partially disassembled, and rebuilt. The joints and methods of construction are designed to facilitate their reuse.

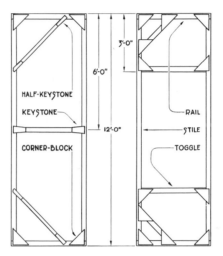

FIGURE 6.1 Traditional and revised framing patterns for flats.

FRAMING COMPONENTS

The standard flat requires seven (or eight) pieces of lumber, and about a dozen small pieces of plywood. When the flat is stood upright on the floor, the two horizontal pieces forming the top and bottom of the frame are called *rails,* and the two vertical pieces are called *stiles.* Fitted between the stiles is a horizontal board called a *toggle.* Two boards are set at an angle across the corners, one at each end of the flat; these are called *diagonal braces.* The four pieces of lumber forming the outside frame of the flat are fastened together with triangles of 1/4" plywood, called *corner-blocks.* In the traditional design, the toggles are attached to the stiles with trapezoidal strips of plywood called *keystones* because they are similar in shape to the keystone of an arch, and the diagonal braces are fastened with *half-keystones,* made by cutting keystones lengthwise on the center line. The plywood fasteners are placed on the back of the flat. When it has been assembled, the frame is turned over and canvas is stretched smoothly across it and glued in place (Figure 6.1).

115

AN ALTERNATIVE DESIGN

Experience has suggested that it is convenient to introduce some slight variations into this traditional design. Two toggles, rather than one, are specified as the basic number, and corner-blocks are used throughout, dispensing with keystones and half-keystones. In addition, toggles are fastened to the stiles with screws rather than nails.

Often special bracing must be added to flats for a particular show. For example it may be necessary to add a toggle to which picture eyes can be fastened, to support a picture or mirror hung on the wall. The extra toggle doubles the chance that the needed brace will already have been built into the flat. Furthermore, the need for such bracing seems to occur most frequently at points three feet from the ends of the flat, so that setting the toggles in those positions makes it much more likely that they can be used without alteration than if a single toggle is put in the center of the flat, where added pieces are seldom hung. If it should be necessary to move a toggle, fastening them with screws makes the alteration easy, whereas if they are nailed removing them takes longer and is likely to destroy the corner-blocks. More important than all of those reasons, the toggles are vital in holding the stiles straight. With first quality lumber, a single toggle in the center of the flat was adequate, but with the lumber which must be used today the extra bracing is distinctly needed.

There are two reasons for the substitution of corner-blocks for keystones and half-keystones. Corner-blocks can be cut faster, and using them throughout means that only one type of fastener need be stocked, with greater convenience in storage. It is desirable to hold the plywood fasteners back from the side edges of the flat by at least 3/4". The half-keystones provide so little nailing space that often they are set closer to the edge, leaving points which must be specially cut off whenever the 3/4" gap is utilized. Keystones can be set back from the edge, but they extend beyond the toggle on both sides, so that if the canvas must be cut out to create a window opening matching the edge of the toggle, the edges of the keystones must be especially trimmed. Corner-blocks provide so much more nailing surface that the entire structure is stronger, and they can easily be held back not only from the edges of the stiles but also from the inner edges of the toggles.

These alterations have been judged more convenient than the traditional pattern, and have been used for years in a number of theaters; they were adopted by at least one New York theater shortly after the publication of *Theatrical Set Design*,[1] in which the new design was first described. The instructions for flat building which follow will conform to this design. If the technical director or set designer in a particular theater prefers the traditional design, the student should have little difficulty in making the few changes which will be necessary.

Flats can be built by one person, but especially at certain stages of the process it is more efficient for two people to work together. The discussion will assume a two-person team.

If it is necessary to check a board for warping more accurately than can be done by eye, mark two points at opposite ends of a sheet of plywood, lay the board so that one edge touches the two points, and draw a line along its edge the full length of the plywood. Flop the board over so that it lies on the other side of the line, with the edge again touching the two points, and draw along it a second time. If the second line exactly matches the first, the board is straight; if there is a gap between the two lines, the board is warped.

STEPS IN BUILDING A PLAIN FLAT, 4'-0" × 12'-0"

1. Study the working drawing carefully, going through the process of construction in imagination. Throughout the actual construction, restudy the drawing frequently whenever you are not sure of the next step.

2. Collect one set of the following tools for each worker:

hammer
work tray of clout nails
screwdriver
container of 7/8" number 9 screws
clinch plate
steel square
try-square
pocket tape measure
pencil.

The try-square, pocket tape, and pencil should be laid on or near the radial-arm saw; the other tools should be carried to the construction area.

The clinch plate is a square sheet of heavy metal. If the scene shop has a template table, it will have clinch plates built into it, and they can be omitted from the list. If the table is in good condition, the corners will be accurately squared and the steel squares can also be omitted.

---

1. David Welker, *Theatrical Set Design: The Basic Techniques* (Boston: Allyn and Bacon, Inc., 1971).

3. Assemble the lumber needed for the stiles, rails, and toggles (it is more convenient to select the lumber for the diagonal braces after the rest of the frame has been assembled). Choose the shortest pieces of 1 X 3 from which the required lengths can be cut. Select the straightest boards available. Especially avoid boards which are warped so that they will not lie flat. Also avoid boards which are split or which have large knot holes that would weaken the flat. If it is not possible to find unwarped lumber, use the straightest pieces for the stiles, the second straightest for the rails, the next straightest for the toggles, and the most badly warped for the diagonal braces. The 1 X 3s should be placed near the saw.

Take twelve 10" corner-blocks from stock and carry them to the area where the flat will be built.

4. Check one end of each board to be used for the rails with a try-square to make sure that they are cut true. If either is off square, if there is a knot within a foot of the end, or if they are split or otherwise damaged, reverse ends or cut the bad end off. (The student should train himself to do this kind of checking whenever he measures a board for cutting, although it is especially important in building flats.) Mark off on one board a dimension equal to the width of the flat. Set it in place on the radial-arm saw, set the second board against it, with the end which has been checked on the same side as the end from which the first board was measured, make sure that they are precisely lined up, check to make sure that the saw will cut exactly at the mark, as described in chapter 3, and cut through both boards with a single pass of the saw.

5. The stiles cannot be cut the full height of the flat, since they must fit between the rails, and if cut to full dimension the assembled flat would be some inches too long. Their actual dimension is 12'-0" minus 2W—that is, the full length of the flat minus the combined width of the two rails.

It would be possible to measure the widths of the rails, add them, and subtract the sum from 12'-0". However, an odd dimension may result, and since boards vary in width it may not precisely match any of the standard marks on the tape. An easier and more accurate method is used.

Lay the two rails on the floor or on a long work table, with the edges tight together. Butt the board from which one stile is to be cut against them, at right angles to the rails. Catch the hook of the tape measure over the far edge of the outside rail, and while your partner holds the hook firmly in place stretch the tape across the rails out on to the stile, and mark the full 12'-0". Picking up the stile and moving it to the saw automatically subtracts the widths of the rails which were included in the original measurement. (This method of measuring should be used whenever it is necessary to subtract the width of one or more boards from the board being marked.)

Set the marked stile on the saw in position for cutting, and fit the other stile beside it. After your partner has checked to make sure that the far ends of the boards are precisely lined up, cut both with a single pass of the saw.

6. Lay the two stiles side by side on the work table or the floor, butt one of the remaining pieces of lumber against them at right angles, catch the tape over the outside edge of the far stile, and measure along the new board the full width of the flat (producing the dimension 4'-0" minus 2W). Set the marked board on the saw, with the remaining board against it, check the alignment of the far ends, and cut both; these are the toggles. (It may be more convenient to use the scraps left from cutting the stiles for measuring the toggle, rather than the stiles themselves.)

7. Carry the lumber, tape measures, try-squares, and pencils to the construction area. Lay the rails and stiles on a flat surface (the floor or a template table; the remaining instructions will assume that the work must be done on the floor). Arrange them in the shape of a picture frame, with the ends of the stiles butted against the side edges of the rails. Sight the rails and stiles for warp. If any is discovered, place the boards so that they curve into the flat.

8. Square one corner of the frame, using the steel square. (Steps 8 through 17 can be carried on simultaneously by the two builders, working with diagonally opposite corners of the flat.)

9. Place a corner-block on the two boards, according to the following rules:

The grain of the outside layer of the corner-block should not be parallel with the crack between the two boards being joined, but should cross it at an angle. Occasionally corner-blocks are cut with the grain parallel with the hypotenuse of the triangle; in that case, any placement will be acceptable. More often, they are cut with the grain parallel with one of the short sides. If the grain is parallel with the crack between the rail and the stile, turn the corner-block over and reposition it; the grain will then cross the joint at right angles.

The corner-block should be held back 1/4" from the outside edge of the rail. This is not a critical dimension, and placement can be done by eye. Since the flat is often moved by sliding it along the floor, holding the corner-block up slightly keeps it from catching and splintering, or ripping up the floor covering. The corner-blocks are 1/4" thick, so if the worker prefers to check the placement precisely, he can use a second corner-block to measure the gap.

The edge of the corner-block should be held back 1" from the edge of the stile. Since it can be expected that the flat will become part of the permanent stock, to be reused in other plays, it may be necessary in the future to fit the edge of another flat against it at the corner of a set. If the corner-blocks were nailed out flush with the edge of a stile, unsightly gaps would appear when a second flat was butted against it from the back.

119

An allowance of 3/4" would actually be sufficient, since that is the thickness of framing lumber, but the corner-block is likely to move slightly when it is nailed, and setting it exactly at 3/4" leaves no margin of error, and requires very precise fastening, with an uneconomical expenditure of time. This dimension is also not extremely precise, so long as at least 3/4" is left clear. An easy method of checking it is to stand a scrap of 1 X 3 on edge at the side of the stile, and then pull the corner-block just slightly farther back.

10. Being careful that the corner-block does not shift, fasten it to the rail with five clout nails; the pattern in which the nails are to be set is discussed in a separate section immediately following this list. Those instructions should be studied before attempting actual construction of a flat.

11. Slip a clinch plate under the rail and drive the nails down firmly.

12. Refit the stile against the rail and check the squareness of the corner with a steel square.

13. Drive a clout nail through the corner-block part way into the stile, placing the nail at one corner of the nailing pattern, near the end of the stile.

14. Resquare the two boards, to make sure they have not shifted when the nail was driven.

15. Drive a second nail part way into the stile, in the nailing-pattern position farthest from the first nail.

16. Check the squareness of the two boards. If the corner is not square, force it into position and hold it while setting a third nail. When it has been fixed square with two nails driven, make sure the clinch plate extends entirely under the nailing area, drive the nails all the way in, and add the remaining nails to complete the nailing pattern.

17. Move to the opposite end of the rail and repeat steps 8 through 16. If the lumber is warped, it will be necessary for one workman to force the boards together at the fourth corner and hold them while the other worker drives the nails.

18. Catch the hook of a tape at one end of a rail, setting it close to the corner so that it can be stretched along the face of the stile in the 3/4" gap, rather than being bent over the corner-block. Mark a point on the stile 3'-0" from the end of the flat. With the try-square, draw a line across the stile through the three-foot mark. (Steps 18–24 can best be done by both members of the team working simultaneously on the same toggle, one at each end.)

19. Set one end of a toggle against the inside edge of the stile, with one edge at the 3' mark and the other edge between the 3' mark and the end of the flat. Force the opposite stile out, if necessary, and press the toggle down flat between the two stiles. Check to make sure that each end of the toggle precisely matches the 3' mark.

If the stiles are warped at all, and have been placed so that they bow into the flat, the toggle will tend to force them straight, and the pressure of the warp will actually tighten the joint. If the stiles have been improperly placed, so that they bow out of the flat, the toggle will not fill the area between them, and to straighten them it will be necessary to push them together and hold them in place while they are nailed. Not only is this difficult, but even if it can be done the warp will tend always to pull the joints open and weaken the flat. It is for these reasons that the in-bow position was specified in step 7.

20. Place a corner-block in position over each stile-toggle joint, following the rules given in step 9. Since the stile-rail joint and the stile-toggle joint are at right angles to each other, notice that the top grain of the plywood will also run in different directions. As with the stile-rail joint, hold the corner-block back an inch from the edge of the stile, and 1/4" from the edge of the toggle which is placed at the 3' mark. Slip clinch plates under both joints and fasten the corner-blocks to the toggle, using the full nailing pattern and driving the nails in all the way.

22. Slipping the fingers under the head of a screw, place it in the area of the plywood over the stile, in one of the standard positions, and set it with a couple of light taps of a hammer. Check to make sure that the inside edge of the toggle is still aligned with the 3' marks and drive the screw down from half to two-thirds of the way with the hammer. Drive it the rest of the way with the screwdriver, sinking the head into the wood until the top is even with or a hair below the surface of the plywood.

23. Fasten the other four screws shown in the standard pattern in the same way.

24. Repeat steps 18–23 for the other toggle.

25. Referring to the working drawing, mark on the inner edges of the stiles and rails the points between which the diagonal braces are to be fastened. Note that the braces are not set in diagonally opposite corners, as might be expected, but that both are fitted against the same stile. The diagonal brace stiffens the frame so as to resist force applied parallel to it; it provides less resistance to force applied at right angles to it. If the braces are put in opposite corners, they are parallel with each other, and provide great strength in one direction but inadequate strength in the other. Setting them against the same stile averages the support, so that the frame resists deformation equally in both directions. In flats with arch or door openings there may not be enough space to set one of the diagonal braces at the bottom; in that case, both braces may be set at the top, in opposite corners, but still out of parallel with each other. The critical

requirement is that one end of each brace must be attached to the same board, for plain flats the stile, for flats with both braces at the top, the rail.

26. With a tape measure, find the approximate length of one brace. Select two boards slightly longer, and cut one end of each at a 45° angle.

27. Lift the corner of the flat off the floor and slip one of the braces under it, fitting the cut end in place against the rail or stile at the point marked, and setting the same edge of the board so that it matches the second mark. Since the lumber is longer than the brace, the uncut end will extend under the flat frame; mark across the diagonal brace by drawing a pencil line along the inside edge of the flat frame where it rests on the brace.

28. Cut the brace along this mark, then lay it on top of the second brace, aligning one end of the finished brace with the previously cut end of the second, and draw along the last edge cut; cut along this line.

29. Give the flat a final check for squareness by measuring the diagonals; if they differ, move the flat until the corner at one end of the long diagonal is against the wall, and force it square by pushing gently against the opposite corner until the two diagonals are equal. It will be necessary for one person to hold the flat in this position while the other attaches the braces. If the check demonstrates that the flat is already square, then both workers can fasten the two braces simultaneously.

30. Fit each brace into one corner of the flat frame, aligning it with the marks which have been made on the stile and rail. Cover the joints with corner-blocks and nail firmly. Again, the grain of the corner-blocks should cross the joint at an angle, and the edges should be held back 1" from the edge of the stile and 1/4" from the edges of the rails; they need not be held back from the edges of the diagonal braces.

31. Turn the frame over and check to make sure that all nails have been properly clinched. If any have been missed, clinch them with a hammer.

NAILING

As with every other detail of flat construction, a great variety of nailing patterns are used, but any effective method of nailing must produce a firm joint with a minimum of play, which will stand up under continued use, and which will not split the framing lumber unacceptably.

Each joint has a line of weakness—the crack between the two boards being joined, and the purpose of the corner-block is to compensate for this weakness and make the joint rigid. It is for that reason that the corner-blocks are always set with the grain running across the joint, since the plywood is much less flexible in that direction. One other practice is essential for a firm joint—the framing lumber must be fastened on both sides of the joint as close to it as possible. Two other factors have already been mentioned—the strength is increased by spreading the nails as far from each other as can be done, and the splitting of the framing lumber must be kept minimal. Since these two considerations tend to push some nails in opposite directions, the actual nailing positions involve a compromise between them. Avoiding splitting depends on three factors, two of which have already been mentioned—holding nails back from the ends of boards far enough that the split does not extend all the way out, and staggering nails so that no two fall in the same grain. The third factor is discussed below.

Corner-blocks can be fastened in various ways, including gluing, screwing, and the use of different types of nails. In most cases the preferred method is to fasten them with *clout nails,* which have been especially designed for the purpose.

Clout nails have cut rather than round shafts, and the tips are shaped like the blade of a screwdriver, forming a straight line rather than coming to a point. If they are driven into wood so that the line is parallel with the grain they cause maximum splitting; if they are set so that the line runs at right angles to the grain, splitting is minimized. The worker should be trained to automatically glance at the point of each clout nail and set it so that it runs across the grain. The difference in the two dimensions may seem small, but the difference in the length of the splits in the two positions is often enormous.

Clout nails are tapered. When first driven in they may hold firmly, but as soon as the joint has loosened even slightly the nails pull up, there is very little contact with the surrounding wood, and the joint falls apart. To prevent that, they must be clinched, that is the points must be driven over at right angles to the wood. The joint will then loosen only if enough force is applied to bend the points straight again. Un-clinched clout nails will not hold anything. Clout nails must *always* be clinched.

The nails are unusually soft, so much so that they can almost be bent with the fingers. If the lumber through which they are to be driven is placed on a hard surface (usually a clinch plate), when the nails strike the plate as they come through the wood they are bent into tiny hooks which turn back and catch in the wood, so that they do not have to be clinched by turning the unit over and bending each one with a hammer. In order to clinch, they must be at least 1/4" longer than the combined thickness of the pieces of wood being joined. Since they are used almost exclusively to attach corner-blocks, the total thickness is 1" (1/4" plywood plus 3/4" lumber). Most scene shops stock clout nails 1¼" long; longer nails can be used, but shorter ones will not clinch.

Unless the heads of the nails are driven firmly into the wood, the point will not stick through far enough for effective clinching. Clout nails should be given one or two blows with the hammer after they have apparently been driven far enough, to make sure that they are fully clinched.

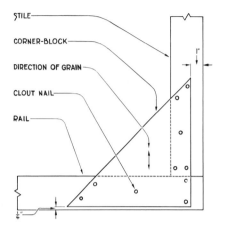

FIGURE 6.2 **The nailing pattern for stile–rail joints.**

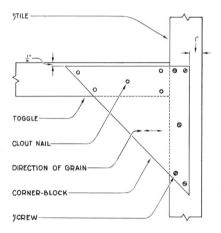

FIGURE 6.3 **The fastening pattern for stile–toggle joints.**

Since the framing lumber is partly hidden by the corner-block, there is some tendency to think of the nailing as designed to fasten the plywood triangle. In fact the purpose of the nails is to hold the framing lumber together, and the placement of the nails depends more on the 1 × 3s than on the corner-block. The plywood must be fastened firmly to each of the two boards being joined; each corner-block thus provides two separate nailing areas, where it is in contact with the two boards, and two nailing patterns must be used.

For most joints, the nailing area has the shape of a rectangle with one end slanted (the nailing area for diagonal braces has both ends slanted). The pattern which is recommended here specifies five nails, arranged like the symbols on a 5-spot playing card, except that at the slanted end of the nailing area the nail at the acute angle is moved up into the point to provide for maximum spreading, and the nails are staggered to prevent their falling in the same grain, rather than being neatly squared like the playing-card symbols (Figure 6.2).

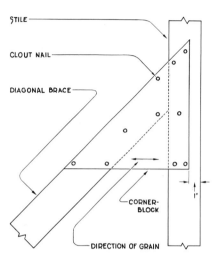

FIGURE 6.4   The nailing pattern for stile–diagonal brace joints.

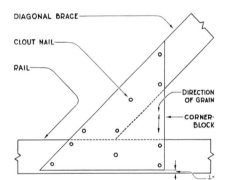

FIGURE 6.5   The nailing pattern for rail–diagonal brace joints.

In each joint, the end of at least one nailing pattern coincides with the end of one of the pieces of lumber. The nails must be held back from this end far enough that the grain will not split out. Since lumber splits parallel with the grain, not crosswise, the nail nearest the joint in the other board can be set much closer to the crack between the boards. The actual placements will depend on the splitting characteristics of the individual pieces of lumber, but it will usually be safe to set nails as close as 3/8" to the side edge of a board, and as close as an inch to the end.

Splitting is most critical at the stile-rail joints; it is much less dangerous for stile-toggle joints, and still less for diagonal braces. However, it is important to remember that the hidden end of a brace is cut at 45°, and to adjust the pattern to it. There is a tendency to set the nails too close to the end of the brace.

Diagrams are given showing the recommended nailing patterns for the four types of joints which occur in a standard flat (Figures 6.2, 6.3, 6.4, 6.5). The screws used to attach the toggle corner-blocks to the stiles are arranged in the same pattern. If key-stones and half-keystones are used instead of full corner-blocks, the nailing areas are greatly reduced, and there will probably be space for only three or four nails.

COVERING THE FLAT

All covering fabrics are often referred to as "canvas," even though they may actually be of other types (on the same principle that filters for spotlights are called "gels," although they are no longer usually made of gelatine, and people still refer to "lead" pencils, although actual lead has not been used for centuries). The inaccurate but convenient term will be used here, but it should be understood to stand for whatever type of fabric is actually used.

The covering can be done on the floor, but it is much less painful if the flat frame is set on sawhorses. Canvassing can be done by one person, but a two-man team can cover three or four flats in the time it takes one workman to canvas one. The instructions below assume that two people are working together. As with construction, canvassing will be described in numbered steps.

1. Set up three sawhorses parallel with each other and about five feet apart; they should be a little longer than the width of the flat. Lay the flat frame on them face up, that is, resting on the side to which the corner-blocks are attached.

2. Pull out a length of canvas from the roll and measure off about 12'-4" or 12'-6"; this measurement is not critical, except that the cloth must be a little longer than the flat. Cut into the side of the cloth and then tear it across, being careful not to let the canvas tear lengthwise; if it shows any tendency to do that, it should be cut the rest of the way with scissors rather than being torn. If the flat is nearly as wide as the canvas, the cloth can be used without further cutting; if the flat is much smaller, it is more convenient to cut or tear off a lengthwise strip. The final piece should be from three to six inches wider than the flat.

3. Get two staplers, one for each worker, and a supply of extra staples.

4. Lay the canvas on top of the flat frame and stretch the selvage along one stile, sticking out slightly beyond the wood. (The selvage is the woven edge of the cloth as it comes from the roll, not the edges which have been cut or torn.) Adjust the canvas so that the flaps which extend beyond the ends of the frame are about equal. (Do not worry about the fact that the free corners of the canvas fall through the frame, and that the sheet sags.) Staple the selvage edge to the wood at the two corners of the frame. Making sure that the selvage is parallel with the edge of the stile, staple it to the lumber halfway between the ends of the stile, close to the inside edge of the board (about 1/4" or 1/2" from the edge); this placement is not critical, and can be judged by eye.

5. One of the workers moves around to the other stile, takes hold of the edge of the canvas at the center, pulls it away from the flat at right angles to the stile, and staples it in the same way, at the center of the stile, close to the inside edge.

6. The two workers go to opposite ends of the flat and take hold of the canvas at the center of the ends and pull it away from the center of the flat, and staple it in the center of the rails, close to their inside edges.

7. Each person then grasps the cloth on each side of one of the staples which were driven into the corners of the flat and lifts up, pulling the staple out of the wood; it should be removed from the cloth and discarded.

8. The workers then return to opposite stiles. Catching the edge of the canvas about a foot to one side of the staples, they pull it smooth and set a new staple in each stile six or eight inches away from the original staple. From this point on, all staples are spaced approximately the same distance apart, and set close to the inside edges of the stiles or rails.

When the first four permanent staples were set in the centers of the stiles and rails, the canvas was pulled at right angles to the two center-lines of the flat. For this and all later steps the direction of pull should be off 90°. Imagine that the center of the flat was marked with a penciled plus sign. From now on, the canvas should be pulled directly away from that center point. It will be seen that as stapling proceeds along the stile the angle shifts steadily, from nearly 90° to less than 45°; this is called pulling on the bias.

All covering fabrics shrink as they dry after being painted. If the canvas is pulled very tight, the shrinkage at best will cause a small unsightly cup to develop around each staple; at worst, the flat frame may be pulled out of shape. If the canvas is left too loose, it will not be taut even after shrinking. Ideally, just enough sag should be left so that when shrunk the canvas will be smooth and flat. Unfortunately, it is difficult to predict how much a piece of unfamiliar fabric will shrink, so that judging how tight to pull canvas taken from a new roll is something of a gamble. Once a flat has been covered and painted, it can be examined, and the tightness adjusted in covering later flats with the same material. A rule of thumb, which can be used as a somewhat inaccurate guide, is that if a canvassed but unpainted 5'-0" flat is laid on the floor face up, the canvas should sag so that it just touches the floor at the center of the flat. The amount of shrinkage varies inversely with the size of the flat, so that for flats as narrow as 1'-0" or 1'-6" it is probably best to pull the covering taut, with little or no shrinkage allowance. Muslin shrinks much more than duck, and heavy canvas least of all. Of course, if the flat is being covered with used canvas which has been previously painted, it will have been preshrunk and should be pulled fully tight.

9. The two workers continue along the edges of the stiles, setting a total of four or five staples. It is essential that they both work in the same half of the flat.

10. Moving to the other half of the stiles, they repeat this process, stopping about a foot and a half short of the end of the flat.

11. They then move to the ends of the flat. It will often be necessary to remove the staple which has been set in the center of the rail, pull the canvas out a little farther

in order to remove wrinkles that have developed, and restaple. When the canvas is smooth, the stapling is continued, starting with the center and carrying it out all the way to the ends. Finally, the gaps at the ends of the stiles are filled in. Wrinkles may occasionally develop which make it necessary to pull up the last staple or two at the ends of the rails, restretch and restaple, although the use of a bias tension most often produces a smooth surface.

12. The staples serve only as a temporary fastening; the canvas is permanently fixed to the frame with glue. Various types of glue may be used; and they are discussed in chapter 9. Rather than anticipate that discussion, it will be assumed here that whatever adhesive is preferred in the particular theater is available and has been properly prepared. One worker flips back the edge of the canvas along a stile, the other paints a liberal coat of glue both on the wood and on the canvas flap. Moving around the flat, he glues the rail, the other stile, and the second rail. As soon as an edge is finished, the first worker turns it over and presses it firmly and smoothly against the wood, most often by running the palm of his hand along it, although some technicians prefer to beat it down with a stiff scrub brush or to press it in place with a small block of wood.

13. The strip of canvas extending around the edges of the flat must be trimmed off. Some workers prefer to let the glue dry first, which makes the job easier and less messy. However, cutting it when wet tends to drive the fibers of the cloth into the wood and makes it less likely to ravel.

The cut is started at one corner (on the worker's right if he stands at the end of the flat facing the rail). The flap hanging over the edge of the rail is cut through, parallel with the stile, and up on to the wood. A knife is usually used for this cut, although it can be done more easily with scissors.

The workman then stands next to the corner of the flat, with the stile on his right, and facing away from the flat. Grasping the flap he has just cut with his left hand, he presses the point of the knife down firmly on the wood and draws it across the end of the rail and along the edge of the stile. The cut should be made close to the edge, although none of the canvas, not even a thread, should be left extending out beyond the edge. Usually the cloth is cut about 1/4" or 1/2" back from the edge of the board. As he cuts, he walks backward along the flat, keeping moderate tension with his left hand on the ribbon of canvas which develops. It will be necessary to stop every few feet to pick up the ribbon closer to the flat. When he reaches the second corner of the flat, the direction of cut is changed, and he proceeds along the rail, walking backwards and cutting off the edge of the cloth. The other stile and rail are trimmed in the same way.

14. As soon as each edge has been cut, the second worker inspects it to make sure that the canvas has not been wrinkled or pulled loose at any point; if so, he presses it back in place.

15. As a final step, the tips of the bristles of the brush are dipped in glue, and it is drawn along the cut edge with the bristles set parallel to the edge so as to deposit a thin, nearly invisible line of glue which helps keep the outside threads from raveling.

A common beginner's error is to assume that the canvas should be stapled and glued to all framing lumber, including toggles and diagonal braces. Since shrinkage depends in part on the size of the open areas of canvas, this breaks the flat into sections which will shrink differently. A much smoother surface is produced by fastening only the outer edges, as described.

There are two exceptions to that practice. If holes are to be cut in the flats, as described in the following section, the canvas must be glued around their edges. In re-working flats taken from stock, it may be necessary to fill in a hole cut, for example, to provide a window opening for a previous set. In that case, a piece of canvas is stretched across the opening and stapled and glued to the lumber framing it. Although the surface of a flat patched in this way is not quite so smooth as if it were entirely recovered with a single piece of canvas, usually the patch will not be noticed by the audience, and there is a significant saving in time and material.

Safety makes it desirable, and local fire laws may make it necessary, that scenery be made fire retardant. Flats should be painted with a mixture of a pound of sal ammoniac and a pound of borax thoroughly dissolved in three quarts of water. It is possible to buy canvas already flameproofed, in which case the frames can be treated before covering. Otherwise, the liquid should be brushed on both frame and canvas. Brushes used for flameproofing should be thoroughly washed as soon as the work is finished, to keep the solution from corroding the bristle case.

At this point the flat is finished. It can be left on the sawhorses, or stood against the wall to dry, with the face out so that the glue will not stick to the wall.

> Some time and material can be saved if two flats can be canvassed at the same time. They are laid side by side on the sawhorses, and their total width must not be greater than the width of the canvas. The canvas is first stapled around the outside edges, as if the two were a single flat. Then it is stapled to the two stiles which are in contact with each other. Finally, they are cut apart by running a knife down the crack between them, and glued separately.

OPENINGS IN FLATS

Most sets require that some flats be built so that doors and windows can be fitted into them. Sometimes such flats will be especially built; often they will be made by cutting openings in standard flats taken from stock. Altering a flat to provide an opening into which a window unit can be set will be used as an illustration of this process.

Let us assume that a window opening must be cut in a 5'-0" × 12'-0" plain flat, that the opening is to be 2'-0" wide and 3'-6" high, and that it is to be placed on the vertical center-line of the flat with the bottom of the opening 3'-0" above the end of the flat. Assume further that the flat as taken from stock matches the design recommended earlier in this chapter.

The first step is to pull the flat from the scene dock and compare it with the working drawing. It will be seen that one toggle is already in the specified position and can be used to frame one edge of the opening, but that the other is set too far away. Laying the flat on the floor, the correct position is marked on the stiles, 6'-6" from the end of the flat. The screws fastening the corner-blocks of the out-of-place toggle to the stiles are removed, the toggle is moved to the new position, and the screws driven in again. At this point, the top and bottom of the window opening have been framed, but additional braces must be provided for the sides. With a tape measure, two points are marked on each toggle, 1'-6" from the outside edges of the stiles; the points are 2'-0" apart, which is the specified width of the window opening.

Two boards are then cut 3'-6" long, fitted between the toggles with the inner edges matching the points which have been marked, and fastened with corner-blocks. Since it is possible that these braces may need to be removed the next time the flat is used, it might be better to screw the corner-blocks to the toggles, although they can be nailed to the added braces themselves.

The flat is then turned over and set on sawhorses (Figure 6.6). The canvas is stapled to the lumber framing the area where the hole is to be cut (that is, to the entire length of the vertical braces, and across part of the toggles). The staples must be placed close to the edges of the lumber away from the planned opening. When they are in place, the canvas covering the hole is cut out, about a quarter of an inch back from the edge of the lumber next to the opening, and the canvas is glued down. It is possible to glue it by forcing it slightly off the wood and slipping the glue brush along between the wood and the cloth. If preferred, each corner can be slit back at 45° so that the canvas flaps can be turned back and brushed directly, as in canvassing a plain flat.

PANELS

A similar method of construction can be used to produce panels sunk below the main surface of the flat. Extra toggles and vertical pieces are added to the flat frame exactly as for a window, the canvas is cut out to match the panel area, and the loose edges glued down. The flat is then turned over and the opening filled in with a piece of can-

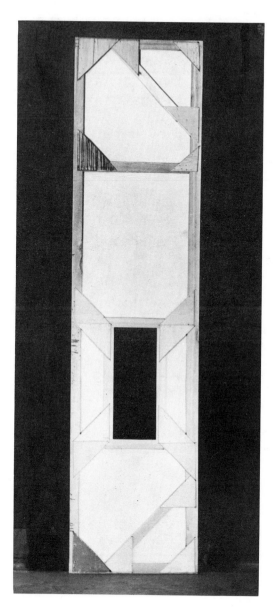

FIGURE 6.6 A flat with a framed opening, shown from the front and back.

vas stapled and glued to the back of the 1 X 3s outlining the opening. Some of the corner-blocks may interfere with fastening the canvas flush with the back surface of the lumber, so that it will be necessary to staple close to the inner edge to pull it flat. Usually the panel will be finished by nailing molding to the inside edges of the framing pieces, on the front side of the flat; if so, it will help conceal any gaps.

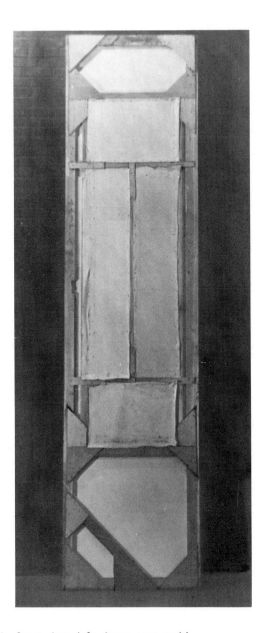

FIGURE 6.7 Sunken panels in flats. The front view, *left*, shows cove molding nailed to the edges of the 1 x 3s to make the panels appear more finished. The back view, *right*, shows the extra toggles and vertical boards added to frame the panels, and the rectangles of canvas tacked to them to fill in the openings.

Panels made in that way are realistically three-dimensional (Figure 6.7). However, this method damages the flats somewhat, and requires extra time and material.

More often paneling is simulated by nailing the molding directly to the front of the flat, and suggesting that the enclosed area is sunken by painting it in a slightly darker shade of the base coat used for the rest of the flat. It may be necessary to move one or both of the toggles to provide a solid support into which the molding can be nailed, and nearly always it will be necessary to add a couple of vertical supports between them on the back of the flat to provide a nailing surface for the molding at the sides of the panels.

SILL IRONS

A set for Shaw's *Misalliance* specified four door openings, three of which stood behind platforms, so that the bottom edges of the openings were some distance off the floor. The same method of altering the flats which has just been described was used for these flats. The fourth door, however, was designed to open at floor level, so that the hole had to be cut down through the rail. It is sometimes possible to use such a flat without further support, but usually some stiffening must be provided to tie the two legs of the flat together strongly enough to hold the flat in shape, but small enough not to be noticed by the audience. The device most commonly used is called a *sill iron*.

Sill irons come in two forms. One is simply a straight metal strap, with holes drilled in it to receive screws. The other type, also called a saddle iron, has two vertical bars welded to the horizontal strap. The straight sill irons are more versatile, since they need not fit the opening precisely. A saddle iron can be used only if the vertical bars are spaced at a distance exactly matching the width of the opening.

Sill irons are fitted against the edge of the rail into which the door opening has been cut, and fastened with screws. The height of the flat is increased by the thickness of the added piece. That causes trouble less often than might be expected, for instance, if a cornice is fastened around the tops of the flats the small difference in height may be completely hidden. If the difference is objectionable, however, the bottom rail must be cut back by the same amount, so that the flat will have true height when the iron is fastened in place. This can be done with a saber saw with considerable difficulty. It is better to use a plane—and this is one of the few instances in the scene shop in which a plane is really essential.

HEADERS

One other type of structure should be mentioned, although it does not involve cutting a hole in an existing flat. Nevertheless, it serves essentially the same purpose.

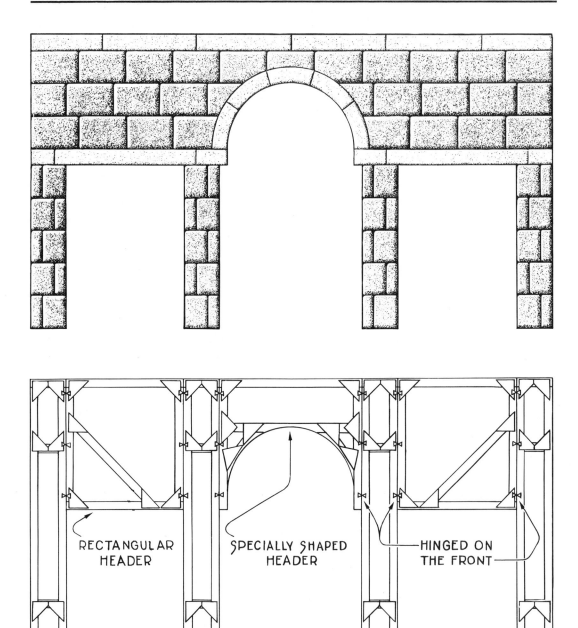

FIGURE 6.8   Headers. The drawing from the back, *bottom*, shows the construction of the headers and the method of fastening them to the stock flats. The drawing, *top*, shows the unit from the front, and illustrates the use of paint to blend the headers and stock flats into a single structure.

Set designers sometimes require openings much larger than any standard flat. There are no theoretical size limitations, but such an opening might well be anywhere from six to ten feet wide, and proportionately high. A flat large enough to frame such an opening might be impossible to transport from the scene shop to the stage, and in any case would be difficult to handle. Instead, the designer or technical director will probably decide to use three separate flats to frame the opening. Stock flats are most often used at the sides, but the wall area across the top will seldom match the dimensions of any flats already on hand; it must therefore be specially built. Such a unit, designed to fill in a wall section over an opening, is called a *header.* It can be a simple rectangle, or elaborately shaped. The construction of special shapes is discussed at the end of the chapter.

Suppose that the back wall of a set is 21'-0" wide, and that an opening must be provided 8'-0" wide and 9'-6" high; the header will therefore be 2'-6" × 8'-0". Suppose a wall section is to be left 4'-6" at one side of the opening, and 8'-6" at the other side.

The rectangular wall sections will be produced by combining stock flats, probably a 3'-0" flat and a 1'-6" flat for the small section, and a 3'-0" flat + a 4'-0" flat + a 1'-6" flat for the large section. The header will be specially built, using standard flat construction methods, although at this size not more than a single toggle will be used.

The entire wall may then be assembled by laying the units face up on the floor and hinging them together (Figure 6.8). The unit will fold, and can be moved through a door opening with a diagonal of slightly more than 8'-0", although it will be somewhat clumsy to handle. Checking its transportability is the responsibility of the technical director. If it cannot be moved from the scene shop to the stage, he will instruct the workers to transport it in sections and assemble them on the stage floor, or he may introduce some variations in the design which will make it possible to fold it to smaller dimensions.

Since sill irons are not usually run across the bottom of wall sections with large headers, it may be difficult to keep the folded units square while transporting them. Not only does that make handling awkward, but if they slip too far out of line the hinges may crack off. The structure can be held straight by driving one or two nails through the layers of flats at the bottom of the wall; they are removed after it has been carried to the stage. If the openings through which the units must be carried are large enough, the bottoms of the flats can be held together by one of two C-clamps, which are easier to remove.

HINGING FLATS

As has been illustrated by the preceding example, walls are usually made up of a series of flats, hinged together so that they can be folded for moving, and so that they will pass through whatever path is provided between scene shop and stage.

Two flats are assembled by laying them side by side on the floor, face up. Hinges are then laid across the joint and screwed in place, spacing them a little less than three feet apart. This spacing is not critical, and can be done by eye. The hinges closest to the ends of the flats must be held back some distance, usually about a foot. Since the screws spread the wood fibers apart, as do nails, to set them close to the ends of the stiles would make it likely that the lumber would split apart.

Usually the square-leaved hinges called back-flaps are used, since they are smaller than the width of the framing lumber. Either tight-pin or loose-pin hinges may be used, but if they are loose-pin care must be taken that the pins do not fall out while the flats are being moved. The heads should be placed toward what will be the top of the flats, and if nails have been used for pins they should be well bent to provide enough friction to keep them from slipping loose. If wires have been used, they should be bent at both ends so that they cannot fall out if the flats are upended in either direction.

The hinges extend out from the surface of the flats, and if stage lights are placed so that the beams are nearly parallel with the surface of the flats, highlights and shadows may appear which make the hinges objectionably visible. In that case, holes must be cut in the surface of the stiles so that the hinges can be set in (countersunk). Usually that is not necessary.

Each leaf of a back-flap hinge has three holes for screws, two close to the pin and the third toward the outer edge of the leaf. Only one of the holes nearest the pin is used, since screws in both holes would fall in the same grain, and would be almost certain to split the wood. Thus, only four screws are needed for each hinge. (Knowing that only one of the two inside holes is used is one of those small things which are used to distinguish between trained craftsmen and novices. Following this rule is not only sound practice, but also an easy way to impress others with one's mastery of stagecraft.)

Each hinge is set so that the pin is centered precisely on the crack between the flats. If well built flats are used, the crack will be dimensionless. Sometimes it may be distressingly wide. That usually makes little difference—it will be invisible after it is covered. It is very important that the bottom rails of the flats be precisely in line, otherwise the unit will not sit firmly on the stage floor.

Once the hinge has been set properly, a screw is tapped into one of the holes nearest the pin (it doesn't make any difference which one), and driven down not more than two-thirds of the way. A screw is then set in one of the nearest-pin holes in the other leaf and hammered down; both screws are driven down solidly with a screwdriver. Screws are next fastened in the outside holes of the two leaves, and the hinge is in place.

Often a hinge will slip out of line when the first screw is tapped in place with a hammer.

1. If possible, move the screw to a new position, at least an inch away.

2. If there is not space to do that, take out the first screw, replace the hinge in its correct position, and carefully set all the other screws, finally driving in the screw which was set incorrectly.

3. As an extra precaution, to prevent the original screw from going back into the original hole and pulling the hinge out of line, force a sliver of wood into the hole and break it off even with the surface before the screw is reset, and drive the screw in at a slant, with the point angled away from the original position and toward the correct position.

4. If hinges frequently shift out of position when the screws are being hammered in place, set the first screw in each leaf in one of the holes next to the pin. Since only one of these two holes is used, if the screw goes in wrong it can be taken out and set in the other hole, in fresh wood. If the hole farthest from the pin is fastened first, it will be difficult to reset it correctly, since the right and wrong holes will overlap.

It is better to fasten the two hinges closest to the ends of the flats first. They will hold the unit securely while the two center hinges are added, and the flats are less likely to swing apart accidentally. If the flats are not too wide, it is best to attach the center hinges by going to the side of the unit and reaching across. If that is awkward, it is possible to walk out along the stiles, squat down, and fasten a hinge while teetering on the flat frames. The two boards combined provide a footing something less than six inches wide, which is adequate but not comfortable. The flats will not be damaged by walking along the frame, but even one slip which sends toe or elbow into the unsupported canvas will punch it through, and cause a reduction in the warmth with which the worker is treated by the technical director and fellow crew members.

DUTCHMANNING

When the hinging has been completed, the entire joint, including the hinges, must be hidden by covering it with a cloth strip. For some reason lost in the mists of theatrical history such strips are called *dutchmen,* and the process of applying them is called *dutchmanning.* The designer's note for such joints will read "hinge and dutchman."

Dutchmen are torn from scrap canvas. It is best if the same type and condition of canvas can be used as appears on the flats. Dutchman new flats with new canvas, painted flats with painted canvas. Dutchmanning is an excellent way to use up scraps of canvas. The pieces must be about 6" wide, so that they will extend a small distance on both sides of the hinges, but short lengths can be used by overlapping the ends. Canvassing flats often leaves full-length canvas strips which are ideal for dutchmen. The instructions will assume that such a strip is available, something more than a foot wide and about 12'-4" long.

1. Tear off the selvage; it shrinks differently from the rest of the canvas, and if left on would make the dutchman pucker. Tear the remaining canvas in two strips, a little over six inches wide; a torn edge is less visible than a neatly cut edge. Tear one of the strips crosswise at about its center point.

2. Paint one of the six-foot strips liberally with the same glue used to canvas flats, but somewhat weaker, since the dutchmen will be removed after the end of the show.

3. Set one end of the strip, glued side down, so as to cover the joint between the flats, placing it about an inch from the end of the flats. Walk backward along the stiles, stretching out the dutchman and pressing it on the surface of the flats, making sure that it extends past both edges of the hinges.

4. When the strip has been smoothed down for its entire length, repeat with the other strip, starting about an inch in from the other end of the flats, and pressing it over the hinges and crack, walking backward again toward the center of the flat. Because each strip was slightly longer than six feet, and each has been held back from the ends of the flats by about an inch, they should overlap by about six inches at the center. The dutchmanning is now finished, and all that remains is to walk carefully off the flat, watching to make sure that the dutchman is not slid askew or wrinkled.

The flats must be left open to dry. If the floor space is needed for another project, it is possible to stand the unit open against a wall, but it should be checked for possible wrinkles which have developed while it was moved, and if any are found they should be spread smooth while the glue is still wet. As soon as the glue has dried, the unit can be folded and stored.

When gluing on a white surface (for instance in dutchmanning the joint between two newly canvassed flats), two or three spoonfuls of paint should be added to the glue, so that it will be easy to see if any area has been skipped by accident. Only enough paint need be added to distinguish the glue from the white surface, and any color may be used.

SPACERS

Any two flats can be hinged and dutchmanned, and when folded they will be no wider than the largest of the two. Three flats can be folded compactly if the center flat is wider than the combined width of the two outside flats. Even a combination of such sizes as 1'-6" + 4'-0" + 3'-0" can be handled fairly easily, although it will not fold entirely flat. More difficult combinations such as 4'-0" + 4'-0" + 3'-0" can be made to fold if a 12'-long 1 × 2 or 1 × 3 board is set between two of the flats. Boards used for this purpose are given various names, including *tumbler* and the unfortunate expression *wooden dutchman;* the term *spacer* is to be preferred.

Each spacer creates an added joint, which must be fastened with its own set of hinges (Figure 6.9). Thus, a 1 × 3 spacer would be fastened to the flat on its left with

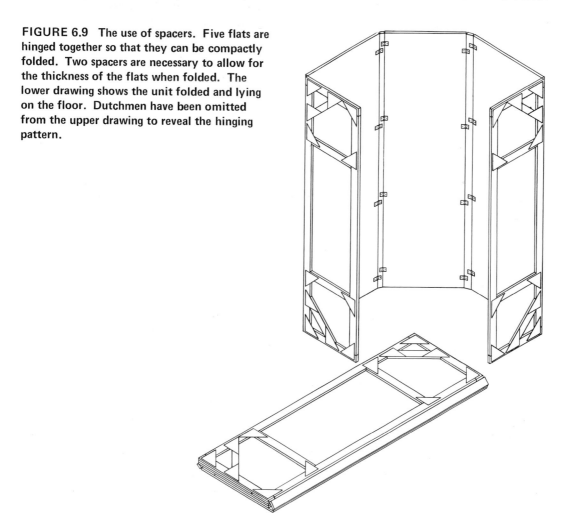

FIGURE 6.9 The use of spacers. Five flats are hinged together so that they can be compactly folded. Two spacers are necessary to allow for the thickness of the flats when folded. The lower drawing shows the unit folded and lying on the floor. Dutchmen have been omitted from the upper drawing to reveal the hinging pattern.

four hinges, and to the flat on its right with four hinges; matching hinges in the two groups should be placed from three to six inches apart, to avoid splitting the spacer. However, the double joint can be covered by a single dutchman wide enough to extend past the outside leaves of both sets of hinges, in this case nine or ten inches. If a 1 × 2 is used as a spacer, smaller hinges must be used, since the commonest size of back-flaps has leaves wider than the board.

Theoretically, any number of flats totalling any size can be hinged for folding if spacers are properly inserted; weight and ease of handling are the limiting factors. The set for *Misalliance* mentioned above required three walls. Each one has hinged and dutchmanned as a unit in the scene shop, and then folded and moved to the stage through a door only a little larger than ordinary size. Planning what size of spacers to use, and where they are to be placed, is the responsibility of the designer or the technical director. A special fact which must not be forgotten is that each spacer adds to the total width of the unit. If the altered dimension would prevent the wall from fitting properly into the set, then the widths of one or more of the flats must be adjusted to compensate.

BOOK CEILINGS

The largest hinged unit that is likely to be made is a foldable ceiling, which is built in the form of two flats hinged together. Because such a unit somewhat resembles the covers of a book, it is referred to as a *book ceiling* (Figure 6.10). Other types of ceiling are also used, but the book is the simplest and perhaps the commonest.

The ceiling is a permanent scenic unit, used for many productions without alteration, except that it may be repainted to match the different color schemes. Conseqeuently, it must be large enough to extend out past the edges of any ordinary set. The hinged joint between the flats is placed parallel with the front edge of the stage, so that the flats extend all the way across the stage from left to right. Because sets are usually trapezoidal in shape, the individual flats built for the book ceiling may also be trapezoids, with the upstage edge of the completed unit shorter than the downstage edge.

Because of their greater size, ceiling flats should be made of 1 × 4s rather than 1 × 3s. The ceiling will be held straight where it rests on the top edge of the back wall, but special stiffening must be provided to keep the downstage edge from sagging. This consists of a narrow flat called a *flipper*, which is hinged on edge to the back of the ceiling itself, at the downstage edge. The flipper extends up above the ceiling, and also helps mask the space overhead. Sagging is less a problem at the hinged center-line, because the ceiling is supported by ropes fastened there, but this edge can also be stiffened by nailing or screwing a 1 × 4 on edge against the back of one of the flats, running the length of the stile.

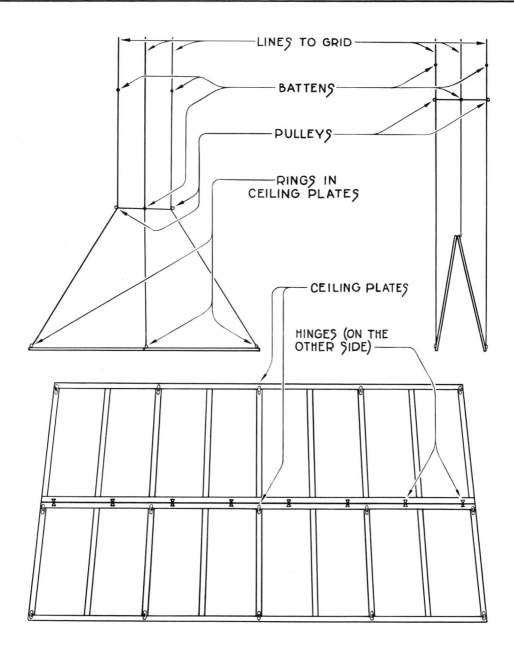

FIGURE 6.10   A book ceiling. *Bottom*, unit laid out on the stage floor; *top*, unit from the end, hanging from the grid; open, *left view*; and, closed for flying, *right*.

All ceilings create lighting problems, especially for the upstage half of the acting area, since the lighting instruments must be set well out beyond the front edge of the stage, and angled so that light shoots in under the downstage edge of the ceiling. For

141

that reason it is customary to place the ceiling on the set so that the front edge is back a foot and a half or two feet from the downstage edges of the flats.

The two leaves of the book ceiling are hinged together on the face; one hinge should be set close to each end of the stiles, and the other hinges spaced not more than 4' apart. The joint is then dutchmanned, and the ceiling painted and finely spattered (see chapter 11).

The ceiling is then turned over, and the stiffeners attached. Finally *ceiling plates* (small metal sheets with rings attached) are bolted to the center, upstage, and downstage edges, and flyropes are tied on. The ceiling is stored overhead by pulling it up into the flyloft (see chapter 13). When it is to be used, the walls of the set are first fastened in place, and the ceiling is then lowered, opened, and adjusted until it rests squarely on the top edges of the wall flats. For a set change, the ceiling is lifted slightly to free the flats, then lowered again after the new set has been put in place, or, if the second set does not require a ceiling, it is pulled up out of sight into the flyloft.

PATCHING

When flats are taken from stock for reuse, it will sometimes be discovered that the canvas has been ripped. Repairs can be made by a method similar to dutchmanning. The flat to be repaired should be placed so that it is possible to reach both sides of it, preferably standing vertically. A patch of canvas is torn out of the same type of cloth, with dimensions at least four inches larger than the tear. The patch is held in place against the back of the flat and coated with glue; when it is lifted off, the glue which has been brushed on the flat around the edge of the patch will define its position. This area is also glued. The patch is then placed against the back of the flat with the glued surfaces in contact, and one person presses against the front of the canvas while another presses the patch flat and smooths it out. The edges of the rip should be pulled smooth and, if they have rolled under, flattened against the patch. Such a repair is practically invisible.

IRREGULAR EDGES

In the nineteeth century, flats of a special type called woodwings were often used to represent trees and bushes. In its simplest form, a woodwing was an ordinary flat with an irregularly curved edge added to it. Trunks and branches were painted on the surface of the flat, and leaf shapes were added, more or less matching the shape of the curving profile. The first use of plywood in the theater was to make woodwing edges.

It consequently came to be called profile-board, a term which is still occasionally found in old-fashioned books.

We no longer use woodwings, except when the older scenic styles are purposely imitated. However, current sets fairly often call for flats with irregular edges. This is probably most frequent for ground-rows, next for false prosceniums, and third for miscellaneous purposes. Not only may the designer ask that the outside edges be given ornamental shapes, but the edges of openings in the flats may need to be of varied pattern.

There are various methods of changing the outlines of flats. Which should be used is determined by the availability of materials, by convenience, by the amount of time required for the alteration, and of course by the effect the designer hopes to produce. The choice is always guided by one consideration—if at all possible the alterations are added to the basic flat, which is changed structurally as little as possible so that they can be removed after the show and a sound flat returned to storage. Only very occasionally will it be necessary to build a special shape from scratch.

Plywood is still the preferred material for cutting unusual edging shapes. It can be easily worked with a saber saw, and it is sturdy enough to last through a production, even if subjected to some abuse. The method can be illustrated by the construction of a ground-row.

GROUND-ROWS

What to do with the back of the stage is always a problem in outdoor sets. Even if a cyclorama is dropped to suggest the sky, the bottom edge of it is unrealistically visible, and if lighting instruments must be placed on the stage floor in front of it, they obviously do not belong in the stage picture. The commonest solution for this problem is to place a low wall in front of them, and then to shape and paint it to suggest distant rolling hills, the skyline of a city, a hedge, or an actual wall. This kind of low horizontal masking device is called a *ground-row.* Occasionally two or more ground-rows are set one behind the other, the first perhaps showing hills and trees in the near background, the second showing distant mountain peaks. By lighting them differently the illusion of solidity and distance can be made especially convincing.

Most often a ground-row is made of a stock flat turned sidewise so that it rests on its stile, with the upper edge shaped to suggest what it represents. Often a ground-row is needed longer than a standard flat. In that case, two will be hinged together, rail to rail, and the joint dutchmanned.

To make the ground-row in Figure 6.11, two twelve-foot flats must first be fastened together. The shaped section above them is then cut from 1/4" plywood. A 1 X 3 is fastened with clout nails to the bottom edge of the plywood, on the back, and a few short pieces of board are run up from it to support the highest sections of the

143

**FIGURE 6.11 A ground–row. Shown from
the front, *top*, and back, *bottom*.**

plywood. All of these pieces are held well back from the edge of the plywood, so that
they will not be visible to the audience.

The combined thickness of the plywood and the 1 × 3 equals the thickness of the
flat, which is also made of 1/4" corner-blocks attached to 1 × 3s. The flats are placed
face down on the floor and the plywood unit fitted against their upper edge. Lengths
of 1 × 3 are placed at strategic angles across the flats and the plywood addition and
nailed firmly with box nails.

The entire unit is then turned over and all cracks dutchmanned. Because the
plywood and canvas have a different texture, a better looking unit can be produced
by gluing canvas over the entire plywood surface, trimming it to match the irregular
edge, about a quarter of an inch back on the wood. The bottom edge of the canvas
should be brought down two or three inches below the upper edge of the flats to hide
the joint. In that case only the joint where the flats are hinged together need be specially dutchmanned.

Edges added to major flats are often smaller than those required for ground-rows.
It may be possible to attach them with strips of plywood instead of lengths of 1 × 3s,
but care should be taken to run the grain straight across the joint, since the plywood
provides less support.

FALSE PROSCENIUMS

Although an increasing number of theaters have been built during the last half-century
with various types of open stages, most older theaters and even many new ones include

a proscenium, a wall which separates the acting area from the auditorium; the audience watches the play through a large hole in the wall, called the proscenium opening. The proscenium has a neutral shape, and its decoration has no special relation to any particular play. Designers sometimes ask for specially shaped and decorated temporary prosceniums which function as an integral part of the stage picture for a specific play. They may be set behind or in front of the permanent proscenium, they may be fitted inside it, or they may entirely enclose it. These temporary structures are called *false prosceniums.*

Although it may be the largest element in the set, a false proscenium is usually designed so that its basic form can be constructed by assembling a group of standard flats, to which specially shaped sections are added. Figure 6.12 illustrates the construction of one false proscenium.

As with doors and windows, fireplace openings must be backed. The most realistic masking is made of miniature flats, hinged together to form a three-fold (Figure 6.13). The center flat is made a little wider than the fireplace opening, and runs up high enough that the audience cannot see its top edge; usually it will be about 3' wide and perhaps 3'-6" high. The side flats are the same height, but need be only a foot or a foot and a half wide. The unit is hinged together, dutchmanned, and painted black. Often it can be placed behind the fireplace flat without special fastening, with the side flats opened at right angles. If there is any chance it might be moved accidentally during performance, it can be fastened to the back of the fireplace flat with hinges or by nailing through the front. If desired, a corner-block can be nailed on the top edges of each corner to hold the angles.

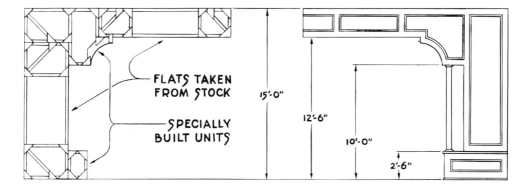

FLATS TAKEN
FROM STOCK

SPECIALLY
BUILT UNITS

15'-0"

12'-6"

10'-0"

2'-6"

FIGURE 6.12   A false proscenium. Half the unit is shown from the back, *left,* **and half from the front. Each half is made from two stock flats, one small rectangular flat, one specially shaped flat, and a rug–center pillar, shown here in the front view only. (Built for a production of Chekhov's** *The Three Sisters.***)**

145

FIGURE 6.13 A fireplace backing. The bottom section of the stock flat is shown, with an opening for the fireplace. The backing consists of three small rectangular flats, specially built, hinged together and fastened at fixed angles by specially shaped corner-blocks. The backing is shown from the back, *center,* and from the front, *right.*

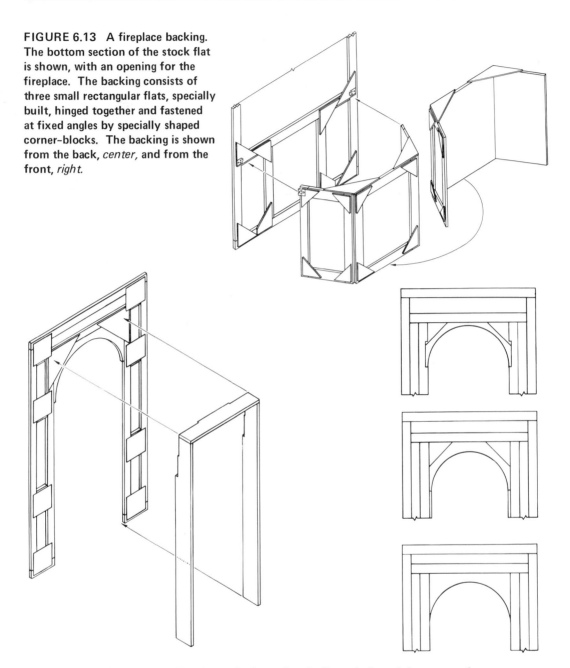

FIGURE 6.14 Framing arched openings in flats. *Left,* arch is cut out of 3/4" plywood and fastened into a rectangular opening with corner-blocks. Tips of inserted piece are 3/4" wide. A thickness piece can be set into the opening from the back and aniled into the edges of the flat frame. *Center right,* the 3/4" gaps can be filled by nailing on 1 x 1 stripping. *Top right,* cut into flat frame so the curve of the arch is tangent to the vertical edge. *Bottom right,* cut the arched shape to points; they may break, but they can be filled in with dutchmen after the unit has been nailed in place.

A shortcut method makes it possible to dispense with plywood stiffening or special framing for a fairly small opening. A sheet of moderate weight cardboard is glued to the back of the canvas, extending at least five or six inches beyond the edges of the opening. When the glue has dried, the opening is cut out with a sharp knife. The glue and cardboard will provide enough stiffness to keep the edges of the canvas from curling.

IRREGULAR OPENINGS IN FLATS

Shaping openings within flats is somewhat simpler because they are likely to be smaller, and are less likely to be damaged in use. One of the commonest internal shaping projects involves providing bracing inside a flat opening to define an arch (Figure 6.14).

The same methods used to frame openings for windows can also be used for rectangular openings for other purposes. Sometimes openings of other shapes will be needed. For example, a fireplace opening may have the corners rounded, or may even have an elaborate outline, perhaps in the shape of a shell. It is possible to cut the opening out of a sheet of plywood, fasten it to the nearest parts of the flat frame, and trim the canvas back a quarter of an inch from the edge of the plywood and glue it tight.

THICKNESS-PIECES

It will sometimes be necessary to create the impression that the solid area around an opening is thicker than the three-quarters of an inch actual thickness of the framing

The three-fold fireplace masking described earlier in effect provides a thickness-piece for the opening, allowing space for logs or a simulated fire, or to throw waste paper into the opening. If nothing need be put into the fireplace, the opening can be masked by stretching a sheet of black canvas across it on the back of the flat, and tacking it to the flat frame. Although the backing will actually be only an inch behind the front surface of the flat, it is usually impossible for the audience to judge its distance, and they will accept it as a normal structure.

lumber. This is done by adding a strip of cardboard or lumber, fastened at right angles to the surface of the flat, and extending behind it. Such a strip is called a *thickness-piece* (Figure 6.15).

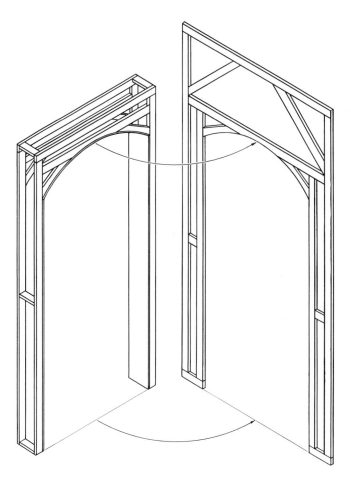

FIGURE 6.15 Independent thickness-pieces. The flat is shown from the back, *right*; the thickness-piece structure, *left.* (Corner-blocks have been omitted from the drawing for greater clarity.)

If an opening is edged with 3/4" lumber, it may be acceptable to glue and tack a strip of smooth cardboard of the desired width directly to the edge of the frame (up-son board is to be preferred for this purpose). More often it will be necessary to attach the thickness-piece behind the framing. In that case, supports must be provided to fasten the edging to. They can be cut from 1 × 4 in lengths equal to the desired thickness minus the thickness of the lumber or plywood framing the opening. They are placed at intervals of six inches to a foot around the opening, one end against the back of the flat, one edge set so that it will touch the thickness-piece; this edge must be held back from the edge of the opening by a distance equal to the thickness of the material to be used for the thickness-piece (1/8" for E-Z curve, 1/4" if plywood is used). The supports can be fastened by nailing from the front edge of the flat.

Finally, strips of cardboard or plywood are cut, the width equalling the total width of the thickness-piece minus the thickness of the edge of the flat. They are stapled or tacked to the supports, and if necessary visible joints are dutchmanned. This method is fast, but the resulting structure is fairly fragile. A sturdier thickness can be constructed by a slightly different method.

In essence, two miniature flat frames are built so as to just outline the opening, except that it is enlarged to allow for the thickness of the edging material. These frames are fastened together with short pieces of 1 × 3 or 1 × 4, so that the total thickness of the unit equals the specified thickness minus the thickness of the flat. A plywood or cardboard strip is cut and fastened to the inner, shaped edge of the unit, which is then fastened to the back of the flat by nailing or with loose-pin hinges. The pins can be pulled if the set must be shifted, and the thickness-piece moved separately.

Thickness-pieces are also regularly provided wherever the audience can see the edges of walls. Door and window units, which are set into openings in the flats, usually have thickness-pieces built into them as integral parts of the structure. Thicknesses are attached to the flats themselves around entrance openings which are not fitted with doors. Often only a very few edges need to be thickneed. In the side walls, the thicknesses at the downstage edges of entrance openings may not be visible, and it will be necessary only to provide thickness for the upstage edges and the horizontal edges above the openings.

The effect of thickness-pieces on the appearance of a set is startling. The audience unconsciously assumes that all walls are as thick as the few edges they are able to see. Thus, an interior supplied with 3″ thicknesses will be seen as a room in a jerry-built apartment house with thin walls; if thickness-pieces a foot and a half wide are applied, and the walls painted to suggest stone, the entire set will have the apparent solidity of an ancient castle. Probably no other small detail changes the appearance of a set so much.

A flickering fire can be simulated effectively with Christmas tree lights. Some strings are designed so that all the lights flash on and off simultaneously, but it is possible to buy bulbs each of which has its own cycle, and which are screwed into ordinary strings. As many strings should be used as possible, at least six, and they should be fitted with white bulbs of the individually flashing type. At any given moment, about a third of the bulbs will be lit, providing a steady glow; at the same time, the irregular flashing will suggest flickering fire. The bulbs must be hidden behind logs, and pieces of colored gel, especially yellows and oranges, should be laid across them. Although this method does not produce visible flames, the effect of dancing light reflected against the fireplace backing and out into the room is strikingly convincing.

7

Building Platforms, Ramps, and Stairs

Actors and directors love platforms, ramps, and stairs. Not only do they make the pattern of movement more interesting, they also make it easy to express interrelationships among the characters in the play. Cleopatra, high above the stage in the last act of Shakespeare's play, finds it easy to dominate Caesar and his entire army, standing on the stage floor below. As the old slave from Corinth is brought in to be interrogated by Oedipus, the king finds it easy to express his superior authority if he can stand on the highest level of the set, with the slave on a lower platform. Then as he is overwhelmed by crushing despair at the slave's answers to his questions, as he in fact becomes dominated by the slave rather than dominating him, he can express the new relationship by rushing straight forward down to the stage floor and falling to his knees, with the slave towering above him. When Horace crawls desperately up the stairs to get the medicine to relieve his heart attack in *The Little Foxes,* and Regina sits coldly watching and waiting for him to die halfway up, the stairs contribute powerfully to the effectiveness of the scene. (For illustrations of sets which make important use of raised areas, see Figures 1.2, 1.4, 1.7, 1.8, 1.9, 1.10, 1.11, 1.12, 2.3, 2.8, 7.6, 7.7, and 7.9.)

More than half the sets for a season of plays are likely to involve the construction of three-dimensional units on which the actors will climb or walk. Such structures can be classified in three groups, the basic ones being platforms, with ramps and stairs as related forms.

RIGID PLATFORMS

Platforms are of two types, rigid and folding. Folding platforms are often called *parallels,* which is a somewhat unfortunate term, since rigid platforms also usually have parallel sides, and occasionally folding platforms do not.

Rigid platforms are easier and faster to build, are generally sturdier, cost a little less, and can be shifted more readily. They have one disadvantage which may overwhelm all their special virtues, and that is that they take an enormous amount of storage space. Parallels, on the other hand, can be stored much more compactly, since they can be taken apart and folded up without damaging them. About ten folding platforms can be stored in the same space as is required for one rigid platform of the same size.

Like flats, the dimensions of platforms are standardized, and when unusual sizes or shapes are needed they are constructed if possible by adding special sections to standard units taken from stock. Platforms vary in height, but usually the tops are 4'-0" X 8'-0". Not only are such platforms readily combinable, but they can be floored with a single sheet of plywood, without cutting or damaging it.

Rigid platforms are essentially boxes with study tops, supported sufficiently to bear the weight of the actors without sagging or swaying. Usually the audience can see only one side of a platform, or at most a side and one end. Whatever areas are visible are covered with 1/4" plywood.

SUPPORT REQUIREMENTS

Platform supports must meet three requirements: they must be held rigidly vertical (if they start to slant, the platform will collapse); they must support the weight of the actors as well as that of any scenic structures which are set on them; and they must stiffen the top so that the audience is unable to detect any sag when they are used, and so that they feel solid underfoot to the actors.

The second requirement listed in the easiest of the three to fulfill. Lumber has great resistance to crushing. If a short section of a 1 X 1 were set in a socket in the floor so that it extended above the floor surface for an inch or two, and then someone stood on it, balancing himself on tiptoe on one foot, the 1 X 1 would be more than adequate to support his weight. From the standpoint of weight alone, then, four 1 X 1s would provide more than enough support for four actors! The additional support which must be built into practical platforms is designed to meet the other two requirements.

Beginners in stagecraft nearly always tend to overbrace, just as they tend to use twice as many nails as they should. One technical director, who regularly lent scene shop facilities for the construction of floats for homecoming parades, reports that he watched in bemused wonder as students showed up year after year with stacks of 2 X 4s, out of which they built massive frames whose purpose was to support wads of cleansing tissue. At another theater, he discovered that it was an established practice to build low platforms out of 2 X 6s. When the stage crew started building platforms under his direction from 1 X 3s, he was met with loud cries—"They'll never last through the performances!" Not only did they hold up for the run of the show, but the same platforms were used in three later shows, and then combined to form a permanent stage in a laboratory theater, where they were used for innumerable productions for seven years and were abandoned, not because they had weakened, but because the theater moved to a new building. Meanwhile, the weight of the 2 X 6s had progressively weakened the joints so much that the platforms made from them had to be retired and torn up for scrap.

Stiffening a sheet of plywood, however, requires much more than four 1 X 1s. If 3/4" plywood is used, the traditional formula is that it must be supported so that no point is more than 2' from a support. That formula would be minimally satisfied by running a support around the outside edge of a 4'-0" X 8'-0" sheet, with a single crosswise support in the center. Experience suggests that that does not stiffen the top quite enough to make it seem firm to the actors. Adequate rigidity is provided either by running the center support lengthwise rather than crosswise, or by using two evenly spaced crosswise supports. If the cheaper 5/8" sheathing is substituted for 3/4" plywood, one more crosswise leg unit must be provided.

Besides supplying adequate stiffening and weight support, the platform legs must be held rigidly vertical, so that they will not sway or collapse. In practical construction, the only rigid geometrical figure is the triangle, and platform supports are made solid by adding diagonal braces which, like those in the corners of flats, produce triangles that hold the frames square.

BUILDING A PLATFORM

The platform shown in Figure 7.1 is made of seven basic parts: the top, the two side supports, and four cross supports. An unaltered sheet of plywood is used for the top, so that the workers need build only the leg supports, in two patterns.

The end and center supports are fitted between the sides, so that they are 3'-10½" wide rather than the full four feet (4'-0" minus the total thickness of the lumber used for the side supports). The sides run the full length of the platform, and so are 8'-0".

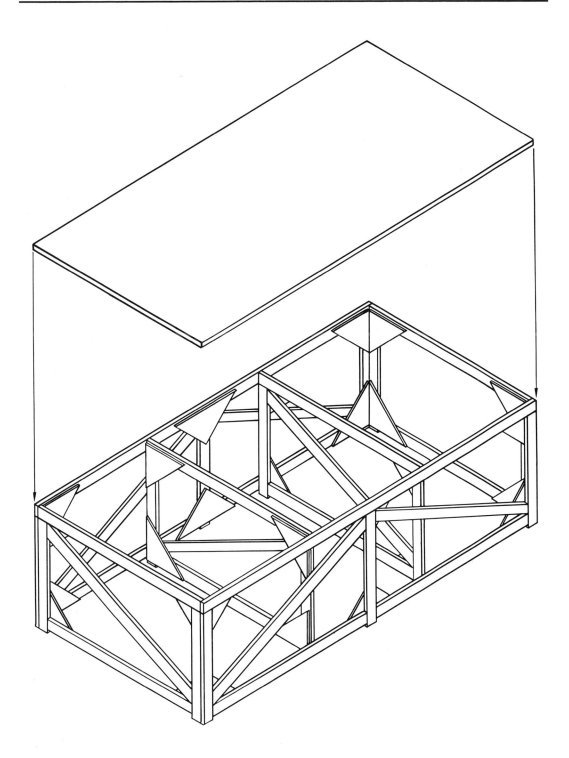

FIGURE 7.1   A rigid platform.

It is most economical to do all the cutting for the platform before beginning assembly, but to simplify the description, instructions will be given for only one of each set of supports.

End or Center Support (4 are needed) (Figure 7.2)

1. Collect: a pocket tape, a hammer, a work tray of clout nails, a carpenter's square, a try-square, a clinch plate, four corner-blocks, and a scrap of 1 × 3 four or five inches long.

2. Cut the following pieces from 1 × 3 lumber:

Top: 3'-10½"
Legs (cut 2): 2'-5¼" minus the width of the top board
Bottom stretcher: 3'-10½" minus the combined width of the two legs.

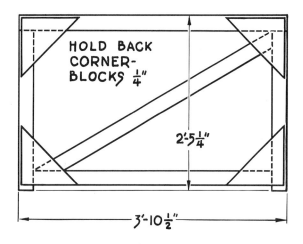

FIGURE 7.2   An end or center support for a rigid platform.

3. Lay out the lumber on the floor or a work table as shown in the drawing. Square one top-leg corner and set a corner-block in place with the grain running across the joint and with the edges of the corner-block held back a little more than 1/4" from the edges of the lumber.

4. Fasten the corner-block with clout nails, driven part way into the 1 × 3s. Recheck for squareness, slip the clinch plate under the joint, and drive the nails all the way down. Repeat for the other top-leg joint.

5. Set the bottom stretcher in place. Notice that it is held up from the ends of the legs; this makes the platform much less likely to rock on unevennesses in the stage floor. The distance it is held up is not critical, but the most convenient dimension is 3/4", since it can be checked easily by using the thickness of the scrap of 1 × 3. Fasten on corner-blocks, following the same procedure as for the other two corners.

6. Check the diagonals of the frame to make sure it is square. If it is not, it will have to be forced square by an assistant and held while the diagonal brace is fastened in.

7. Turn the frame over and measure the distance between opposite inside corners of the frame, and get a board which is slightly longer. Lay it across the frame where the brace is to go, with the full width of the board resting on the frame at each end. Lay the 1 × 3 scrap on top of the diagonal brace, with one edge matching the edge of the frame below it, and draw along the diagonal board; repeat for the other end. Cut along these lines with a hand saw, a saber saw, or a radial-arm saw.

8. Fit the brace in place; each end will rest on one of the corner-blocks used for the top-leg or leg-stretcher joints. Slip the clinch plate under the frame and drive a single nail down solidly at each end of the brace. Turn the unit over, set it on the clinch plate, and add two more nails at each end. The clinched points do not hold well against plywood; the first two nails will hold the brace in place while it is turned over and the nailing is completed.

Side Support (two are needed) (Figure 7.3)

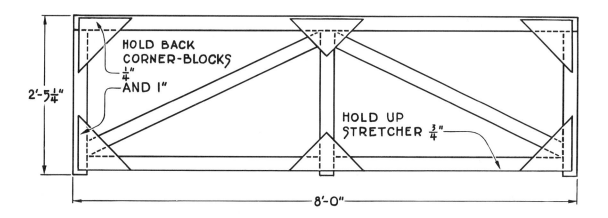

FIGURE 7.3 A side support for a rigid platform.

1. The same tools can be used as for the ends, except that 6 corner-blocks are needed.

2. Cut from 1 × 3:

Top: 8'-0"
Legs (cut 3): 2'-5¼" minus the width of the board used for the top
Bottom stretchers (cut 2): one half of 8'-0" minus the width of the three
   legs.

3. Lay out the lumber on the work table as shown in the drawing. Fasten the leg-top joints as previously described, except that the edges of the corner-blocks must be held back an inch from the outside edges of the legs.

4. Mark two points along the top board, 3'-10½" from each end. The gap between them will be just slightly wider than the third leg; set it in place with the end butted against the bottom edge of the top board, and centered in the space between the two marks.

5. Slip a clinch plate under the joint, square the boards, and set a corner-block on top of the joint with the hypotenuse parallel with the edge of the top board, held back about 1/4". Holding the corner-block and leg carefully so that they will not shift, set two widely spaced nails part way into each board; recheck for squareness, adjust if necessary, and drive the nails all the way down. Complete the nailing pattern.

6. Fit the two stretchers in place, holding them up 3/4" from the ends of the legs, and fasten them to the outside legs, holding the corner-blocks back 1" from the outside edges of the legs. Fasten the ends of the stretchers to the center leg with a single corner-block, placed so that the hypotenuse runs along the bottom edge of the stretchers.

7. Turn the unit over and place a board across the frame where one of the diagonals is to go, marking it as described previously; cut two boards at the same angles and of the same length.

8. Set the diagonal braces in place and check the entire frame for squareness by comparing its full diagonal measurements. If it is off square, it must be forced into shape by an assistant and held while the braces are fastened. Drive one nail in fully at each end of each brace. Turn the unit over and add two more nails to each joint.

Assembly

1. Set one end unit against the inside face of one of the side units, turning both so that the corner blocks are on the inside. Nail them together by driving 2″ common or box nails through the side support into the end support. Fasten the other end support the same way.

2. Turn the entire unit on its side and lay it on the floor with the end supports pointing up. Lay the second side support on top of them, and fasten the joints; it will be helpful to get an assistant to hold the free ends together while the first joint is being nailed.

3. Make marks on the top board and stretchers 2′-7″ from each end of the frame. Set one of the inner supports into the frame so that the leg is centered on one set of the marks. Adjust the leg unit so it is at right angles to the side support (this can be done with a square or by eye). Fasten them together by nailing through the side support into the leg of the inner support. Repeat for the other inner support.

4. Carefully turn the entire unit over so that it is resting on the side support to which the center supports have been attached. Mark the side support which is now at the top as in step 2, move the inner supports until the legs are centered on the marks, and nail them in place.

5. Turn the assembled support over so that it rests on its legs in the position in which it will be used. Lay a sheet of 3/4″ plywood on top and adjust it so that one end exactly matches the end of the frame; drive a nail through the edge of the plywood, close to the center of the end, and into the support. Adjust the frame so that the other end exactly matches the end of the plywood, and nail it in the center. Two-inch coated box nails are preferred for fastening on the top, since they provide much greater friction than common nails, and the top is less likely to loosen and develop a spring when it is used.

6. Moving to one side, adjust the frame so that the edge of the plywood matches the face of the frame, and nail them together close to the midpoint of the long edge of the plywood; drive a matching nail into the other side edge of the plywood.

7. Drive two nails at each corner, about 3″ from the corner, one into the side support and the other into the end support. Each edge of the plywood is now fastened by three nails. Add two more for each end, spacing them halfway between the nails which have already been driven. Six more nails should be driven into each side edge, spaced approximately evenly. Finally three nails are driven through the plywood into each inner support, one at the center, the other two placed halfway between the center nail and the side edges of the plywood.

The ability to start a nail somewhere out in the center of a sheet of plywood and drive it down solidly into a hidden brace below seems to be unlearnable. Either you have it or you don't. If you don't, carefully mark directly above the leg support at each edge of the plywood, and run a line across the sheet between the two points, either with a pencil or a snap line, and use this as a guide in placing the nails.

If there is the slightest doubt about whether a nail has gone squarely into the supporting board, it is important to check it before it is driven all the way down. Even if the support is missed, the nail is likely to be close enough to it so there is not space to drive it back up with a hammer, and if it is left hanging in air it may work up when the platform is used and produce a lump under the padding. While it takes a second longer to check each nail, it may take fifteen or twenty minutes of struggling to dig up one which has been driven down flush.

SURFACING

If surfacing is added to the sides of such a platform, its dimensions will be changed by the thickness of the surfacing material; 1/4" plywood added to each end would produce a total length of 8'-½". That will often be unobjectionable, but the designer may specify that the platforms be built so that the surfacing will not change their dimensions. The only alteration required is that the frame must be built 3'-11½" × 7'-11½" instead of the full 4'-0" × 8'-0". The top must then be set on with a quarter-inch overhang at each edge. This can be done most easily by pressing a corner-block against the face of the leg units at the top, and then adjusting the plywood sheet until its edge matches the outer surface of the corner-block. When the corner-block is removed, the top will be set out exactly the right distance beyond the edge of the frame.

A rectangle of 1/4" plywood is used to cover the side or end of such a platform, wherever they are visible to the audience. The sheets should be 2'-5" wide. They are fitted under the 3/4" platform top, tight against its overhanging edge, and fastened by nailing them to the frame. Coated box nails should not be used, because it may be necessary to remove the facing for later plays, and the box nails are very difficult to pull out.

The width recommended is less than the full height of the platform, so that a 1/4" gap is left along the bottom. That is done for the same reason that the stretchers are held up from the ends of the legs. The platform is less likely to rock on irregularities in the stage floor, and there is much less danger that the facing will be pulled loose when the platform is moved along the floor. The gap is almost never noticeable from the audience.

COVERING

Before the platform can be used it must be padded, since the bare plywood would resound hollowly when the actors walked across it. The padding is laid across the top of the platform and cut to fit. Often it may be made by combining smaller pieces. The padding is then fastened down so that it will not shift. Traditionally, large, sharp-pointed carpet tacks were used. 1/2" or 5/8" staples hold satisfactorily, and can be driven much faster.

Several layers of ordinary newspaper make an acceptable padding for platforms and stairs. The commercial rug padding usually used produces a softer surface, but the newspaper deadens sound about as effectively.

Most padding materials must be covered with a layer of scenery canvas. A sheet of the canvas is spread over the top of the platform and cut to about 4'-6" X 8'-6", allowing a 3" overhang for each edge. This is brought down on the side of the platform and stapled just under the 3/4" plywood top, either to the side surfacing or to the supporting frame. The extra layers of the cloth at the corners should be removed with cuts at 45°. The underside of the edge is painted with glue and pressed firmly against the side of the platform, as in canvassing flats. The unit is now finished, and ready to be painted.

Upson board or any moderately heavy cardboard can be used to pad platforms and stair treads. Corrugated cardboard tends to dent in use, but it is only slightly less satisfactory. The cardboard can be tacked firmly and painted without further covering, or it can be canvassed, as must be done when rug padding is used. The cardboard padding has the advantage that it alters the height of the platforms less than rug padding, which is not only thicker but which tends to soften the outlines slightly. The cardboard is less resilient and produces a somewhat firmer surface underfoot, but it tends to deaden sound almost as effectively as rug padding.

Platforms of this type taller than three or four feet should be supported on 1 X 4s, up to about six feet high. For higher platforms, 2 X 4s should be used, and for extremely high structures the designer may specify larger lumber, and is sure to design a more elaborate bracing pattern, including the use of bolts for greater strength.

159

BOLTED PLATFORMS

A somewhat different type of construction is often preferred even for the lower plat-forms (Figure 7.4). First a rectangular frame is built of four 2 × 4s, set on edge; the plywood top is then nailed to this structure. Four legs are cut from 2 × 4 lumber to a length matching the height of the platform minus the thickness of the top. These are set inside the corners of the 2 × 4 frame, with their upper ends pressed against the underside of the plywood top. They are usually fastened to the frame by bolts, al-though they can be nailed. The legs are tied together by a frame of 1 × 4s running all the way around the platform, with the bottom edge held up 3/4" from the ends of the legs. A 1 × 4 diagonal brace is fastened to each leg, just above the 1 × 4 stiffeners, and run up the center of the long side of the frame, inside the 2 × 4. The brace must be twisted slightly and forced into place; the resulting tension will tend to pull out nails, so that these joints must be bolted. A similar brace is run from each leg to the center of the 2 × 4s at the ends of the platform.

This type of platform has some advantages over the one previously described. It can be made faster, and the legs and braces can be unbolted and legs of different length substituted. It is heavier than the other type of platform, and slightly more difficult to surface, since the side supports are not all in the same plane.

FIGURE 7.4   A bolted platform.

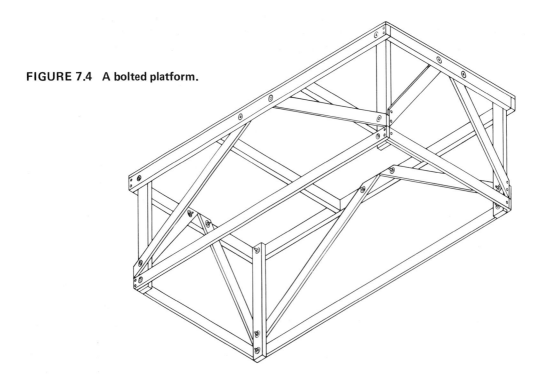

FOLDING PLATFORMS

Several types of folding platforms (parallels) have been devised. They are alike in that the supporting units are hinged together, so that they can be folded compactly after the top has been removed, although the arrangement of the hinges varies with the different designs. What is called the *continental platform* is perhaps the most convenient, although it takes slightly more time to build than the others. It is illustrated in Figure 7.5. At first glance the frame looks very much like the rigid platform shown in Figure 7.1. Rather than analyzing the construction by individual steps, the differences will be pointed out.

FIGURE 7.5   A folding platform.

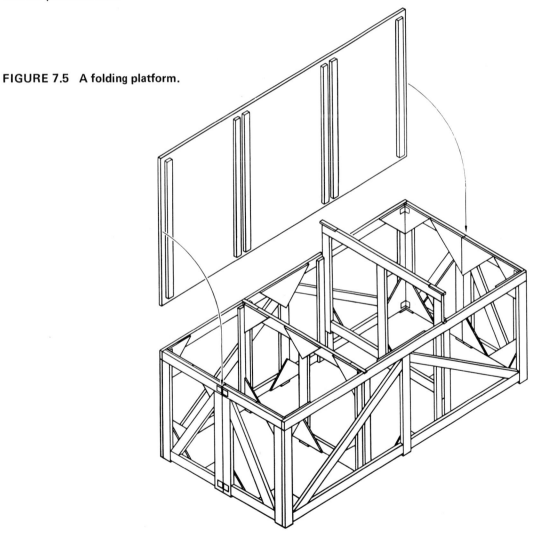

The most obvious is that each end support is made in two pieces, which are hinged together on the outside of the platform so that they will fold into the structure for storage. The internal crosswise supports do not fold, and so must be removable. They can be fastened to the sides with loose-pin hinges, or vertical 1 × 2s can be nailed to the inside of the side supports to form slots into which the inner supports can be slipped. If the platform were lifted, they would fall through, so they must have a metal strip screwed to each end of the top edge, projecting for 3/4" so that it catches on the top of the side support. Notches must be cut in the top edges of both the inner and side supports so that these metal strips will not stick up above the surface of the wood.

The plywood tops cannot be fastened permanently to the supports for any type of folding platform. They are kept from shifting in use by nailing 1 × 3 guides to the underside of the top, placed so that they fit tightly against the supports. Since the canvassing cannot be glued to the sides of the platform, it must be brought around the edges of the plywood and glued to the underside. When the top is set in place it rests on this under layer of fabric. Even with 1 × 3 guides, the assembly is less than ideally stable. The top can be made firmer by nailing it temporarily to the outside framing, using common nails so that they can be easily removed. From four to six nails should be adequate.

RAMPS

A ramp is simply a platform with a slanted top. The dimensions and the angle of slant will be specified by the designer. It is possible to make ramps that will fold, but usually they are built as rigid structures. The slant slows the work somewhat and makes construction a little more difficult, but the techniques used are very much like those described for building a rigid platform.

Some centuries ago, entire stage floors were sloped, highest at the back and lowest at the edge of the stage. Such fully ramped structures are called *raked stages.* One of the sharpest rakes ever used in the theater covered the entire stage for the Broadway production of *Gideon* some years ago. The angle was so extreme that cleats had to be driven all over the surface to provide enough footing that the actors could walk without falling down. Fully raked stages are occasionally extremely effective, as was the *Gideon* one, but most often ramps are used as only one of several scenic elements. An especially large one is the 50-foot curving ramp for the *Tempest* set which has already been mentioned (Figures 1.7 and 7.6). Occasionally a director with conservative or traditional tastes may demand the use of a raked stage for a series of plays. In that case, it is better to build it in the form of a group of ramps 4'-0" wide which can be set side by side to cover the stage floor, but which can be moved individually and stacked for storage.

FIGURE 7.6   A ramp used for *The Tempest*. Only part of the ramp is shown; the entire structure was 50' long.

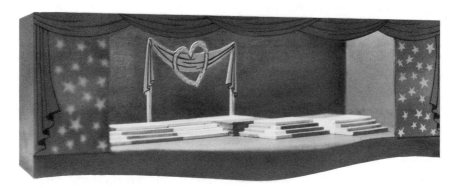

FIGURE 7.7   The use of stairs and platforms. These photographs of the designer's models show two arrangements of platform and stair units for the musical comedy *Of Thee I Sing*, by Kaufman, Ryskind, Gershwin, and Gershwin. *Top*, the steps of the national capitol with a speaker's stand in place for a presidential inauguration. *Bottom*, a runway used for a beauty contest scene. (Notice the false proscenium, used to narrow the excessively wide stage opening.) Other sets making more or less extensive use of platforms and stairs are shown in Figures 1.2, 13.4; 1.4, 1.9, 2.3; 1.7, 7.6; 1.8, 1.12, 8.2; 1.10; 1.11; 2.2; 2.9; 8.4; and 8.15.

STAIRS

Almost all sets which make use of platforms also require flights of stairs to enable the actors to reach them, not only on stage but also behind the set (Figure 7.7). Offstage step units hidden from the audience are called *access stairs* (or sometimes escape stairs, depending on whether the actors are envisioned as using them for entrances or exits).

Whether onstage stairs have railings or not depends on the effect intended by the designer, and on how the actors must use them. If railings are intended to be primarily ornamental, they are usually built as an integral part of a *plug,* in essence a small flat shaped to fit the side of the steps, but covered with plywood or rigid cardboard rather than canvas, so that it will not shake when the stairs are used. If a more solid railing is needed, for example so that an actor can lean on it or vault over it, the banisters are likely to be built as part of the outside carriage of the stairs, by extending the legs two and a half or three feet above the tread supports.

If the backstage area is likely to be inadequately lit during performance, offstage access stairs with more than two or three steps should be provided with railings. These need not be attractive, since they will not be seen by the audience, but they should serve as guides in using the stairs, and should be strong enough to withstand an actor's weight if he should stumble and fall against them. The railing itself can be a 1 X 3 nailed to the inside edges of the banisters, which are formed by extending the outside legs up to a convenient height.

Stairs for stage use can be classified as dependent or independent, and straight or curved. *Independent stairs* are self-contained, free-standing structures, which are simply pushed against platforms, and fastened only to prevent their shifting when they are used. The bottom of *dependent stairs* rests on the stage floor, but the top is fastened structurally to the side of the platform up to which they run. Curved stairs are nearly always independent, and the majority of straight stairs made for the theater are also of that type.

Stairs outside the theater are supported by wide boards fastened on edge (called *carriages*), with notches cut in them to which the treads and risers are fastened. The *treads* are the boards on which a person steps when climbing the stairs. The word *riser* is used in two slightly different senses, to indicate the vertical distance between the tops of adjacent steps, or, if the spaces are filled in with surfacing, the pieces of material used. This type of carriage is also frequently used in the theater, although cutting carriages for curved stairs is one of the most difficult, irritating, and frustrating of construction projects, and a different method, described below, is to be preferred. Even for straight flights of stairs, the cut-carriage method of support is expensive, the units are unnecessarily heavy, and the job is difficult for all but experienced workers. An easier method will be described here.

BUILDING STRAIGHT STAIRS

The supports for straight stairs shown in Figure 7.8 are assembled with lap joints. Usually two supports are adequate for a flight of stairs. They are identical except that they are mirror-images, that is if they are laid side by side on the floor identically oriented, the legs of one support will be next to the floor, and the legs of the other will be on top.

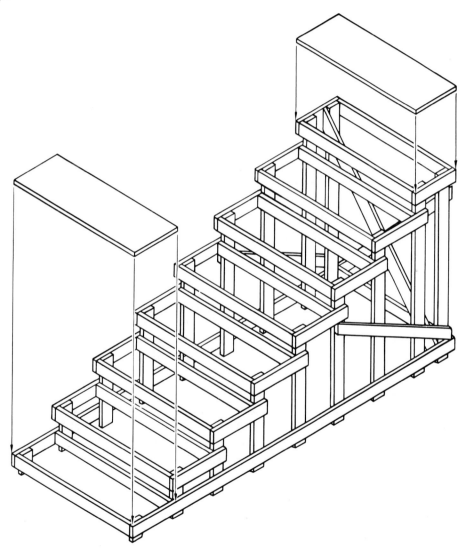

FIGURE 7.8   The construction of straight stairs. (The riser facings have been omitted from the drawing, as well as all but the top and bottom treads.)

For each of the support units, each step requires one leg except the top step, which needs two; the length of the bottom leg equals the height of the step (that is, the riser) minus the thickness of the tread. Usually 3/4" plywood is used for the treads. Thus, for a flight of stairs with 6" risers the bottom leg would be 5¼" high. The height of the leg for the second step equals the height of the leg for the bottom step plus the full height of the riser, in this case 11¼". Each higher step rests on a leg the height of the leg below it plus the full riser distance.

The tread allowance for the top step will vary according to the particular design. Usually it will be equal to the depth of the tread minus the thickness of the material used for the riser. For each step below it, the horizontal space between adjacent legs equals the full depth of the tread.

In building one of the carriages, the legs are first cut to the specified lengths. They are tied together at the bottom by a piece of lumber which starts at the front leg and runs horizontally all the way to the back leg, its top edge being set at the height of the shortest leg. Each two adjacent legs are also joined at the top by a horizontal board which runs from the front of the short leg to the back of the next higher one. All of these boards are of the same length (= depth of tread + width of one leg) except the one joining the two legs which support the top step.

After the lumber has been cut, a line is drawn across each leg at the height of the shortest leg. This can be done most easily by laying the short leg on top of each and marking along its upper edge. Each leg is then laid on top of the next taller leg, with the bottom ends of the boards aligned, and the height of the shorter marked on the other. The long horizontal board is marked off at intervals matching the depth of the treads (the space at one end will be shorter than the others, since the legs supporting the highest step are closer together than the other legs).

The legs are laid on a work table, and the long bottom crosspiece placed across them. Its top edge is lined up with the mark on the back leg, the two boards are squared, and a nail driven solidly through them near one corner of the square nailing surface—the area in which they are in contact. A second nail is driven part way into the top board in the diagonally opposite corner of the nailing area, the boards are again checked for squareness and held firmly while the nail is driven in all the way.

The other legs are fastened on in the same way, placed so that the top edge of the horizontal precisely matches the lower mark on each leg, and so that the front edge of each leg matches the corresponding mark across the horizontal. These placements must be made accurately if the unit is to stand solidly without rocking. The legs are then tied together at the top with the short boards, which are lined up with the end of the shorter of each pair of legs, and with the mark which has been drawn across the taller leg, six inches down from the top. Finally a diagonal brace is added, running from the back leg just above the long horizontal, up to just under the short horizontal near the top of the center leg. This need not be fitted precisely, and it is not even necessary to miter the ends, so long as the corners are not allowed to extend out past the legs. One or two nails driven through the brace into each leg it touches will hold it securely. All of the nails which have been driven must be clinched.

When a large number of identical support units must be assembled (for a raked stage, for several matching flights of stairs, etc.), the work can be speeded by drawing a full-scale pattern on 3/4" plywood. The boards can then be assembled by matching them to the drawing, and if it has been done carefully it will not be necessary to use a square. If the unit is larger than 4' X 8', two or more sheets of plywood can be battened together by running a 1 X 3 along each edge and one or more in the center. The unit is then turned over and the unbattened side used for assembly.

The other carriage unit is assembled in the same way, except that it must be a mirror-image of the first. The easiest way to achieve this is to arrange the lumber as for the first, except that if the longest leg was set on the left and the shortest on the right for the first unit, these positions should be reversed for the second. This method cannot be used if the placement of the lumber has been guided by a pattern drawn on plywood. The same result can be achieved by reversing the two layers of lumber. If the first unit was built by laying the legs on the plywood and putting the horizontal boards on top, the second unit should be arranged with the horizontals laid directly on the plywood, and the legs laid on top of them.

When using a guide drawn on plywood to assemble a supporting frame, it is better to drive the nails all the way into the plywood. Once key nails have been set, this will hold the boards in place. After all the nails have been driven, the unit should be carefully pried loose and turned over, and the nails clinched.

In the final assembly, the carriages may be placed at the outside edges of the treads, or they may be held back. They should be set so that the horizontal boards are toward the sides of the stairs and the legs toward the center. It will be necessary to tie the two units together with other horizontals, running parallel with the treads. Exactly how the unit is to be fitted together will be indicated by the drawing. Besides the boards supporting the treads, it will be necessary to tie the two back legs together at the bottom, and to run a diagonal brace across just in front of them. It will be necessary to cut the ends of this brace at a slant, since there is less nailing area and it must not stick out past the edges of the legs.

Finally treads and risers are added. Treads are usually made of 3/4" plywood, and risers of 1/4" plywood. Most often the risers are set just under the tread above and extend down behind the tread below. They are nailed to the framing, and then coated box nails are driven through from behind into the back edge of the lower tread. This method automatically stiffens the back edge of the tread. If it is not used, an additional board must be run across just under the tread at the back.

Finally, the treads must be padded and the padding covered with canvas, and if either side of the stairs will be visible to the audience it must be faced, usually with 1/4" plywood or composition board. If a railing is to be provided, it is built as a separate unit which includes the facing; it can be fastened to the stairs with loose-pin hinges, or, for greater rigidity, with screws or bolts.

CURVED STAIRS

A different method of construction is used for curved stairs (Figure 7.9). A separate rectangular support is built for each step, plus an extra one for the highest. All supports have a height equal to the height of the step which rests on them minus the thickness of the tread. Their width will be specified by the designer's working drawings, and depends on whether both sides are visible to the audience or only one, whether the treads are to overhang at the ends, and whether the side surfacing is to be fitted under the treads or run all the way up to cover the ends of the treads. The legs of each support are tied together at the top by a horizontal board on which the front edge of the

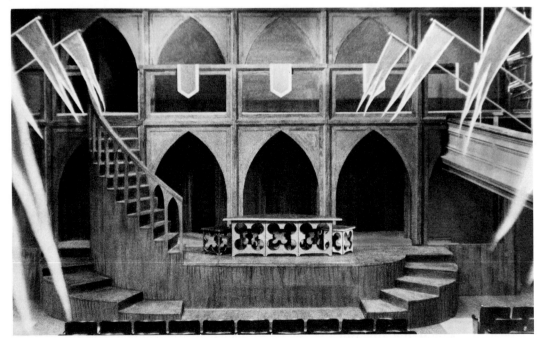

FIGURE 7.9   The use of curved stairs. All three of the stair units shown were especially built for this production of Shakespeare's *The Taming of the Shrew*.

FIGURE 7.10   The construction of curved stairs. The completed unit, *top left*; the individual supports are shown in orthographic, *left and bottom*; the supports are shown assembled, with the surfacing omitted, as well as the boards tying the near ends of the legs together, *right center*.

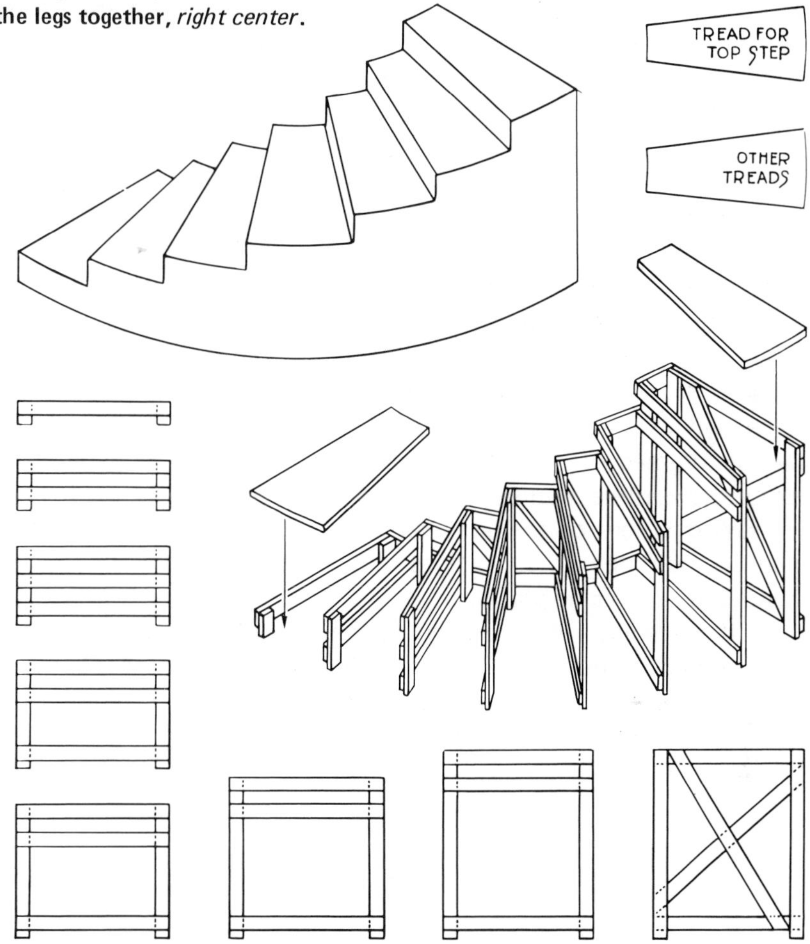

TREAD FOR TOP STEP

OTHER TREADS

tread will rest. In addition, each support except the first and last (that is, for the front edge of the lowest step and the back edge of the highest) has a second support parallel with the top board but set below it at the height of the next lowest step; the back edge of the tread for that step rests on this second board. Steps higher than 1'-0" should have an additional crosspiece, identical with the tread supports except that it is nailed across at the height of the crosspiece for the lowest step. Each support unit higher than 2'-6" should also have a diagonal brace.

The curvature is provided not by these supports but by the treads. They are cut from 3/4" plywood in the shape of a trapezoid with each end curved; the radii of these curves and the angle between the side edges will be indicated by the drawing.

The supports are built with lap joints, as shown in Figure 7.10. In assembling the unit, the two lowest supports are tied together by nailing the lowest tread in place. Boards are then cut to join their ends and nailed on. The second tread is attached, the end boards added, and so on until the basic structure is completed. Diagonal braces are added between successive leg units wherever possible. There will probably not be space for one for the lowest step. The legs must be carefully squared with the floor when these braces are fastened on. Finally, surfacing is applied to the convex side of the stairs. Usually 1/4" plywood is used for surfacing. If possible, it should be set with the grain running horizontally. If the curve is too sharp for it to be bent in that position, the grain can be run vertically, although it will probably be necessary to make the surfacing out of more than one piece of plywood. It is nailed to the horizontal and diagonal side supports where they join the legs. Since the plywood will exert constant pressure against the nails, coated box nails should be used.

The surfacing must be cut to match the treads and risers. It is very difficult to do this accurately before it is applied. If possible, the plywood should be cut roughly at an angle approximating the slant of the stairs, but wider than needed, so that three or four inches will extend above each step. When it has been nailed in place, the extra plywood can be trimmed off with a saber saw. An alternative is to nail the surfacing on temporarily, draw a line along the edges of the treads and risers where they touch it, remove the surfacing, cut on the line, and then nail it on permanently. The surfacing should be held up from the bottom edges of the legs by about 1/4" of an inch, as was recommended for surfacing platforms.

If the stairs will be placed so that the concave side is visible to the audience, it will also have to be surfaced. Since its curve has a shorter radius, it will probably not be possible to run the grain of the wood horizontally. Even when set vertical it may be difficult to force the plywood into position. In that case, upson board or other more flexible material should be used.

STAIR RAILINGS

If a railing must be provided, the banisters will usually be fastened individually to the treads. Alternatively, the design may specify that they be built as an integral part of the step supports.

The pattern for the railing can be developed by standard drafting methods, and may be supplied by the designer. If not, it can be drawn as follows. Before the banisters have been attached, lay a large sheet of cardboard on the steps, extending out slightly from the corners at the side where the railing is to be fastened. While one person holds the cardboard in contact with the front edges of the treads, another person takes a pencil or a felt pen and marks on the underside of the cardboard the point at which it touches the front corner of each tread. The cardboard is then removed, laid on a flat surface with the marked side up, and the marks joined free-hand with a smooth curve. Let us suppose that the outside edge of the railing will be held back 1" from the side of the stairs, and that the railing itself will be 2½″ wide. A second curve is drawn inside the first, parallel with it, and 1″ from it; a third curve is then drawn 2½″ inside the second. These last two curves define the shape of the railing. The strip is cut out of the cardboard, and used as a pattern to lay out the railing on plywood.

> To draw a curve parallel with another, open the legs of a small compass to the distance between the curves. Set the point of the compass near the end of the original curve and draw a half-circle on the side of the line where the new line is to be drawn. Reset the compass where the half-circle touches the line, and draw another half-circle. Repeat for the entire length of the line. Draw the second curve free-hand, joining the midpoints of the half-circles ina smooth curve (Figure 7.11).

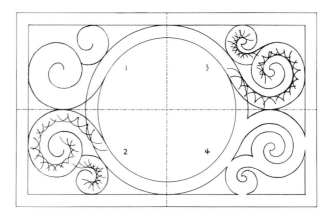

FIGURE 7.11 Drawing parallel curves. The procedure is shown in four steps: *1*, the original curve is drawn; *2*, a compass is set for a radius equal to the desired distance between the two curves and used to make a series of arcs, with points on the original curve as the centers; *3*, lines are drawn freehand joining the outer edges of the curves; *4*, construction lines are erased.

Usually it will be necessary to make the railing out of more than one piece of plywood. Joining the pieces is difficult if the railing is cut from plywood as thick as the railing itself. It is better to cut it from two or three layers of 1/4″ plywood; the lengths can then be glued and nailed so that the joints of individual layers are staggered (running lap joints). The edges of such a railing must be carefully smoothed with a wood rasp and perhaps sandpaper. If necessary, a strip of canvas (in essence a dutchman) can be glued around them to protect the actors' hands against splinters.

If the steps form an arc of a circle, the cardboard pattern need not extend all the way. The full pattern can be drawn on the plywood by merely slipping it along. If the steps are arranged in any other curve, then the cardboard pattern must extend for the full distance.

Stairs, platforms, and ramps contribute greatly to the effectiveness of a set; not only are they visually interesting, but they provide valuable assistance to the actors and the director. The descriptions which have been given demonstrate that they require sizable amounts of work time to construct, so wherever possible they should be built to standardized dimensions so that they can be reused.

8

Building Furniture and Three-Dimensional Properties

Which crew is assigned to supply furniture for a set depends on the policy of the individual theater and the crew chiefs' resistance to persuasion. Usually, if the furniture is to be borrowed, rented, bought, or taken from stock, its selection and collection are the responsibility of the set properties crew. If it is to be specially built for the production, the work will probably be assigned to the set construction crew. The two crews overlap in a grey area involving alteration of existing furniture. If only minor repairs, reupholstering, decorating, and painting need to be done, the properties crew will be responsible; if major repairs or rebuilding are necessary, the work will be turned over to the set crew. Obviously, the line between major and minor is fine and subject to being shifted.

It is desirable that no piece of furniture (or indeed any other scenic element) be used in a set which the audience will recognize from a previous production. Consequently, furniture of distinctive appearance—an elaborately carved Victorian sofa, for instance—is likely to be rented or borrowed for a particular show. Only the simpler pieces of furniture, which lack individuality or which can easily be reshaped or redecorated, are likely to be stored for reuse. (For examples of furniture specially built for particular plays, see Figures 1.2, 1.7, 1.8, 1.12, 2.9, 8.2, 8.3, 8.4, 8.5, 8.6, 8.16, 12.1, 12.2, 14.1, 14.2, and 14.4).

REPAIRING FURNITURE

Often discarded or broken furniture can be bought cheaply enough for one-time use. It must of course be repaired so that it will stand up under whatever use is made of it in the play. One of the most convenient additions to scenic resources within the last couple of decades is the development of a number of new adhesives (see chapter 9). Each has its own properties, and by matching them to the needs of a particular job, repair work can be done easily which would formerly have been prohibitively time-consuming. Some of the adhesives, for instance, set so quickly that the pieces joined can be held together until the glue has dried, instead of having to clamp them for over-night setting.

Alterations involve both strength and appearance. One-by-threes or corner-blocks can seldom be used to strengthen weak joints, but L-braces and I-braces are unobtrusive enough. Missing sections of molding or carved ornaments can be replaced by plastic wood or other pastes, shaped to match the design. If the end has been broken off the leg of a sofa, a hole can be drilled in the leg, a 1/2" or 3/4" dowel inserted, glued, and cut off at the correct angle, and when the glue has set the shape of the foot can be built around it with plastic paste. Driving a few brads into the surface of the dowel, leaving the heads sticking out for an eighth of an inch or so, will help anchor the plastic, and holding it up slightly from the tip of the leg will make it less likely to break off. Cane seats which have been punched through can be replaced with sheets of 1/4" plywood.

Even with fast-setting glue it may be necessary to use clamps to draw the broken pieces together. C-clamps will often be too small, and bar clamps must be substituted. An alternative is to run a loop of wire or strong string across the joint, preferably held up in the air, for instance by looping it around opposite legs (Figure 8.1). The ends of

FIGURE 8.1 The use of a rope loop for clamping furniture.

the wire should be tied together to form a moderately tight loop. A screwdriver, bolt, or length of doweling is run between the two wires and turned round and round so as to twist them together and tighten the joint. If the wire has to be left in place to give the glue time to dry, it must be prevented from untwisting. The easiest way to do that is to use a twisting device which is somewhat longer than the space between the wire and the nearest surface of the furniture; the twisting device is slanted at an angle while it is turned to tighten the wire, then it is swung straight, and one end caught against the furniture.

ALTERING FURNITURE

Since furniture is damaged in a variety of ways, to some extent repair methods must be improvised after an analysis of each particular piece. The commonest method of changing the appearance of a piece of furniture is to reupholster and repaint it. Usually borrowed furniture cannot be repainted, but with permission it may be possible to reupholster it. The original covering is not removed; the new fabric is simply spread over it and tacked or stapled in place. The major problem in upholstering is to stretch the fabric smoothly around curves. The solution is to lay the material so that the threads run at 45° angles to the edges of the areas to be covered; bias pulls can then be used in fitting it, facilitating covering it smoothly just as they do in canvassing flats. Especially for large units such as sofas the bias placement requires very wide fabric, although two or more lengths can be sewn together to provide the necessary size. The pattern of the fabric may make a bias placement impossible. For instance, striped material is nearly always applied so that the stripes run parallel with the center-line of the furniture.

It is possible to buy liquids which can be safely painted on wooden furniture to protect it. The color which is specified for the furniture is then painted on as a second coat. After the play, both coats can be stripped off with the fingers, leaving the furniture at least theoretically clean and undamaged. Such treatment is more usable for ornamental shelving or chests of drawers than for chairs or sofas, where the coating may be rubbed off when they are used. Of course furniture taken from the theater's own stock can be rebuilt, redecorated, and freely painted without having to worry about protecting it.

FURNITURE CONSTRUCTION

The set crew is most likely to be asked to build furniture from scratch if the scenery has been designed in a distinctive style for which matching furniture is not available.

FIGURE 8.2   Furniture for the stage. A chair, a throne, and stools were especially designed and built for a production of *The Lark*. (See also Figures 14.1 and 14.2.)

Feydeau's farce *A Flea in Her Ear* requires two sets. For one production, the director asked that the scenery be designed in the art nouveau style which was current at the turn of the last century, and that the furniture be specially built (Figure 8.3; also Figures 2.7 and 14.4). Furniture was designed and constructed for both sets, but the list for the first-act set alone included a love seat, two tables, four side chairs, an arm chair, a bench, a highboy, and a filing cabinet with one practical drawer. (In the theater the term *practical* is used to identify a property or scenic element which is actually used by the actors, rather than simply serving as decoration; thus, a practical

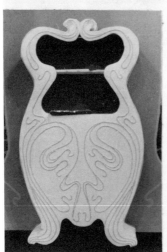

FIGURE 8.3 Furniture designed in the art nouveau style for *A Flea in Her Ear*. The filing cabinet has only one practical drawer (shown both closed and open). The linear decoration was produced by fastening on 1/4'' cotton rope with a glue gun, and painting it gold. (See also Figures 14.3 and 14.4 for a ground-plan and painting of the entire set with the furniture in place.)

window is one which can be raised and lowered, a practical rock is one on which actors can sit or stand, a practical drawer is one which can be pulled out. Units which serve only as decoration and are not used by the actors are called nonpractical.)

If a practical floor lamp is to be constructed, the wire can be concealed by making the shaft of the lamp out of four quarter-rounds. The corner of each is planed or trimmed off with a knife, so that when they are joined a space is left in the center through which the wire can be run. The flat surfaces of the quarter-rounds are coated with glue and held together to form a pole, with a length of electric wire covered with waterproof insulation run through the hole in the center. The rod can be wound at various points with masking tape until the glue has dried, or the pieces can be joined with brads, so long as care is taken not to pierce the wire.

The techniques used in furniture construction vary more than for other scenic elements because different styles require widely varying shapes and patterns of assembly. The construction methods which are commercially used to strengthen furniture can seldom be used in the theater because they require a prohibitive amount of time. The designer will furnish detailed working drawings showing more practical methods. They should be studied closely before the lumber is cut, and referred to frequently while the furniture is being built.

Most pieces of furniture can be analyzed most simply by relating them to boxes of similar dimensions. Thus, a bench or stool is essentially a box with the sides left open and the top extended out slightly at the edges. An armless chair is a box with the sides flared and one of them extended to form the chair back. A chest of drawers is a box with holes cut in one side into which other boxes can be slid to serve as drawers.

A continuing problem in building furniture for the theater is providing adequate bracing. Corner-blocks and diagonal braces can be used if they will be hidden from the audience. For example, if a table is to be covered with a full cloth it will be possible to attach the legs with corner-blocks. More often, such bracing would be unsightly and inharmonious with the style of the design.

Often joints can be reinforced unobtrusively by metal fasteners, either simple straps or T- or L-braces; it may be possible to set them invisibly on the back of the furniture, or under shelves or seats. Halved joints can be used, especially for screens, rather than butt joints. Gluing and clamping them until they are dry will help hold them solid. As a last resort, it may be possible to use relatively fine wire for additional bracing, and unless the furniture is set in front of a very light background the wire is likely to go unnoticed.

Plywood is used more frequently in furniture for the stage, especially for chair, stool, and bench seats. Typically, a solid frame is built of 1 X 2 lumber, and then plywood is used to fill in the open areas. Occasionally part of the framing itself may be cut from 5/8" or 3/4" plywood.

One of the advantages of plywood is that it can be cut into complicated shapes with freely varying outlines. Smaller shapes can be glued to background areas to simulate carving, perhaps with the edges rounded with a rasp before the pieces are attached. Curved surfaces are especially difficult to form on furniture built in the scene shop, but 1/4" plywood can be bent by forcing it against a shaped frame, often producing a curve visible enough to express a particular style of design. The plywood can be made slightly more flexible by painting it with boiling water, fastening it securely while wet. It is possible to cut a series of parallel grooves through one layer of the plywood, parallel with the grain, thus in effect making the sheet thinner, and then bend it somewhat more sharply, although there will be some loss of strength. If surfaces need not bear weight, they can be covered with cardboard or other materials more flexible than plywood.

Finally, the appearance of the furniture can be altered greatly by the application of three-dimensional decoration and by painting. The decorative elements may consist of hardware (ornamental drawer pulls, etc.), moldings, papier-mache, or rope glued on in various patterns. The methods of applying such materials are discussed in chapter 9; their use is illustrated by a number of the pictures in this chapter and throughout the book. Often decorative elements are improvised from whatever happens to be on hand in the scene shop. An example is a pair of stools made for a production of *Macbeth*. They were decorated by setting rows of ornaments around the edge of the seats, each one made of two washers of different size fastened in place by square-headed roofing nails. The stools were painted dark brown, the ornaments were painted gold, and a square of bright red rug was cut to fit the seat and glued in place.

It is unusual for a piece of furniture to be made entirely of plywood, without 1 × 2 or 1 × 3 framing. Figure 8.4 shows one example. Two screens, designed in Russian Victorian style, were built for Chekhov's *The Three Sisters*. Each screen had four leaves outlined with 5/8" plywood, each one cut with a saber saw from a single sheet. The opening was filled by a sheet of 1/4" plywood cut in an elaborate pattern and glued and nailed to the back of the 5/8" edging. Finally, a stiffening shape cut from 5/8" plywood was fastened to the front of the 1/4" sheet.

Smooth rope was glued on in a shell pattern, and rough string was added elsewhere. The entire structure was then painted dark brown and grained to simulate wood, and the upper surface of the rope and string was painted gold. The two screens were seven feet high and had a combined width of twenty-four feet. From the audience, they looked like fine furniture. In fact, many members of the audience assumed that they had been bought or borrowed.

Ordinary hinges can seldom be used on screens because they are obtrusively visible and do not fit into the design. Instead piano hinges are preferred. They can be fastened to the face of the screen on the back, if the leaves will be set on stage so that the corner formed by the joint points toward the audience. More often, they are screwed to the edges of the leaves. If the leaves of the screen must be folded in different directions during the performance, small double-acting hinges can be used which will permit each leaf to move either forward or back.

THE STRUCTURAL USE OF CORRUGATED CARDBOARD

Twenty years ago, a method of building furniture out of corrugated cardboard was developed in order to speed up shifts during television programs by reducing the weight of the pieces. The method has proved equally effective for the stage. The resulting furniture is not only light but amazingly strong and durable; cardboard

FIGURE 8.4   The dining table for a scene in *The Three Sisters* is backed by two screens totaling 24′ in width. They are made from plywood, with decoration of gilded string and rope. (The banisters are made from short lengths of cardboard tubing used for rug centers.)

stools and tables have held up through numerous plays and years of use and abuse. In fact, this book was written while sitting on a cardboard stool that was originally made for the theater, and has now lasted through one show, two books, and five years of office use (Figure 8.5; for illustrations of other cardboard furniture see Figures 1.7, 2.7, 7.9, 8.3, 8.6, and 8.7).

New sheets of corrugated cardboard can be bought fairly cheaply, but it can also be obtained at no cost by salvaging discarded packing boxes. With proper design, sturdy furniture can be made from single layers of the cardboard; more often it is laminated for better appearance and greater strength.

In laminating, a layer of the cardboard is laid on a sheet of plywood, with the grain of all the pieces (that is, the corrugations) running in the same direction. The top surface of the layer is painted with a medium-to-thick coating of glue. Any glue can be used, but ground carpenter's glue is most convenient, mixed with whiting in the same

FIGURE 8.5 Cardboard furniture for *The Taming of the Shrew*. Made entirely from corrugated cardboard, glue, and a few scraps of cloth, decorated with rope and paint. (See also Figure 7.9 for the full set of stools with a larger cardboard table.)

proportions as for gluing canvas to flats. A second layer is then laid over the first, with the grain running at right angles to that of the first layer. Further layers are added with grain alternating until the desired thickness is reached. A sheet of heavy plywood is then laid on top, weighted (with work trays, lumber, or more plywood) and the cardboard is left to dry. Drying is slow because of the plywood surfacing, and may take from three or four days to a week. When the glue has dried, the plywood and weights are removed, and the material is ready for use in construction.

The sheets can be cut readily with a saber saw, using blades designed for plywood. The pieces are assembled by gluing the edges. They can be clamped, although driving a few nails into each joint will usually hold them together until the glue has dried. If any raw edges are visible, revealing the corrugations, they can be covered by gluing on strips of thin cloth. The tough paper forming the outside layers of the cardboard can also be used for this purpose. If scraps of the cardboard are soaked for a few moments in hot water, the layers separate and the paper can easily be pulled off to use in covering joints.

The completed units can be decorated with glued-on rope, pieces of cardboard, papier-mache, gesso, or any other materials which are available. They take scene paint well, and if a glossier finish is desired they can be given a final coat or two of varnish or shellac.

A single sheet of the cardboard will not support much weight if placed level and supported at each end; however, a sheet held upright on edge offers considerable resistance to crushing. It is possible to make sturdy furniture by designing it so that the weight is supported by single sheets fixed so that they remain vertical.

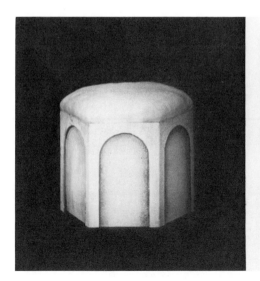 

FIGURE 8.6   A footstool and Victorian table made from cardboard. (The footstool has a cushion of foam rubber covered with cloth.)

The stool shown in Figure 8.7 is an example of such a structure. The seat is supported by a single layer of cardboard. Two strips were cut 17" wide and totaling 9'-0" in length, with the grain running across the strips. They were then folded accordion-fashion at 9" intervals. One side of the strips was coated with glue and they were folded compactly so that adjacent glued surfaces were in contact, and weighted and left to dry.

When the glue had set, the cardboard was stood on edge and the folds opened to form a star shape. A hexagonal seat was cut from a laminated sheet of the cardboard, 1" thick, the top edges of the star were coated with glue and the seat set in place and weighted down. Finally, a single sheet of cardboard was bent in six sections, fitted around the star support, and glued in place. Decorative openings were cut in the sides, ornamental rope added, and the stool painted.

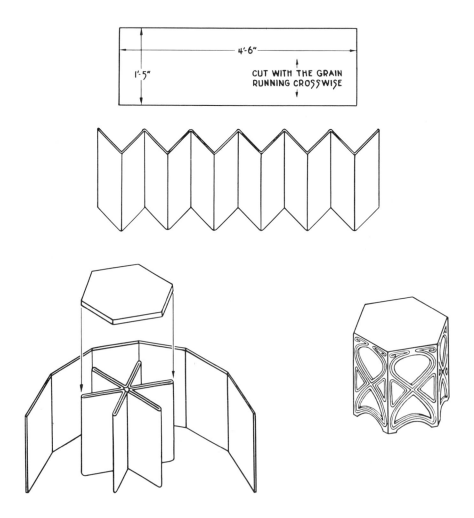

FIGURE 8.7   Working drawings for a footstool to be made from corrugated cardboard.

Obviously, corrugated cardboard is not going to replace lumber for structural purposes, but as a supplementary material with its own characteristics it is a useful addition to the scene shop. The saving in weight may be significant, especially if shows are toured. The furniture can often be made somewhat faster than similar pieces built from wood, and there may be some reduction in cost, although the cost of the glue must be considered, even if the cardboard is free. The strength of properly designed and well built units must be seen to be imagined. A cardboard stool will support more people than can stand on it, even if they climb on each others' shoulders. The cardboard will withstand the force of an actor running across the stage and jumping up on a table or stool. So far it has not been possible to determine the crush point of such units, because they supported all of the weight available in the scene shop when it was piled on to test them.

WINDOWS

Doors and windows are constructed as separate units, which are fastened into holes in the flats especially built to receive them (Figure 8.8). The first part of the window to be built is the thickness, which is made of four boards set on edge with the boards

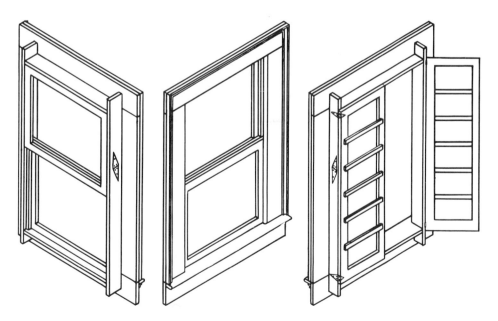

FIGURE 8.8 Windows for the stage. Double hung (back view, *left*; front view, *center*), and casement, *right*.

joined end-to-face. Four boards are then nailed to the edges on one side of the thickness, forming a kind of picture frame, the inside dimensions of which are the same as the inside dimensions of the thickness unit. If the facing boards are to be decorated, cove molding or quarter-round can be fastened on the front, or wide molding can be used instead of the framing lumber. In that case, the molding will have to be mitered at the corners. It will be necessary to fasten the boards together at the outside edge. If the corners are mitered, small nails can be toenailed across the joints; if they are left square, a small flat **L**-brace can be screwed to the back of each corner to hold the boards in line.

If the windows are not practical (that is, if they need not be opened during the performance), four additional boards (usually 1 X 2s) should be nailed inside the thickness to represent the frame which encloses the glass, with narrow strips of plywood nailed across at the back to represent crossbars.

If the window is of the double-hung type and must be opened during the show, the two glass frames are built separately, and 1 X 1 strips are nailed to the inside of the thickness to guide their movement. It is possible to control their setting by running sash cord from the upper corner of each frame through holes drilled in the top thickness piece. The cords run over small pulleys fastened to the top of the thickness piece, and out beyond it, with weights tied to the ends. Heavy bolts loaded with washers are convenient, since the weight can be adjusted by adding or removing washers. More commonly, the windows are held in position by carefully setting the 1 X 1s so that they provide just enough friction, without making it too difficult to open them. A more satisfactory method is to fasten strips of spring metal to the edges. Casement windows, which swing like doors, are set behind the frame and hinged to the offstage face of the thickness.

Glass is not used in making stage windows because of the danger of breakage, but also because it is possible for the glass to catch a spotlight and reflect it blindingly into the eyes of the viewers. If the glass effect is necessary, a rigid sheet of clear plastic can be used, although it too may produce an unwanted reflection. Traditionally, shiny screenwire substitutes for glass, providing something of its sheen without producing a mirrorlike reflection. Most often, however, the windows are simply left unglazed; if curtains are provided the absence of glass is indetectable, and it is unlikely to be noticed even without curtains.

> Real mirrors are avoided on stage for the same reasons that glass is not used in windows. Moderately smooth cardboard should be substituted for the glass, and sprayed or brushed with silver-colored paint. Not only will it look completely convincing from the audience, but after the mirror is hung on the set more than one actor or technician is sure to walk up to it to check his (or her) hair arrangement, on the assumption that it is the real thing.

DOORS

Door frames are similar to window frames, except that they are three-sided. The fourth side, which would rest on the floor, is omitted (Figure 8.9). The doors themselves are usually built 1½" wider than the inside opening (that is, the width matches the outside width of the thickness), and are set behind the thickness, with the hinges fastened to the outside face of the thickness frame. This provides automatic masking for the edges when the door is closed, and avoids the precise fitting which would be necessary if the doors were set inside the thickness frame. It is not necessary to make the door higher than the opening in the frame, since it is raised 1/4" or 1/2" when it is hinged to the frame, to make sure it clears the stage floor and swings freely.

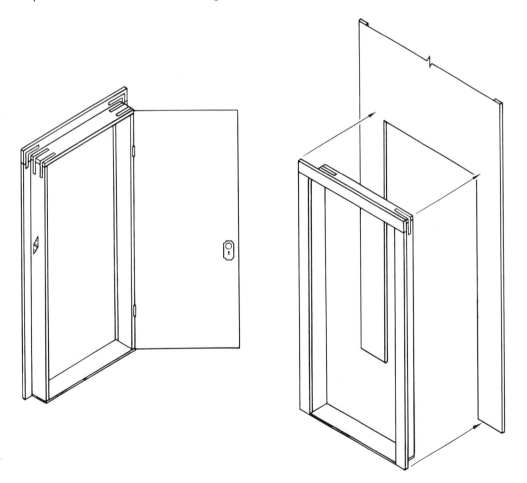

FIGURE 8.9   A scenic door frame.   Shown from the back, *left*, and from the front, *right*, with the door removed, and in position to fit into the opening in the flat.

When hinging a door to a door frame, rest the bottom of the door on one or two layers of 1/4" plywood (corner-blocks are convenient). Then when the hinging is finished and the plywood is pulled out, the door will clear the floor and swing freely.

The doors may be built of a sheet of 1/4" plywood, with a frame of 1" lumber nailed or screwed on (Figure 8.10). For a flush door, the frame is fastened on the back of the plywood. For a conventional door, it is fastened to the front, and additional verticals and horizontals are set in as needed to match the designer's pattern. Cove molding is nailed to the visible edges of the lumber to frame the panels.

In hinging a door to a door frame, always fasten the top hinge first, then the middle hinge if one is used, and finally the bottom hinge. If the bottom hinge is fastened first and the door should be knocked ajar the weight and leverage of the door would tear the hinge off. When a door is removed, either by taking off the hinges or pulling the pins, the order should be reversed, and the hinges unfastened starting with the bottom one and finishing with the top.

FIGURE 8.10 Doors for scenery. *Left*, the frame for a paneled door is shown separated from the backing plywood; *center*, the same door assembled, and with molding added around the panels. *Right*, a flush door with frame. (See Figures 1.2 and 8.16 for photographs of a flush door and a paneled door in use on stage.)

If the set need not be shifted, it is possible to fasten the door frame permanently to the flat; the thickness boards and the casing are nailed to the edges and face of the lumber framing the door opening in the flat. In that case, the opening will have to be somewhat smaller than when the frames are built separately, since no space need be left for the hinge fasteners.

FASTENING INTO THE SET

Door and window units are fastened in place after the flats have been set up on stage. A strap hinge is screwed to each of the vertical thickness boards, on the outside face, where they will be hidden from the audience. The hinges are first opened flat and placed vertically against the thickness face down, with the pin in contact with the surface of the board; the bottom leaf of the hinge is screwed to the thickness. The hinges must be placed so that when the top leaf is flipped down it will firmly pinch a 1" board placed between the hinge and the casing. This position can be checked by laying a scrap of 1 × 3 against the casing and opening the hinge. It should then be swung flat again, and the bottom leaf fastened in place. Because the pin holds the hinge out from the surface of the wood, somewhat longer screws will be needed.

When the frames are to be set in place, the loose flaps of the hinges are flipped up so that they lie flat against the surface of the thickness-pieces, and the unit is pushed through the opening in the flat from the onstage side until the casing fits against the flat; the opening must have been made large enough to allow the hinges to pass through. The top leaf of each hinge is then forced down to horizontal, so that the vertical board framing the opening of the flat is held firmly between the casing and the edge of the hinge. The units are removed for shifting by reversing this procedure; as soon as the hinge leaves are flipped up, the frame is freed and can be removed by pulling it forward through the opening.

If a door must be slammed during performance, neither of the methods of fastening which have been described can be used, since the canvas of the flats would vibrate. For a *floating door frame* the construction is identical with the hinge-fastened unit, except that the hinges are omitted. The door is set in place so that it is not in contact with the frame of the flat, centered in the opening and with a 1/4" gap between the casing and the front surface of the flat. A stage-brace or jack is fastened to each side of the thickness-piece, angled slightly away from the door so that the braces will not be seen by the audience or get in the way of the actors, and the bottom of each thickness is fastened to the stage floor with a foot-iron to prevent the frame from shifting back against the flat when it is used.

JACKS

Various types of jacks are used in the theater. The simplest, which serve the same purpose as stage braces, have the shape of an open triangle formed from three pieces of 1 X 3 or 1 X 4. Three methods of construction are shown in Figure 8.11; other patterns vary in minor ways.

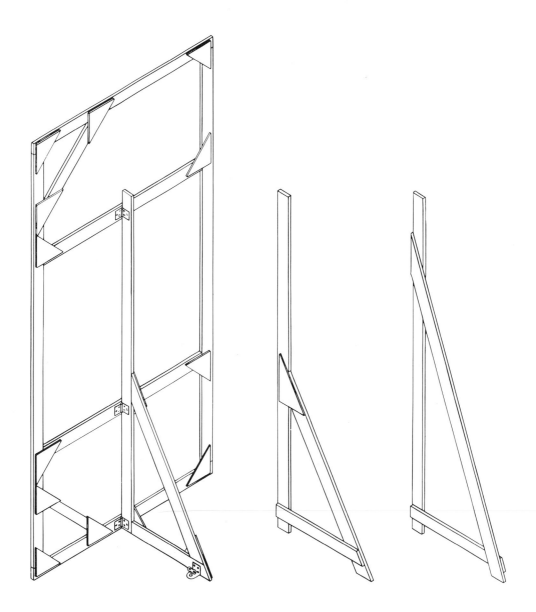

FIGURE 8.11   Jacks. Three types of construction are shown. The jack attached to the flat, *left*, is fastened together with corner–blocks, and all the boards are in the same plane. The jack, *center*, uses one corner–block, and the lapped crosspiece allows it to fold against the flat in only one direction. The jack, *right*, is fastest to make, but the sides of the triangle are in three different planes, resulting in some slight twisting.

Jacks may be used simply as substitutes for stage braces, although they are effective in some instances where stage braces cannot be used. In one theater, it was necessary to anchor a silhouetted bush for a children's play. Since the bush was much too low to use even the smallest stage brace, a 3'-6" jack was especially built to support it. Jacks also have the advantage that they can be hinged to a flat and swung out of the way against it; they can be anchored to the flat throughout almost its entire length, rather than at a single point as with stage braces; they tend to use up less space back stage, and it may be easier to swing them out of sight than to conceal the standard braces. Jacks can be made so quickly that they are often built for one-time use, and are disassembled after production, but if they are built to support full-sized flats they can be readily reused, and are worth saving if storage space is available.

ROCKS

Besides platforms, stairs, and furniture, the most commonly built three-dimensional scenic properties are rocks and pillars. It is customary to distinguish between practical and nonpractical rocks, the practical rocks being defined as those on which actors must sit or stand. Unfortunate experience demonstrates that actors treat all rocks as practical; even if a boulder is not touched during performance, some actor is sure to sit on it during a lull in rehearsal, or a technician may pull it aside and climb on it to reach a piece of equipment over his head. It is suggested therefore that all rocks be built sturdy enough to stand up under considerable abuse in addition to their intended use.

The designer will provide a drawing or a scale model of rocks which must be built for a set. He will probably also prepare working drawings showing their internal structure, although occasionally the technical staff will be asked to improvise the construction. The first step in planning the framework for a practical rock is to find out from the director how it is to be used, specifically where on it actors will stand or sit. These surfaces must be supported with sufficient strength to bear their weight.

The simplest approach to designing weight-bearing surfaces is to think of each as the top of a stool. If an actor climbs the rock by stepping from one surface to another, then the ledges correspond to a short flight of stairs. Even if the rock is apparently free-form, these weight-bearing areas must be fairly close to horizontal.

The internal structure is then designed in the form of one or more stools, or of a short flight of steps. The treads and tops of the stools will probably be at least slightly slanted, and they may well not be square or rectangular, but it is easiest to think of them as pieces of furniture of odd shape.

If more than one is incorporated in the rock, they must be tied together, which can be done by running boards between them, placed so that they will be entirely hidden when the rock is completed. Other areas of the rock surface must be given some support, even if they are not weight-bearing. Boards are attached to the basic stool or step structure, extending toward key points of the rock shape, with the ends cut off where they touch the surface of the rock, at angles which match its shape. A little experience will enable the worker to judge how many such supports are needed. Because this entire structure will be hidden when the rock is completed, it is possible to use the easiest and fastest joints, lap joints.

When the basic structure has been completed, sizable pieces of ordinary chicken-wire are fastened to it with heavy staples (The U-shaped kind which must be driven with a hammer, not the type used in staplers). Coated box nails can also be used, each nail set beside one of the wires, driven in about two-thirds of the way and then bent over the wire with the edge of the head pounded into the wood so that the wire cannot slip out. The chickenwire should be applied somewhat loosely. When it is fastened, it is shaped with the hands to match the surface of the rock as designed, pushing it in for hollows and pulling it out for convex areas; the wire can even be pressed into sharp folds to suggest crevices where rock ledges join. The chickenwire is somewhat intractable and troublesome, but with a fair amount of effort it can be molded to a close approximation of the shape of the finished rock.

Next a heavy surfacing of papier-mache is added, finished with a layer of cloth (see chapter 9). When it is first applied, the papier-maché forms a gelatinous mass, which can be given some shaping with the hands; ridges and cracks can be formed or emphasized. If it is desired that the rock surface be rough, it can be painted with glue and sawdust or ground-up foam plastic sprinkled over it.

It will take some time for the papier-maché to dry, perhaps two or three days. It can then be painted; the color should be varied to suggest natural rock, and the shape should be reinforced by painting highlights and shadows. Very realistic rocks can be made by the method described; more than one member of an audience has accepted property rocks as the real thing.

PILLARS

Occasionally, it is necessary to provide scenic units precisely or approximately cylindrical in shape, most often for pillars or tree trunks. If the cylinders are precise, it is worth going to some trouble to find manufactured ones which can be used. Sturdy cardboard tubes are made for use as forms in pouring cement. They are available in a wide range of diameters, and long enough for almost any stage purpose. Although they are expensive, they can be reused, and the saving in construction time makes them the first choice. Cardboard tubes with a diameter of four to six inches are used as centers around which rugs are rolled for delivery to carpet stores. As the rugs are sold, the centers are discarded and either burned or hauled to the dump. They can be had free, and can be used for small pillars and a variety of other purposes in the theater.

If pillars must be tapered or if cylinders of the right diameter are unavailable, it will be necessary to build them. They are made of a series of wood strips running the length of the cylinder, and fastened to horizontal discs. The discs are made with a radius equal to that of the completed cylinder minus the thickness of the wood strips.

The most obvious material for the discs, 3/4" plywood, cannot be used because nails driven into the edge of plywood tend to split the layers apart and do not hold well enough. The simplest way to construct the discs is to draw a circle of the right size on a piece of cardboard and then lay two layers of ordinary boards on top of it so that each part of the circle is covered by a board in one layer or the other. The layers are then nailed together, the circle marked on them with a cardboard pattern, and the edge cut off with a saber saw (Figure 8.12).

It is better to construct the discs for the top and bottom of the pillar so that a continuous circle is formed in a single plane. One layer of boards is arranged to cover the edge of the pattern; it may be necessary to miter one or two of the boards. They

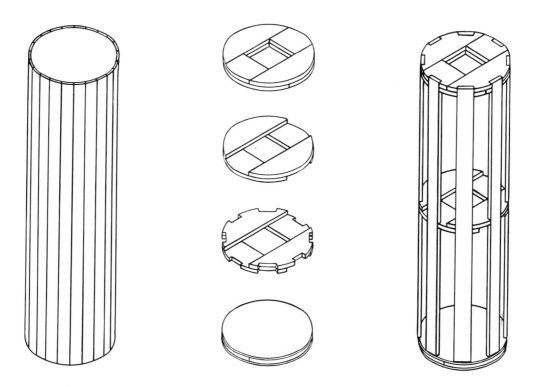

FIGURE 8.12 Pillars. Various construction patterns are shown. The pillar, *left*, is solidly surfaced with lath nailed against the edges of the circular supports; *right*, 1 x 3s are set into notches cut in the circles, *top and center*; the bottom circle is set against their tips, and nails driven through it into the ends of the boards. The bottom disc, *center*, is made from a plywood sandwich with a 1 x 4 filling; the top disc is made entirely of lapped 1 x 4s. The second and third discs are alike except that the second is smooth, for use in the pillar, *left*, while the third is notched, to fit into the pillar, *right*.

are then fastened together with a sheet of 1/4" plywood, and a second piece is nailed to the other side for greater rigidity. The circle needed is traced on one of the plywood pieces and cut out with a saber saw.

The discs are used as a support for wood strips, which may be lath or strips of quarter-inch plywood. These are nailed to the edges of the discs, running the length of the pillar. They need not be fitted together; usually gaps of an inch or two are left between them. Finally, the entire pillar is wrapped in flexible material such as medium-weight cardboard and painted.

If the pillars are to be tapered, the discs must be cut to different diameters, which must be carefully set at the heights at which they match the diameter of the pillar as indicated in the working drawings.

TREE TRUNKS

Tree trunks are constructed by the same method, except that they will have irregular cross-sections. The shape of the trunk at various levels must be determined from the designer's drawings, and the horizontal supports cut to match. The vertical strips will fit the shape of the trunk more closely if they join only adjacent cross-sectional pieces, rather than running all the way.

Instead of covering the trunks with cardboard, it is better simply to glue on scenery canvas. When it has dried, a second layer of canvas can be added, using sections about a foot wide and three or four feet long. These are dipped in glue, set on the trunk at an angle, and given a bias pull, so that they wrinkle; the wrinkles can be shaped and pressed against the first layer of cloth to suggest bark.

PILASTERS

Occasionally, set designs call for square pillars, or for pilasters, which have a rectangular cross-section and are set against the walls. Square pillars a foot or more on a side are usually made of standard flats. They are assembled by setting the edge of one flat against the back surface of the stile of another, and nailing them together. Almost never will the audience be able to see all four sides of a pillar; the invisible side or sides are omitted, but that results in one side's being 3/4" too narrow. This can be corrected by nailing a 1 X 1 strip along the edge of the stile (Figure 8.13).

In order to hold the sides at right angles it will be necessary to provide internal bracing. These braces should be made of four 1 X 3s set together to form an open square of the right size and fastened together by lap joints. Flats of normal size will

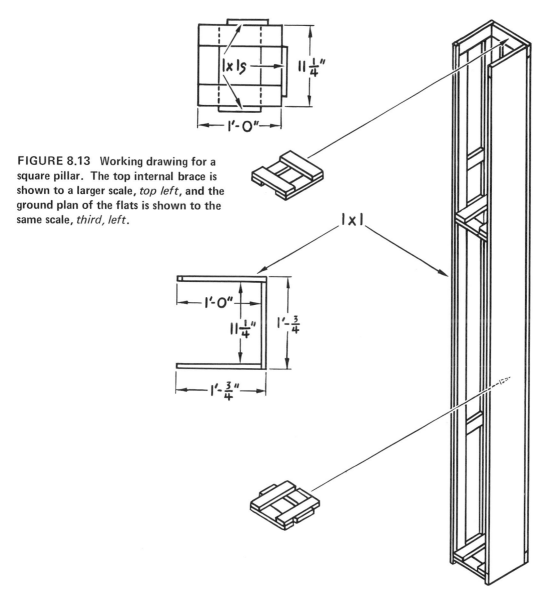

FIGURE 8.13 Working drawing for a square pillar. The top internal brace is shown to a larger scale, *top left*, and the ground plan of the flats is shown to the same scale, *third, left*.

require four such braces, one at the top of the pillar, one at the bottom, and two approximately evenly spaced in between. These braces will not touch the canvas. If it is necessary to nail molding on the surface of the flat, pieces of 1 × 1 stripping nailed to the edges of the braces will extend them to the back surface of the canvas, and will form supports into which the molding can be nailed. These strips cannot extend the entire length of the brace edges, but must be held back at each end by the width of the stiles of the flats.

Pilasters are usually too shallow to be built entirely of flats. If the width is 1'-0" or more, a stock flat can be used for the front surface. The sides can be cut from

1/4" plywood and nailed to the edges of the flat. A vertical 1 X 3 can be nailed at the edge of the plywood sides, inside the pilaster, and the unit fastened in place by driving nails through from the backs of the flats into these boards. Alternatively, lengths of 1 X 3 can be nailed to the front of the flat against which the pilaster is to be fastened, spaced so that the outside edges of the boards just fit inside the plywood strips when the pilaster is set in place; it is fastened by nailing through the back edges of the sides into the battens. If the pilaster must be removed during a scene shift, it can be fastened to the flat by loose-pin hinges or picture hooks-and-eyes.

> Designers' drawings often indicate the dimensions of repeated units as "on centers"; thus, pickets for a fence might be described as spaced *on 4" centers.* In actual construction, it is often difficult to measure from center to center; the same spacing will result if any matching parts of the units are spaced to the same dimension— which parts are used can be chosen on the basis of convenience. With pickets, for example, it is more convenient to catch the tape on one edge of the first one (say the left edge), and then set the second picket so that its left edge is at the prescribed distance.

CORNICES

Cornices are ornamental moldings fastened around the top edge of the walls of a set. They may be extremely simple, perhaps only a piece of 3" molding, or they can be apparently massive structures with a horizontal dimension as much as two feet and a height of as much as three.

Cornices for the stage differ from those used outside the theater in being bolder in design and much lighter in weight, since they must be supported by the flats. Usually large cornices are hollow, with ordinary lumber, simple moldings, and cardboard or other flexible material combined to form a complex shape. The designer's drawing must be studied to determine the shape of the inside surfaces of the elements which are combined to produce the visible ornamental surface. A pattern should then be drawn matching this shape, with horizontal and vertical edges meeting at right angles where the cornice, if solid, would touch the ceiling and wall. If solid lumber is available wide enough to draw the pattern on it, the supports should be cut from it. Otherwise, it will be necessary to build them in the shape of an open right triangle, with the hypotenuse made from a board wide enough that the irregular edge of the pattern can be cut from it without weakening it too much. An alternative method is to cut the entire shape from 3/4" plywood, but in that case a horizontal board must be nailed along the side of the plywood at the ceiling line, since the screws by which the cornice is held in place will not hold in the edge of the plywood (Figure 8.14).

One of these shaped braces should be made for each end of each section of the cornice. If the walls of the set are simple in shape, only three sections will be needed, but if the outline of the walls is broken by bays or extensions, more will be needed. Enough additional braces must be built to fit between the ends of the cornice sections so that the maximum unbraced area is not longer than three or four feet.

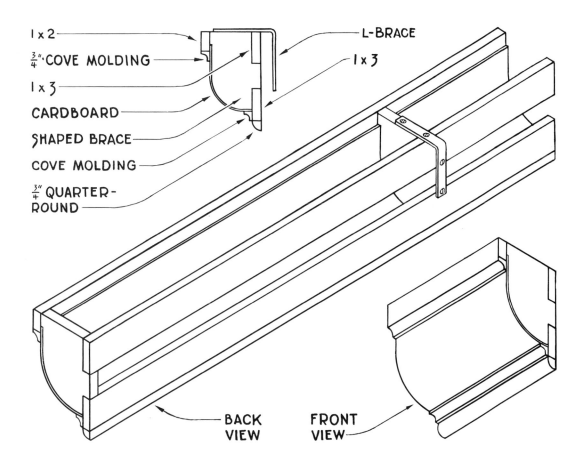

FIGURE 8.14   A cornice for the stage.

The cornice sections are then assembled by nailing the ornamental units to the shaped edges of the braces. Where the ends of the sections will have to be mitered when they are fitted together on the set it is important to hold back the end braces far enough that they will not be cut into when the joints are sawed.

The sections can be stiffened and made easier to assemble by cutting a notch at the corner where the ceiling and wall meet. This should cut into the ceiling edge by 3/4″ and should extend down along the wall edge by the width of a 1 × 3 or a little more. The first step in assembling is to fit a horizontal board into these notches and nail it to the bracing units. If desired, a similar notch can be made at the bottom edge of the wall line, and a second board fastened in; the ornamental surfacing is then applied.

Of all cuts which must be made in the theater, mitering cornices is the most difficult. It is hard to mark the angles, the cornice sections are large and unmanageable, and the irregular shape makes it hard to guide the saw accurately. Fortunately, the cornice will be less brightly lit than any other scenic element, and it is possible to cover gaps with masking tape or paper dutchmen, and touch them up with paint after the cornice has been set in place.

It is easiest to fit the cornices after the walls of the set have been placed on stage. At a corner into or around which the cornice must fit, a chalk line is drawn on the stage floor bisecting the angle of the walls. If it is an outside corner, the cornice is then set on the floor in contact with the flat. While one or two workmen hold it in this position, another takes a carpenter's square and sets it so that the edge of one leg rests on the floor at right angles to the chalk line, with the corner of the square touching the line. The square is then moved until its other leg touches the outside upper edge of the cornice section, and this point is marked. It is essential that the face of the square be held vertical; if that cannot be done accurately enough by eye, it can be checked by a second square set at right angles to the face of the first. The point where the corner of the flats touches the back edge of the cornice is then marked, and the cornice is moved out from the wall.

A yardstick or other straight-edge is laid across the ceiling surface of the cornice, connecting the two points, and a line is drawn across any lumber which the straight-edge touches. Using a square, the point at the wall-ceiling corner of the cornice is carried down the back and marked at the bottom edge. This point and the first one marked are carried around by eye and marked on the edges of the shaped surface. A chalk-line is then stretched between these two points, around the shaped surface, carefully adjusting it so that it defines as straight a section of the cornice as possible, and snapped to mark the cut line. The cornice is then cut along these lines with a saber saw.

If the cornice is to be fitted inside the angle, the bisecting line is first drawn as described, and then a line is drawn parallel to it a foot or so away, extending out from the surface of the flat. Using a square, a vertical line is drawn on the flat from the point where the parallel touches the rail, and slightly higher than the height of the cornice. The cornice is set in place so that its end crosses the second line drawn on the floor parallel with the bisector. The cutting line is marked as described for an outside corner, except that all marks are based on the second, parallel line drawn rather than on the bisector.

> When measurements or guide marks must be recorded on finished scenery, press a piece of masking tape on the surface and make the mark on it. When the mark is no longer needed, the tape can be removed, thus saving having to paint it out as would be necessary if it had been drawn directly on the scenery.

After the cornice sections have been cut, **L**-braces are screwed to the tops of the shaped cornice braces. They must be of the three-dimensional rather than the flat type, formed by bending a strip of metal rather than simply being cut from a sheet. They are set to match the square corner of the cornice braces, except that a 1″ gap must be left between the back leg of the **L**-brace and the back edge of the cornice brace.

When the cornice is to be fastened in place, it is lifted slightly above the flats until the back ends of the **L**-braces are cleared, and then fitted over the flats by pushing the **L**-brace legs down behind the top edge of the rails. Where the legs strike a corner-block they will fit tight; where there is no corner-block a scrap of 1/4″ plywood should be slipped between the leg and the rail, and fastened with a couple of small nails. One person can set a three- or four-foot cornice section in place, but for longer pieces two people will be needed, and for very long sections it will be necessary for other workmen to help support the weight between the ends.

There are other methods of fastening up cornices, but the one described is generally the most convenient. It is possible to remove a cornice during a scene shift, but at considerable expenditure of time. An entire wall section can be moved without disturbing the cornice, and it may be possible to fly the longer cornice sections. The best practice, however, is to dispense with cornices on sets which must be shifted, and use them only for one-set shows.

> Sometimes a number of identical plywood pieces must be cut in a complicated shape, and after the first has been carefully drawn and cut it may be easier to mark the others by tracing around it. Each time a new one is drawn, some deviation from the pattern is likely, and although it may be too small to matter, if the third unit is drawn by tracing around the second, and the fourth by tracing around the third, the errors can multiply. If each one is enlarged by only 1/16″, and sixteen are traced in this way, the last one will be a full inch too big. To prevent that, the first one cut should be marked in some way, perhaps by penciling a star or the word "pattern" on it, and it should be used to mark all of the separate pieces.

ROOF TILES

Rug centers can be used for a variety of purposes besides pillars. One is to simulate curved roof tiles (Figure 8.15). The tubes are cut crosswise in sections a couple of inches longer than the finished tiles. Each section is then cut lengthwise in thirds.

FIGURE 8.15 Roof tiles made from cardboard tubes, for a production of *A Funny Thing Happened on the Way to the Forum*, by Shevelove, Gelbart, and Sondheim.

This can be done with a hand saw or saber saw, although a radial-arm saw will cut them faster; however, it must be used with care. The blade is raised very high, so that it is in position to cut through the top section of the tubing when it has been laid on its side. Two boards are nailed temporarily to the saw table, parallel with the saw blade, one on each side of it, and spaced so that they will hold a section of the tube in place. The tubing is pressed down at the left, keeping the fingers well away from the blade, and cut carefully. The tube is then turned and a second cut made, leaving two sections, one a third of the tube and the other two-thirds. This is done for all of the sections which are needed, and then the lumber guides are reset farther apart to fit the width of the two-thirds sections. These are placed between them with the cut sides down, the saw blade is lowered, and each section is cut in halves. It is usually most convenient to paint the tubing before it is nailed on to the roof.

Each tile is laid on a work table with the concave side up, and a hole made by driving a nail through it in the center, about an inch and a half from one end; the nail is then removed. The row of tile at the bottom edge of the roof is fastened on first. A long nail is inserted in the hole which has been made in each tile, and driven down into the wooden frame. The second row is then added, with the bottom ends overlapping the upper ends of the first row so that the visible area is of the size desired. The last row of tiles, at the top of the roof, must be cut short by the amount of the overlap.

If heavier tiles are preferred, two of the sections can be glued together. The convex side of one tile and the concave side of another are coated with glue and forced together with the glued surfaces in contact. They must be weighted until the glue has dried.

Tiles made in this way are extremely realistic, and in fact indistinguishable from the real thing at audience distance. If desired, the top edge of the roof and the peaks where roof surfaces meet at an angle can be finished by running smaller tubing along them, from which a 1/3 section has been removed.

FLUTING

Cove molding can be used to suggest fluting on pillars. Alternate lengths of molding are turned in opposite directions, so that the concave quarter-circles join to form half-circle indentations. This works best with pilasters. For round pillars the edges of the molding must be trimmed in order to fit them together, or the gaps between them must be filled with wood paste or strips of masking tape. The individual fluting indentations produced by 3/4" molding are an inch wide; smaller fluting can be made by using 1/2" or 3/8" molding, although it will probably have to be specially ordered. Reeding can be simulated with the use of half-round or paired lengths of quarter-round. These are readily available in various sizes.

BENDING MOLDING

It is sometimes necessary to bend molding, perhaps to follow the shape of a gothic arch, or to produce curved corners for panels (Figure 8.16). Decorating the side of a curved flight of stairs, the back of a davenport, or the frame of a round mirror may also require bending the molding.

FIGURE 8.16   Bent molding. The arcs at the center edges of the doors were made from 3/4″ cove molding, cut at intervals, bent, and nailed to the door frames. (A set for Moliere's *The Imaginary Invalid*.)

Cove molding can be bent around a shorter radius than might be expected, and 3/4″ quarter-round will bend somewhat. Both are subject to considerable warping, and it is worth taking a moment or two to find the most sharply warped pieces, which can be bent farther without breaking than a straight piece. Nevertheless, the molding will break if forced beyond a certain point. It can be made more flexible by cutting a series of grooves in it. The blade of the radial-arm saw is raised so that it does not cut entirely through the wood; about an eighth of an inch of solid wood should be left. The molding is laid against the guide fence and a series of cuts made across it. The sharper the curve, the shorter must be the distance between cuts. Two or three inches is about the closest practical spacing. The piece of molding is then set in place on the flat or other scenic unit to which it is to be fastened, and nailed with the thinnest brads available. It is less likely to split if it is nailed in the gaps, through the 1/8" solid strip, but that is not always possible. If pieces break off, they can be fastened back with contact cement or white glue. The slits which have been cut will be visible after nailing. They can be covered with masking tape, or, better, with paste maché (see chapter 9).

MACHÉ MOLDING

An alternative method is to make the entire molding out of cardboard and maché (Figure 8.17). Suppose that a circular mirror frame, 2'-0" in diameter, is to be decorated with a strip of 3/4" cove molding, to be run around its outside edge. First cut a ring from 1/8" upson board, with an outside radius of 11 7/8" and an inside radius of 11¼". Glue this to the frame, leaving an eighth-inch edge around it. Next cut a strip of upson board 3/4" wide and a little over three feet long. Spread the outside rim of the frame liberally with glue and curve the strip around it, the edge resting on the surface of the frame and the face of the strip pressed against the edge of the ring

FIGURE 8.17 Maché molding. A circular picture frame is shown, made from cardboard and paste maché in the shape of bent 3/4" cove molding. Three stages are illustrated. *Left*, a 3/4" strip of upson board is glued around the edge of a cardboard ring. *Center*, maché paste is pressed into the cardboard form and shaped with the thumb. Inside the circle are a lump of the maché and a piece which has been rolled out between the hands into a pencil shape. Nearby is a small dish of water, used to moisten the fingers as an aid in smoothing the applied maché. *Right*, the finished frame, hung against a wallpaper background, with a mat and a copy of a period photograph inserted (Mrs. Aleen Manning, taken about 1899). The frame has been painted with tempera and varnished.

which has been glued on. It will be necessary to trim the strip so that the ends meet precisely without an overlap. They should be glued and taped together and the unit weighted so that it will hold together until the glue sets.

Next a small quantity of paste maché is prepared, rolled across a flat surface to form a cylinder about as thick as a pencil, and then pressed into the corner formed by the ring and the strip of upson board. It is pressed with the thumb into the shape of cove molding, pulling out some of the maché or adding more as it is needed; it is easier to shape if the thumb is occasionally dipped in water. The frame is then set aside to dry, after which it can be smoothed with sandpaper and painted.

IMPROVISED DECORATION

Structures of the types which have been discussed in this chapter are likely to involve more improvisation than any other scenic elements. Designers often ask that effects be produced for which there are no established techniques. Construction workers are very likely to invent new methods of using materials. Many examples are scattered through this text, and probably almost every experienced craftsman could assemble a similar collection. Familiar techniques and materials are always the first choice when they will do the job. When some new effect is intended, a flexible analysis of the materials available will frequently uncover a novel method of achieving exactly what is needed.

9

Plastics

During the last thirty years a large number of synthetic plastics have been developed that are proving to be of great value in building scenery and properties. Only one or two were specifically designed for theatrical use, but inventive stagecraft workers have appropriated others and adapted them to scenery. Their use is irregular, but spreading fast. Some theaters use enormous amounts of various plastics, others use them minimally or not at all. Even in the theaters which rely on them most, as for example the Tyrone Guthrie theater in Minneapolis, the use of plastics is still exploratory and experimental; their full potential is yet to be discovered.

The term *plastic* comes ultimately from a Greek word meaning *to mold,* and in the broadest sense it would include such materials as papier-maché, which has been used in the theater for centuries, but in recent years there has been a tendency to restrict the use of the word to the new synthetics, many of them derived from petroleum. Closely related to the plastics are a number of new adhesives which are valuable in the scene shop. In fact, in some cases identical materials are used for gluing, molding, binders for paint, and even the production of thread and fabrics. Casting resin, originally sold as a clear molding material, has within the last few years begun to be used as a high-gloss varnish. It is consequently impossible to divide the materials into rigidly separated categories on the basis of their composition. This discussion will include not only the synthetics but the other materials which serve similar functions, even though they have very different chemical structures.

As with all resources, plastics have both advantages and disadvantages. The chemical plastics vary greatly in characteristics, so that they can be readily adapted to different uses, such as the construction of tombstones, very lightweight simulated wooden beams, or resilient pads for platform tops. They have two disadvantages. One is that they tend to be very expensive, and the continuing shortage of petroleum can be expected to make them still more costly and more difficult to obtain.

HAZARDS

The second disadvantage is of profound importance, and one which may surprise scene shop workers who use plastics regularly, and that is that they are at least potentially extremely dangerous. Furthermore, the hazards have not yet been fully identified, and even our present partial knowledge has not been widely publicized.

There are apparently four sources of danger in handling plastics in the scene shop. The first is that some of the liquids used are extremely flammable. The second danger is that some of the chemicals can be absorbed through the skin. Third, some plastics when heated give off poisonous fumes. And finally, it seems likely that if plastics are shaped with power tools which create fine dust, breathing in the particles might produce lung damage.

The first and last dangers are readily avoidable. Plastics should be shaped with knives or rasps rather than with power saws, so that the material will not be removed in particles small enough to float through the air. If power saws or grinders must be used, the worker should wear a filter mask. If liquids are marked as flammable, the greatest care should be taken to isolate them from sparks or fire.

The other two dangers are particularly insidious, because some of the gases do not produce early symptoms, but build up in the body and may reach dangerous levels of toxicity only after extended use. A related hazard occurs in some commercial sprays, including aerosol paint. Unfortunately, many aerosol containers do not indicate what type of propellant is used, and it is the propellant which is most likely to be toxic.

In working with plastics, poisonous vapors come either from chemical solvents or are released from the plastics themselves when they are wet with the solvents or are shaped by heat. Painting with liquid solvents is a common method of texturing foam plastics, and heated wires are often used to shape them.

As with all work in the theater, safety should take precedence over all other considerations, and plastics should be used not simply with a sensible concern for safety, but with fanatical care. All instructions provided by the manufacturer should be studied carefully, and any precautions recommended should be considered minimal. Workers should be *more* careful than the manufacturers prescribe. Apparently, so long as shaping is done with rasps, scissors, or knives there will be no danger. If texturing or carving is done with liquids or heat, the work should be done out of doors if at all possible. If it is done in doors, at the minimum it should be done in the largest possible room (not in a small properties laboratory), with doors and windows open. The same comments apply to the use of sprays with toxic or unknown ingredients.

Nevertheless, if scrupulous precautions are observed, plastics are a valuable addition to scenic resources. Even if the use of heat and toxic liquids is forbidden, plastics of various types can solve many scene shop problems with a great saving in time and work—although often at a higher cost.

TYPES OF PLASTICS

The different plastics vary greatly in their characteristics, and can be classified in many ways. Following are some of the sets of categories which are significant for scenic use.

Plastics are clear, translucent, or opaque. The opaque plastics are available in a variety of colors, many of them unattractive, but they can easily be painted. Some plastics are solid, some in the form of cellular foam. Some are rigid and brittle, others are flexible. Some of the foam plastics are elastic, and will spring back to shape after being compressed; others can be dented or compressed but will not return to shape. Plastics are available ready formed, or as liquids or sprays. The preformed plastics are available in thin sheets, in blocks of various sizes and thicknesses, and as rods or tubes.

> The plastic tubes, of various diameters, are extremely flexible and can be bent to follow decorative patterns, but they will not hold a shape, and so must be stiffened. The easiest method is to bend heavy wire in the pattern desired, and then slip the tubing over the wire. Coat-hanger wire is excellent for this purpose.

SHAPING

Plastics can be shaped by woodworking tools or hot wires. They can be softened by heat (thermoplastics) and pressed into molds; or they can be mixed as liquids and poured into molds or sprayed on supports.

Large plastic sheets can be shaped by laying them over a mold, softening them by heat, and then forcing them into the mold either by pumping the air out beneath them (vacuforming) or by forcing them down with compressed air from above. This method requires special equipment which few scene shops have at present.

Rigid polystyrene foam (usually identified by the trade name styrofoam) can be shaped by pressure alone. The plastic block is laid on a sheet of 3/4" plywood, and a carved wooden mold laid on top of it. The entire sandwich is then subjected to pressure, by piling on weights, by a vise, or by clamps, and the mold presses into the plastic block, which will retain its new shape when the pressure is released.

For three-dimensional objects such as cornices, moldings, banisters, and fireplace mantels, the rigid foam can be most easily shaped with a hot wire cutter. In its simplest form, the cutter consists of a resistance wire fastened to a support about a foot and a half above a table surface. The wire extends vertically down through a hole in the table, and forms part of an electrical circuit. When the switch is turned on the resistance wire becomes hot and the plastic is shaped by moving it against the wire, which cuts it by melting it.

A more versatile version of the hot wire cutter looks like a soldering gun, and is held in the hand. A moderately heavy resistance wire (about 12 gauge) is bent with pliers to the shape desired, and each end inserted into the holes in the cutter and fastened with set screws. As the heated wire is drawn through the plastic it cuts it to shape. A styrofoam block set in a lathe can be quickly formed into a banister or newel post by holding the shaped wire against it as it turns. The hand cutter can also be used like a carving tool to form irregular shapes. Plastics can be readily carved with hand tools, including saws, knives, and rasps.

Finally, texturing and moderate shaping can be done with liquid solvents such as paint thinners. The solvent can be spattered on, which will produce a surface like pitted stone, or it can be drybrushed or patted on with a wadded piece of cloth.

Solvent painted on with a brush can be used to imitate simple carving, with repeated coats applied to produce deeper cutting. An especially valuable use for solvent is to simulate bricks. Mortar lines are drawn on the surface of plastic foam and painted with solvent, using a narrow brush; the plastic dissolves, so that the mortar lines sink below the surface. The bricks can be textured by touching them with a brush, by spattering with the solvent, or by drybrushing them to produce striations. Stone walls can be simulated in the same way, and the mortar lines can be sunk deeper and the corners of the stones rounded by careful application of the solvent with a brush. Texturing can also be done mechanically by striking the surface of the plastic with a wire brush, drawing a saw blade across it, denting it with light blows of a hammer, or pounding it with a chain.

SHEET PLASTIC

Most nonporous sheet plastic is too shiny for stage use, but it may be valuable for special effects. For example, a sheet of cellulose acetate film might be spattered on one side with bright greens and then cut into leaf shapes and used for bushes and trees for a fantasy, a musical comedy, or a children's play. Heavier clear sheets can be cut into prisms and used to decorate a chandelier.

CASTING

The casting resins are of limited value in the scene shop. They are sold in the form of a clear liquid and a hardener, which must be mixed together in carefully measured proportions when the resin is to be used. Occasionally, a property such as a paper weight or a crystal ball will be cast, but more often the resin is used as a binder and stiffener for fiber glass. The most useful form of the glass is as a woven sheet. Typically, it is draped over a rough base of wood or chickenwire and then painted or sprayed with the resin. Brick walls, logs, fence posts, tree trunks, and stones are sometimes made in this way, although the glass-resin combination is less frequently used in the theater than other materials.

PLASTIC PADDING

One of the most frequently useful plastic products is designed as a pad for rugs. It is about a half-inch thick and comes in large wide rolls. In the theater, it is ideal for padding platform tops and stair treads. It can be readily cut with scissors or a sharp knife, and can be quickly fastened down with staples. It forms a soft surface which deadens sound but it is not too thick, and although it has an unpleasant color it is of course hidden by the top layer of canvas, which can then be painted. Not only is the foam plastic fairly cheap, but it is almost entirely salvageable, and can be pieced easily. It is faster, cheaper, and more effective than the conventional rug pads which were formerly used in the theater, and it is one of the most welcome recent additions to scenic resources.

ADHESIVES

In their liquid form, many of the plastics also can serve as adhesives, and as new plastics have been developed related glues have also appeared. Especially during the last ten years so many new adhesives have been put on the market that it is nearly impossible to keep track of them. Each has its own characteristics, and nearly all are of some value in the theater, either for general use or to meet special needs. The most useful are the traditional ground carpenter's glue, white glue, wheat paste, contact cement, and epoxy.

> When scenic units must be pressed down while glue is drying, trays of hardware taken from the storage shelves make excellent weights. Not only are they readily transportable, but they provide a surprising amount of weight. Boxes of nails, bolts, washers, or any other heavy materials can be used.

GROUND GLUE

Carpenter's glue may well be the oldest or second oldest glue. Although it was invented in prehistoric times, it was the standard theatrical glue until this century, it is still thoroughly usable, and is the preferred adhesive in many scene shops. It is an animal product, and is sold in the form of a coarse powder or flakes. It is a versatile glue, and with some alteration can be used for almost every scene shop purpose, including fastening wood joints, gluing canvas to flats, and even as a binder for paint. It is readily soluble in water, which makes it unsuited for scenery which is to be used outdoors, but which may be an advantage. For instance, paint in which it is used as a binder can easily be washed off flats to produce a clean surface for another coat. One of its greatest advantages is that it is the cheapest adhesive of those normally used in the scene shop.

> Ground glue mixed with sawdust forms a paste which can be used like plastic wood to fill knotholes or gaps in joints. Adding a little whiting will make a smoother paste which can be used for modeling, to simulate wood carving on furniture or picture frames.

Before the glue is used it must be melted. It is put in a metal container (an ordinary cooking pan) and covered with water to perhaps a half inch above the surface of the glue. A larger pan is then partly filled with water and half a brick put in the bottom; the glue pan is set on the brick and the two containers put on an electric stove. It is important that the larger pan not be allowed to boil dry, and that the glue not be put directly on the fire; it will readily scorch at temperatures only a little above the boiling point of water, with a strong smell like burning feathers. As the water in the larger pot boils, the glue flakes dissolve. Just before the glue is ready to use it will have a milky appearance, because of the tiny particles of undissolved glue, but when it is fully dissolved it will be clear and slightly brown. It is also possible to buy electric glue pots which are constructed so that the heat does not reach the burning point, so that the two-pan double-boiler arrangement need not be used.

The glue will dissolve more readily if it has been left to soak overnight. When considerable gluing is to be done, three glue pots should be used, one for soaking, one on the stove melting, and the third to hold the melted glue being used. In this way a continuous supply of glue can be maintained.

The melted glue is at full strength, and is used for gluing wood joints. It must be weakened for gluing canvas to flats because scene paint will not adhere satisfactorily to the pure glue. Discarded powdered pigment can be mixed with it as well as additional warm water; if no waste paint is available, whiting is used, since it is by far the cheapest pigment. Usually wheat paste (a mixture of flour and water) is also added to the glue-paint-and-water mixture, although it is not absolutely necessary. The use of ground glue as an adhesive for paint is discussed in chapter 10.

Occasionally, a flat is accidentally stepped on or punched with the hand, leaving an unsightly dent in the canvas from six inches to a foot in diameter. If the flat has been painted the cloth will have shrunk, and cannot be retightened by wetting it. However, if the dented area is painted on the back with a mixture of paint and ground glue a little stronger than that used for painting, the glue itself will shrink as it dries, and pull the dent taut again. If necessary, the treatment can be repeated, but care must be taken to avoid too strong a coating of glue, which would overshrink and pucker the area.

The glue will congeal into a solid or gelatinous mass if it is allowed to cool, but it can be readily redissolved by adding a little water and setting it on the fire in a pan of water to reheat.

When replacing a screw top on a container of glue, turn it all the way down and then unscrew it by a full turn. That will prevent it from sticking, so that it can be easily removed later.

WHITE GLUE

White glue is preferred by many stagecraft workers for its greater convenience. It is sold under various brand names, the most familiar of which is Elmer's. It is not water soluble when thoroughly dry, with the advantage that it can be used for outdoor scenery but the disadvantage that brushes and containers must be thoroughly cleaned after use before the glue has had a chance to dry. White glue is more expensive than ground glue; it is cheapest if bought by the barrel, and most expensive in small bottles containing only a few ounces. It is readily available in gallon containers, but must be especially ordered for larger quantities.

> The plastic bottles in which dishwashing detergent is sold make excellent containers for white glue, especially those which have a perforated button at the top for opening and closing. The screw top is removed to fill them, and then replaced, and the button used to open and close the containers.

At full strength white glue is usable for wood joints. It can be weakened for canvassing flats by mixing it with water alone, or with water and whiting.

> If difficulty is encountered in pouring glue from gallon jugs into smaller containers, the glue can be guided by inserting a length of coathanger wire, a small dowel, or even a pencil into the mouth of the smaller bottle, holding it at a slight angle so that it does not touch the sides of the opening, and pouring the glue against the wire or dowel.

MISCELLANEOUS GLUES

Contact cement and epoxy are infrequently used in the theater. The contact cement has the great advantage that it bonds instantly, so that glued units need not be clamped. However, they must be very precisely aligned before they are pressed together, because the cement holds at the slightest touch. The great advantage of epoxy is that it can be used on any type of material, even to join metals. It is available in various forms, most of which require that separate pastes be mixed together. Its major disadvantage is its cost, so that it should be reserved for joints where other glues will not work.

THE GLUE GUN

One last type of glue requires the use of a special instrument called a glue gun (Figure 9.1). It is essentially an electric heater into which is inserted a waxy white cylinder about the shape and size of a piece of chalk. The glue melts and flows out of the tip of the gun when the upper end of the glue stick is pressed with the thumb. The glue gun is useful for fastening ornamental rope to furniture. A line of glue is run across the surface for a distance of up to a foot and the rope is pressed against it. The glue does not bond strongly, and so it cannot be used for joints which must resist force; it hardens as it cools, but can be remelted by running the heated tip of the gun along the surface of the glue.

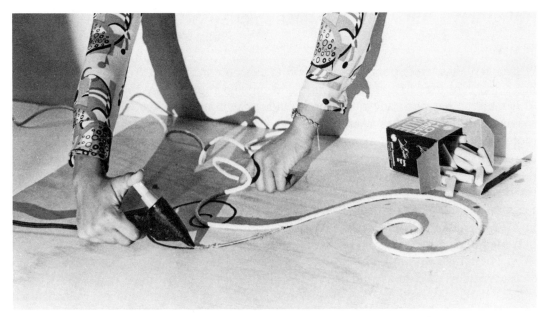

FIGURE 9.1   The glue gun.   The worker has drawn the pattern of a decorative spiral on the plywood, and fastened cotton rope along part of it.   She is laying down a further stripe of glue, and will press the rope into it while it is still melted.   A box containing glue cylinders lies at the right.

IMPREGNATED FABRICS

The use of glass fabric for stage properties has been described. The material is shaped over a support and then coated with liquid plastic to make it stiff. Various products have been developed which produce much the same effect, the most familiar being sold under the trade name of celastic. This is a cloth already impregnated with plastic. When it is used it is dipped into a special solvent and pressed in a mold or shaped by hand while wet; after it dries it forms a tough structure which can be painted or decorated with glued-on ornaments. If celastic is to be shaped in a mold, it is convenient to buy a special mold release. Celastic is excellent for units requiring strength and lightness, such as masks and armor. Its major disadvantages are that using it involves some toxic hazard, and it is so expensive that it can seldom be afforded for large structures. Some other products have been marketed for similar purposes but of different materials, for instance sheet rubber which can be softened by applying moderate heat. They are less widely used than the impregnated fabrics, and experience suggests that they are somewhat less satisfactory.

PAPIER-MACHÉ

With a very few exceptions, the same units can be constructed from a material which has some centuries of use both inside and outside the theater, called papier-maché.[1] This material has both advantages and disadvantages as compared with the recent commercial products: it takes a good deal more time to make objects from it, and they dry more slowly; the finished material is somewhat thicker; with the most frequently used adhesives the finished objects have some tendency to mold during long storage, and may be attacked by mice. Its greatest advantage is its cheapness. Since it is made from scrap materials, the only cost is the adhesive. It would be possible to cover all the surfaces of a set with papier-maché without wrecking the theater budget, whereas making just a few masks and two or three suits of armor out of the impregnated-fabric products might put a serious strain on the expense account.

The longer drying time required for papier-mache may be both an advantage and a disadvantage. If a large number of identical units must be made in a mold (for instance, if the set requires that twenty ornamental capitals be made for pillars), each one will have to be left in the mold for several hours until it is firm enough to remove safely. As a result, it may be necessary to make several molds and to spread the work out over a week or more. On the other hand, if rocks, tree trunks, brick walls, or ornamental wood carving are simulated in papier-mache, the fact that it dries slowly gives the workers time to do careful shaping and to refine details, pressing crevices into rock surfaces, forming bark, and adjusting the lines of the carving.

A significant factor in choosing among the various materials is the individual taste of the worker. Some set builders find papier-mache messy and troublesome, others prefer it. Certainly it is still an extremely valuable scenic resource.

---

1. Although the French spelling is used for this term, for centuries *papier* has been pronounced like the English word *paper*. In fact, George Washington so pronounced it. When Mount Vernon was redecorated, he specified that the ceilings be made out of this material.

PASTE MACHÉ

The term is applied to two products which are made from the same materials but which are handled very differently. In French, *papier-maché* means "chewed paper," which more accurately describes the older of the two forms. It is sold commercially as a dry greyish powder with a soft texture, a combination of dry glue and powdered paper. This is mixed with water and kneaded to form a mass having the consistency of modeling clay (see Figure 8.17). This type of papier-maché can be used for direct modeling, for example to simulate carving on a panel or a piece of furniture. The glue already present in the mixture will make it stick to the surface to which it is applied, although a stronger bond will be produced if some white glue is added when the water is kneaded into the powder. This type of maché is especially useful for filling cracks in wood joints, especially miter joints, which are difficult to make accurately. It can also be used to restore damaged sections of picture frames. The material shrinks somewhat as it dries, so that it cannot be used for solid modeling of three-dimensional objects larger than a few inches.

STRIP MACHÉ

The second type of papier-mache is much more frequently used in the theater, and is adaptable to objects as small as a piece of jewelry and as large as a rock cliff ten feet high and forty feet wide.

THE MOLD METHOD

This type of maché must be formed in a mold or over a supporting frame. The construction of units in a mold will be described first. Suppose that a set shows a formal garden, that four or five pillars are to be topped with ornamental stone urns, and that the technical director decides to build them from papier-maché. A real urn may be used as a model, or a half-urn can be shaped from modeling clay. A plaster cast is made of half the urn, using either the real urn or the clay shape; when the plaster has hardened the urn is removed.

   The inside of the mold is covered with aluminum foil, pressed down tight, to keep the maché from sticking to the plaster. Thin cloth, preferably with a flannel-like surface, is torn into strips or squares, which are immersed in a glue mixture. They are removed one at a time, some of the glue is removed by running them through the fingers, and they are pressed into the mold in a criss-cross pattern so that they completely cover the foil. Next, sheets of newspaper are torn into strips of convenient width and length, thrown into the glue, the excess glue wiped off with the fingers, and the strips criss-crossed so as to completely cover the layer of cloth. Two more layers of paper are laid on top of the first, and finally a layer of cloth. The material is pressed down firmly to make sure that it fits solidly in the mold, and the entire unit is set aside to dry. Although it may not be entirely dry by the next day, it will probably be firm enough that the cloth-and-paper structure can be removed from the mold without damaging it. It is carefully set aside to finish drying, and the entire process repeated.

When the two halves have thoroughly dried, the edges are trimmed to remove any irregularities, and the halves are fitted together and joined by gluing strips of cloth across the crack, both inside and outside the urn. When these have dried, the unit is ready to paint.

Any type of adhesive can be used for papier-maché, including flour paste, ground glue, and white glue. Probably the most frequently used is the combination of ground glue, wheat paste, whiting, and water which is also used for fastening canvas to flats.

Objects made in this way are surprisingly strong. One teacher of stagecraft used to demonstrate that fact by bringing a bowl to class which his wife had made of papier-maché, turning it upside down on the floor, and standing on it on tiptoe with one foot. Most of the strength comes from the layers of cloth. If paper alone is used, the structure will be brittle and easily damaged. For nearly all scenic purposes, a single layer of cloth applied to the outside surface is adequate, although if it is convenient to cover both the inside and outside of the paper layers with cloth the unit will be still stronger.

The mold method is frequently used to make property bottles, and is especially adapted to quantity production of such things as elaborately shaped ceiling tiles. Because the modeling or carving need be done only once, the set crew can afford to prepare a heavily decorated mold which can then be used to shape as many maché panels as are needed (this is probably the method used for the Mount Vernon ceilings).

THE FRAMEWORK METHOD

Still more frequently, the strip type of papier-maché is used to construct objects like large rocks or tree stumps. A supporting structure is first built, and the maché applied to the outside. Usually the support is not removed, but remains as an integral part of the unit.

The method can be illustrated by describing the construction of a stump. First two shapes are cut from plywood, one matching the top of the stump as shown in the designer's drawing, and the other the bottom of the stump where it stands on the floor. These are then fastened together with 1 × 3s set vertically between them so as to form a firm structure. Wherever possible, the lumber should match the final shape of the stump, and the boards at the edge can be slanted and trimmed to shape if desired.

Next, pieces of ordinary chickenwire are stapled to the edges of the plywood forms, stretching somewhat loosely between them so as to form a continuous surface around the structure. The chickenwire is somewhat intractable and troublesome to work with, but with a little care it can be squeezed, stretched, curved, and folded so that it takes the shape specified for the finished stump.

The chickenwire is then covered with a layer of paper strips. (Cloth can be used for the first layer, although the chickenwire provides enough strength so that the inner cloth layer is usually omitted.) The paper will not stick to the wire, so the first strips must be especially attached. Each strip is laid across the wire surface, and the ends pushed through the openings in the chickenwire, bent around the wire, and pressed against the back side of the strip, gluing the strip to itself. These self-glued strips are scattered across the surface so that the spaces between them are about half as wide as the lengths of the strips being used. The surfacing is completed by laying additional strips across the gaps in criss-cross fashion so that each end overlaps one of the self-glued strips.

Additional layers of paper strips are then applied. The larger the object, the more layers are needed, but three layers of paper is the practical minimum, and seldom would more than six or seven layers be necessary. Finally, the surface is coated with a layer of cloth.

In applying strips of paper for papier-maché, alternate layers should be made out of ordinary black-and-white sheets of newspaper and colored Sunday comics. There is a chance that some areas will be skipped in applying each layer after the first, and if alternate layers are of different colors, any areas missed can be identified and filled in.

At this point, the papier-maché forms a somewhat gelatinous mass, matching the shape of the supporting chickenwire-and-wood structure. A good deal of detailing and texturing can still be done to the surface, as well as some adjustment of the modeling. For example, grooves can be deepened, rounded surfaces emphasized or trued, and the cloth can be pulled and shaped into wrinkles to suggest bark. When the shaping is finished, the unit is left to dry, which may take two or three days, and then it is painted, often so as to emphasize the shape, with deeper areas darkened to suggest shadows and raised areas painted lighter.

The size and shape of the strips used for papier-maché depend on the shape of the object to be covered. If it has compound curves or curves of small radius it may be necessary to use short, narrow strips of paper and cloth; if the curves are simple and large, as for the surface of a boulder, it may be possible to use pieces of paper as much as six inches wide and a foot and a half long. Usually the strips are torn about an inch and a half wide and from six to eight inches long. Cut strips should not be used for the outside layer; the irregular edges produced by tearing are much less visible than the straight lines produced by cutting.

Structures of any size and shape can be covered with papier-maché. If they are weight-bearing (for instance, if actors must climb up a papier-maché cliff), the interior frame should be planned so that it will support the weight, so that the upper surface of the rock ledges is solid wood, on which the actors can step. The papier-maché surfacing applied to the sides of the cliff can be carried around so that it covers the wooden steps, but the necessary support will still be supplied by the frame.

USES FOR MACHÉ

Papier-maché is one of the most versatile decorative materials available for building scenery, so much so that it is not possible to provide even a representative list of units which can be built from it. It can be used for hand properties, for decorating furniture, for simulating carved marble, for statues, in making logs for cabins or rails for rustic fences, in imitating stone or brick walls, in making roof tiles, for armor or masks, and even for jewelry. Necessity and ingenuity will suggest variations in the techniques described. Just one will be given as an illustration—the construction of a brick wall.

BRICK WALLS

Cut ordinary lumber or 3/4" plywood into rectangles the length and width of bricks. Lay them out on a sheet of plywood with spaces between them for mortar and nail them to the plywood. Lightly coat the entire structure with oil so that the papier-maché will not stick to it.

Lay on a layer of cloth which has been dipped in glue; good-sized squares or rectangles of cloth can be used. Press the cloth down into the spaces left for mortar. Add two layers of paper, and then a final layer of cloth, and press well down into the mortar spaces. The edges of the bricks can be rounded and indentations pressed into them to suggest striations or pieces chipped out, if it is intended that the wall look old. When the maché has dried, it is pulled up gently off the mold, fastened to a frame, and painted to simulate brick and mortar.

216

Although this method involves the use of a mold, as did the construction of the urns described above, the brick mold is positive while the urn mold was negative; that is, the finished surface of the urns, which is visible to the audience, is the surface which was in contact with the mold; the surface of the bricks which was next to the mold is hidden, and it is the outer surface which the audience sees. The positive process results in some loss of definition. If it is intended that the wall represent new bricks, with sharp edges, a negative mold must be made. This is produced by nailing down the mortar lines rather than the bricks; narrow plywood strips can be used, or 1/2" stripping bought from the lumber yard. Horizontal strips are first nailed to the plywood sheet, spaced the width of a brick apart, and then a series of short strips are nailed vertically between them separated by spaces equal to the length of a brick. The layers of papier-maché are pressed firmly in place as with the positive mold, and when dry the sheet is fastened to a frame with the surface which was in contact with the mold turned out toward the audience.

The positive process can also be used to reproduce urns, capitals, or statues without the necessity of making a plaster mold, although the loss of definition makes this method unsuited to small objects or fine details. If it is desired to duplicate an actual vase, the surface is first coated with a thin film of petroleum jelly (or, if the oil would damage it, a layer of aluminum foil). The entire object is then covered with papier-maché and allowed to dry. In this case, it is necessary to use two layers of cloth, on the inside and outside of the maché. Taking a sharp knife, the papier-maché is cut in halves and removed from the vase, and the edges rejoined with strips of cloth. This method involves some chance of damaging the object being reproduced, and so of course should not be used with borrowed or valuable properties.

FINISHING MACHÉ

Usually maché objects are finished with ordinary scene paint, but any type of paint will do, and the surface can be treated to produce different effects. For instance, the vase described can be sanded smooth and painted with two or three coats of enamel, with a final coat of high-gloss varnish to simulate ceramic glaze. Wrought iron or armor can be sprayed with metallic paint, and will then be indistinguishable from actual metal. Rock surfaces can be spattered to suggest pitting, and tree trunks drybrushed to emphasize the pattern of the bark.

Although working with papier-maché is undeniably messy, and requires a sizable amount of time, if it is carefully planned it can contribute greatly to the appearance of a set, and a few maché ornaments may make a set which would otherwise seem bare look richly decorated and interesting.

10

Paint Mixing

With few exceptions, all scenic elements are painted before they are transported to the stage. Stagecraft workers need to know something about the composition and preparation of paint, they need to be able to mix colors so as to match the designer's specifications, and they need to be familiar with the various methods of applying paint, and to have developed skill in using them.

THE COMPOSITION OF PAINT

Paint is, theoretically, a combination of three materials: the pigment, which provides the color; the vehicle, which holds the pigment in suspension so that it can be brushed; and the binder, which makes the pigment adhere to the surface after the vehicle has dried. Occasionally a single material will serve two of these functions. In artists' oil paint, for example, the oil is both vehicle and binder, although usually turpentine is added as a supplementary vehicle.

TYPES OF PAINT

Paint is usually classified according to the binder used, for example, oil paint, latex paint, acrylic paint, and casein paint, where oil, rubber, synthetic acrylic, and casein serve to glue the pigment to the surface. As new types of glue have been developed in recent decades, many of them have been adapted for use in paint, so that there are a very large number of kinds of paint currently on the market which were not available twenty years ago. The special characteristics of each glue affect the paint in which it is used; for example, the extremely strong epoxy glue, when used as a paint binder, produces a waterproof surface almost like ceramic tile.

SCENE PAINT

While many types of paint may occasionally be used in the scene shop for special purposes, in the overwhelming majority of cases scenery is painted with tempera, that is, opaque pigment mixed with water as a vehicle, and producing a dull or matte rather than a shiny finish. Traditionally, ground carpenter's glue has been used as a binder, although more and more scene shops are adopting casein paint. The use of both types will be discussed in this chapter.

As with other areas of stagecraft, the choice of type of paint depends to a large extent on the individual taste of the technical director. Traditional scene paint is somewhat more troublesome to prepare; casein paint is more convenient. The traditional is the cheapest paint available; the casein more expensive, although not prohibitively so. The most significant difference between the two is that the traditional paint, if mixed with animal glue, can be redissolved after it dries, while the casein paint is essentially permanent. Either characteristic may be desirable. For instance, the traditional paint is unaccpetable for scenery which is to be used outdoors, since a sudden rain might wash the flats clean, and even a moderate sprinkle will leave them spotted and unsightly. On the other hand, if a designer frequently asks that different colors of paint be blended on the scenery the casein paint is much less convenient, since each area must be blended while it is still wet. With the traditional paint, an entire varicolored pattern can be painted on a flat, and then the areas to be blended redissolved with a damp brush.

TRADITIONAL SCENE PAINT

The traditional scene paint is sold in the form of a dry powder. It is available with the glue already mixed with it, but the pure pigment is preferable because it will not spoil in storage and it is often convenient to vary the strength of the glue-pigment mixture, which is more difficult when they are already in combination.

In preparing the paint for use, a bucket is filled about two-thirds full with the dry pigment, and then warm water is stirred into it; it will take about two-thirds of a bucket of water. It might seem that the bucket would overflow, but as the pigment dissolves in the water it occupies much less space than when it is dry. Next a quantity of ground carpenter's glue is poured in (previously melted as described in chapter 9), and the mixture thoroughly stirred.

If too little glue is used, the paint will not stick to the scenery; if too much is used, the paint will have a hard, dark, shiny appearance and will crack when the scenery is handled. The acceptable range in proportion of glue is wide, but it must not be exceeded. Two tests are suggested for determining whether the proportions are acceptable; both are literally rules of thumb. One gives an approximate indication, the other is more definitive.

When the glue is thoroughly mixed, stick your hand well into the paint and rub the thumb hard against the forefinger. If the paint is in a metal container, a gritty or grating sound will be heard which becomes louder as more glue is added. A little experience will enable the painter to identify the proper loudness for acceptable proportions.

When this thumb test indicates that the mixture is right, a little of the paint should be spread near the edge of a sheet of paper and force-dried by holding it over a hot plate or a candle, being careful not to burn it. Before drying it, the painter should wash his hands clean and dry them thoroughly, because the test requires a clean and absolutely dry thumb. After the paint has completely dried, remove it from the fire, and wait a few seconds—it will be hotter than you think. Then grasp the paper between the thumb and finger, press them together hard, and rub the thumb from the painted area out into the unpainted area. If the paint smears, not enough glue has been used. Flex the paper across the painted area. If the paint breaks in a straight line and looks darker than expected, too much glue has been used.

The paint must be further thinned to brushing consistency by adding more water. Some painters prefer to mix the glue with the water rather than with the pigment. This mixture is called *size water*. Which method is used is a matter of personal preference.

The proportions of water and pigment also can vary acceptably over a fairly wide range. If too much water is used, the paint will not cover adequately and the previous coat or the raw canvas will show through. If too little water is used the paint will be hard to brush, and an unnecessarily thick layer will be deposited. It is easier to test this on the scenery itself. It is better to start with the paint a little too thick, and then cautiously add water after a few experimental strokes of the brush.

This type of paint will partially jell as it cools, and become steadily harder to apply. As soon as this happens, the workers should add a little more hot water. If the paint is to be used after having been left in the bucket overnight it will be necessary to warm it. Theoretically, this should be done with the same kind of double-boiler arrangement used to melt the pure glue. In practice, it is more often set directly on the hot plate turned to low heat, but the paint must be stirred constantly, and it should not be left unattended even for a moment.

The pigments vary in chemical composition and in weight. French orange, for instance, is very heavy, while black is so light that it may float on the surface of the water. If the paint used is mixed from several pigments, they therefore tend to separate while it is used, sometimes with striking and disastrous alterations in the color. To prevent this, the paint should be stirred after every one or two square yards of scenery have been covered. Of course paint which has been left overnight will have separated maximally, and should be thoroughly stirred before it is warmed; especially if there is a heavy layer of pigment at the bottom it will tend to trap the heat and burn while the liquid above it is still cool to the touch.

Dry black pigment is so light that it floats on the surface of the water and is very difficult to mix. Adding a little rubbing alcohol or ordinary dishwashing detergent lowers the surface tension of the water and greatly speeds the mixing.

CASEIN PAINT

Casein paint is sold in gallon buckets in paste form which varies greatly in viscosity; some of it is so thin that all of the paint will readily pour out of the can, other brands or colors may be as thick as axle grease, and cannot be poured at all, but must be dug out with a stick or spoon.

The casein binder is already mixed with the pigment, but the paint must be thinned with additional water to brushing consistency. Traditional scene paint is usually mixed to the thickness of fairly heavy cream; casein paint is thinned to about the consistency of milk. The correct thickness can be determined by the same tests used with traditional paint. If too much water is added the casein paint will not hide the background; if too little has been added the brush will drag and the work will go slowly. Again, it is better to start with the paint a little too thick, and then adjust by adding water after a few test strokes with the brush on the actual scenery. Cold water can be used, but fairly warm water improves brushability.

Casein paint is often too stiff to pour cleanly out of the containers in which it is bought. After most of the paint is removed, about a cupful of water should be added to the bucket and the paint scraped down off the sides and the sludge from the bottom stirred into the water so that it can be poured out. However, if three or four buckets of paint are to be mixed together, and water is put into each one separately, there is danger of getting the total mix too thin. Instead, put a cup of water or a little more into the first bucket and stir in all the remaining paint, then pour the same water into the second bucket and repeat. In this way, the buckets can be cleaned without using an unaccpetable quantity of water.

COLOR MIXING

Included in the designer's instructions for the stagecraft crew will be samples of the colors to be used in painting the set. Only very rarely will one of the specified colors be exactly the same as one of the manufacturers' paints which are carried in stock. In nearly every case, special mixes must be prepared. Skill in analyzing colors, and in duplicating them by combining stock paints, is consequently an essential part of the workers' mastery of stagecraft. The theory of color mixing is fairly simple; its application is somewhat more difficult. Once the theory is clearly understood, the student can expect that his ability to apply it will grow with practice, and that after mixing paints for several stage sets he will become able to match color specifications with precision.

STANDARDS OF ACCURACY

At the highest level of skill, it is possible to prepare mixes which match a prescribed color sample indetectably, that is, accurately enough so that the human eye cannot distinguish between the two mixes (although electronic machines may still be able to identify differences). Such close matching is seldom necessary in the theater. As standards of accuracy increase, the amount of time required for preparing mixes rises sharply. It might well take eight or ten hours to prepare an indetectable match for a paint sample, whereas a fully acceptable close approximation would hardly ever require more than an hour to mix.

The designer's color scheme is intended to produce a particular emotional and esthetic effect, depending in part on the individual colors but even more on their inter-relationships. So long as the intended impression is created, the colors mixed will be satisfactory. In case of doubt the technical director or designer can be asked to check and approve the colors before they are applied to the scenery. Nevertheless, the student worker should push toward the greatest accuracy achievable in the time he has available, and should never be satisfied with an approximation of the designer's samples when a more accurate mix can be achieved.

This discussion will be divided into two parts, the first dealing with the theory of color mixing, the second including some hints for its practical application. Almost every color to be seen in nature can be analyzed as a combination of four different pigments, black, white, and two taken from the three primary colors red, yellow, and blue. In theory, then, duplicating a designer's sample requires identifying which two primaries it contains, and the relative proportions of the four pigments. In studying mixing theory it is easiest if we begin with the first of those problems, identifying the primaries, and leave the black-white factors for later consideration.

THE COLOR WHEEL

Let us imagine three jars of paint in the pure colors of red, yellow, and blue, each one free of any black or white contamination. In imagination, take three small cards and paint each one with one of the three pigments, and then arrange them on the desk at the points of an equilateral triangle, spread well apart.

If we take an equal quantity of two of these colors and mix them together, a third color will be produced which is distinctively different but clearly related to the two which were used to make it. Thus, equal quantities of blue and yellow will mix to form green. If we visualize the first three color samples as lying at equidistant points on an imaginary circle, the green we have mixed will fit visually on the circumference of the circle halfway between the blue and yellow. The other two pairs of colors can then be similarly mixed, red-and-yellow producing orange and red-and-blue producing purple.

With these six colors in position, we have a clearly defined circle, with each color standing between the other two to which it is most closely related. What would happen if the mixing process were continued, again mixing equal quantities of color which appear side by side in the circle?

Let us experiment with the green mix. Since it was produced by combining blue and yellow in equal amounts, it can be described as made up of 1 part blue + 1 part yellow = 2 parts green. If we then combine the green with an equal quantity of the adjacent yellow, the resulting mixture will have the formula of 2 parts yellow + 2 parts green, which can be restated in terms of the colors used to make the green as 3 parts yellow + 1 part blue.

Inspection of the color produced by actually mixing the pigments as described would demonstrate that the new color is related to the color circle exactly as might be expected: if we fit it on the circle we must put it halfway between the green and the yellow. Each adjacent pair of colors on the circle can be mixed in the same way, resulting in twelve different colors.

THE PRIMARIES AND SECONDARIES

Nine of these colors have been produced by mixing. The three original colors have the peculiarity of being unmixable; red, yellow, or blue paint can be prepared only by finding materials in nature which already have those colors and using them as pigments. Since all color mixing must start with these colors, that is, since they are the first colors from which others can be mixed, they are called *primaries.* The second colors which we produced (by mixing pairs of the primaries) are called *secondaries.* (There is no special name for the third set of mixes. They have sometimes been called tertiaries, but that term should be avoided because it is also applied to mixes which are quite different in appearance and formula.) The circle of colors which we have produced is technically called a *color wheel* (Figure 10.1).

NOMENCLATURE

There is fair agreement on the names of the twelve colors which have been described. The primaries are red, yellow, and blue, and the secondaries are green, purple, and orange. The last six colors which we mixed are identified by combining the names of the pair of colors between which each stands, using the nearest primary as an adjective and the nearest secondary as a noun. These are consequently called blue-green, yellow-green, yellow-orange, red-orange, red-purple, and blue-purple. It will be noticed that although there is a distinctive name for each color, the nomenclature suggests a special relationship among the mixed colors; there is only one red, one blue, and one yellow, but three colors are identified as green, three as orange, and three as purple. The names of the secondary colors are often used generically, so that *green* is applied to the entire range of colors from blue to yellow, that is, to all colors prepared by mixing blue and

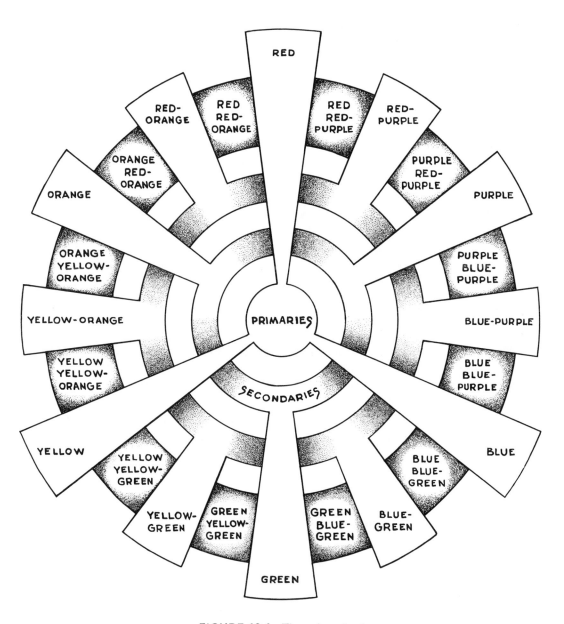

FIGURE 10.1   The color wheel.

yellow in any proportions. If it is necessary to indicate that only the half-and-half mixture is intended, the term *central green* can be used.

Carrying the mixing pattern one step further would result in twelve additional colors, each one placed halfway between two of the colors already on the wheel. There are no standard names for these added mixes, but they can be clearly (although somewhat clumsily) identified by an extension of the traditional nomenclature, again combining the names of the adjacent colors to form yellow yellow-green, yellow yellow-orange, orange yellow-orange, orange red-orange, red red-orange, red red-purple, purple red-purple, purple blue-purple, blue blue-purple, blue blue-green, green blue-green, and green yellow-green.

This mixing process could be carried on ad infinitum, producing any number of intermediate mixes desired. As the added colors become more and more alike, we would finally reach the point where they could no longer be distinguished by eye, and the color wheel would seem continuous, with the colors flowing around it smoothly, blending from red through the purples to blue, then through the greens to yellow, and finally through the oranges back to red. The more steps there are on the color wheel the more accurately we could use it to find a color matching a prescribed sample. However, as steps are added the wheel becomes more complex and difficult to use. As with a ruler, if we divide each inch into thirty-seconds or sixty-fourths we will be able to match the dimensions of something we measure more precisely than if the ruler is marked only in quarter-inches, but to have smaller divisions than we actually need complicates rather than facilitates making measurements.

Most discussions of color describe a 12-step color wheel; experience suggests that a 24-step wheel is more useful in matching colors for scenery, but that more divisions complicate its use rather than making it easier. Even so, the steps in an actual or imagined color wheel should be thought of simply as measuring points rather than restrictions, and we can freely mix colors which would fall between them, just as in using a ruler we can, if we like, cut lengths of lumber which fall between the points marked on the ruler.

ANALYZING COLOR SAMPLES

The first step in matching a color sample is to determine whether it is a primary or secondary (using "secondary" to refer to the entire group of mixed colors). In nearly all cases the designer's sample will fall in one of the secondary areas. The next step is to determine which secondary. Let us suppose that a particular paint sample is one of the greens. It should then be checked against the color wheel (either an actual wheel or an imagined one) to determine whether it is central green or not. If it is not a central green, the next question is to decide on which side of the center point it falls, that is, whether it is a yellow-green or one of the blue-greens.

It will be seen that this process of identification involves a steady narrowing of the area of the color wheel considered. It is continued until the precise position of the paint sample on the color wheel has been determined; if it does not exactly match one of the steps, then the two steps between which it would lie are identified. Let us suppose that in this example the green is identified as lying between blue-green and green blue-green.

BLACK AND WHITE

In order to make this identification, it will be necessary to ignore any admixtures of black and white in the color sample. Especially if large quantities of black have been added to darken the color, or if the sample is a pastel color with a heavy admixture of white, that may be difficult. Continued experience in color mixing will develop the painter's skill in this assessment, although at first he may find it difficult to subtract the admixtures in imagination and focus only on the pure color-wheel hues.

Visualizing the color minus its black content may be especially difficult in one curious instance—brown. All colors may be darkened by the addition of black, and the shades thus produced are usually given the name of the basic pigment (dark blue, dark green, dark red, etc.). However, when black is added to orange the resulting mixture is given, in English, the distinctive name of brown. Not all languages have a matching term (Latin, for instance, has no word for brown). Perhaps because of this linguistic quirk, it is difficult for us to see brown as what in fact it is, darkened orange. Oranges range throughout a full third of the color wheel, from red red-orange to yellow yellow-orange, and the various oranges are matched by related browns. In addition, white may be added to brown in any quantity, producing tints such as straw, tan, or eggshell.

When the matching mix is prepared, of course black and white must be added to the primaries in the proper proportions, and so having identified the position of the sample on the color wheel the painter must reverse his pattern of attention, focusing on the quantities of black and white present in the paint sample.

Like the color-wheel primaries, white cannot be mixed from other pigments, but must be found in nature. The white pigment used for traditional scene paint is simply chalk dust, dug out of chalk cliffs and prepared by grinding it to powder and sifting it. Even though white is unmixable, it is not usually called a primary because it does not fit on the color wheel.[1]

---

1. It should be mentioned that there are two methods of mixing color, one applicable to pigments and combinations of colored plastics used as filters for spotlights, the other used in mixing colored lights. Not only are the primaries different for the two methods, but many of the rules are different. For example, white light can be readily produced by mixing colored lights, although white pigment cannot be mixed from colored pigments. The process of mixing colored light is called *additive,* the mixture of pigments is called *subtractive.* Lighting crews in the theater are concerned with both methods, but paint for scenery is mixed by the subtractive method (with one exception—spattering), so that this discussion is limited to the subtractive procedure.

MIXING BLACK

The student may have wondered why the formula for color given at the beginning of this discussion specified only four variables, black, white, and two primaries. Why not the third primary? The reason is that the three primaries mixed in equal quantities produce black, so that if all three are combined in preparing a paint sample, at least one of them will be changed to black, and will appear in the formula as part of the quantity of black which the paint contains.

MIXING TO SAMPLE

Having identified the position of the color sample on the color wheel, and having estimated the percentages of black and white which it contains, the painter is ready to match it by mixing the scene paint. Theoretically, it would be simplest to mix from the four basic colors, red, yellow, blue, and white (perhaps with the addition of black). In practice, the painter is more likely to start with prepared paints which are already complex mixtures. However, it may be clearer to describe first the theoretically simpler

Let us assume that the sample supplied by the designer has been identified as falling between green blue-green and blue-green on the color wheel, that it contains a very small quantity of black, and a large amount of white, constituting about a third of the total mixture.

If he is working from black, white, and the primary colors alone, the painter would begin by mixing blue and yellow to match the color-wheel position of the sample. Since the color lies between central green and blue on the color wheel, it will be necessary to use somewhat more blue than yellow. When the mixture has been matched as closely as possible to the color-wheel position which he has determined, the painter begins to add white, starting with less than he needs and cautiously increasing the amount until it seems to match the sample. Finally black is added in small quantities until a very close approximation is achieved.

Since the paint will change color as it dries, as the mixture comes closer and closer to the sample the painter should spread a little on a sheet of paper and force-dry it over a candle or hot-plate. The paint should be spread all the way out to the edge of the paper so that when it is dry it can be laid across the designer's sample and the two colors compared side by side. Any differences should be analyzed (perhaps there is not quite enough black in the mixture) and more of the short pigment added. When it has been thoroughly stirred, another sample should be force-dried and again compared with the designer's color. In this way, matching can be carried out to any degree of accuracy.

CONTAMINATION

The procedure described is theoretically sound, but it contains one error of great practical significance. It assumes that pure primary pigments are available, and in fact they are so rare that in most scene shops not a single container of an uncontaminated primary will be found in stock. (Manufacturers often identify their paints as "primary" or "spectrum," a synonymous term, but such labels should be disregarded, since they are almost never accurate.) As a result, the painter must assess the contaminations or intermixtures of colors in the paints which he has in stock, and adjust his formula to allow for them.

Contaminations of primaries as supplied by the manufacturers are of two types: a pigment labeled primary may contain a small quantity of a second primary, or it may contain an admixture of black or white (seldom both). Occasionally, the second primary may be present in such small amount as to be unnoticeable, and it might seem that it could therefore be ignored. However, the contaminating primary may become strikingly visible when the paint is mixed with other colors.

The reason for that is the operation of the formula for mixing black. Let us suppose that we need to mix a clear yellow-green, and that we combine a blue and a yellow which are apparently pure primaries but which contain an unnoticeable quantity of red. For illustration, let us suppose that the total amount of red present in a bucket of the two colors equals one spoonful. Since equal quantities of the three primaries produce black, the single spoonful of red will combine with one spoonful of the yellow and one spoonful of the blue to produce three spoonfuls of black. The original contaminant, when tripled, may become painfully visible, and may make it impossible ever to mix the clear yellow-green at which we are aiming.

An actual example of unexpected contamination occurred in preparing paint for a set for Sheridan's *The Rivals.* A false proscenium had been designed, which was to be painted a wine red (that is, a red red-purple). Unfortunately, the supposed primary red was strongly contaminated with yellow, with the result that the addition of purple produced an unacceptable brown. The problem was not discovered until too late to place an emergency order, so that it was necessary to abandon the wine color and substitute blue, an alteration which the director found somewhat distressing.

THE USE OF NEAR-PRIMARIES

The solution to this problem is to purposely choose colors near the primaries (since the pure primaries are unobtainable), but contaminated in such a way as not to disturb the mixture we are trying to achieve. In making yellow-green, we would choose a yellow with a slight blue contamination and a blue with a slight yellow contamination; these would then combine to produce a clear yellow-green. It might be thought that these colors also could have invisible red admixtures; however, even if the blue (with a touch of yellow) does contain some red, it will already have combined with the other two colors to produce black. If the black element is so minute as to be invisible, it will become no more visible when the colors are mixed, and in fact is more likely to be diluted by the addition of the (faintly greenish) yellow. In any case, it will not suddenly multiply.

> The ability to remove a color from a mixture by turning it to black can be used to extend a short supply of paint, if the final color is intended to include a considerable quantity of black. One set for a production of *Macbeth* required large quantities of very dark red—more red than the total supply on hand. However, there was a good deal of purple and a little orange in stock. The painters multiplied the supply of red paint by mixing some of the orange with the purple, just enough to neutralize the blue in the purple by turning it to black, leaving the red in the purple unaltered. The resulting color was thus a pure red combined with a heavy quantity of black. Mixing this with the supply of red on hand produced exactly the color needed. The same procedure could be used to increase the quantity of any color so long as the added black is acceptable.

In practical mixing, then, we tend to avoid the actual primaries, and to use instead secondaries which are so close to the primaries as to be almost indistinguishable, but which would nevertheless stand at one side of them on the color wheel.

The theoretical primaries are thus replaced in actual practice by six colors, a very red red-orange, an extreme red red-purple, a blue blue-purple, a blue blue-green, a yellow yellow-green, and a yellow yellow-orange, each one as close to the adjacent primary as possible.

PSYCHOLOGICAL TEMPERATURE

At these points on the color wheel, it may be difficult even for an experienced worker to visualize the contaminants in terms of added primaries. Rather, they can be identified by a peculiar characteristic of color—its psychological temperature. It is a familiar part of color theory that colors seem to differ in warmth (colors also differ in actual temperature, but the differences do not match the psychological impressions). Colors are traditionally divided into warm and cool groups. There is not total agreement on the line between the two groups, but the oranges are generally identified as warm, and the greens as cool. Of the primaries, red is warmest, blue coolest, and yellow in between. Even a little admixture of a second primary produces a noticeable difference in its psychological temperature, so that if a true primary red were divided into two parts, and a very small quantity of yellow mixed with one and an equal quantity of blue mixed with the other, one of the two mixes would seem clearly warmer than the other.

In using near-primaries as bases for mixing, the painter can therefore most easily guide his choice by noticing differences in psychological temperature, as indicated in the following table.

Psychological Temperature		Basic Primary	Minute Admixture
Cool Red	=	Red	+ Blue (or Purple)
Warm Red	=	Red	+ Yellow (or Orange)
Cool Blue	=	Blue	+ Yellow (or Green)
Warm Blue	=	Blue	+ Red (or Purple)
Cool Yellow	=	Yellow	+ Blue (or Green)
Warm Yellow	=	Yellow	+ Red (or Orange)

BLACK AND WHITE CONTAMINATION

Black and white contaminents are less troublesome. Almost all colors specified by the designer will include some of both black and white, so that starting a mix with colors in which they are already present will not usually interfere with the match. Pigments vary greatly in cost. In particular, the cheapest pigment (other than white) available in traditional scene paint costs from six to ten times as much as whiting. As a result, manufacturers often mix black or white into paint to reduce the cost, where they feel the additions will not be noticed. Yellow is especially likely to be contaminated with white, and blue or purple with black.

> If more yellow paint is needed than is available in stock, a true yellow which has not already been adulterated can be stretched by adding from a third to half a gallon of white paint to each gallon of yellow. There will be some loss of brilliance, which can be partly restored by mixing in a very little orange. If a pure and vivid yellow is needed, this method will not work, but for most purposes the difference in effect is not likely to be noticeable.

231

Even these contaminations may occasionally cause trouble, especially if the painter is attempting to mix black. Theoretically, one quart of primary yellow mixed with two quarts of central purple will produce three quarts of black. But if the yellow contains an admixture of white, it will combine with the black to produce not black but grey. Consequently, black paint for scenery is usually bought in true color, although with care an acceptable black can be mixed from other colors, and the formula for mixing black can be used to darken mixes which already contain some white.

It should be noted that each drop of a primary added to its matching secondary produces three drops of black, so that if paint is darkened by adding a primary, it must be done very cautiously. Pairs of primaries and secondaries which mix to form black are called *complementaries.* A comparison of the formula for black with the color wheel will demonstrate that there are three sets of complementary colors, red and green, blue and orange, and yellow and purple.

A MODIFIED PROCEDURE

Two procedures for mixing paint have been described, one based on theoretical primaries, the other using six near-primaries, in both cases with the addition of white and (for convenience) black. It is perfectly possible to mix any colors except pure primaries by these methods. However, two practical considerations result in a modification of these procedures.

One is cost. The price of paint depends on many factors, including the scarcity of the materials used to make the pigment and the complexity of the manufacturing processes needed to prepare it for use in painting. It is the availability of chalk and the simplicity of its preparation which explain why whiting is so much cheaper than other paints. Although there are many exceptions, in general the clearer and brighter colors are significantly more expensive than the duller colors, particularly the earth colors. It is easy to mix a dull brown by combining orange, yellow, black, and white in the proper proportions, but it is much cheaper to start with one of the ready-prepared earth colors, and then alter it to the shade desired by the addition of only a small quantity of the more expensive colors.

Furthermore, if a color at a point on the wheel is matched by starting with colors at a considerable distance from it, they must be moved toward the hue desired by cautious mixing, at some cost in time. In practice, then, the painter is more likely to start his mixture by identifying the paint on hand which is closest to the color desired, and then to alter it by small additions. In principle, this method follows the same rules which have been described. In practice, the use of paints which are themselves complex mixtures greatly complicates the analysis and the choice of colors needed to match the sample. Nevertheless, the beginning painter should train himself to use his paint as economically as possible, not only with regard to cost in money but also in the expenditure of time. At first he will have to run through the theory of color mixing consciously as he analyzes the sample and chooses colors from stock, but with a little experience the decisions will become easier and can be made quickly and automatically.

RECORDING FORMULAS

In matching a color, including the designer's sample, it is important to assess the rate of change producing by successive additions of pigments. This can be done most easily by keeping a sample of the color produced by each addition. Before mixing has started, a small spot of each color to be used in the first trial mixture should be painted at the edge of a sheet of white paper, and the manufacturer's name for the color written below it. The first mixture should be painted on in the same way. As each pigment is added, the paint should be thoroughly stirred, and a sample of the new mix added to the paper, with a note identifying the new pigment. Although this may seem like busy work, it is very easy to forget what colors have been used, and a few minutes taken to jot down the formulas may save more than an hour of work. These records should be kept until the scenery is painted, so that if it should be necessary to mix additional paint it will be easy to identify the basic pigments used (Figure 10.2).

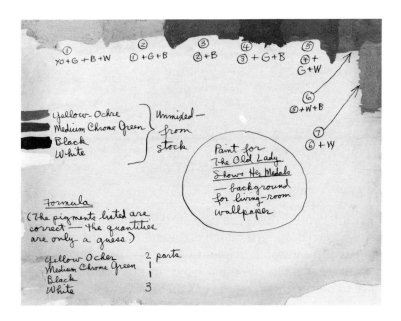

FIGURE 10.2   A color–mixing record sheet.

When a series of paint samples are applied to the edge of a piece of paper to test the progress of mixing, it is easier to compare them if each sample is painted on so that it slightly overlaps the previous one. The colors can then be judged side by side, without an intervening strip of white paper.

As the successive mixes move closer and closer to the color desired, the spots of paint around the edge of the paper will form a smooth progression, starting with the original unmixed colors and changing in the direction of the designer's sample. At first, pigments should be added cautiously. Each new mix should be evaluated not only to make sure that the alteration is in the right direction, but to identify what part of the distance the color has been moved. If for instance a small quantity of blue has been added, observation may demonstrate that five or ten times as much may be safely poured in. As the mixture approaches the sample, additions should be made more cautiously.

When one color heavily predominates, the other colors should be added to it. For example, in mixing pink, red should be added to white rather than the reverse. If this rule is violated it may be impossible to achieve the correct mix without flooding the color with great quantities of the predominant pigment, and winding up with many times as much paint as is actually needed.

It is most efficient to mix only a very small quantity of paint when first matching the designer's sample, not more than a cupful or two. This trial mixture will identify the pigments which must be combined, and will give some indication of their proportions. The entire amount needed for the set can then be mixed without waste of time or paint.

QUANTITY

Running out of paint two-thirds of the way through the job may cause serious delays. If additional paint is mixed, it must match precisely, or the difference will be visible to the audience, and as the allowable margin of error narrows, the length of time needed for mixing increases greatly. On the other hand, to mix vast quantities of paint, much of which will have to be discarded, results in expensive waste.

When a large quantity of paint of a single color must be mixed, there may be no container large enough for the entire amount, so that it must be prepared as three or four separate mixes, in different buckets. However, they are certain to vary slightly in color, and must be intermixed to make the entire supply uniform. Assuming that three bucketfuls must be combined, take two clean buckets and pour a third of one bucketful into each, thus dividing the mix into three equal parts (counting the original container). Then take a second full bucket and add a third of it to each of the partially filled containers, and finally add a third of the last bucket to each of the new containers. When the three buckets of paint have been thoroughly stirred, any differences in color should be indetectable.

Ideally, about a third of a bucket of paint should be left over after the scenery has been painted. Unfortunately, the area a particular quantity of paint will cover varies so much that it is impossible to give a usable formula; as a very approximate guide, seven or eight gallons of paint (measured after thinning to brushing consistency) should cover all the walls of an ordinary box set. Experience and observation in their own scene shop will help the painters estimate more accurately the amount of paint required.

If a special mix of paint runs out before all the flats have been covered and an additional quantity must be mixed to match it, do not start painting with the new mix in the middle of a flat or wall. Instead, go back and repaint so that the two mixes meet at a corner of the set; any difference in color will then be unnoticeable.

If a set requires many different paint mixes, even a well stocked scene shop may run out of containers. Some space can be saved by adding only enough water to the paint to facilitate mixing; when it is to be used, only the quantity immediately needed is poured out and thinned to brushing consistency. If some of the thinned paint is left after the day's work it can be poured into the thicker mix.

Left-over paint especially mixed for a set should be labeled and saved until the end of the last performance. If the scenery is damaged—a glass of water accidentally spilled on a flat, the edge of a door unit smudged with dirt when the set is assembled— the defect can be retouched without having to spend hours remixing to match the original color. It should be an inviolable rule in every scene shop that no specially mixed paint be used for any purpose except the intended one, and the label not only helps identify the mix, but also serves as a hands-off notice. It is distressing to discover that someone has snatched up a special mix and used it to paint a table or a play poster, with the result that there is not quite enough left for finishing the job it was mixed for.

If more paint must be mixed, it should be put in a fresh bucket, so that it can be compared with what is left of the original mix. When a satisfactory match has been achieved, the paint left over from the first mix can be added to it.

> When more of a special color must be mixed, an extremely accurate method of testing whether the new mix matches the old is to dribble a little of one mix into the other. The dribbled paint will float on the surface, and even a slight difference in color will be clearly visible.

SPOILAGE

Casein paint will stay fresh indefinitely in unopened cans. Once they have been opened, the paint may begin to spoil. The pigments used in traditional scene paint will not deteriorate even when mixed with water, but the animal glue will begin to rot within a couple of days. Spoilage can be delayed somewhat if a small quantity of a germicide such as carbolic acid is added. A better method is to prepare the complete mix for each color using only pigment and water. Since the glue alters the color somewhat, it will be necessary to add glue to a small quantity of the mix for the final color tests. The paint is then stored in buckets as a thick pigment-water mix, and quantities are taken out and glued and further thinned as needed for immediate use.

Left-over paint to which glue has not been added can be allowed to dry thoroughly and returned to stock. It may solidify slightly, but can easily be broken up by pounding it with a hammer. Even if the color is unsuited for use in a later show, it can be used to weaken glue or to tint the mixture used to size flats. If left-over casein paint in the thicker mix has a usable color it may be worthwhile to try to save it, especially if it might be used for the next show, but even if it is returned to paint cans and kept tightly closed it may have developed a strong enough odor to be unusable later. Paint mixed to brushing consistency should be thrown out.

> Special mixes of color left over from one show may be difficult to incorporate in the paint mixed for the next show because the color schemes are unrelated. However, much of the paint can be salvaged. All the remainders should be mixed together to form a single color. Fresh paint in the complementary color should then

be added in the right quantity to neutralize the color of the mix (that is, to turn the color-wheel hues to black). The result will be one of the greys, its lightness depending on the amount of white in the original mixes. Since most of the new mixes will probably include some grey, this can be used for that purpose. If the grey needed is darker or lighter, the salvaged paint can be altered by adding black or white.

Paint which must be left overnight will lose some of its water, and must be further diluted when it is used again. This is especially true of the thicker mixes, which may dry to a hard layer on the top of the bucket. It should be standard procedure at the end of each day's painting to consolidate all the paint of a single color into as few containers as possible, and then to gently pour about half a cup of water into each one. This will float on the surface of the paint and keep it moist, and will have disappeared overnight, so that the paint should be about the right consistency for use the next day. The small quantities of paint left over after the work has been finished, which are saved for touch-ups in case the set should be damaged, can be put in jars or empty paint cans and tightly sealed. They will remain moist throughout the run of the show, after which they can be discarded.

LABELING

Often a set will require that several groups of closely related colors be mixed. For instance, as many as a dozen browns might be used for painting a stone wall, and perhaps two or three more for use on tree trunks, and the foliage might involve the use of a half dozen greens. A great deal of time will be lost if the painters must puzzle over which shade to use for a particular area of the set, and the accidental use of the wrong color might make it necessary to spend hours in repainting. Efficiency can be greatly increased by taking a few minutes to label the various containers, not only those in which the thick major supply is stored but also each bucket as it is prepared for immediate use. The most convenient way to label is to press a strip of masking tape on the side of each bucket or can and print the identification on it with a felt pen. If the container is emptied and used for a second color, the tape can be taken off and a fresh label put on. Labels should be put on the sides of the containers, not the lids. It is very easy for lids to be removed or switched, so that their labels would be inaccurate.

> When specially mixed colors are stored in the cans in which paint was purchased, the manufacturer's labels should be torn off, to prevent misidentification and misuse of the paint.

The identification can be done by describing the use for the particular mix of paint: "tree trunk base," "tree trunk highlight," "distant foliage dark," "distant foliage light." An alternative method is to number each color, perhaps with the addition of general names: "brown 1," "brown 2," "blue 1," etc. This method requires that a master list be prepared identifying how each mix is to be used; often such a list will have been supplied by the designer. The longer labels take a little more time to prepare, but can be used more easily by the painters. The numbered labels are especially useful if areas on the flats must be marked. For instance, if a complicated wallpaper pattern is laid out on the flats, the work can be speeded up by marking all of the areas to be painted with a particular color by writing a code designation in each in light chalk: "G 1," "P 3," "R 1," "R 4," (green 1, purple 3, red 1, red 4). The painters can then choose the colors to be used by checking the similar labels on the containers, and are unlikely to make mistakes.

> When hammering the lid back on a paint can, the paint can be prevented from spattering by covering the top with an unfolded newspaper or a good-sized scrap of canvas, and pounding on top of the paper or cloth.

There are so many variables in the preparation and use of scene paint that it is impossible to give precise formulas which can be rigidly followed. Skilled scene painters operate by maintaining a constant alertness to how the work is going—whether the paint covers adequately, whether it brushes at normal speed, whether the colors remain true as the paint is applied, and especially whether the general effect specified by the designer is achieved. They watch steadily for any problems or difficulties, and then correct them as soon as they appear. Since almost all of the visible surface of a set is covered with paint, the ability to mix colors accurately and apply them effectively and economically is a very important part of the set worker's skill.

11

Base
Painting and Texturing

Nearly all elements of scenery are covered with a solid coat of paint, and then one or more coats of other colors are applied over the first, covering only part of the surface. The first coat of paint applied is called the *base coat.*

PRIMING

Raw surfaces may have to be prepared to receive paint before the base coat is applied. This is especially true of flats, which must be primed so that the fabric is shrunk tight and the threads coated and filled. The priming coat is essentially a very thin layer of paint. The water shrinks the canvas, and the glue and pigment fill the pores to facilitate applying the base coat. The flats can be stood vertically or laid horizontally, and covered quickly with a thoroughly wet brush. Any type of brush can be used, but the special priming brushes are large and make the work go faster. The color of paint used for priming is not significant, although it should not contrast so vividly with the base coat that it will be difficult to hide. Priming is an ideal way to use left-over paint, and small quantities can be thrown together without worrying about the color of the final mixture. Usually it is better to keep the priming color rather light, and whiting or white casein paint can be added if the discarded paint produces a vivid or dark mix.

THE BASE COAT

The base coat is applied after the prime coat has dried. For the base coat also the flats can be placed horizontally or vertically, in a paint frame or against the wall of the scene shop.

"Laying-in" brushes are used for the base coat. They are flat brushes about four or five inches wide, similar to the priming brushes but smaller and lighter. The paint can also be applied with a compressed-air spray with a considerable saving of time, although the coat of paint is thinner than if it is brushed on. Casein paint sprays well. Traditional scene paint is ground less finely and uniformly and tends to clog the nozzle.

Brush marks will not entirely level out of traditional scene paint, so that it dries with a somewhat striated surface. That is not objectionable, except that if all the striations run in the same direction different amounts of light will be reflected from individual flats. Consequently, it is recommended that the paint be applied in cross strokes of the brush, forming a series of overlapping X's. This is not necessary for the thinner casein paint, which can be brushed in any direction and can consequently be applied a little faster.

After finishing a base coat, it is wise to check the flat to make sure that no spots have been missed. These are called *holidays,* an old term of obscure origin, but first adopted by house painters. It has the ring of American humor—they are areas where the painter took time off from work.

The manufacture of paint has been revolutionized in recent decades. Correct application of paints available fifty years ago required repeated brushing. This is unnecessary with most modern paints, and must not be done with traditional scene paint. Base coats should be applied with a thoroughly wet brush. If the workers can resist their instinctive tendency to wipe the brush off on the edge of the paint container, the work will go much faster. Simply dipping in and out and brushing away is undeniably messier, but it is the preferred method. For detail painting, much more brushing with a drier brush may be necessary, and wiping the brush after each dip may be desirable.

When painting from a can with a sunken rim, either with oil-based or water-based paint, the paint can be kept from collecting in the groove if the brush is wiped against the edge farthest from the painter rather than against the nearest edge.

Overbrushing casein paint only wastes time, but traditional scene paint is so soluble that if a previously painted flat is covered with a different color even moderate brushing melts the original coat, which will begin to mix with the new paint and alter its color. The rule is that no spot should be brushed more than three times (right, left, and back). If some of the first coat is picked up, the spot should be left to dry thoroughly, and then the area repainted, preferably with a single brush stroke. Further application of the new paint while the surface is wet will only pick up more of the original paint and spread the discoloration.

PUDDLING

Most often the base coat is applied as a solid color, but for special effects two or more colors may be combined by a technique called *puddling*.[1] If two colors are used, a small area of irregular shape is first painted with one of the colors, and while the paint is still wet a similar area of the second color is laid beside it and the edges between the two areas blended by brushing across the joint. Any number of colors can be combined, although usually they will be closely related variations of the same basic mix. This technique can be used for various purposes, for example in painting a stone wall. Four or five shades of brown might be puddled across the surface of the flat, and then, after the paint has dried, details such as mortar lines, shadows, and highlights could be added with smaller brushes. The puddled coat suggests the kind of variation in color to be found in natural stone. Sometimes puddling in cool shades of green is used as a base for foliage, representing the more distant and shadowed leaves; the nearer leaf shapes are then painted over it, allowing the base to show through as an indistinct mass of foliage.

Occasionally, the base coat for an entire flat will be blended by mixing two related shades of the same color. For instance a flat intended to represent the sky as seen through a window might be painted with a moderately dark blue at the top and a light blue at the bottom, the blending being carried all the way across the flat from one end to the other. Blending techniques are described in chapter 12.

Almost always one or more further coats of paint are applied over the base coat, but not covering the entire surface of the flat. These are of two types—applied patterns (wallpaper designs, foliage, painted molding, etc.), and texturing of various types.

---

1. This term is used for various painting techniques, some of which are quite different from the one described here.

SPATTERING

One method of texturing is so common as to be standard. It is called *spattering*. Although other techniques may occasionally be substituted for it, it may be used either alone or as a supplement to other methods of texturing, and it is used so frequently that it would be possible that all of the scenic elements for an entire season's shows would be spattered. Consequently, skill in spattering is essential for a mastery of stagecraft.

In this technique, the tips of the bristles of a laying-in brush are dipped into very thin scene paint and the brush is swung toward the flat or other scenic element and stopped with a sudden snap of the wrist. The bristles continue to swing down, and as they stop spots of paint fly out and fall on the surface of the scenery.

Within certain limits, spattering is subject to fairly delicate control: the placement of the spattered paint, the amount of spatter deposited, the smoothness with which it is applied, and the size of the individual spots of paint can all be varied. Four factors determine the size of the spots. They are largest when the paint is thick, when the brush is heavily loaded with paint, when it is swung hard, and when it is stopped close to the surface of the flat. Spatter can be applied so finely that the dots are indistinguishable from the first row of the audience, or so coarsely that the individual dots are visible from the back row.

The coat of spatter can be spread uniformly across the surface of the scenery, or it can be applied heavily in one area and faded smoothly out beyond it. Usually each flat is spattered in two colors, the darker being applied heavily at the top of the flat and faded smoothly to the bottom, and the lighter applied heavily at the bottom and faded smoothly toward the top.

THE FUNCTIONS OF SPATTERING

Spattering serves several purposes, the most important of which is that a spattered flat has a vibrancy and interest which are lacking in a flat painted solid, even though the two flats are apparently of the same color. A second function which is of great practical value is that spatter conceals defects to an astonishing degree. If a flat has been patched, the edges of the tear will be clearly visible at a distance after the application of the base coat; when it has been well spattered, they will have become completely invisible from the audience, and may be difficult to find even from a distance of three or four feet. A much less significant advantage of spattering is that it can be used to correct an error in the color of a base coat without remixing and repainting. Thus, if a set has been painted with a red which proves to be too bright, it can be toned by spattering it with black or dark brown.

242

Finally, spattering is of great value in providing texture. A brick or stone wall can be antiqued—aged and pitted—by spattering it, a wallpaper pattern made less vivid, foliage blended, or platforms spattered so as to look worn and dirty. Spatter can even be used to apply fairly well-defined patterns by applying the paint through a stencil (see Figure 8.16, showing a wallpaper pattern applied by spattering through a stencil). The technique is in fact so versatile that its total range of possibilities cannot be described, and ingenious set painters constantly invent adaptations to produce special effects.

The two-color spatter pattern, in which flats are faded from dark at the top to light at the bottom, serves to reinforce the stage lights, which are usually pointed toward the lower half of the set, and to focus the attention of the audience in the areas through which the actors move, because the eye tends to turn toward the lighter area (Figure 11.1). Since most flats are spattered this way, the method used will be described in detail.

FIGURE 11.1 Two flats spattered in the traditional light–to–dark pattern. They are shown reversed to emphasize the variation in spatter color.

The two main variables in spatter are the size of the individual dots and how fully the background is covered (Figure 11.2). Dot size is indicated by such terms as "extra large," "large," "medium," "fine," and "extra fine"; coverage is described as "solid," "extra heavy," "heavy," "medium," "light," "extra light," and "zero." The designer's specifications might read: "Medium spatter, fading from heavy at the top of the flats to zero at the bottom for dark spatter; light spatter reversed." If a more precise description is necessary, he will discuss it with the painters or the technical director, and may provide spatter samples or supervise the workers as they begin spattering.

243

SPATTER COLORS

Occasionally, the designer will rely on the spatter to provide significant color for the flats. If so, he will supply color samples. More often the spatter will be used to produce texture and reinforce the lighting without noticeably altering the base coat. In that case, the designer is likely to leave the choice of spatter colors to the set crew.

Two patterns of color can be used to produce this effect. Both involve altering quantities of the paint used for the base coat. In the first method, some of the base paint is put into two buckets, and a quantity of white mixed with one and black mixed with the other. The two mixes should be clearly different from the base, but clearly related to it. The light spatter should have about the color of the base coat in the center of a bright spotlight, the dark spatter should match the appearance of the base coat in shadow. Flats spattered with these two mixes will seem almost identical in color to unspattered flats painted with the base coat, but the spatter will still serve to create greater vibrancy, reinforce the lighting, and conceal defects.

The second method produces an even more vivid and interesting effect. Suppose that one of the greens has been used for the base coat. The formula will probably be made up of blue, yellow, black, and white. Quantities of the base paint are put into two containers, and a little blue and black mixed with one (the darker colors) and a little yellow and white mixed with the other, as before producing colors related to the base but distinct from it.

If the base coat is made from a single primary (for example red), then the colors mixed with it should be the secondaries which stand beside it on the color wheel. A little orange is added to one container of the base coat, and a little purple to the other. If desired, some white can be included with the orange (the lighter of the two secondaries), and some black with the purple.

Paint for spattering should be much thinner than for brushing. A quantity of water should be added, equal to from a third to half of the paint as mixed for brushing, although of course the thickness depends also on how large the spatter spots are intended to be.

THE APPLICATION OF SPATTER

In spattering, the flats are laid on the floor and both colors of paint carried in and set beside them. One laying-in brush is needed for each color, and they should be dipped in water and then squeezed dry before beginning to spatter.

Since the spatter pattern depends on how heavily the brush is loaded with paint, it is important that it be tested each time it is dipped into the bucket, before any paint is applied to the flat. The tips of the bristles should be dipped for about a half inch or an inch into the paint, and then the spatter pattern tested on a spare flat, sheets of

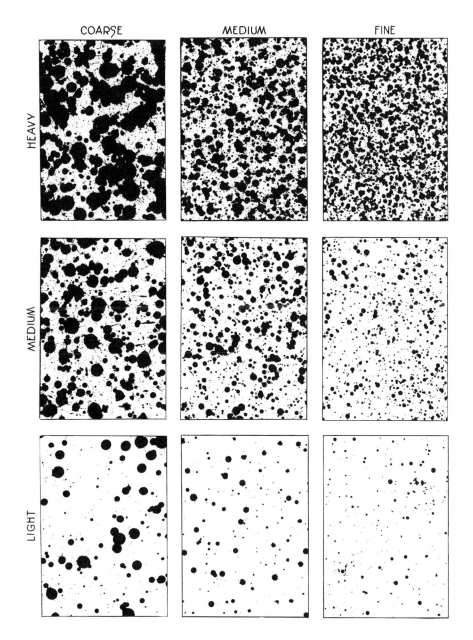

COARSE   MEDIUM   FINE

HEAVY

MEDIUM

LIGHT

FIGURE 11.2   The range of spatter. The rows vary in size of dots, the columns in the amount of paint spattered on the surface. The spatter is shown half size. (Spatter effects can also be studied by examining Figures 1.2, 1.6, 1.10, 1.11, 1.12, 8.2, 14.1, 14.2, 12.4, 12.12, and 12.24.)

newspaper, or a piece of cardboard. If the spatter is heavier than desired, the brush should be swung repeatedly to shake off some of the paint; when the size and distribution of the spots match what is intended for the set, the painter should move to one corner of the flat and begin to spatter it.

Although the distribution of the spatter can be controlled to some extent, it is not possible to produce a smooth coat with a single application. Any number of spatter coats may be applied, but the practical minimum is four. Each coat must therefore be spattered lightly, depositing at the most a fourth of the paint needed for the flat. The beginner's mistake of trying to apply all of the spatter in one or two coats is the major reason for ineffective spattering (Figure 11.3).

Let us suppose that the painter is applying the dark spatter. He should walk toward what will be the top end of the flat and, standing erect, swing the brush down, stopping it three or four feet above the surface of the flat, directing the swing so that the spatter will fall in a long vaguely rectangular area across the corner at an angle of 45°. He then moves along the stile, covering the flat with a series of swings at the same angle, and being careful to overlap the edges of adjacent spatter patterns so as to produce as smooth a coating as possible.

The spatter should be heaviest at the top end of the flat, and should fade almost to nothing at the bottom. As more and more paint flies out of the brush, the spatter automatically becomes steadily fainter. If it fades too slowly, the painter should gradually reduce the force of his swing. If the spatter fades too fast, he should increase the force of the swing as he moves toward the bottom of the flat. Often, the automatic fading produced by the gradual drying of the brush will match the pattern desired, and the swings can be kept uniform.

For a flat two or three feet wide it may be possible to cover the entire surface in this way. If the flat is wider, the painter should redip the brush and start again at the top of the flat, walking along the other stile, being careful to slant the spatter parallel with the first application.

If the flat is large, it may not be possible to carry the spatter all the way to the bottom with a single dip. Each time the brush is redipped, however, the spattering should be started again at the end of the flat, rather than in the middle where the paint gave out. The new spatter should be carried along more quickly until the end of the previously spattered area is reached, and then the remainder of the flat spattered at normal speed. To begin the second spatter in the center is almost certain to result in a large heavily spattered area which would destroy the smooth fade intended.

For the second coat, the entire process is repeated except that the spatter is thrown at right angles to the first, that is at 45° to the edges of the flat but in the opposite direction. For the third coat, the spatter is thrown directly across the flat parallel with the rails, and for the final coat the spatter is set vertically, parallel with the stiles. This is the most difficult coat to apply. For the dark spatter, the painter should begin by standing just beyond the top rail of the flat, facing the flat directly, and spatter the top quarter of the flat (for a distance of 3', if the flat is 12' high). As the spatter begins to fade, he raises his brush and throws it out beyond the 3' strip and

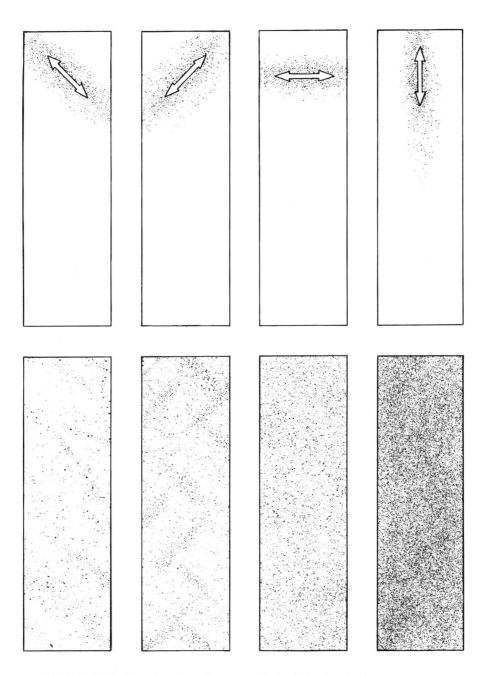

FIGURE 11.3 The direction of spatter. Each of the four basic coats necessary for smooth spatter is illustrated by two flats. *Top*, the spatter deposited by a single swing of the brush, the bottom flat entirely covered. *Bottom*, flats are spattered cumulatively, so that the last one has all four coats, spattered in different directions.

up to the horizontal center-line of the flat. He then moves around to the bottom rail of the flat, spatters from the center-line about 3' toward the bottom, and finally when the brush is nearly dry applies a faint coat to the bottom quarter of the surface.

It is easier to spatter a single flat than a large wall. However, with care and a little practice, spatter can be thrown in a controlled spray as far as ten or twelve feet, so that a wall of any size can be spattered.

Each added coat, applied at a new angle, tends to cancel out irregularities in the previous coats. It is possible in this way to produce a spatter which fades uniformly without visible variation from heavy at the top to light at the bottom. Nevertheless, if large deviations are left in a particular coat they may remain visible, so that each one should be applied as uniformly as is practical.

Exactly the same procedure is followed for the light spatter, except that it is applied heavily at the bottom of the flat and faded to faint at the top. Both colors should be carried all the way along the flat, to prevent sharp breaks in the pattern, but when finished the faint end of each spatter pattern should be unnoticeable.

If an area of the flat is accidentally spattered too heavily, the error can be corrected by taking a clean brush and spattering it with some of the base coat. This will cover up part of the excess spatter. This method cannot be used if the spatter is being applied over an area on which detail painting has been done (for instance, if a brick wall or a wallpaper area is being spattered). Correction of spatter in that case can be done only by laboriously painting out individual dots with a fine brush dipped in the background colors. Consequently, such surfaces should be spattered with great care.

The four coats specified for spattering each color are a minimum if the spatter is to be applied smoothly. Any number of additional coats may be applied, in order to deposit as much spatter on the flat as is desired. Each coat beyond the basic four should be angled according to the same pattern. Flats are usually allowed to dry before spattering. If they are spattered while wet, the drops of paint tend to blend with the background color and to lose definition. Occasionally, that effect may be exactly what is desired.

It is important that the spattering applied to each wall of a set match the other walls. After the first flat is spattered, it should be laid parallel with the next flat, far enough away so that the new spatter will not strike it. While the second flat is being spattered, it should be compared frequently with the first to make sure that the patterns are acceptably similar. Further flats should also be tested against the first one spattered, to prevent a gradual shift in the application.

Each worker tends to produce his own individual spatter pattern. Consequently, it is undesirable to have matching flats spattered by different crew members. However, it is possible to plan the work so that more than one person can take part. If two workers are available, one should apply all the light spatter and the other all the dark. If more than two painters are to be used, each one should apply all of a single coat. Thus, one person could spatter all of the flats with the first 45° coat, another apply the second coat at the opposite angle, a third the horizontal coat, and a fourth the vertical coat. The two colors can be spattered simultaneously, so that it is possible for eight people to work on a set at the same time.

Spattering is an inherently messy technique. Not only does the paint tend to stain the floor, but after the bristles have swung down and expelled the spots of paint on the flat they swing back and throw at least some paint upward. If the painter holds his brush in the natural position, directly in front of himself, the paint thrown out when the bristles rebound will fly directly at his face. A few experiences with a thoroughly peppered face and glasses coated with spots of paint will remind him to hold the brush slightly to the side, so that the paint flies over his shoulder.

A scene shop which does not have an area where spattering can be done freely without worrying about floor or walls is not adequately equipped. Nevertheless it is possible to control the mess with some care. Flats can be taken from stock and used to protect furniture or drapes, cardboard or paper can be laid over areas of the floor. As the painters develop skill, they will be able to control the distribution of the spatter so as to keep it off articles which must not be soiled. Needless to say, the most skillful painter cannot prevent some of the paint from getting on his clothing. Discarded shirts and jeans or dresses should always be used, as well as worn-out shoes. A protective smock is not sufficient.

Spattering is hard work, and a painter may be reminded of a long spatter session every time he moves his arm for a day or two. Nevertheless, it can be done with surprising speed. Two workers can spatter an entire set in a single evening. Spatter can be applied with a spray somewhat faster, and with considerably less muscle strain. An electric spray can be used, or even an ordinary hand-pumped garden spray. The range of effects possible with a spray is narrower than with a brush. The hand application provides subtler control and a broader choice of patterns.

MISCELLANEOUS TEXTURES

Although spattering is by far the commonest method of texturing a base coat, many other techniques are possible, each of which produces its own effect. Often they may be invented for a special purpose, but some of the more familiar will be described.

At the largest, the spots of paint thrown from a brush are about the size of the head of a spike. A feather-duster can be used to produce still larger spots. The tips of the feathers are dipped into paint, and then set down gently on the flat, leaving irregular blobs. The flat can be uniformly covered, or by altering the pressure and the amount of paint on the duster the coating can be faded from heavy to light.

Wadded cloth, paper towels, or newspaper can be dipped in paint and pressed against the flat, leaving an irregular mass of color with open areas between the wrinkles of the cloth or paper (Figures 11.4, 11.5). The material can be folded accordion-fashion, held loosely, and pressed down to print irregular parallel lines. This method, for instance, is effective in imitating certain kinds of bricks. The cloth can be twisted into a large roll, taped, sewn, or tied, and then dipped into paint and rolled across the surface of the flat, so that the wrinkles print. This method is especially effective in sug-

FIGURE 11.4   Texturing with wadded cloth or paper. The three rectangles were given a base coat of medium grey, and then the left two-thirds of each was overprinted with light grey, and the right two-thirds with dark grey. Tightly wadded cloth was used for printing the left rectangle, loosely wadded cloth for the center rectangle, and wadded newspaper for the right one. Buckets of paint in the two colors stand ready for use, *left*. The paint is brushed across one of the squares, *bottom*, and the wadded cloth or paper pressed into the paint and then used to print on the surface to be textured.

FIGURE 11.5   Texturing with folded cloth. The technique is similar to that illustrated in Figure 11.4, except that the cloth is folded in accordion pleats, so that it prints in parallel streaks, and only one color has been used for texturing in these examples. The rectangle, *upper right*, has been printed in opposite directions, producing the effect of a coarse weave. The rectangle, *center*, is being printed horizontally. The rectangle, *lower right*, has been printed horizontally, and then mortar added to suggest a section of a wall made from bricks with a striated surface.

gesting the pattern of bark on a tree trunk. Natural or synthetic sponges can be used similarly.

Natural sponges are often to be preferred for printing on flats, since synthetic sponges tend to have too uniform a texture (Figure 11.6). They can be improved by carefully tearing each sponge in two, and then using the torn rather than the cut surface for applying the scene paint.

Any of these methods can be used to print through stencils, or to provide an overall texture across an entire flat. For texturing, two colors are generally used, both related to the base coat. For example, a wallpaper area might be painted a medium pink, and then a dark and light pink printed over it. The resulting surface can be used by itself, or it could serve as a background for a repeated pattern.

Strips of cloth fastened to a dowel can be dipped in paint and then beaten against the flat. Various types of brushes have been used to produce special effects. A soft-bristled rectangular brush can be dipped in paint and set down gently on the flat to produce a kind of stipple. Even pushbrooms have been used similarly.

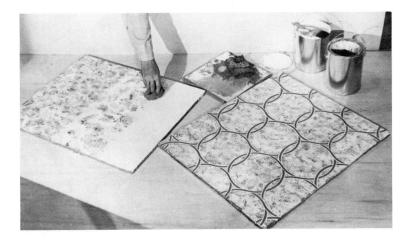

FIGURE 11.6 Texturing with sponges. The texture paint is brushed on a scrap of plywood or cardboard, *top center*, the sponge pressed against it and then printed on the surface to be textured. The rectangle, *left*, has been given a base coat of white; the left two–thirds has been textured in dark blue, and the left third also in light blue. The rectangle, *right*, has been textured in dark red and green, and white and gold circles have been painted across it to suggest a linoleum pattern.

DRY-BRUSHING

One texturing method, second in frequency of use only to spattering, is called *dry-brushing*. This involves painting with a brush which has so little paint in it that it makes a series of streaks rather than laying down a solid area of color. Dry-brushing can be done more easily with a specially prepared brush. The brush is pressed down on a wood surface at an angle so that the bristles are spread out, and they are cut off with a razor blade or a very sharp knife to form an irregular toothed edge (Figure 11.7).

Dry-brushing is used to produce striations, to simulate thatch or combed plywood. It can be used to suggest the texture of bricks or rough stone, to imitate bark, or to roughen lumber so as to make it look hand-hewn. Shadows and highlights on rough surfaces can be dry-brushed. If a flat is covered uniformly with two coats of dry-brushing, one vertical and the other horizontal, it will have the appearance of coarse cloth. An inventive painter will undoubtedly be able to think of other uses for this technique, of which these are only representative examples.

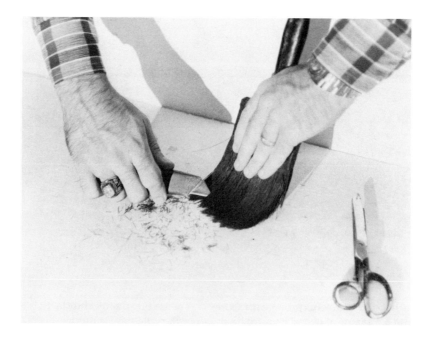

FIGURE 11.7 Trimming a brush for dry-brushing. Having done rough shaping with a pair of scissors, the painter forces the brush down so that the bristles are spread out, and cuts the tips off irregularly with a knife to produce a serrated edge.

GRAINING

Dry-brushing is most often used to simulate the grain of wood. This technique is centuries old, and in fact dry-brush graining was a highly respected profession in prerevolutionary America, and superb examples are still to be seen in some eighteenth-century homes. It is possible to simulate grain with completely convincing fidelity, including imitations of the grain of various species of wood. Usually such verisimilitude is unnecessary in the theater, and a moderately faithful imitation of grain is more than adequate.

Effective graining requires some analysis of the characteristics of actual wood. Grain is visible because the alternating layers of hard and soft wood are different in color. Most lumber has a background of soft wood, with streaks of darker hard wood running through it in a direction nearly parallel to the edges of the boards. Stresses during growth distort the grain, and the structure of the tree produces irregularities, for example where limbs branch out from the main trunk.

A minimum of four related colors are needed for effective graining, differing in darkness. The first step is to lay in the base coat with a variation of the puddling technique (Figure 11.8). If the colors are numbered from lightest to darkest, the base is

FIGURE 11.8 Graining: the base coat.

painted with numbers 1 and 3. They are painted in irregular streaks running generally in the direction of the board, and with the edges blurred but not fully blended. The grain is then painted on with color 4. If this is done while the base is still wet, the grain will be less distinct; if sharper grain lines are desired, the base should be allowed to dry.

A brush specially clipped for dry-brushing should be used. The bristles are dipped into the paint, and the brush pulled lightly across the surface to be grained, approximately parallel with the edges of the boards which are being represented. The brush should be passed along the entire length of the lumber in a single movement. It should be held lightly, not pressed down (Figure 11.9). At first some of the weight of the brush should be supported in the hand. As the painted stripes become fainter, the weight should be gradually released so that the hand is used only to hold the brush upright. Toward the end of the stroke it may be necessary to provide some slight pressure.

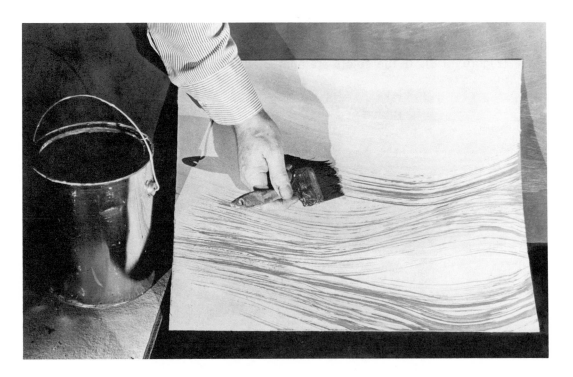

FIGURE 11.9   Graining: dry–brushing the dark grain.

The stroke should not be straight, but should curve slightly out of parallel with the board. Altering the angle of the brush will vary the width of the painted area. As it is moved along, the brush should be gradually turned so that it is moving sidewise, and then gradually turned back to paint a wider stripe.

After recharging the brush with paint, a second stroke should be laid beside the first, again carrying it the full length of the board. This stroke should be generally but not precisely parallel to the first. If the brush is swung so as to make a narrow line at the same point as the first stroke but away from it, a two-pointed opening will be left. A spot of dark paint should be dropped in the center of this area, the thumb pressed down on it and revolved. The result will be an imitation of a knot.

Because the brush prints more faintly as it becomes drier, the grain at one end of the board will be distinctly darker than at the other end. The brush should be recharged and the grain repainted, starting at the light end. The entire area is then regrained in the same way, using the second lightest paint (Figure 11.10).

FIGURE 11.10 Graining: the finished product. The light graining has been painted on, and then cracks added.

Graining produced in this way will amost always be satisfactory. If a still more accurate imitation is needed, and especially if a particular kind of wood must be represented (knotty pine, for example), it will be necessary to sketch in the grain lightly with charcoal or a sharpened piece of chalk, and paint it with small brushes, using examples of actual lumber as a guide. Cracks between boards can be marked with a snap line and painted with a fine brush or drawn with a felt-tip pen, perhaps with some added highlighting and shadow. Usually that degree of precision will not be necessary.

SCUMBLING

Dry-brushing is also used to blend or texture a base coat by applying the paint with a circular scrubbing motion; this technique is called *scumbling*. It can be used for shading or antiquing. For instance, a dark brown might be scumbled in the corners and around the edges of a panel; or the edge between two adjacent areas of color (say blue and green) might be blended by scumbling with blue out into the green area, gradually fading the amount of color deposited, and similarly scumbling from the green area into the blue (Figure 11.11).

GLAZING

Sometimes a very thin layer of paint is used to tone a base coat or to reduce contrast in a design. This is called *glazing*. Ordinary scene paint is used, but so heavily diluted that the pigment does not cover the surface, which remains visible as the major color of the flat. Glazing can be applied uniformly, or it can be varied to suggest antiquing, by applying successive coats to smaller and smaller areas.

BLEEDING

Some felt-pen inks bleed; that is, they soak through paint applied over them, and remain visible. Usually it is best to work only with nonbleeding inks. They can be identified by making a sample mark on scrap material, letting it dry, painting over it with a light color, and then checking to see whether the original mark is visible.

Bleeding paint can be identified by sticking a finger in the paint and then rinsing it off. If the color bleeds, it will leave a vivid stain on the finger which cannot be easily washed off.

A few scene paints also contain bleeding pigments, and since the colors which bleed vary from brand to brand they may show up accidentally in stock. They should not be used for permanent scenery which will have to be repainted for a later show. Even for scenery to be used only once they may create problems, since a mistake cannot be easily corrected.

FIGURE 11.11 Scumbling. Although the effect of scumbling is similar to that of blending, it differs in that the two colors of paint are not mixed together, but laid over each other. Scumbling can be carried out to any degree of smoothness, but usually it is left rougher than blending.

If it is necessary to apply a different color over bleeding paint, the bleeding can be stopped by first painting the area with a thinned mixture of white glue (1 part glue to 1 or 2 parts of water). After it has dried, the bleeding should be tested, and if it persists, a second coat of the glue mixture should be painted on.

THREE-DIMENSIONAL TEXTURING

Textures simulated with paint alone are accepted as real by the audience more frequently than might be expected, and painted simulations may save time, expense, and difficulty in shifting. Sometimes, however, the designer may choose to use actual textures. One method is to cover the flats or other scenic units with textured cloth. Tobacco cloth or burlap has a bold enough weave to be visible from the audience. Powders of various degrees of coarseness may be added to scene paint to produce texturing, including sawdust, papier-maché powder, or rough-ground foam plastic. Instead of mixing them with the paint, the scenery can be coated with glue, the powders spread on it, and loose particles shaken off after the glue dries; scene paint is then applied over the textured surface.

Such techniques are likely to be invented to produce special effects, rather than being standard. Two examples involving the use of corrugated cardboard will be given as illustrations of what can be done. A set for *Rosencrantz and Guildenstern Are Dead* included a large number of rectangular platforms. The director objected to the impression created by the hard edges, and asked if they could be made to seem less rigid. After some analysis, the problem was solved by spattering the edges heavily with black paint, faded to zero about six inches in on the surface. Strips of corrugated cardboard were then torn, about three inches wide, with one irregular edge and one straight edge. These were painted and drybrushed in two shades of a neutral color which contrasted with the rather brightly painted sides of the platforms. Each surface was edged with a cardboard strip, the irregular edges being turned toward the center of the area; the black spatter extended for two or three inches inside them to suggest antiquing (Figure 1.10). The alteration in the appearance of the set was striking, and the director liked it so well that he suggested the same technique be used for a later play.

One set for *The Tempest* included a very large expanse of wall intended to suggest a surface formed from rock ledges (Figure 7.6). It was not shaped, and the designer felt that paint alone would not produce a sufficiently three-dimensional effect. Long strips of corrugated cardboard were cut with somewhat irregular edges, varying from two to eight inches wide. These were glued to the flat surface with gaps between them, in an irregular but approximately horizontal arrangement, and then covered with strips of canvas, which were pressed tightly into the gaps between the cardboard. The entire surface was painted a base coat, the gapped areas painted dark to suggest shadows, and shadows and highlights added to the raised areas. In essence a large texture was produced in this way which, when reinforced with paint, produced exactly the effect of rock ledges which was intended.

BRUSHES

Many different types of brushes have been used in painting scenery, including even such oddities as scrub brushes, shoe brushes, and the push brooms and feather dusters which have already been mentioned. Most painting, however, is done with brushes specially designed for the theater. They are often divided into overlapping categories, including priming brushes, laying-in brushes, liners, and detail brushes; these vary primarily in the size of the bristle clusters. For most of them, the bristles are fastened in the shape of a flat rectangle, although some of the detail brushes hold them in a pencil-like cylindrical shape, which may form a point when they are wet.

Little attention is paid to the theoretical categories in actual use; the brushes are chosen for their adaptation to the job at hand, so that laying-in brushes may be used for priming, and vice versa, and lining brushes may be used for detail work if they will do the job satisfactorily. Obviously, the largest brush which can be used for a particular purpose will make the work go fastest, but the weight of the bigger brushes is significant, and for example most painters would choose laying-in brushes for spattering rather than primers simply to keep from having their arms worn out too quickly.

THE PLACEMENT OF FLATS

Probably most flats are laid on sawhorses for painting, but many workers prefer to stand them vertically, either against the wall or in a paint frame. Preferably a frame should be movable, so that the flat can be lowered into a slot in the floor in order to paint the top half. If the frame is fixed rigidly, or if the flats are simply leaned against the wall, the workers must climb up on some support in order to reach the top. Ladders can be used, but the preferred support is a rolling platform with two or three levels and provided with lock casters so that it will not shift while in use.

Painting with the flats horizontal has several disadvantages. The painters cannot step back and check on their work as a whole, the flats eat up an enormous amount of floor space (at least 14 square yards for a 4' × 12' flat, including space for the workers to stand), and especially for detail painting it may not be possible for the workers to reach the center of the flat, or to control the brush marks even if they can reach it. It is not unusual for several flats to be hinged together and dutchmanned to form an entire wall, with total dimensions as great as 12' × 20'; only the outer edges of such a unit could be painted if it were placed on sawhorses. The wall can be laid on the floor, and the center painting done by walking out along the stiles; each pair of stiles provides a walking surface about 5½" wide, and the toggles and diagonal braces may be used as auxiliary supports. Painters should slip off their shoes to avoid dirtying the flat, and can then teeter out along the stiles, squat down, and start painting in the center of the unit, moving backward along the stiles until the area remaining can be reached from outside the flat. Not only is this method uncomfortable, but an incautious step out on the unsupported canvas will punch it through, and even a momentary loss of balance may result in swinging the paint container and slopping paint out on the flat.

As a last objection, this method imposes an order on the painting (since the center must necessarily be painted first) which may not be the most convenient. Nevertheless, many set workers regularly do floor painting of large wall sections, and it is more often used than not for painting large drops, even in professional studios, since they are more difficult to hang vertically. Spattering is almost always done with the flats on the floor; the spatter can easily be thrown to the center of even a large wall, and the spots are likely to run down a vertical surface.

Flats laid horizontally eat up a great deal of floor space, and there is a temptation to stand each flat up against the wall out of the way as soon as it has been painted. However, it is important to wait until the paint has had time to set; it need not be bone dry, but it should not be stood upright while there is any chance that the paint will run, necessitating troublesome retouching.

If the scene shop is heated by forced air, a little investigation will identify one or two areas where the heat is blown most directly against the floor. If these are kept clear, flats can be laid in them as soon as painting has been finished and the paint will set in a few minutes so that they can be stood against the wall without damage.

Running and sagging of paint, as well as accidental dripping on the flat from the brush, are almost the only defects of vertical painting. All of the problems of painting on a horizontal surface are corrected by this method. For instance, it is easy to step back and check the work at a distance to make sure that widely separated parts match correctly. The choice of flat placement depends essentially on the tastes of the painters. Both arrangements are acceptable, and both are widely used.

12

Detail Painting

The painting methods which have been described in chapter 11 provide a textured basic coat, and they are used for almost all scenery, both flat and three-dimensional. More than half the scenic units require further painting, to represent wallpaper patterns, molding and paneling, trees and bushes, and a miscellany of other elements. These require special techniques, which can be generally identified as detail painting.

THE ORDER OF PAINTING

Except for the standard base and spatter coats, every paint job should be analyzed to determine the most efficient order for doing the painting. The decision should be guided by the ease and speed with which the details can be painted, rather than by broad rules such as "paint the background areas first, then the foreground details"—sometimes it is more efficient to leave the background to the last.

Ease of painting depends primarily on three factors: the shape of the areas, their size, and whether the paint is to be blended or laid in solid. Smooth blending requires free and fast brushing, and it is difficult to blend an area without carrying some of the paint out into the background. In that case, it is often more efficient to paint the blended sections first and then true up the edges by painting in the background.

It is easier to paint a curve from the concave side. The natural swing of the arm and wrist follows the circumference of a circle with the elbow at the center. Even if the curve is not an arc of a circle, only a little adjustment of the natural movement is required to follow it from the concave side. Painting a curve from the convex side requires that the arm first be stretched out away from the body, awkwardly pulled around toward the body, and then pushed out again. Inspection may make it possible to plan the work so that most of the painting can be done with the easier movement. For instance if a flat is to be hand painted with a wallpaper motif, it may be easiest to paint one element of the design first, running the paint out into the background area, and then painting the background up to the correct line, if the background can be reached from the concave side of the edge. The relation of a curve to the worker's position of course depends on where the worker must stand to reach the area, so that for the pattern described it might be most efficient to paint the motif first in one area of the flat and the background first in another area.

When adjacent areas of a flat, painted in different colors, are intended to meet in a sharp line, it is most efficient to paint the first area a little beyond the edge. When the paint has dried, the adjoining area is then painted precisely to the correct line. This prevents leaving even the smallest gap between the areas, but more importantly speeds up the work greatly, since the edge of the first area can be painted much more quickly, and the time necessary for precise work need be spent only on the edge of the second area.

The wetter a brush the wider the stripe of paint it lays down. If an area is painted with a precise edge until the brush has lost most of its paint, and the brush redipped and set down in the same position to continue the edge, the paint is likely to flow out beyond the line, producing a blob. Each time the brush has been recharged with paint, it should be started a little back from the edge of the area being painted, and then moved up in a curve tangent to the edge. This technique is unnecessary for broad painting, but for precise or detail painting it will save a good deal of the time would otherwise have to be spent in making corrections.

Especially with a complicated design, work can be speeded by marking each area which is to be painted with a particular color. This is especially true when similar areas are to be painted differently, for example where a lattice pattern requires that a blended shadow be painted on one side of the points at which the boards cross for alternate motifs, and in the reverse position for the other motifs. Marking should be done with ordinary chalk, which is least likely to discolor the paint. Arbitrary symbols can be used, although if different areas are being painted simultaneously by separate painters, the symbols must be distinctive. If desired, initials such as "H," "B," and "S" can be used for highlight, base, and shadow, or, if the containers of paint have been labeled by number, the code numbers can be used.

Another method is to dip a detail brush in the paint to be used and touch it to each area to be painted, leaving a small dot of color. This can be done only if the colors used are distinctly different. Not only does marking the areas save the painters from having to stop and analyze the design to determine which part of each motif must be painted a certain color, but the markings can be checked before the painting has progressed very far, and errors caught in time. One of the worst of small disasters encountered in the scene shop is to finish painting a flat and discover that two-thirds of the highlights have been painted in the wrong areas.

BLENDING

Blending takes considerably more time than applying solid color, but its special effect greatly alters the appearance of a set, and the ability to make a smooth blend is an essential part of the painter's skill.

The colors to be blended, the smoothness of the blend, and the space over which the blend must be carried will all be specified by the designer. Blending has already been mentioned in connection with puddling and graining, and the cross-faded application of two colors of spatter produces a blend, although the term is usually reserved for work done directly on the surface.

As an illustration of the process, let us imagine that a small flat, 5' wide and 8' high, is to be placed at a little distance behind a window to suggest the sky, and that the designer has specified that it is to be painted a medium blue at the top and a very light blue at the bottom, and that the surface fade smoothly from one color to the other. The first step is to paint the top half with the darker color and the bottom half with the lighter. The sharp edge between the two areas must be destroyed. While both areas are still wet, a clean damp brush is swung back and forth across the joint, then moved up a little way into the dark area and back down into the light. The brushing picks up some of each color of paint and mixes them together to produce an intermediate tint. Continuing a steady swing, the painter then moves the brush slowly up toward the top edge of the flat, picking up more and more of the darker mix, and brushing each area until the colors are smoothly blended before moving on.

At this point a little more than the upper half of the flat will have been blended. The painter then moves back down the flat, continuing to brush across the surface, carrying the work down past the center-line and on toward the bottom edge. It is important that the brush not be lifted from the flat at the top and blending be restarted at the center-line. The brush picks up paint from the surface as it is used, so that when the top edge is reached the paint on the brush will be almost entirely the dark blue; if it were then used at the center-line, a dark streak would be left. By continuing to brush down from the top edge, the paint in the brush is gradually lightened, so that by the time it reaches the center-line it matches the color of the flat at that point. At least a small area of the solid, unblended color should be left at each end of the blend.

Blending is not quite so simple as this description suggests. Like spattering, skill depends on constant analysis and some practice. The painter must begin with a clear picture of the way the finished blend is to look, and must check the appearance of the work constantly against that picture. As the brush picks up paint from one area and then is moved into the second, the color of the first area is intermixed. Often when the brush moves, for example, from the dark area into the light it may carry too much of the dark paint with it. When that happens the brush should be rinsed and the blending started again well down in the light area and moved up. Repeated adjustments will produce the effect wanted. If one area has been greatly discolored, it may be better to dip the cleaned brush into some of the pure color, start again at the edge, and then blend along the flat and into the other area. In fact, skilled painters may do the entire blend with one or two brushes dipped into the pure paints, rather than using a clean damp brush.

If the colors to be blended are distinctly different it is better to use a different brush for each color. Blending mixes the colors not only on the flat but also in the brush, so a bucket of water should be set nearby in which the brushes can be rinsed off before they are returned to the paint. It is not necessary to clear them of all paint, but to prevent progressive dilution of the paint supply the excess water should be removed by wiping them on the edge of the rinse bucket after each cleaning.

Since blending removes some of the paint which has been applied to the flat, the paint should be mixed a little thicker than usual, and a heavier quantity applied. Blending can be done only while the paint is wet. Traditional scene paint will readily redissolve, and so is especially easy to blend. Casein paint cannot be remoistened after it has dried, so that often small areas must be blended at a time, a difficult process since it is hard to match blends in adjacent areas. Although the casein paint cannot be redissolved, new paint can be laid over the first coat and blended while still wet.

The more alike the two colors are the easier it is to blend them. Thus, two closely related shades of green could be blended easily, but to blend pure black through an even series of greys to pure white would be much more difficult. Nearly always where blending is specified, the colors will be similar, often dark and light versions of essentially the same mix.

The example of blending described specifies a smooth area of color with no visible irregularities. Blending may be done as roughly or smoothly as desired. For example, the designer may ask that five or six browns be blended as the base coat for a stone wall, with the blended areas rough and varied.

Blending is a versatile technique which can be used for extremely varied purposes. It is adaptable to all styles and types of scenery, ranging from the fully abstract to the romantic or realistic. It is probably most often used in realistic or trompe l'oeil painting (see below), but may be specified by the designer for quite different types of scenery.

REALISTIC PAINTING

Like everything else in the theater, almost all of the functions of scenery serve the single purpose of communication. A set is intended to express the underlying mood of a play, whether it is one of lighthearted and stylish playfulness, as in *Twelfth Night,* tragic despair, as in *King Lear,* or low comedy, as in *The Merry Wives of Windsor.* Scenery is also often, although not always, intended to identify the locale in which the action takes place—a sleazy nightclub in *Cabaret,* the Ascot race track in *My Fair Lady,* the steps of the national capitol in *Of Thee I Sing.* But its most important communicative function is indirect—the assistance it gives the actors in expressing their characters' personalities, feelings, thinking, and experiences to the audience.

The means by which such communication is achieved are more centrally part of the skill of the designer than of the construction workers, who carry out his instructions rather than making the essential communicative decisions themselves. Seldom are objects or elements transported from ordinary life to the stage without alteration, and even apparently realistic scenic elements such as wallpaper are nearly always especially designed for the theater. Realism, then, is an effect or a style, and it is seldom used in the theater in its extreme sense of a precise reproduction of objects found outside the theater.

TROMPE L'OEIL PAINTING

The extreme degree of realism is usually given the French name *trompe l'oeil,* which means "fool the eye." Totally naturalistic painting is almost never done in the theater, and yet audiences are so suggestible, so ready to be fooled, that even conventionalized suggestions of objects actually fool audiences' eyes with astonishing frequency. Every experienced set builder can supply instances where members of the audience believed that papier-maché rocks were the real thing, that the flats were covered with actual wallpaper, that an ornamental screen built in the scene shop was an expensive hand-carved piece of furniture bought from a store, that cobblestones painted on the stage floor were actually three-dimensional, that a tower was really round, even though it was painted on a flat surface (and all of these examples are taken from actual experience). In the literal sense, then, *trompe l'oeil* often accurately describes scenery,

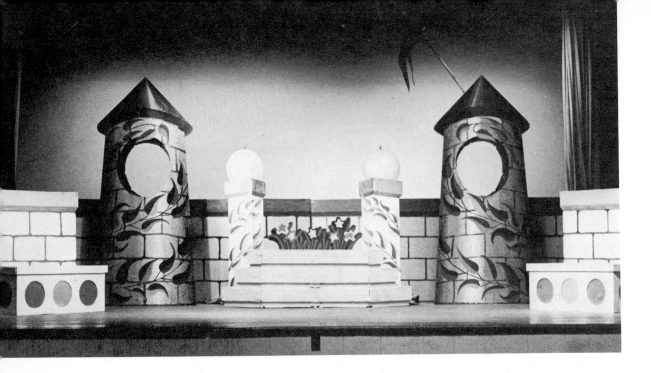

FIGURE 12.1 Trompe l'oeil painting. The towers are painted on flats, including the thickness–pieces on the windows. In addition, the ornamental balls at the tops of the pillars are painted on flat plywood, and some of the angles and other details of the walls are painted rather than being built three–dimensionally.

although it is nearly always simplified, projected, and otherwise altered from the appearance of similar objects outside the theater (Figures 12.1, 12.2, 12.3, 12.4, 12.5).

Even as an effect or style, trompe l'oeil painting is only one of a large variety of styles used in scenery. From the standpoint of the painter, however, it requires the greatest precision and skill, and the techniques used for it are adaptable to other styles which are purely decorative or abstract and which make no attempt to reproduce off-stage reality. Consequently, it seems desirable to make some suggestions with regard to realistic painting.

Fully three-dimensional objects, for example papier-maché boulders, must be painted to match the appearance of the real stones. Some hints for such painting will be given later. The present discussion is concerned primarily with the representation of three dimensions on a flat surface.

THE PATTERN OF REFLECTION

A three-dimensional object (for instance, a white pillar) does not reflect light uniformly. The pattern of reflectivity will depend on whether it stands in bright sunlight

FIGURE 12.2 Trompe l'oeil painting. All of the details except the furniture are painted on flat surfaces, including the pillars, the ornament on the front beam, and the false proscenium (notice the thickness–pieces). (Oscar Wilde, *The Importance of Being Earnest,* Act I.)

FIGURE 12.3 Trompe l'oeil painting: *The Importance of Being Earnest,* Act III. Like the set shown in Figure 12.2, all of the scenery in this third–act set except the furniture is painted on flat surfaces.

FIGURE 12.4 Trompe l'oeil painting: *A Funny Thing Happened on the Way to the Forum*. In Erronius's house, *right*, the left window is practical and fully three-dimensional; the right one is painted on the surface of the flat. The window of Hero's house, at the *left*, is also painted on the wall, and the ball at the top of the pillar, *center, at the back*, is painted on a circle of plywood.

FIGURE 12.5 Trompe l'oeil painting. In this set for Tom Taylor's *Our American Cousin*, the desk is practical and three-dimensional; everything else, including the bulletin board and the sheets pinned to it, is painted on the flats.

or in shadow, on the direction of the light source, and on its texture—a highly polished column of bright marble will reflect differently from a rough wooden pillar which has been painted white (Figure 12.6).

A moderately smooth but not polished pillar, in reflected light, with the light source behind the observer, will show essentially three areas of differing brightness. At each of the visible edges of the pillar there will be a vertical streak considerably darker than the rest of the pillar; about halfway between the edges there will be a vertical streak lighter than the rest of the pillar. These areas fade gradually toward each other, so that the pattern of color can be described as a dark streak fading gradually into a

FIGURE 12.6 Steps in painting a pillar. The left and center pillars show the areas of paint laid in solid, before blending; the left pillar is painted with highlight, base, and shadow; the center pillar has extreme highlight and shadow added. The pillar, *right*, after blending.

medium area, which then fades to a light streak, on to a second medium area, and finally to a second dark streak.

The color of the medium areas is given various names, but the most convenient for set painters is *base;* the lightest color is called *highlight,* and the darkest *shadow.* The pillar described displays a simple pattern. With different lighting or a different base color, the areas might show greater contrast, and two additional colors might appear beyond the edges of the list given, producing a five-step range:

> extreme highlight,
> highlight,
> base,
> shadow, and
> extreme shadow.

Theoretically, the range of tints and shades may be infinite. In practice, scene painters very seldom need more than these five steps, which are used not only in planning how the painting is to be carried out, but in mixing the various colors.

The variations in color in the different areas of the column are produced by the fact that the various parts of the column are turned at different angles to the light. Where they are turned so that the light is reflected directly toward the eye, the column seems brightest. At the edges, where very little of the light is reflected to the eye, it seems darkest. The effect of the angle of a surface can be demonstrated easily by glancing around the walls of a room, particularly if they are painted with a solid color. Where two walls come together, in almost every case one will seem much lighter and brighter than the other because they stand at different angles to the source of light. It is by interpreting this pattern of reflectivity that we are able to identify the shape of objects we see. If a column were lit so that all areas of it reflected exactly the same amount of light to the eye, we would be unable to tell whether it was round or flat.

REFLECTION PATTERNS IN PAINT

Different colors of paint themselves vary greatly in the amount and kind of light they reflect. Theoretical black absorbs all light, theoretical white reflects all of it (these two colors do not actually exist in nature or pigment—paint which we call black reflects some light, and white absorbs some). The various colors of pigment show a still more complex pattern of reflectivity, a fact which makes one bucket of paint look red and another green or blue. Nevertheless, they also differ in the amounts of light reflected, so that a dark green reflects less light than a light green of the same basic chroma.

The process of painting a flat surface so that the viewer will interpret it as three-dimensional, then, consists of using the reflectivity characteristics of pigment to paint it so that the pattern of reflection matches that of the real object. For the white pillar described above, for example, we would begin by mixing three buckets of paint, representing the base, the shadow, and the highlight. We would then paint a vertical rectangle on a flat, matching the outline of the pillar, using the base color. A stripe of the shadow would next be painted at each edge of the rectangle, and a stripe of the highlight painted down the center. Each of these would be smoothly blended into the base color, and the pillar would seem to be round.

This is about the simplest example that could be described. Painting more complex shapes, however, requires only a more detailed and complicated application of the same methods. One useful generalization which can be made from this example is that objects or areas which extend out toward the viewer tend to be light, while sunken areas tend to be dark. Observation would demonstrate thousands of exceptions to that rule, but since we are interested only in communicating a general effect, they can usually be ignored in painting scenery, and the simplified principle followed.

Just two examples will be given. If a sunken panel, edged with molding, must be represented on a flat, painting the panel just faintly darker than the surrounding area will help make it look as though it were set back in behind the molding. In representing latticework (Figure 12.7), the interweaving of the strips can be effectively suggested by painting a shadow streak across the back strip, above and below the front strip, with a sharp line at the edge of the front strip and with the other edge of the shadow fading smoothly into the base color of the back strip. A comparison of this treatment with real lattice will demonstrate that it is very different, and yet the pattern produced by the simplified formula will be accepted without question by the audience.

FIGURE 12.7 A simplified method of painting lattice. Where the strips cross behind they have been darkened, as described in the text. It would be interesting to hold this picture up near real lattice, under ordinary lighting conditions, and notice the differences.

GEOMETRICAL SHAPES

Columns are often tapered. A cone may be thought of as a cylinder which tapers to a point. The same method of painting applies, except that the various areas (base, high-light, shadow) get steadily narrower from the base to the point. A doughnut shape (torus) is essentially a cylinder bent into a circle. Painting the torus is somewhat more complicated than painting a cylinder or a cone, but essentially the same formula applies. The difficulty is that in some areas the outside edge of the doughnut is toward the source of light, and so must be highlighted, whereas in other areas it is away from the source of light, and so must be shadowed (and of course the same statement also applies to the inside edge). The transition from highlight to shadow involves placing an area of base between the two and blending each smoothly into it (Figure 12.8).

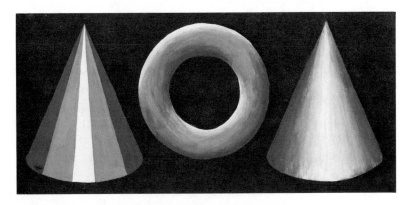

FIGURE 12.8 Painting a cone and torus. The cone unblended, *left*; after blending, *right*.

A sphere lit from some angle behind the viewer will display a circle of bright light, fading to base, with the edge of the sphere shadowed, also fading to base. If the highlight is off center because of the angle of light, the shadow will be darkest and widest at the edge of the sphere farthest from the highlight, and the edge closest to the highlight will show the least shadow (see the spheres in Figures 8.15, 12.1, 12.10, and 12.5, all of which were painted on flat surfaces).

In all curved shapes smooth fading between the areas is produced by the fact that the angle between the surface and the source of light changes steadily, with a smooth alteration in the amount of light reflected. In an object made up of flat surfaces, the amount of light reflected will be uniform throughout each area, and there will be a sharp-edged change of color where the surfaces come together, without blending. A cube, a hexagon, and an octagonal pyramid are used to illustrate this effect (Figure 12.9).

Three other patterns of reflection are frequently needed for painting scenery. In one, a flat surface must be painted so that its edges seem to curve away from the

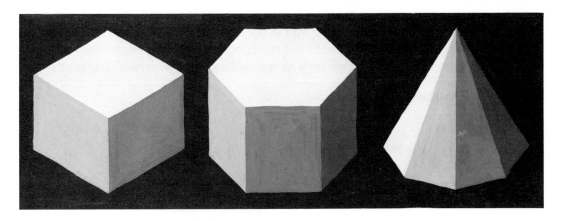

FIGURE 12.9   Painting objects with flat surfaces.

viewer. This is frequently the case in stones used to build a wall. A thin highlight is drawn along the edges of the stones which the light strikes directly, and a thin shadow line is run along the opposite edges; both highlight and shadow are faded into the base coat (Figure 12.10, the left section).

A crack is produced when two such patterns join. For instance, if the stones were shown in contact, without mortar, a crack would appear between them. This is represented by the same formula which has just been described. Assuming that the light comes from overhead, and that the crack is horizontal, a thin streak of shadow is painted just above the line of the crack, and a thin streak of highlight painted just below it. Where the two streaks meet their common edge is left unblended, but the other edges are faded into the base.

FIGURE 12.10   Painting stone walls. *Left*, cut stone without mortar; *left center*, with mortar; *right center*, fieldstone cut flat on one side; *right*, natural fieldstone.

273

Sometimes, especially in painting molding, it is necessary to represent the shape of a half-cylinder, extending out from the surface of the flat (Figure 12.11). Imagine such a shape running horizontally, with the light coming from overhead. The most light would be reflected from the upper edge of the half-cylinder, where it rests on the flat,

FIGURE 12.11   Painting convex and concave surfaces.

and the least light would be reflected from the lower edge. The shape is painted by first drawing two pencil lines marking the upper and lower edges, and then by painting a streak of highlight just below the upper line and a streak of shadow just above the lower edge; the outside edges are left sharp, and the inside edges smoothly faded toward each other into the base. A half-cylinder cut into the surface of the flat is painted similarly, except that the shadow and highlight are reversed.

Three-dimensional objects often interrupt the light falling on nearby surfaces, producing what are called cast shadows. For instance, a horizontal half-cylinder projecting from a flat would shadow the surface of the wall directly below it. Some designers and painters may choose to represent these also, but usually such accuracy of detail is unnecessary even in scenery painted with extreme realism.

Almost all three-dimensional shapes which must be represented by paint can be analyzed as combinations or variations of those which have been discussed. Even these are interrelated. For example, the curved edge of a shaped block of stone can be thought of as a quarter-cylinder. Once the painter has developed skill in painting these rather simple shapes, he will be able to produce convincing representations of molding, carving, irregular stones, tile, tree trunks, the stems of vines, latticework, or any other objects. A few hints will be given which may be of some practical value.

PAINT MIXES

Usually it is most economical to begin by painting the entire area to be shaped with the base coat. The shaping is then done as a second step. Most often only highlight, base, and shadow mixes are necessary. For small areas, it is convenient to put the paint in lightweight containers that can be set on the surface of the flat, rather than using large buckets. Small cans or plastic milk bottles with the tops cut off make good containers. In addition to the paint, the workman should have a container of water. Some painters prefer to use a different brush for each color of paint, but if the areas are to be blended it may be as efficient to use a single brush and swish it through the water a few times whenever it must be dipped into a new color.

The shadow and highlight should be prepared by altering the base mixture. A little white is added to it for the highlight, and a little black for the shadow. More interesting and effective colors can be produced by also changing the proportion of color-wheel pigments. Usually the base will have been made from one of the secondaries, so that it will be a combination of two primaries, one of which will be darker and one lighter. A little of the darker should be added along with the black to form the shadow, and a little of the lighter for the white. The pattern of mixture is shown in the following table:

With an orange (or brown) base:
    add white and yellow for the highlight;
    add black and red for the shadow.

With a purple base:
    add white and red for the highlight;
    add black and blue for the shadow.

With a green base:
    add white and yellow for the highlight;
    add black and blue for the shadow.

If the base is made from a single primary, then the adjacent secondaries (with one exception) should be used to lighten and darken it:

With a red base:
    add white and orange for the highlight;
    add black and purple for the shadow.

With a blue base:
    add white and green for the highlight;
    add black and purple for the shadow.

With a yellow base:
    add white alone for the highlight (since orange is darker than the yellow);
    add black and green for the shadow.

Occasionally it will be necessary to extend the 3-color series by an extreme highlight and an extreme shadow; in that case the shadow and highlight are further altered by additions of the same colors which were used to distinguish them from the base.

LIGHTING PATTERNS

As has been suggested, the pattern of light and shadow depends on the direction of the light. Suppose for example that a simple half-cylinder molding is used throughout a set. If the light is from overhead, the top edge of each horizontal piece of molding would be brightest, but if a floor lamp were placed so that the light shone up on a strip of molding above it, the bottom edge would be more brightly lit than the top. Even a molding running along the top of a fireplace opening might be more brightly lit along the bottom edge, where the firelight shone on it.

MATCHING LIGHT SOURCES

Three patterns of light can be used as a guide in simulating three-dimensional scenic elements in paint. The most realistic is to determine all of the light sources to be used on the set, and paint the elements with reference to them. Only this pattern is completely realistic, and it may be followed in small scenic areas of the type described, where an individual source of light can be distinguished and predicted. In most cases, however, this pattern is impractical, for several reasons. Stage lighting is extremely complex, and often the lighting design will not have been completed by the time the flats are ready for painting. But even more importantly, the degree of realism achieved by this method is almost never needed in the theater, and simpler patterns may actually communicate with greater clarity.

CENTER-STAGE SOURCE

Although dozens of different sources of light may be used for a set, the stage space is likely to be most brightly lit in an area about six or seven feet above the stage floor, in the center of the space outlined by the walls of the set. If the flats are painted to show the appearance of three-dimensional scenic elements lit from that point, the result is likely to be completely convincing for the audience. In this pattern, for example, a vertical molding at the right of the stage would have a highlight along its left edge; an identical molding on the opposite sight of the stage would show a highlight along its right edge.

UPPER LEFT SOURCE

The third pattern is the simplest of all. It depends on a psychological phenomenon which has not yet been explained, although it is easy to demonstrate. Unless the source of light is strongly indicated, viewers always subconsciously assume that the light strikes the object at which they are looking, at an angle of 45° from the upper left corner. All the elements of a set can be painted to show the effect of that angle of illumination. In this case the molding mentioned above would be painted with the shadow on the same side, no matter where it was placed on the set. This pattern is the least realistic of the three, but also the simplest and fastest to use. It can be effectively combined with the other patterns. For example, if a set is to be painted to suggest that it is made of cut stone, all of the stones can be painted as if lit from the upper left, and isolated carved decorations painted with reference to the second pattern (with the light source at center stage) (Figure 12.12).

FIGURE 12.12   The upper left source of light. Some of the panels appear sunken, and some raised; if the picture is turned upside down, they reverse, due to the fact that the positions of shadows and highlights reverse, and that they are subconsciously interpreted as being caused by light from the upper left, whether they are viewed right–side–up or upside down. (The same effect appears in the panels in Figures 1.11 and 6.7, and the bulletin board in 12.5, if the pictures are viewed right–side–up and upside down.)

STEREOSCOPIC COMPENSATION

Identifying the shape of three-dimensional objects depends on one additional factor besides the interpretation of patterns of reflectivity. This is stereoscopy. The visual field is slightly different for each eye—the left eye sees a little more of the left side of objects, the right eye a little more of the right side. Although these differences are usually small, they provide distance and spatial clues which help in identifying shapes.

The stereoscopic effect cannot be duplicated in scene painting; consequently, even if the reflectivity patterns of three-dimensional objects were reproduced with precise fidelity in paint, the result would seem somewhat flatter than the actual objects. In particular, the line between two planes which meet at an angle would be seen less vividly than in the actual object.

This loss of stereoscopic clues to the shapes painted should be compensated by artificially emphasizing such lines. When two lengths of molding meet at an angle, one is likely to catch more light than the other, and so appear brighter. This difference should be emphasized by painting the end of the lighter molding with still brighter paint than is used for the rest of it, and darkening the end of the darker molding still more. In each case, the paint should be blended out to the basic colors of the two lengths of molding, away from the joint. The same techniques should be used wherever paint is used to represent planes meeting at an angle. For example, if a ground row shows angled sections of a brick wall, the edge of the darker section should be reinforced with still darker paint where the two sections meet, and the edge of the light section should be made a little lighter.

Stereoscopic compensation also requires a slight modification of the painting pattern which assumes a light source at 45° to the left and above objects represented. If a rectangle of molding were lit from that angle, the top would reflect exactly as brightly as the left side, and the right and bottom edges would be identically dark, so that the different directions of the two planes meeting at the upper left or lower right corners would be indistinguishable. The two areas in each pair should be painted with different mixes, using a slightly brighter highlight color for the top surface and a slightly darker mix for the left edge, and a shadow mix for the right side slightly lighter than the natural color, and a slightly darker mix for the bottom of the molding. In effect, this shifts the source of light a little to the right, so that the top of the object represented reflects the light a little more directly than the left side. In addition, the edges of the planes should be emphasized as has been described.

Although these alterations are so subtle that it is hoped they will not be consciously noticed by the viewers, their effect on expressing the shapes of three-dimensional objects is enormous. Like the thickness pieces added to the walls of a set, these very small adjustments make a very great difference in how the audience inteprets the shape of the scenery.

TRANSFERRING DESIGNS

Unless a design is to be painted free hand, guide lines must first be drawn on the flats. They may be as simple as straight lines marking the outside edges of molding, panels, or pillars, or they may require the drawing of extremely detailed shapes, such as the stems of a vine and even the individual leaves.

PROJECTION

Various methods are available for transferring the designer's drawings to the flats in preparation for painting them. One of the simplest is to put the drawing in an opaque projector and shine it on the flats, which have been stood upright against the wall. As an alternative, the drawing can be photographed to produce a slide, which can also be projected. This method is especially useful for large drops, where other methods are difficult because of the lack of complete framing.

STENCIL

A second method is to prepare a full-scale stencil, with the pattern areas cut out. This method is standard for small repeated patterns, especially those used to represent wallpaper, but it is also adaptable to entire flats. It is seldom used because preparing the stencils is difficult and time-consuming. Nevertheless, it is helpful in two situations: where guide marks cannot be removed from the surface to be painted, and where the painting must be delayed for any reason.

For one production of Kopit's *Indians* both those situations occurred. The designer specified a series of specially shaped flats to be covered with tightly-woven very light-colored burlap, on which Indian motifs were to be painted. It was felt that guidelines would show permanently on the burlap, even if made with pencil or light chalk. Furthermore, the burlap was not delivered on time, so that the painting was delayed long enough to produce a small crisis. For special reasons it was not possible to work on the set at night. The technical director spent his evenings drawing the patterns full-scale on sheets of bristol board taped together; these were then cut out with a mat knife. When the burlap arrived, it was quickly applied to the flats, the stencils laid in place, and the patterns traced. As soon as the pattern had been drawn on the first flat the painters started to work, and by the time they had finished it all of the other patterns had been traced. A single emergency all-night painting session completed the work. To have laid out the patterns by any other method would itself have been an all-night job for the crew.

GRIDDING

As a standard, rather than emergency, procedure, gridding is more often employed. The designer's drawing is covered with two sets of parallel lines at right angles to each other, which form a network of squares. The surface of the flat is then marked with matching squares, although they will be larger (Figure 12.13). Where the lines of the

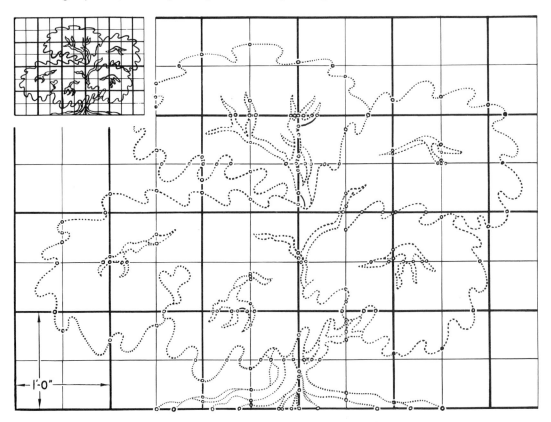

FIGURE 12.13 Enlarging by gridding. The two grids are identical except in size. The grid lines are in alternating colors (shown here as heavy and light lines). The points at which the lines of the pattern cross the lines of the smaller grid have been copied (shown as small circles), and the lines of the pattern have been sketched in free hand (shown as dotted lines).

designer's drawing cross gridlines, points are marked on the matching lines of the grid on the flat, and the design is finished by connecting these points freehand.

This is an irksome method of transferring a drawing, but it goes faster than it seems to, and it can be done with any degree of accuracy desired. If workers are alert, the largest possible error is something less than half the width of one of the squares, so that by adjusting the number of squares used, the margin of possible error can be set as small as desired. Increasing the number of squares slows the work, so as many squares should be used as are necessary for maintaining the desirable degree of accuracy, but not more. If much of the design is made up of large elements, with small details concentrated in specific areas, the over-all grid can be adjusted to the major areas of the flat, and the squares in the detailed sections subdivided to provide more guidelines.

The simplest way to lay out the squares is to mark the edges of the flat at the specified intervals, and then stretch a chalk line across between matching points and snap the string to mark the guidelines. These lines must be removed after the design has been drawn, so they should be as faint as possible; a color of chalk should be used which contrasts only very slightly with the background, and the string snapped gently. A little experience will demonstrate how clear the lines need to be for drawing the design, but beginners tend to make them unnecessarily vivid, and consequently difficult to remove. A faint, almost invisible pattern of lines is entirely adequate, and can be used as a guide in transferring the design almost as fast as a brightly contrasting grid.

It is extremely important in copying the design that the points for each square in the designer's drawing be transferred to the matching square on the flat. Especially if a large number of squares have been used, it is easy to jump one or two squares and throw the entire design off.

Accuracy also depends on a psychological set which seems awkward and unnatural. The design itself should be ignored while the key points are being marked. Each point should be copied in isolation, placing it by assessing its position on the grid line on which it falls. It is identified as being at the center of the short segment of the grid line, or to one side or the other of the center, and a particular distance from the center or the end of the line segment on which it lies. Thus, the worker should say, "This point is on the vertical grid-line segment just a little more than a third of the way down from the top end," and then should mark that position on the large grid.

When all the points have been recorded on the flat, the worker's attention should be turned to the design as a whole, and a check to make sure that the pattern of points matches the shape of the drawing being copied should be made. The entire outline is filled in free hand, the line passing through all of the points which have been marked, and constantly compared with the original drawing. Finally, the enlarged drawing is checked as a whole, and any necessary corrections made. After the design has been painted, the grid lines should be removed by dusting the flat with a soft brush or by standing it against the wall and beating it with the flat side of a yardstick.

WALLPAPER

Most often, wallpaper is applied to flats by means of a full-sized stencil in which one motif of the design is cut. The spacing of the motifs will have been specified by the designer, and will nearly always match key points on a simple geometric grid, which may be of various types but which is likely to be formed by two sets of slanted parallel lines forming an all-over diamond pattern, with each motif framed by the four sides of one of the diamonds.

The first step in laying out the wallpaper design is to mark this underlying geometrical pattern. The lines can be printed with a chalkline, or, if it is felt that they are likely to show after the design has been applied, the marks can be made only at the corners of the diamonds, with chalk or pencil. The stencil should have four small holes in it matching the corners of the enclosing diamond. When the grid has been completed, the stencil is laid on the flat so that the four corners of one of the grid areas show through the holes in the stencil, and the pattern is printed through the stencil on the flat. The stencil is then moved to a new area and the pattern printed again, continuing until the entire wallpaper area is covered with the motif.

The design can be applied in various ways. One is to spray paint through the holes of the stencil while it is lying on the flat; another is to paint through the holes with an ordinary brush or a special stencil brush. It is even possible to print a large and simple design by spattering over the stencil, using the standard method for spattering flats, although usually the brush is held much closer to the surface of the flat. If either spraying or spattering is done, the rest of the flat must be protected by covering it with newspaper or cardboard.

Applying paint directly to the stencil, either by brushing, spattering, or spraying, creates certain problems. The paint may creep under the stencil and leave unsightly blobs; at best, the underside of the stencil must be wiped clean after each application. Stencils are seldom ideally rugged, and as they are repeatedly wet they may begin to disintegrate. Their life can be extended by covering them with hot paraffin or painting them with two or three coats of varnish, and by fastening them to a frame made of 1 X 3s set on edge.

The pattern can also be transferred in various ways that do not involve the use of paint. A *pounce bag* is made by putting a few spoonfuls of powdered chalk or pigment in the center of a square of cloth, about eight inches on a side. The corners and sides are then pulled up together, so that the pigment forms a little ball. Holding the loose edges, the worker then swings the cloth down so that the end containing the ball of pigment is struck on the surface of the stencil. Some of the pigment is forced through the pores of the cloth, and prints on the flat through the holes in the stencil. Any kind of porous cloth can be used; two or three layers of cheesecloth are probably best, although light scenery canvas works acceptably, and muslin works well. Since the areas printed will be covered with paint, the marking can be brighter than for a grid, although the color chosen should be compatible with the paint to be applied: for instance, green should not be used to print an area which is to be painted in red or yellow.

Usually wallpaper patterns for stage use are bold and simple enough that they can be cut out of the stencil paper as open areas. If cutting the entire pattern out would weaken the stencil impractically, bridges can be left to tie the solid areas together. In painting, the blank areas left by these bridges are painted out to match the intended design. In adding bridges, it is essential that the design not be obscured, so that they should not be put at the ends of open spaces, but rather toward the middle, where the painters can easily identify the lines which are to be continued across the protected areas. If there is likely to be any confusion, each bridge can be cut with a zigzag edge, to distinguish it from the lines of the design.

If a pattern is to be transferred which is too complicated to be cut out of the stencil paper, the lines of the design can be perforated by running a stencil wheel along them, and the design pounced through; it will then appear on the flat as if drawn with dotted lines. A final method is to trace around the holes in the stencil with pencil or chalk; this is slower than the other methods, but may be preferable for delicate designs or when the surface might be damaged by even a little of the pounce powder's getting on it. This method was used for the *Indians* flats mentioned earlier. Patterns marked in this way must be painted by hand.

FIGURE 12.14   Printing wallpaper. Background stripes have been painted on the rectangle as the base for the wallpaper, and a number of leaf shapes have been printed over them. The worker is brushing paint on the specially made leaf stamp, preparatory to continuing printing the leaves. The stamp is made of a piece of upson board, flexed and tied to hold a curve, with a leaf–shaped piece of foam rug padding glued to it.

A new method of printing wallpaper designs has just been devised, and although there has not been time to experiment with it fully, it is clearly a valuable one which should be added to the supply of stagecraft techniques. The design motif is cut with a knife or scissors from a sheet of plastic foam rug padding, and then glued to a rectangle of heavy cardboard (upson board) which has been flexed until it forms a permanent curve. Scene paint is applied to the padding with a brush, or the paint is brushed on a flat surface and the padding pressed against it. The pattern is printed on the flat by pressing the wet pad down with a rolling motion. This method was used for the wallpaper for a set for *Hedda Gabler,* and the technical director estimated that it saved from three to four hours' work for each flat (Figure 12.15).

With any method, errors or blobs are likely to appear. They can be corrected by touching them up with the base color of the flat, after the wallpaper paint has dried. Usually wallpaper needs to be toned down or reduced in contrast after it is finished. This is done by glazing or by spattering it lightly, in colors related either to the background or the motifs.

FIGURE 12.15   Printed wallpaper.   This set for *Hedda Gabler* shows wallpaper printed with several rug–pad stamps similar to the one shown in Figure 12.14.

FOLIAGE

Often the background of wallpaper is puddled with closely related mixes. The same technique is applicable to foliage, which is frequently required for outdoor sets, and may even be needed for flats placed beyond windows in interior sets. As with other types of scenery, foliage is usually simplified, generalized, and expressed suggestively and abstractly. Nevertheless, effective representation depends on the observation of some of the characteristics of actual shrubs and trees.

As tree trunks divide in branches, the total quantity of wood remains about the same. Thus, when a trunk splits into two branches, the two together contain about the same amount of material as the solid trunk below them. As they further divide, the individual branches and twigs become smaller and smaller, but the combined material at equal distances from the trunk remains the same.

Where the branches join the trunk (or other branches), the edges flow together in tangential curves, not angles. Furthermore, there is a slight thickening to form a solid connection. Failure to apply those two facts destroys the feeling of reality more than any other error in painting trees.

The leaves tend to appear in roughly cloud-shaped masses, fairly flat at the bottom and irregularly rounded on top. A few of the outside leaves, especially toward the top of the masses, will be turned so that they catch the light more directly, and will show as patches of individual brightness. These brightest leaves are seen as separate shapes; the masses of leaves of which they are a part are much less precisely defined, and the leaves beyond them are seen as indistinct masses of darker color.

A final fact is that in trees, as in most natural objects, symmetry and straight lines are extremely unusual. Trees tend to be precisely balanced, unless they have grown under the continued stress of strong winds, but the balance is asymmetrical, with perhaps two smaller branches on one side matching a larger branch on the other.

The first step in painting a tree, after the background of sky has been painted, is to outline the trunk and branches, using light charcoal, chalk, or pencil lines. If the designer's plans do not require gridding, the work can be done freehand. It is easiest to work with the flats standing against the wall or in a paint frame, so that the painter can step back frequently to check the effect as a whole. When this has been done satisfactorily, the outlines of the leaf masses are sketched in (Figure 12.16).

The trunk and branches require at least three mixes of paint, and more often five. They are first painted with the base coat, and then the shadows and highlights are added and blended, and finally the extreme shadows and highlights. The degree of blending depends on the effect desired, although usually the paint will be left rather rough.

The leaves require six colors. The two darkest are used to paint the entire leaf area, in irregular patches which are blended roughly to produce a puddled surface. The edges of the area, especially the lower edges, should be painted irregularly in something of a sawtooth pattern, with points of individual leaves extending down; patches of

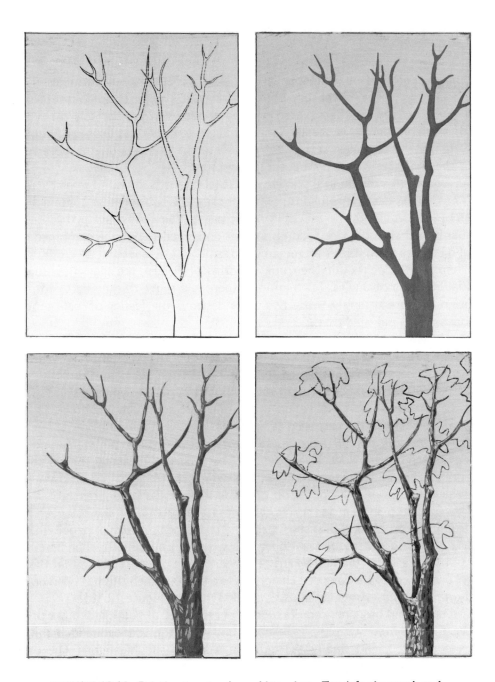

FIGURE 12.16 Painting tree trunks and branches. *Top left*, the trunk and branches have been outlined in black chalk; *right*, the base coat has been painted on. *Bottom left*, the shadows and highlights have been added; *right*, they have been slightly blended, the extreme shadows and highlights added, and the darker leaf shapes sketched in.

FIGURE 12.17   Painting leaves. *Top left*, the leaf shapes have been puddled in the two darkest colors; *right*, the ligher leaves have been outlined. *Bottom left*, the lighter leaves have been painted, with highlights and shadows added; *right*, the painting has been completed by painting a few of the upper leaves with extreme highlight.

open sky should be left here and there. This coat of paint represents the masses of shadowed leaves seen indistinctly beyond the more sharply defined outside foliage.

If the painter is unsure of his skill, he should next sketch in the outer leaf masses (Figure 12.17). With more experience, he may be able to paint them directly without further drawing. They should extend generally to the outside of the first areas painted, but should be narrower, so that some of the indistinct foliage is visible below and between them. These areas are painted with the third lightest mix, again serrating the edges irregularly in imitation of leaf shapes. They are varied by adding spots of highlight and shadow (mixes 2 and 4). The highlight should be concentrated toward the top of each mass, and the shadow toward the bottom, but they should be placed irregularly, and the areas should not be precisely defined. The lightest color (mix 1) is then used to spot the cloud-shaped masses, especially along their upper and left edges. Since these spots of color will be seen individually, they should be shaped more carefully, but usually it is enough just to avoid any simple geometrical shape, rather than attempting to imitate leaf shapes precisely.

Finally, the painter should step back to check the flat from audience viewing distance, and make any corrections or adjustments necessary. The most likely change will be that the foliage will seem too spotty, and some of the shadows and highlights will have to be toned down or reinforced so that the foliage is seen as made up of broad masses rather than individual leaves.

The method which has been described is a generalized one. If it is intended that a particular kind of tree be represented (for instance, the birches which are emphasized in Chekhov's *The Three Sisters*), then actual trees or photographs will have to be analyzed to determine their special characteristics. Often the designer will plan some special effect which may not match any natural tree; for example, the set for one production of Paul Sills' *Story Theatre* included trees intended to look like the pop-up illustrations for children's books. Each one was split down the middle and the two halves set at an angle of 45°; the trunks and branches were heavily twisted, and each branch ended in a clutching three-fingered hand.

An ordinary medium-sized paint brush can be used to print a pointed leaf shape (Figure 12.18). The brush is dipped in the paint and then the side edge pressed down on the surface of the flat, with the brush held at about a 45° angle. The tips of the bristles will spread out, and where they are fastened to the handle they stay together, so that a long leaf shape is printed, with one end round and the other pointed. Several leaves can be printed with a single dip of the brush, and at great speed. Although only one kind of leaf shape can be painted with this method, it is frequently usable for trees or bushes, unless a recognizable species must be represented.

AERIAL PERSPECTIVE

If trees, bushes, or any outdoor scenic units such as mountains, fields, or distant buildings, are intended to be seen as standing at different distances, they can be made more convincing by the use of what is called *aerial perspective.* Any dust, haze, or mist in the atmosphere alters the colors of outdoor objects, and progressively more so as they stand farther away from the viewer. Usually the colors are pastelled, but also made cooler. This effect can be produced by adding white and a little blue to the paint mixes. This method is especially effective in painting ground-rows. If trees and rolling hills are represented at different distances, the nearest ones should be painted with the clearest colors, and more white and blue added as the foliage areas stretch progressively into the distance.

DRAPERY

It may have been noticed that the trunks and larger branches of trees require painting techniques which are related to those used for pillars. The same methods are basic to

FIGURE 12.18 Printing leaves. Each leaf has been produced by pressing the edge of a small brush down firmly on the surface at a slant. *Upper right,* square of scrap cardboard is used to test the pattern after recharging the brush, before applying it to the good surface.

painting drapery. A full heavy drape, hanging straight, can be analyzed as a series of columns placed side by side, some with vertical edges, some wider at the top and others wider at the bottom (Figure 12.19).

Such a drape is first laid out by drawing or snapping a series of nearly vertical lines, varying them so that they are not uniformly parallel, and spacing them to match the folds of the actual drapery material. The heavier the material, the larger the folds. The top and bottom edges are then drawn with chalk, charcoal, or pencil, bowing them out between adjacent vertical lines.

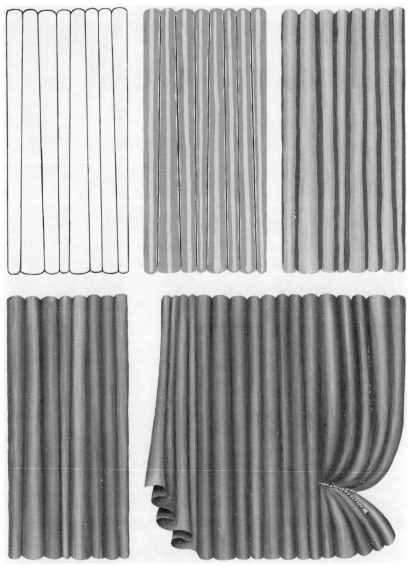

FIGURE 12.19 Painting drapery. *Top left*, the folds are outlined; *center*, the base and highlight are added; *right*, base and highlight are blended, and the shadow laid in. *Bottom left*, the painting is completed by blending the shadow. *Bottom right*, drapery is shown with a slanted lower edge and caught up with an ornamental rope.

The base is painted on first, holding it back slightly from the verticals so as not to lose them. A vertical stripe is then painted in the highlight color up the center of each area of base and blended at the edges. The shadow color is painted over the lines and also blended into the base. The edges between the shadow, base, and highlight areas will be sharpest with shiny and smooth materials such as satin, and widest and most gradually blended with dull and rough materials.

If the folds are caught up so that they do not hang vertically, for instance in a swag, they are drawn freehand to follow the cloth. Details such as fringing, ornamental rope, and tassels can be added.

MOLDING

Molding and paneling also regularly involve shapes related to the column, or to half- or quarter-round, and in some cases also to the groove (Figure 12.20). First the outside

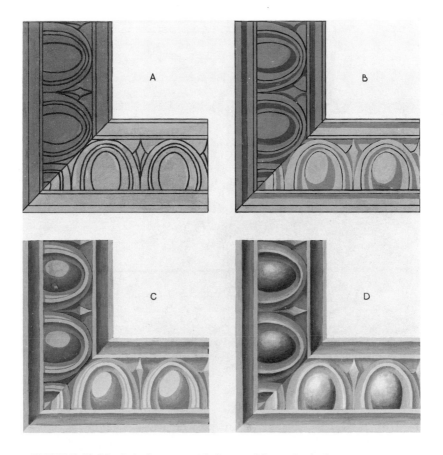

FIGURE 12.20 Painting egg–and–dart molding. *A*, the base coats are painted and the shapes outlined; *B*, the shadows are painted in; *C*, the shadows are blended and highlights added; *D*, the highlights are blended.

edges of the molding are drawn, and the entire area painted with base. The pattern is analyzed to determine which areas will be brightly lit, which in shadow, and which will be of the base color. The shadows are then painted in and blended over the rounded surfaces, and the highlights added and blended.

The design for the molding may not show a uniform cross-section. For instance, the pattern called egg-and-dart includes repeated half- or quarter-oval shapes, with raised pointed shapes between them. These must be painted individually, with variations of the techniques used for spheres and cones. Reeding or fluting for pillars is imitated with methods similar to molding, using the techniques described earlier for half-cylinders and grooves.

An effective striping guide can be made from a length of ordinary molding (Figure 12.21). Cut it about three or four feet long, and screw a metal drawer-pull to the center of the back of the strip. In use, it is held against the flat face down, with the thin edge facing away from the painter, and used as a guide for the brush in the same way that a metal-edged ruler is used to draw ink lines.

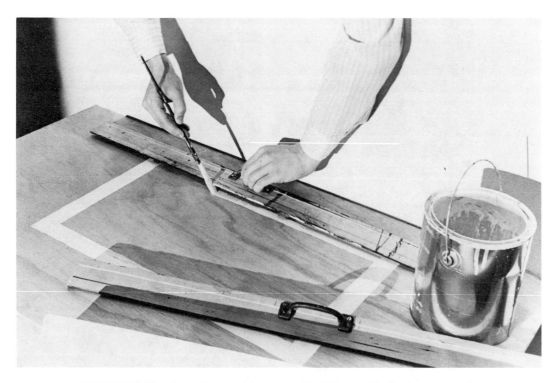

FIGURE 12.21   The striping guide in use. Holding a guide firmly against a sheet of plywood, the painter uses it to control his brush as he paints a stripe. A second guide, *bottom*, in front of the paint can.

BRICKS

Of the remaining three-dimensional objects simulated by painting, the two most frequently needed for scenery are brick and stone walls. Bricks can be laid in various patterns, called *bonds*. The bricks themselves may be of various colors, shiny or mat, flat or textured, new or used and chipped. The mortar may be wide or narrow, squeezed out between the bricks, smoothed level with them, or scraped back in below the brick surfaces. Which of these different characteristics are to be represented for a set will usually be specified by the designer. The method of painting one type of wall will be described; the others can be handled as variations of it.

Some painters prefer to cover the entire flat with the mortar color and then add the brick shapes over it; others prefer to use the brick color as the base coat and paint the mortar lines last. Four colors are needed for the bricks: a light and a dark base, and a highlight and shadow. Using the brick-first method, the entire flat is painted with the lighter of the two base colors; the second color is then drybrushed horizontally across the surface. The paint should be applied irregularly, so that some areas have little or no new paint, and others are fairly heavily colored. This will produce the effect of somewhat worn brick. If new brick is intended, the drybrushing should be subtler and more uniform (Figures 12.22, 12.23, 12.24).

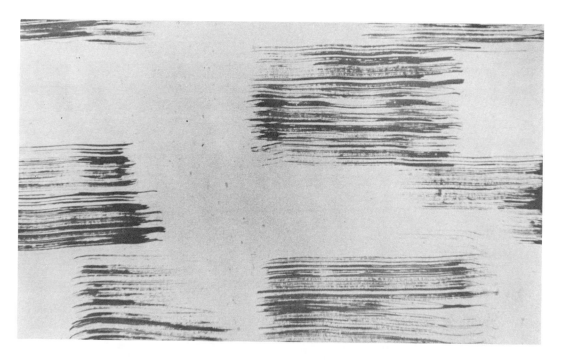

FIGURE 12.22 Painting bricks. The wall section has been painted with a light base, and a darker color has been drybrushed randomly in approximately brick–shaped areas.

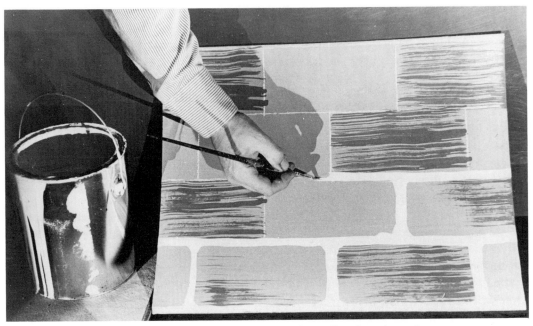

FIGURE 12.23   Bricks: the second step. Mortar lines have been drawn across the surface shown in Figure 12.22, the drybrushing has been touched up, and the mortar is being laid on.

FIGURE 12.24   Finished bricks. The wall section has been completed by adding shadows and highlights to the bricks and applying a coat of fine spatter.

Horizontal mortar lines are then snapped across the flat, spacing them 4¼" apart. Starting at one end of the bottom row of bricks, vertical mortar lines are drawn with chalk across the row, spacing them 8½" apart. Unless a very regular mechanical effect is desired, these lines can be drawn freehand, but the spacing should be measured. That can be done most conveniently by cutting a card to the right dimension and moving it along as the lines are marked. (These dimensions provide for a mortar thickness of 1/2", leaving brick faces 3¾" × 8", which is the commonest size. Of course, other dimensions can be used if desired.)

The second row is then marked, centering each mortar line above a brick in the bottom row. This can be done by eye. This pattern is the commonest, although one of the less interesting, brick arrangements. It is called a running bond; other bonds would require a different spacing of the mortar lines.

Using a narrow brush and, if desired, a striping guide, the mortar is then painted. Rounding each corner slightly where the vertical and horizontal mortar lines join makes the wall look a little less mechanical and more convincing. The drybrushing should then be retouched. If a dark area starts in the middle of a brick, it should be extended to cover the entire surface. Individual bricks can be drybrushed with either of the brick base colors to produce a more uniform or more varied texture for the wall as a whole.

The brick highlight and shadow colors are then brushed roughly in fine lines along the edges of the bricks. The third lighting pattern described earlier is usually satisfactory for brickwork, in which case the highlight color is painted along the upper and left edges of each brick, and the shadow color along the right and bottom edges. These stripes need not be blended; if they are painted irregularly, they will produce more texture. For the greatest realism, the mortar lines could also be highlighted and shadowed, although that is almost never necessary.

Finally the entire surface should be moderately spattered to provide further texture, to tone down the mortar, and to help blend the different areas.

STONES

Similar techniques are used in painting a stone wall, except that stones vary more in size, shape, color, finish, and arrangement. The wall may be built of unworked field stone, the stone may be cut into uniform rectangular blocks, the surface may be polished, smoothed, or given a variety of textures.

For the *Story Theatre* set which has been mentioned, a hut was constructed with a stone foundation four feet high, the stones flat but irregularly shaped, as if large fieldstones had been sawed through and fitted together to form the wall. First the entire surface was painted with a base coat. Individual stones were then outlined in chalk, irregular in shape but roughly circular. Several mixes were prepared by adding different colors to quantities of the base coat, and these were printed on the stones with wadded up canvas, taking care that no two adjacent stones were of the same color, with the paint covering from a third to two-thirds of the base coat. Finally, the mortar lines were painted in.

Since the set was intended to imitate the illustration for a child's book, the wall was handled symbolically rather than realistically. The colors were brighter than ordinary stone would have been, the stones were left flat, rather than being shaped with shadows and highlights, and the finished wall was not blended by spattering. For a more realistic wall, the painting would have been done less broadly, and more of the techniques described for brickwork would have been used. (Illustrations of stones simulated with paint appear in Figures 1.2, 1.4, 1.9, 6.8, 7.6, 12.1, 12.2, 12.4, 12.10, and 12.22.)

Since stone constructions vary so greatly in appearance, it is difficult to give a single typical example. Errors are most likely to be made in imitating rough stone walls. The individual stone shapes must be probable, and should be thought of as essentially circular; a mortar joint which creates the impression that a field boulder set into the wall has a pointed corner will look disturbingly unconvincing. At the same time, the mortar lines must be kept within reasonable limits, and if three stones come together so as to leave a large space between them, they should be redesigned, or a fourth small stone drawn in, rather than painting an enormous and unlikely blob of mortar to fill the hole.

PAINTING THREE-DIMENSIONAL OBJECTS

This discussion has been concerned with the representation of textured and three-dimensional shapes on flat surfaces; but most actually shaped objects must be painted also. Rather than being simulated by trompe-l'oeil painting, rocks and tree trunks may be made fully rounded, and brick and stone walls shaped in realistic thickness. Carving over a mantel or on furniture may be represented by paint, or it may be constructed three-dimensionally. All of these things must also be painted before they are used on stage.

It is possible simply to paint them with a base coat, or to vary it only to represent the different colors of the real objects. More often, however, they are painted so as to emphasize and reinforce the actual three-dimensionality. Thus, highlights and shadows would be added even to a fully rounded boulder, and cracks in it would not only be molded but emphasized by shadowing and highlighting them. The same techniques are used as for painting on a flat surface.

It is sometimes necessary to paint a curving stripe parallel with a raised structural element, for example the edge of an arch. The edges of the stripe can be marked most accurately and quickly by the use of cardboard circles (Figure 12.25).

From light upson board, heavy drawing board, or even corrugated cardboard, carefully cut a circle with a radius equal to the distance between the raised edge and the nearest edge of the stripe. Punch a hole in the center of the circle with a nail. Insert a pencil in the hole and lay the circle on the flat so that the edge is in contact with the raised edge. Holding the pencil, roll the circle along the raised edge, marking a line on the surface of the flat. A second circle is then cut with a radius equal to the distance between the raised edge and the farthest edge of the stripe, and that edge is marked in the same way.

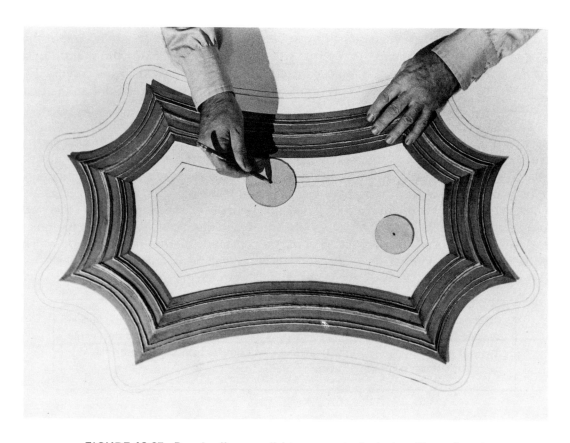

FIGURE 12.25   Drawing lines parallel to a curved raised edge. Upson–board circles have been cut as described in the box, and used to draw lines parallel with the ornamental shape. The lines closest to the shape, drawn by using the small circle, have been completed. The other line has been fully drawn outside the ornamental shape, and the worker is finishing the last section of the inside line.

ANTIQUING

A slightly different technique is often useful for highlighting carving or texturing which is raised only slightly from the supporting surface. Suppose for instance that rope has been glued in an intricate pattern on a picture frame or a table to simulate carving. The object is first painted all over with the shadow color. It is then painted with the base color, in a modification of the drybrush technique. The major areas should be covered solidly, but the shadow should be left visible beside and between the ropes. This is done by painting lightly at right angles to the rope, avoiding pressure which would force the bristles of the brush down onto the surface. Finally, the top edges of the rope are touched with the highlight color, applied with the flat side of the brush, with the bristles almost parallel with the surface of the wood, so that a thin line of paint is deposited along the upper surface of the rope. If desired, gold paint can be used in place of an ordinary highlight color, to emphasize the raised areas more clearly.

As an alternative, the base color can be painted first and then a thin wash of the shadow laid on. Immediately, while it is still wet, it is rubbed hard with a cloth or a paper towel so that all of it is removed except in the areas closest to the carving. Finally the highlighting is added. This produces a somewhat subtler effect than the first method described.

Ordinary shoe polish has occasionally been used to antique scenery, especially carving on picture frames, furniture, or panels. Brown or black polish is rubbed on the surface in areas in which soil would naturally accumulate, allowed to dry, and then slightly polished. Shoe brushes are best for this purpose, and they can also be used in a variety of other ways in the scene shop, including blending paint. Since designers are constantly asking for unusual effects, ingenuity must often be employed to solve new problems. Although established materials and techniques can be used in the great majority of instances, the best set painters are constantly alert to new products which will extend their resources, or to old products which can be used in new ways.

> Cardboard, including upson board and corrugated board, tends to warp and buckle when it is painted. This can be prevented by painting the back first and then while it is still wet painting the front. If the back will not be seen by the audience, discarded or leftover paint can be used.

GLOSS FINISHES

Usually mat-finished paints are preferred for scenery, so as to avoid the stage lighting's being annoyingly reflected into the eyes of the audience. Occasionally, it may be desirable to produce a shiny surface for a special effect, for instance to imitate the sheen of ornamental tile set around a fireplace opening, or to suggest shiny linoleum or floor tile. Special gloss paint can be used, although it would be needed so seldom that it is uneconomical to stock a supply of various colors. Instead, ordinary scene paint can be used, and then one or two coats of shellac or clear varnish applied over it. (Shellac comes in two colors, which are called orange and white, although the white is in fact clear; the orange cannot be used because it greatly alters the color of the paint over which it is applied.) Plastic or other coatings supplied in pressure cans and sprayed on the scenery are not acceptable. Not only do they involve at least two hazards, but they produce a slightly grainy finish which does not have the sheen desired.

Shellac and varnish share the disadvantage that brushes used for them cannot be cleaned with water. Alcohol must be used for shellac, and paint thinner for varnish. A substitute has just recently been discovered which can be cleaned from brushes with water alone, which is readily available in most scene shops, and which is cheaper than either shellac or varnish—what is called white glue, although it is white only in the container and dries almost colorless. It can be diluted with water, in as weak as a half-and-half mixture, although adding water somewhat reduces the sheen.

Occasionally, it is desirable to seal the surface of scenery for reasons other than its appearance. If water must be spilled on it during the performance, or if actors' hands soil it, as for instance in using a stair rail, the surface can be made waterproof by any of the methods which have been described. In the production of *Story Theatre*, the director asked that the stage floor be coated so that actors could crawl and roll around on it without soiling their costumes. This was done by painting it with a moderately strong coat of white glue. Clear varnish has been used for the same purpose, although it is more expensive and takes considerably longer to dry.

METALLIC PAINT

The use of metallic paint has already been mentioned. Any coloring material can be used on scenery, and for special effects unusual products may be chosen. Recently metallic pastes in a range of colors have been put on the market by several manufacturers; some of them come in jars, others in metal tubes. They have the consistency of paste shoe polish, and much the same smell. They are intended to be rubbed on a surface such as a picture frame, allowed to dry, and then polished with a soft cloth or brush. They are relatively expensive, but are convenient for producing a metallic sheen on small scenic units. They can be stretched greatly by diluting them with alcohol or paint thinner. The brush is first wet in the liquid and a little of the paste picked up on it and spread on the surface to be decorated.

Ordinary scene paint can be given a sheen by mixing a little gold- or silver-colored metallic powder with it. Because the powder is light, it will float to the surface as the paint dries, and increase the amount of light reflected. It is not necessary to add glue to the mixture, since there is enough binder in the paint to hold the small quantity of metallic pigment to the surface.

The scene shop is more likely to stock metallic paint in the form of pure metal ground to an extremely fine powder. It must be mixed with a vehicle and binder before it is used. White glue and water are often used because they are readily available, although the mixture is a little difficult to brush, and may slightly dull the pigment. White shellac or clear varnish are more satisfactory, as well as a special bronzing liquid; these combine both vehicle and binder.

MAINTENANCE

An essential part of good painting practice is the care of equipment. Since casein paint is insoluble after it has dried, brushes must be washed thoroughly while they are still wet. Soap or a liquid detergent makes the work easier. The brushes should be washed until water run through them comes clear. The paint tends to collect where the bristles are attached to the handle, so the detergent should be worked well into that area, and the bristles separated and flushed with water running at some force from the faucet. If the brushes are stood on the bristles to dry, they will be permanently angled. Large brushes should be hung up, and small brushes laid flat after the bristles have been smoothed to a point.

It is possible to clean paint buckets even after they have dried, especially if they are plastic rather than metal. However, dried paint takes much longer to clean out, so they should be scoured as soon as they are emptied. In an emergency, they can be filled with water, and then cleaned as soon as convenient. The life of brushes is significantly shortened by soaking them in water, and they should be left in a bucket of water only in the direst emergencies; even this is preferable to allowing paint or glue to dry in them, because once they have hardened they are irretrievable.

A great deal of mess and clean-up can be saved by covering counters with newspaper before beginning to mix paint or before pouring it from one container to another. Although this seems like an irksome interruption of the work, three or four minutes spent in spreading newspapers can save an hour or two of the time needed to dig up dried paint and scour the surfaces clean.

13

Set-Up and Strike

Before the first rehearsal of a play, the set crew is expected to mark the position of the scenic elements on the stage floor. The director is also likely to ask that platforms, ramps, and stairs be built first and set up on stage so that the actors can practice using them. Other parts of the scenery are finished in the scene shop, including painting, before they are transported to the stage.

The scenery is usually moved to the stage, assembled, and fastened in place during the weekend before the show opens, although the precise date will depend on the traditions of the local theater and the nature of the scenery. A set incorporating trick effects like the revolving bed in *A Flea in Her Ear* may need to be assembled earlier than usual so that any unforeseen problems may be solved well before opening night.

About a week before opening, one rehearsal, called the technical rehearsal, is set aside in which little attention is paid to the actors and instead all of the other elements of the production are checked and evaluated—costumes, makeup, lighting, sound, properties, and scenery. Since the light crew must do a large part of their work after the set is in place, the deadline for the scenery crew is a day or two before the technical rehearsal.

STAGE GEOGRAPHY

Throughout the preparation of a play, technicians, actors, and the director constantly need to describe positions on the stage floor. This is especially necessary for the scenery crew during set-up. Methods of identifying areas on the various types of open stage (arena stages, thrust stages, etc.) have not yet been standardized. Although use of the traditional proscenium stage is declining, each stagecraft worker should be familiar with the established terminology and methods of identifying stage areas.

Scenery on a proscenium stage usually encloses an approximately trapezoidal area of the stage floor. The front edge of the trapezoid matches an imaginary line joining the back corners of the proscenium opening. The back edge of the trapezoid is parallel but shorter, and approximately fifteen feet beyond the front line. The side edges are marked by slanted lines connecting the matching ends of the front and back lines (Figure 13.1).

This trapezoid is subdivided into smaller areas, each of which is given a distinctive name. The number of subareas varies from theater to theater, but perhaps the commonest is a nine-part division. Each edge of the trapezoid is divided in thirds, and lines are drawn between matching points on opposite edges. The middle division is called *center,* the area immediately in front of it (toward the audience) is called *down center,*

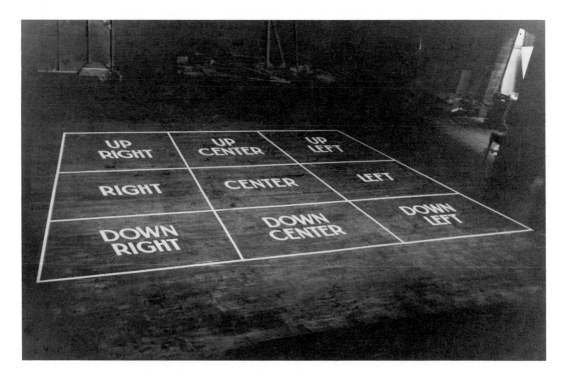

FIGURE 13.1 Conventional divisions of the acting area.

and the division just behind it is called *up center.* The other divisions are named from the viewpoint of someone standing at center, facing the audience. The area directly to his right is called *right center,* the area next to it toward the audience is called *down right,* and the area above it is called *up right;* matching terms are used for the three areas on the left. Eight of these terms, plus five others, are also used directionally. The omitted term is *center,* and the additional terms are *on stage, off stage, above, below,* and *level.*

Two points on stage are said to be level when they are at the same distance from the front edge of the acting area. Thus, a table placed in the center area would be level with a door in the middle of the right wall. One point is said to be below another if it is closer to the audience; a chair set against the side wall between the door and the audience would thus be described as below the door. *On stage* and *off stage* are used less precisely and with more than one meaning. Directionally, *on stage* generally means toward the center area, and *off stage* away from the center. Thus, a technician who was asked to move a platform a little farther on stage would push it toward the center.

When *left, right, up,* and *down* (and their combinations) are used directionally, they do not refer to areas of the stage floor, but are based on a point regarded as center which may be set anywhere in the acting area, although *left* and *right* are still identified in terms of someone directly facing the front of the stage (Figure 13.2). Suppose for example that a chair is placed at the point where the edges of the right-center, center, down-right, and down-center areas meet, and that a technician were instructed to move

FIGURE 13.2 Indicating directions within the acting area. When used directionally, "center" is understood as indicating the point where the actor or scenic unit is standing, no matter where it is located on the stage floor.

it a foot up left; the correct adjustment would be toward center. Moving it down left would move it into the down-center area, up right would put it in the right-center area, and down right in the down-right area. *Up* and *down,* used directionally, mean away from and toward the audience, and *left* and *right,* used alone, mean straight across the stage parallel with the front edge of the acting area, oriented as for someone facing the audience.

These terms may be somewhat confusing at first, especially *left* and *right.* Actors and technicians frequently stand on stage facing in other directions than toward the audience, and the director most often works from a position in the audience, so that the standard directions are the reverse of his own—the right side of the stage is on his left, and the left side is on his right. However, to adjust the terminology to the actual position of each person or scenic element would introduce still more confusion, and after a little experience set crew members should have little trouble using the terminology correctly.

PREPARATION FOR MARKING

As a preliminary to assembling the scenery, the stage must be cleared of the furniture which has been used for rehearsal. In addition, platforms and step units should be moved out of the way.

Some stages are covered with a permanent canvas surfacing. If that is not the case, a floor cloth must be fastened down before the set-up begins. Usually it consists of a single sheet of heavy canvas, hemmed and with grommets set in on three sides. The down-stage edge is fastened to the stage floor with large tacks, and the cloth stretched out to cover the acting area and fastened at the sides and back with large-headed roofing nails driven through the grommets.

MARKING THE GROUND PLAN

After the floorcloth is in place, the first step in assembling the scenery is to mark the positions of the walls, furniture, and other scenic elements on the ground cloth. If this is done before the first rehearsal, it is best to make the marks with lengths of masking tape. If it is done immediately before setting up the scenery, chalk can be used.

The placement of the scenery is indicated by the designer's ground plan (or floor plan) of the stage. Each significant point will be identified by indicating its distance from two basic measuring lines. One of these is the center-line of the stage, running from the front of the stage straight back to the back wall, through the center of the proscenium opening. The other measuring line may be the front edge of the stage, or a line connecting the back corners of the proscenium opening.

FINDING THE CENTER-LINE

The up-stage end of the center-line should be permanently marked by driving a roofing nail into the floor next to the back wall. If it has not been marked, it can be found as follows.

Take a long steel tape and stretch it from one corner of the proscenium opening diagonally across the stage toward the center of the back wall, keeping it two or three feet short of the wall; the free end of the tape should be up stage. The worker holding the tape reel sets the tape at the nearest full foot against one corner of the proscenium wall and holds it firmly against the floor with his thumb. The worker holding the free end of the tape slips a piece of chalk through the metal tab at the end of the tape and swings the tape like a compass, marking an arc of a circle on the stage floor long enough that he is sure it passes through the center-line. The worker should keep the tape taut while marking, and should watch to make sure it does not catch on the floor cloth and bend, thus altering the radius. The other worker then moves to the other side of the stage opening, sets the tape at the same foot mark in the matching position, and holds it while a second arc is marked crossing the first. The center-line will run through the point where the two arcs cross.

The tape is then stretched across the proscenium opening, and the center-point marked. If the width of the opening is not expressible in full feet, the easiest way to find the center is as follows. Two people stretch the tape from the inside edge of the proscenium opening across the stage to the matching edge. A third worker marks the full foot which is closest to the center. The other two workers then reverse positions, stretch the tape out in the opposite direction, and the same dimension is marked on the floor. The center-point will be halfway between these two marks. If they are close together it can be marked by eye. Otherwise, the tape can be used to find the point.

The center-line is then snapped on the floor cloth by stretching a chalk line so that it runs through both points, or it can be drawn by hand in chalk. If the designer has used the edge of the stage as his second measuring line, the workers can proceed to lay out the positions of the scenery. If he has used the line connecting the back corners of the proscenium opening, that line should also be drawn or snapped.

305

When a triangle has sides measuring 3, 4, and 5 units long, the short sides form a right angle. That fact can be used to draw the center-line of the stage at right angles to the front edge. First the center of the edge is marked, and then a point 12′ to one side, on the edge of the stage. One tape is caught at the edge of the stage, at the center-point, and stretched up stage; another tape is run from the second point marked on the edge of the stage, stretched diagonally toward the first tape, and the two tapes are adjusted so that the 16′ mark on the first tape matches the 20′ mark on the slanted tape; the first tape will then be at right angles to the edge of the stage. (In this case, 4′ is taken as the unit of measure; any convenient multiples of 3, 4, and 5 can be used.)

COPYING KEY POINTS

It is usually not necessary to measure every line shown in a ground plan. If a series of platforms are grouped together, it may be possible to measure only one, and then simply push the others into their proper places against it. A few minutes' study of the ground plan, aimed at analyzing the most efficient method of measurement, may save several man-hours of work. In one set for *The Lion in Winter,* the placement of all of the scenery depended on two basic lines, which met at a right angle (Figure 13.3). Their dimensions were as follows:

> *Right wall*
> Downstage corner: 17′-0″ right of the center-line,
>   7′-0″ above the horizontal measuring line
> Upstage corner: 7′-0″ left of the center-line,
>   23′-0″ from the horizontal measuring line
>
> *Left wall*
> Upstage corner: same as for the right wall (they
>   meet at this point)
> Downstage corner: 17′-0″ left of the center-line,
>   8′-0″ above the horizontal measuring line.

Against the walls defined by these two lines several platform and step units were placed. When they were set on stage in the correct order, their positions were automatically determined. In addition, a 6′-0″ wall section extended from the downstage end of the left wall straight toward the audience, stopping 2′-0″ above the horizontal

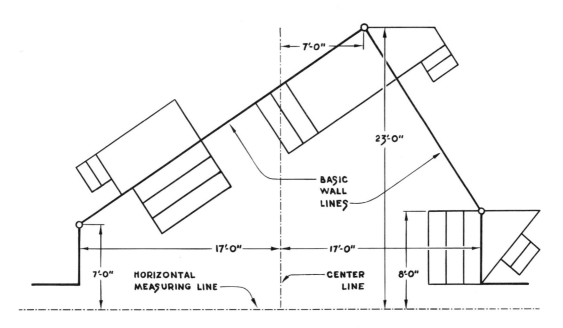

FIGURE 13.3 Laying out basic wall lines for a set on the stage floor.

measuring line, and a similar 5'-0" wall extended from the downstage end of the right wall straight toward the audience, also stopping 2'-0" above the horizontal measuring line. From the downstage edge of each of these walls, a 4'-0" flat ran directly off stage, as a return. Although this description does not include the placement of furniture, which required somewhat more measurement, it was nevertheless possible to lay out the plan of the set on the stage floor efficiently and accurately from a relatively few measurements.

In marking a ground plan on the floor of the stage, a carpenter's steel square is too small to use as a guide for setting the measuring tape at right angles to the front edge of the stage. The most convenient guide is a full sheet of corrugated cardboard; upson board or even 1/4" plywood can also be used. The dimension left or right of the center-line is first marked on the edge of the stage, then the sheet laid beside it, about an inch away, and the short side aligned with the edge of the stage. The tape is held at the mark and stretched back parallel with the edge of the sheet to measure the second dimension for the point being located.

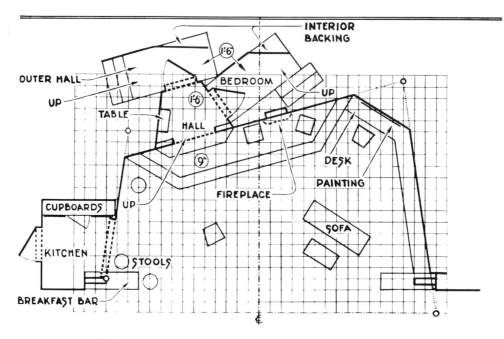

FIGURE 13.4   Laying out wall lines which do not match grid points.

The dimensions are not always quite so simple. Often one edge of a wall section will not fall at any easily measurable point. However, if the designer has planned with desirable efficiency, it will be possible to draw a line along which the wall is to stand and to determine the point at which the other corner is to be set. When the wall matches that point and line, it will then be in the correct position.

As an example, in one set for Neil Simon's *Come Blow Your Horn,* the downstage edge of the right wall was placed 14'-0" right of the center-line, and 3'-0" above the horizontal measuring line (Figure 13.4). The upper corner did not fall at an easily identifiable point, but when the line of the wall was extended it passed through a point 12'-0" right of the center-line and 16'-0" above the horizontal measuring line. The workmen first drew this entire line, and then set the wall in place with the downstage corner at the end of the line and the flats extending along the line. They did not reach all the way, but the measurements defined the angle at which the wall was to stand, and when it had been set in place the upper corner was in its correct position, even though that had been determined indirectly. Obviously, it is extremely helpful if the designer has indicated the simplest method of measuring on his ground plan, and in fact one of the marks of a skilled designer is the ease with which his plan for the set can be drawn full-scale on the stage floor.

The positions of the furniture may be drawn at the same time as the outlines of walls and platforms, or, if they are not too complicated, they can be set by eye after the major scenic elements are in place.

THE ASSEMBLY SEQUENCE

The design of the set enforces a particular order of assembly. For instance, door frames cannot be fastened in place until the flats which support them have been set up, and a flat which is to stand on a platform cannot be fastened up until the platform has been put in position. Of course, decorative elements such as cornices, pictures, and drapes can be hung only after the walls are assembled.

Probably most often the flats are fastened together first. The back wall is moved into position, so that one flat is in its proper place, but with the rest of the wall left partially folded so that it will stand by itself. The first flat is fastened with a stage brace, the rest of the wall unfolded and moved into position, and fastened with as many additional braces as necessary. If stiffening is needed, it is added, either by setting battens in S-hooks, by fastening them to the back of the flats with hinges, or by nailing them directly to the stiles.

As soon as the first flat has been fastened, the adjacent side wall is moved into place and fastened with stage braces, and the corner where the two walls meet is lashed tight. Meanwhile the rest of the back wall will have been set, and the other side wall brought into position and fastened tight.

When flats are placed so that the corner points toward the audience at an angle other than 90°, the edges of the flats form an unsightly joint (Figure 13.5). Sometimes it can be concealed by hinging the flats on the offstage side so that the back edges of the stiles are in contact, and then nailing a strip of 3/4″ quarter-round between the stiles, on the front, and painting it to match the flats.

FIGURE 13.5 Concealing joints between angled flats. When the houses were assembled, ugly gaps appeared where the edges of the flats came together. These were filled in by nailing vertical strips of 3/4″ quarter-round into the gaps, and painting them to match the flats.

When the walls have been properly placed and fastened, any work involving ladders is done, for example, fastening up beams or a cornice. Usually platforms and stair units are kept off stage to keep the floor clear for the ladders, but if large platforms are to be used in the set it may sometimes be more convenient to move them on stage so that the ladders can be set on top of them. When these jobs have been finished, the ceiling is lowered until it rests on the top edges of the wall. This will help to stiffen them. The platform and step units are then moved into position.

> In setting up a stepladder to work on scenery, the natural instinct is to place the base of the ladder directly under the point where the work must be done; then the worker climbs up and discovers he is two or three feet away from where he should be. Instead, he should decide approximately which step he will be standing on, and then set the ladder so that that step is under the work point. It is dangerous to work while reaching far out beyond a ladder; in fact, that is the cause of more than half the accidents involving ladders.

Finally, attached pieces are added, window and door frames, mopboards, pictures, and drapes; the set is finished by laying rugs if they are to be used, and setting the furniture in place. Although additional decorative touches may be used—vases of flowers, books on shelves, ashtrays, a telephone, dishes, etc.—they are likely to be supplied and arranged by the properties crew rather than the set crew.

> Sometimes a door in scenery will tend to ooze open after it is closed. If it is set in a back wall which is not joined rigidly to side walls (for instance, the wall of a hall placed some distance behind the back wall of the main set), it can be made self-closing as follows. Loosen the stage braces supporting the wall and open the door halfway. Very slowly tilt the wall forward. At some point the door will begin to close. Fasten the stage braces in this position. The door will then stay shut during performance.

The scenic units must be fastened so that they will not move during the final rehearsals and the performances of the show. In particular platforms and stairs must be prevented from teetering or shifting in use. If they stand against flats, it may be possible to nail through the stiles or bottom diagonal braces of the flats into the frames of the platforms and stairs, preferably using double-headed nails which will be easy to remove. If platforms, ramps, or stair units stand beside other structures, they can often be joined to each other with loose-pin hinges or by nails driven through adjacent legs or braces. This may be difficult at the downstage edges, which are visible to the audience and consequently enclosed, but by pulling the structures out from the wall it will be possible to nail them together at the offstage or upstage sides, which have not been surfaced. If the units are high enough it may be possible for a crew member to crawl inside them and drive a few strategic nails close to the on-stage edges. The legs of adjacent platforms can also be fastened together by C-clamps, placed so that they are inside the structures, not only out of sight but so that they will not strike the flats when the units are pushed back into place.

Fine adjustments can be made in fitting doors on frames and in slanting the doors so that they will stay shut, by putting cardboard shims under the hinges. Decide whether the top or bottom of the door should be moved, and then turn the screws to loosen the hinge. Slip one or more strips of cardboard under the leaf of the hinge and retighten the screws. If the cardboard shims are fairly thick, it will be necessary to replace the screws with longer ones.

It may be difficult to nail off-stage access stairs or platforms to flats or other units. They can be prevented from shifting by nailing small blocks of wood to the floor beside the legs, so that the units cannot move in any direction. The backstage areas are usually dark during a performance, so it is important that the blocks be placed where the actors are not likely to step on or trip over them; they can be placed between the legs rather than outside them. In addition, luminous tape should be pressed along the edge of each step as a guide to using them in the dark.

Monofilament nylon fishline is nearly invisible on stage; it can be used to suspend light scenic units in the air or as guylines to stabilize hanging pieces, and will be unnoticed by the audience. Stovepipe wire can be used for the same purpose, although it is somewhat more visible and cannot be used in front of a light background.

The method described applies primarily to a one-set show which does not require shifting during performance, and to a set fastened on the stage floor rather than being flown. The procedures for flown and shifted scenery are discussed in the next chapter.

Masking flats are usually moved into position after all the rest of the set has been assembled. They serve the double purpose of hiding backstage areas from the audience and suggesting what the audience would see through the doors and windows if they were looking at the real room represented by the stage set—a patch of sky beyond a window, with perhaps a distant skyline painted on it and a tree branch or two extending into view; the wall of an adjoining room, glimpsed when an actor walks through a door.

The audience will be able to see only a small area beyond a door of normal size, and it is nearly impossible for them to judge the distance between the masking and the door; consequently, only a small wall section will be provided, and it will usually be placed close behind the opening.

Like the major walls of the set, the positions of the masking flats will be indicated on the designer's ground plan, but it is seldom necessary to measure them; they can be judged by eye. The flats must be set so that the edges are hidden from each member of the audience, but the placement need not be checked for every seat in the house. Instead, only two critical seats need be tested, usually those at the ends of the first row. If the backing flats mask fully for those two seats, no one in the audience will be able to see past them.

The visible areas can be checked before the masking is set in place by going backstage and standing behind the opening. The workman looks through the opening toward one of the end seats and moves sideways until he reaches the point where he can no longer see the seat. This point is then marked in chalk on the floor of the stage. He then moves back in the other direction until the seat again disappears, and marks that point. If lines are drawn between these two points and the edges of the door, they will enclose the entire backstage area which can be seen from the seat tested (these are called *sight lines*). A pair of lines can be similarly drawn for the seat at the other end of the row, and the two outside lines will then mark the area visible to anyone in the audience. (A little experience will demonstrate which two of the four lines are critical, so that only they need actually to be drawn.)

The backing must be placed so that it runs entirely across the visible area, and so that the edges are beyond the lines marked. Usually the masking will have been designed so that it extends at least half a foot beyond the sight lines; if backstage space is very restricted the fitting may be tighter, and if there is a great deal of space it may have been designed to stretch farther by several feet. Often the masking will be in the form of a two-fold or booked flats, which will stand by themselves if they are placed at an angle not too far from 90°, and so may not need stage braces or other fastening. This is an advantage if the set must be shifted, since the backing can be folded and moved aside without having to remove a stage screw.

The sight lines fan out beyond the opening, so that the closer the masking is placed to the door the farther it will extend out beyond the visible area. However, backing must not get in the way of the actors. Not only must it be possible for them to open the door freely, but the masking flats should not interfere with their movements, forcing them to curve sharply so as to walk around them.

After the masking has been set in position, it should be checked by actually sitting in the critical seats and leaning from side to side to make sure that the edges will be invisible even if the viewers should not sit perfectly straight.

LIFTING TECHNIQUES

Although scenic structures tend to be much lighter than their counterparts outside the theater, they are nevertheless often too heavy for easy handling, and even a simple flat is awkward because of its size. Efficient lifting depends at least as much on mind as on muscle, and a worker of only moderate strength who uses sound techniques can move weights that would stagger a far larger and stronger person who was not using his power efficiently.

Efficiency in handling scenery depends on two fundamental secrets. One is the relation between the center of gravity and the support. If the scenic unit is not to fall over when it is picked up, the center of gravity must be between the supports, either in the same plane or directly above or below them. It may seem incredible that two workers would try to pick up a flat by lifting a rail and a stile. What is even more staggering is that, having lifted one flat off sawhorses from those positions and watched it collapse on the floor, they would walk to a second flat and attempt to lift it in the same way—but that painful example is not imaginary. Obviously, if two workers are to pick up a horizontal flat, they must lift it by both rails or both stiles. The center of gravity then lies between their supporting hands.

The center of gravity is the point inside a unit at which the structure would hang evenly balanced, if a rope could be fastened to it. It is not always in the dimensional center of the structure. For example, something like half the weight of a platform is supplied by the flooring. Thus, when a platform is turned on its side to carry it through a door, the center of gravity is much closer to the plywood top than to the ends of the legs, and if it is to be carried easily the hands must be placed off the dimensional center, closer to the flooring.

The second secret of efficient handling is related; scenic units are most manageable if carried vertically or horizontally, and least easy to control if they are slanted. If two workmen are carrying an upright flat, each one holding one of the stiles, and the flat begins to tilt, the center of gravity falls away from them out past their hands, and great force must be used to keep the flat from falling over. Much greater control results from spreading the hands vertically on the stile a little farther apart than is comfortable, and that should be done automatically whenever a flat is held upright, either by one or a pair of workers. This seems awkward at first, but having a flat or two fall over is enough to persuade crew members that they should use the spread-hand grip.

There are standard techniques which make it possible for one person to raise a flat from the floor to vertical position, to set it on sawhorses or take it down, to move it across the stage, and to maneuver it in almost any way desired. Indeed, one long-suffering technical director on dozens of occasions has laid an entire wall as high as twelve feet and as long as thirty on sawhorses by himself, taken it down, moved it into the theater, and set it upright on stage. In most theaters, however, enough workers are available for each flat or platform to be handled by at least two people, with much greater ease and with a saving in work time.

Moving flats by hand is called *running,* which suggests a fact of value when a single worker must move a flat standing vertically. The faster it is moved the easier it is to hold it upright. The stile closest to the position to which the flat is to be moved is grasped, with the worker standing beside the flat and facing toward where it is to be moved. The front corner of the flat is raised slightly from the floor and the flat is then pulled forward quickly to its new position, sliding on the back corner of the rail. The pressure of air against the canvas helps hold it upright, and the faster the flat is moved the more assistance is provided.

Air pressure can also be used to lower an upright flat to the floor; this is called *floating.* A plain flat of ordinary size or wider has a large canvas surface in relation to its weight. If a worker sets one foot against the center of the bottom rail of a flat standing vertically, gives it a slight push and then lets go, the flat compresses the air in front of it as it falls, so that rather than crashing to the floor it floats down and settles gently into place. This is a rather startling sight, and some workers like to amaze beginners by floating a flat without explanation. Thinking the flat is about to crash, a new worker is likely to run forward and grab a stile, but the momentary pause enables the compressed air to escape—and then it will crash.

If the flat has door or window openings, the air can escape through them, and the flat will not float. The method will also not work with narrow flats, where the ratio of canvas to framing is too small, or with flats to which a great deal of additional bracing has been added, which may increase the weight beyond the ability of the air cushion to support it. Of course, before a flat is floated, the worker must make sure that the area in which it will fall is clear of furniture, scenic elements, or other workers, and he should give the traditional warning, "Heads up!" As the flat settles down, the escaping air blows out any dust which is lying on the floor, often in a billowing cloud. Nevertheless, floating is a useful and easy way to lower a flat in order to work on it.

If a flat must be lowered by hand, two workers are required. They stand facing the side of the flat which is to rest on the floor, one at each stile, and then *walk it down,* first leaning it slightly toward them and walking backward, shifting their support of it hand-over-hand, and lowering it at approximately the same speed so as to keep it level. The flat must be supported by the stiles; pressing against the open canvas is likely to punch it out of shape. A flat can be raised in the same way, first picking up the top rail and lifting it to head height, then walking toward the flat, moving the hands down hand-over-hand, until it is standing upright. There is a tendency for the bottom rail to slide along the floor when it is walked either up or down, so it is helpful if a third worker can *foot it,* holding his toe against the bottom rail until the flat has been raised or lowered.

Book flats, that is, two flats hinged together, will remain stable as long as they are opened at approximately 45°. By standing between them, facing away from them, grasping a stile with each hand, lifting the front corners slightly off the floor, and walking forward briskly, one person can move a book rather easily. When a book flat has been moved into place, there is a tendency to open it fully, but it must then be manually supported while it is fastened. It is better to set one flat in place and to leave the other at the 45° angle. Once the first flat is fastened firmly, it will support the entire unit as the second flat is opened and swung into place.

A final suggestion is that before any piece of scenery is picked up, the workers should have decided where it is to be moved to. If it is necessary to turn it, they should agree on which direction it is to be swung; and the path along which it must be moved should be checked to make sure that the space is clear. Few experiences make one feel sillier than picking up a flat or platform, taking two steps with it, and then discovering that there is no visible spot to which it can be moved, and that it must be carried back and set down in its original spot while a new area is found or cleared. A little foresight is always valuable in the scene shop. Many a worker has tried to turn over a flat resting on sawhorses by grasping the center of one stile and lifting and swinging it away from him, only to discover that when he had turned it past vertical he could no longer reach far enough to lay it down, could not drop it (a flat will not float down on sawhorses), and could only wrestle it back into its original position or call frantically for assistance.

STRIKING

For no known reason, the process of removing a set from its position on stage is referred to as *striking*. The term is also used for other theatrical units such as lights and properties. Sets are struck following the last performance of the play, dismantled, permanent units placed in storage, usable materials salvaged, and the rest scrapped and sent to the dump.

In most theaters, it is traditional to strike the set on the same evening as the last performance, beginning as soon as the last member of the audience has left the theater. The usual explanation for that rather late work session is that the actors are on hand to help, whereas if the strike were delayed till the next day, the dispirited set crew would have to do it alone in the cold light of morning. Certainly, large numbers typically turn out for strike, including all the members of the various crews, the actors, and perhaps even a director or designer. The combination of performance tension and the release produced by the final fall of the curtain, as well as the euphoria of fatigue, produce a somewhat hectically festive atmosphere, in which the theater workers attack the scenery with enthusiasm, even if not always with a desirable degree of restraint. At the Wake Forest University theater, it has become traditional to have cake, cookies, and punch provided for each strike, and not only are staggering quantities consumed during the hours of work, but it is rumored that strikes are sometimes followed by off-campus parties at local pizza parlors. In any case, strike is a fitting climax to the weeks of work which have gone into any successful theatrical production, and is an experience not to be missed, in which the enthusiasm and camaraderie of theater people at their best are most vividly displayed.

SUPERVISION

The excitement of the strike may tempt the technical director to snatch up a hammer and take an active part. This is a mistake. Because the work is necessarily chaotic, and because many of the workers are inexperienced, they need constant supervision. The shop foreman should be assigned the responsibility for actually running the strike. He operates on stage most of the time, making work assignments, indicating the order in which projects should be done, and giving assistance when it is needed. He may also take frequent trips to the scene shop to check on the work being done there, to make sure that units are properly stored, and to solve any problems that may have arisen.

It is better for the technical director to stay out in front of the stage during most of the strike, also ready to answer the questions of the workers, and available for consultation with the foreman if need be. His second most important responsibility is to make sure that locally established policies are followed—that units to be saved are not torn apart, that hardware is removed and stored properly, that the stage is returned to its normal condition at the end of the strike. His most important responsibility is to watch constantly to make sure that the work is being done safely, something which he can assess more accurately than the foreman can from his position on stage.

SAFETY DURING STRIKE

The strike session involves special dangers. Many different jobs are carried on simultaneously. Large quantities of trash are handled, and even if it is steadily picked up and put in containers, debris will be lying on the floor during most of the strike, including some boards with nails pointing up; large and heavy units may have to be moved, and in the case of flats, workers must walk backward across the stage as they are lowered. Many members of the strike crew may have had no experience in scene shop work, and all of them are likely to be tired; even though fatigue may be masked by the excitement of the strike and by the enthusiasm produced by the end of a successful run of the show, those feelings in themselves may decrease the care with which the work is done.

The crew should be given a few instructions about safety before the strike begins. It will probably not be possible to list a complicated set of rules, but the necessity for care and safety should be stressed. The traditional, "Heads up!" warning should be mentioned, and the workers should be urged not only to react to it instantaneously, but to give the warning whenever a flat is to be lowered or a heavy platform turned on edge. In addition, the technical director and his supervisory staff should remain alert to dangerous work procedures, and should stop them whenever they are detected.

Without such a procedure, serious accidents are possible during strike, but with reasonable care and sound precautions, the work can be done as safely as other theatrical tasks.

THE STRIKING SEQUENCE

Before the fall of the curtain at the end of the last performance, the equipment needed for the strike should be assembled. This includes all of the screwdrivers, crowbars, nail-pullers, and hammers available (excluding tack hammers). Usually wrenches should also be provided, perhaps supplemented by some borrowed from the light crew. Half a dozen large waste containers, preferably on casters, will be needed.

Storage trays should be brought out so that hardware can be put in them as it is removed from the scenery. Probably the "unsorted" trays should be brought out for nails, screws, and bolts, since workers are unlikely to sort them out carefully during the frenzy of strike. Besides these, trays should be included for hinges, cleats, stage screws, foot-irons, and any other types of hardware used on the set.

The basic pattern of strike is the reverse of that of set-up. First furniture and decorative elements such as drapes and pictures are removed. Simultaneously the properties crew will be collecting the props which are on stage and taking them to the prop room for storage. Meanwhile the set crew can raise the ceiling to clear the flats, if one has been used.

Next platforms and stair units are pulled out, the nails, clamps, bolts, or hinges which were used to fasten them together are taken off, and the platforms are sent to storage. Architectural elements attached to the walls are removed (pilasters, cornices and mopboards, door frames, window frames). As many of the wall supports are removed as can safely be done, stiffening battens are taken off, even some of the stage braces. When the stage has been cleared of furniture and debris, the walls are walked down to the floor and disassembled.

STORAGE

Strike procedures vary a good deal from theater to theater, depending on the particular policies which have been established. For example, in one theater platforms will be sent to storage intact. In another theater they will be disassembled and only the usable lumber saved. It may be the policy to remove all hardware from flats before storage; other theaters may regularly leave the hardware on. Such variations depend on the amount of storage space (it takes much more space to store platforms intact than when they have been disassembled), on how well stocked the scene shop is (if flat hardware is in short supply, it will probably have to be removed before the flats are put in the scene dock), and on budget. (A theater operating with an inadequate budget may save even very short boards for reuse. With a generous budget, only the best and longest pieces of scrap lumber may be saved.) Suggestions made here are therefore subject to adaptation for different theaters, and the local policy should take precedence over them.

In almost every theater, flats are stored individually. Consequently each wall section must be separated. The flats are first laid face up on the floor and the dutchmen pulled off by loosening the ends in the center of the stiles, and pulling the strips off while walking backwards along the adjoining stiles. Next the hinges are removed. The flats are then turned over and hardware such as lash cleats or stop cleats taken off. However, sill irons at the bottom of door openings are considered permanent parts of the flats, and should be left on. Each flat must then be carefully inspected on both sides to make sure that no nails have been left (except of course the clout nails which are an essential part of the structure). It is very easy to miss nails, and more than a fast glance should be given the flat. Projecting nails are likely to punch into other flats when the scenery is stored, but more important they can cause dangerous wounds or scratches when unsuspecting crew members pick up the flats to carry them to the scene dock.

SALVAGING

Which materials are to be saved and which discarded depends on the policies of the individual theater. In case of doubt, workers should ask the technical director. As a fundamental policy, no piece of furniture or scenic unit can be reused if the audience will recognize it from a previous play. If the character of a piece of furniture is structurally determined, that is, if the basic frame is distinctively shaped, as in the case of an elaborate Victorian sofa, reuse will usually be impossible. On the other hand, the appearance of the unit may depend on applied decoration—carving glued on, painted motifs, the pattern of the upholstery material. In that case it may be possible to strip off the decoration and replace it so as to produce a very different appearance and style. Even then, the amount of work required for effective alteration must be balanced against the cost in time and material of making a new unit from scratch.

> Although it may seem surprising, there is a ready market for furniture specially built for stage use, and in fact for salvageable decorative units such as papier-maché plaques. Instead of sending such things to the dump, a theater can make a considerable sum of money by holding well publicized sales once or twice a season.

Odd-shaped platforms and stairs are unlikely to be used again. Square or rectangular rigid platforms of standard dimensions are readily reusable, but require a great deal of storage space. Folding platforms should always be saved; they will have been specifically designed for storage.

> If platforms and stairs are kept for reuse, the padding and canvas covering should be left intact, since it would be needed whenever they were used again.

When platforms are discarded, all usable lumber should be removed, processed, and stored. Nearly always the plywood tops will be worth saving. The supporting lumber may require too much work to justify trying to salvage it, especially if many nails must be unclinched and pulled. However, even short lengths of lumber are useful in the scene shop, and it may be possible to retrieve some of the framing by simply cutting out the sections where the pieces have been nailed. Badly split or warped lumber should be discarded.

All salvaged lumber, including plywood, should be carefully denailed before it is stored. This can be done on stage, or the boards carried back to the scene shop for processing. Workers should be discouraged from clinching nails as a supposed safety precaution. Not only must they be unclinched before they are removed but it is easy to overlook them, and when a board is pulled out of the lumber rack an unsuspected clinched nail can cut a long slash across the hand. Clinched nails are safer only if the boards are left on the floor with the points up. They should be denailed as soon as they have been removed from the scenery, so that clinching is not even temporarily necessary as a safety measure.

With a very few exceptions, all flats are salvageable. Even if flats of odd shapes or dimensions have been used in the set, the best design practice is to plan them so that the unusual elements can be easily removed, leaving standard flats.

Sections of canvas as small as a square yard may be valuable for covering openings in flats or patching holes. Even smaller pieces are usable for papier-mâché; however, if the canvas is stiff from having been painted several times, it is worthless. Strips of canvas six inches wide and five or six feet long are useful as dutchmen, if the canvas is in good condition.

Heavy plywood can be used to make chair seats or stair treads. For seats, the minimum usable size is a square 1'-6" on a side; stair treads require pieces a foot wide and at least three feet long; plywood pieces smaller than these dimensions should be discarded. In designing scenery, every effort is made to avoid cutting into a sheet of heavy plywood, so that where possible the platforms will have been built a full 4'-0" × 8'-0". If the platforms are taken apart, the full-sheet tops should be pried up, the nails removed, and the plywood stored with the supply of new sheets.

Much smaller scraps of 1/4" plywood are salvageable, since they can be cut up into corner-blocks. Any piece from which a 10" square can be cut is usable, but strips 7" wide can also be cut into corner-blocks of standard size by running the grain parallel with the hypotenuse of the triangle. Within a day or two after strike, it is established practice for the set crew to cut up all scrap 1/4" plywood into corner-blocks, so that the wood can be carried to the scene shop and left near the saw, rather than being put in the regular plywood bins.

Nearly all hardware is reusable, and discarded scenic units or even broken boards should be carefully checked to make sure that no hinges or bolts are left attached to them when they are thrown away. Nails are so cheap that it is uneconomical to straighten them. Tacks should be removed from plywood before it is put back in storage, and unless they have been bent they should be saved.

Occasionally, a long bolt may be usable even if it has been slightly bent, and it may be worthwhile attempting to straighten it, but if the threads have been damaged it should be discarded, since it will be difficult or impossible to attach a nut. Thread damage can be identified by inspection; the threads will have been flattened, and the area may appear brighter than the rest of the bolt.

Screws should be discarded if they are bent or have blunted points or worn slots. For some reason, undoubtedly associated with gremlins or poltergeists, if two bad screws are put in a work tray among a hundred good ones, one of the bad ones will be picked up ninety-seven times out of a hundred; not only during strike but throughout construction, workers should be instructed to discard defective screws in the waste basket as soon as they are discovered, not throw them back into the regular supply.

HARDWARE STORAGE

After the scenery has been processed and stored, and the scraps set out for collection and disposal, all tools and hardware should be returned to their proper places, and the tool rack should be carefully checked to make sure that all the tools have been accounted for. The different types of hardware should be sorted out and stored properly (loose-pin hinges separated from tight-pins, bolts sorted by size, lash cleats separated from stop cleats, etc.). And at long last the crew is ready to turn out the lights, lock up, and take off for the nearest pizzaria or their homes for a well deserved rest.

Few things contribute so much to scene shop efficiency as a tradition of thorough, efficient, and orderly striking. Nails bent down and left in lumber which is put in storage can cause painful and dangerous wounds. Tools tossed down in the corner of the stage may require hours of searching when work is started on the next show; hardware thrown together in an unsorted mess will delay its future use. Half hinges carelessly left on flats when they are stored may create serious difficulties when they are next needed; and the reckless destruction of scenic units which could have been used again can result in a distressing and unnecessary expenditure of money and time when they are needed for a later show. A well planned and orderly strike avoids those problems, contributes greatly to the general efficiency of the theater operation, and is probably the most vivid indication of a properly organized and operated drama program.

14

Shifting

All of the action of a play may take place in one room (Shaw's *Candida*), or different episodes may occur in a variety of locales (Shaw's *Saint Joan* specifies seven settings, three interior and four outdoors). No esthetic principle requires that the backgrounds of the action be reproduced in full and realistic detail; nevertheless, it will often be necessary to provide more than one scenic background for a play, one of which will have to be moved off stage and a second put in place for the following episode. This process is called *shifting*.

The use of multiple settings may contribute greatly to the effectiveness of a production, not only by identifying the different locales of the action for the audience, but also by providing visual variety, giving the actors different patterns of movement, and making it possible to underline the varying moods or emotions of different scenes. At the same time, the use of several sets creates several problems. The most important is that the flow of the performance must be interrupted while the scenery is being changed. The less important problems are technical or practical—with each added set, the time needed for design and construction is increased, and the technical director must spend several hours planning the shifts and training a special crew to carry them out, and of course the cost of materials rises steadily as the amount of scenery which must be provided increases.

For those reasons, there is a strong tendency to plan productions so as to require as few sets as possible. One collection of Ibsen's drama includes eleven plays, ten of which specify scenery as follows:

>4 plays—1 interior setting for each
>2 plays—2 interiors
>2 plays—2 interiors, 1 exterior
>1 play—4 interiors
>1 play—4 interiors, 1 exterior

The eleventh play, *Peer Gynt,* specifies thirty-one different exterior settings and three interiors; in only three instances is the same set used twice during the play; in addition, one scene is described as being played in total darkness, and so would not require a special setting. The locales vary enormously, including mountain and desert scenes, the deck of a ship, the interior of an Arab tent, an insane asylum in Egypt, and a cave in which trolls live. It is easy to see why the play is generally considered almost impossible to stage, and any production of it is viewed as a tour de force.

But even if the playscript lists several different settings, the designer may reduce their number. The traditional texts identify the action of Shakespeare's *Taming of the Shrew* as taking place in eleven different places, six interiors and five out of doors. For one production the designer developed a single complex structure which could be used for all of the scenes, and the only shifting needed was for the servants to bring out and arrange one small and one large table, and five stools.

Whatever the form of the scenery, it is the designer's responsibility to plan it so that it is shiftable within the physical limitations of the stage, with the available man-power, and so that shifts do not unduly interrupt the flow of the performance.

SPECIAL SOLUTIONS TO SHIFTING PROBLEMS

When working with plays which make unusual scenic demands, or in theaters with inadequate stage facilities, designers' ingenuity may be severely tested. The solutions developed to problems of shiftability may involve adaptations of established methods or the invention of new techniques, some of them almost reaching the level of magic tricks. A detailed discussion of such solutions would be more appropriate to a book on set design, but a couple of examples will be given.

The first makes use of what is called a unit set, in which the major scenic structure is relatively neutral and unobtrusive, given character by the addition of smaller but more noticeable units, which suggest the different locales. This is a larger application of the method often used for adapting furniture, in which a simple table or chair is restyled by the addition of applied ornaments.

Brecht and Weill's *Threepenny Opera* is set in early nineteenth-century England, and the action takes place in half a dozen locales, including a London street, a clothing store, a barn, a brothel, and Newgate prison, one of the prison scenes showing the outside of a cell, another with a scaffold and gallows ready for an execution. One production was given in a theater with extremely limited off-stage storage space. The designer developed a relatively neutral structure which could remain in place throughout the performance, with the different settings suggested by adding furniture and relatively small scenic elements to change its appearance.

The basic structure consisted of three long platforms placed parallel with the front edge of the stage, one behind the other, with the front edge of the group ten feet back from the edge of the stage. A false proscenium was placed just in front of the curtain line, and a similar structure was set against the front edge of each platform and immediately behind the last; they had rectangular openings and were decorated with three-dimensional beams simulating rough-hewn timber. The entire structure was designed in forced perspective to make the stage seem deeper: the openings varied in width from 29'-4" at the front of the stage to 8'-0" at the back. To suggest the period, it was decided to paint all of the scenery in imitation of a faded etching: the beams were painted dark brown and grained, the flats were given a faded tan base and cross-hatched with brown. The stage floor was covered with cobblestones.

For the street scenes, the act curtain was closed, the scenes played in front of it, and the locale suggested only by the cobblestones, the pattern of the actors' movements, and the lines of the play.

The clothing store was suggested by setting a specially made structure in the center of the stage immediately in front of the first platform, combining a counter, a display case, and a stand-up desk. For the brothel scene, special furniture was placed on stage and the acting area was defined by screens set on the stage floor, backed against the front edge of the first platform. A window was cut at center and a free-standing street lamp was placed beyond it on the lowest platform, which then served as a sidewalk along which actors could stroll and occasionally stop outside the window for a discussion with other actors inside the house.

Large crude gates, designed in forced perspective, were used to close the space between the two down-stage inner prosceniums for the scenes in the barn, and furniture specified by the script was brought on—kegs for the actors to sit on, a table, and a sofa.

Overhead tracks were constructed behind the first and second of the inner prosceniums, and for the prison scenes large uncanvassed flat frames were slid on from each side so that they met in the center. They were covered with bars, creating the effect of a prison cell, with a barred door set in the down-stage frames; the stage floor in front of the cell became a prison corridor. For the execution scene the two barred frames at the front were pulled apart and a platform placed in the center with a short flight of stairs hinged to its front edge, which were flopped down to rest on the stage floor. A gallows was set down in a socket at the back of the platform.

The appearance of the setting was altered strikingly by these rather simple changes. It was possible to store the scenic structures not being used at the moment without interfering with the free movement of the large cast back stage, and a couple of hours rehearsal was sufficient to enable the shift crew to make the changes quickly and unobtrusively.

In a production of *The Lark* in the same theater, a problem arose when it was discovered that both a showy altar and a desk for three judges had to be provided, but that there was not enough backstage space to store both of them when they were not in use. The designer's solution was to create a single structure which could be used for both purposes but which could be altered greatly in appearance without stopping the performance for an undue length of time (Figures 14.1, 14.2).

The desk was used first. It was designed in medieval style, with decorative triangular shapes at the front, and painted a uniform dark grey. The two triangles were fastened to rectangular bases which were hinged so as to form part of the top surface of the desk. In addition, a section at the center of the back edge was hinged and a cross

FIGURE 14.1 The desk–altar for *The Lark*, shown here in use as a desk for the three judges.

FIGURE 14.2   The desk for *The Lark* transformed into an altar, shown here as a model.

attached to its underside which was invisible to the audience during the trial scene.

The desk was transformed to an altar during a momentary blackout. The two triangular sections were flipped back so that their bases rested on the solid top surface of the desk, and the hinged section at the back was swung up and forward. Behind the triangular sections a white lace altar cloth had been fastened in place, hidden from the audience when the unit was first seen but revealed when the sections were set upright. The inside surfaces were decorated with molding and carving, and were painted a bright gold. Attached to each triangle was a half-arch, unobtrusive when they hung down but joining to form a complete arch of gold in the upright position, and framing the gold cross. The change in appearance was so great that it is probable no one in the audience realized he was seeing the same piece of furniture twice, and since the shift required only three quick flips it could be done by a single actor in not much more than one second.

When sets of different sizes are required for a play, it may be possible to leave the largest permanently in position, and to place the other set or sets inside it as needed. In the production of *A Flea in Her Ear* which has already been mentioned, the revolving bed needed for the hotel scene was too heavy and complicated to shift, and too large to store off stage. The two sets for the play were designed so that the hotel set could

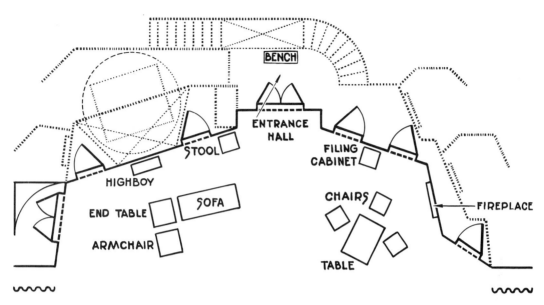

FIGURE 14.3 Nesting sets. The first–act set for *A Flea in Her Ear* (*shown in heavy lines*) is placed in front of the act-two set (*dotted lines*), which remains in place throughout the performance.

remain in place except for one short wall section, which was arranged to fold back out of the way, and the living room set could be fitted in front of and inside the other (Figures 14.3, 14.4).

The kind of shifting methods which have been described may be especially invented by the designer, and so are likely to vary greatly. There are standard methods of shifting which are used over and over again, and with which all set workers should become familiar. Shifting methods can be divided into two basic groups—those in which the scenery is moved vertically, and those in which it is moved horizontally.

FIGURE 14.4 The designer's painting of the first–act set for *A Flea in Her Ear*.

FLYING

Two or three methods of vertical shifting have been tried, but by far the commonest is *flying.* This requires that a high open space be provided over the stage area, called the *flyloft,* and that support be supplied for fastening pulleys over which cables can be run and the scenery fastened to them and pulled safely up out of sight of the audience.

Two systems of flying are used, the sandbag and counterweight systems. This last term is misleading, since the sandbags also serve as counterweights, but it is reserved for an arrangement involving battens from which the scenery is hung, and metal weights running in a protective cage. The pulleys are attached to an open horizontal ceiling formed of steel beams running parallel with the front edge of the stage, set close to the actual ceiling of the flyloft, with just enough space above it so that workmen can walk out on the beams and adjust the pulleys. This is called a *grid.* Normally three pulleys are fastened in each of the slots between the beams, and cables run through them and tied to battens made of metal pipe. The other ends of the cables run to pulleys attached to the side wall of the stage, and then down to a lock rail to which they can be fastened. This may be placed so that it can be reached from the stage floor, or it may be set some distance up on the wall, with a catwalk in front of it on which the workers stand while raising or lowering the scenery. Between the lock rail and the grid, devices called *arbors* are fastened to the cables, into which heavy weights can be set so as to approximately match the weight of the scenery being raised. The only manual force required is whatever is needed to lift the difference in weight between the counterweights and the scenery, plus enough to overcome the friction of the pulleys.

The counterweight system functions most simply in flying a drop or the back wall of a set, since those units are likely to be parallel with the battens. The batten nearest the position of the back wall is lowered and fastened to the top edge of the flats with ropes or to hanger irons caught under the bottom edge. Weights are then placed in the arbor until they almost but not quite equal the weight of the wall, the entire wall is raised out of sight by pulling on the ropes at the side of the stage, and they are fastened firmly at the lock rail.

When the back wall is lowered into place for performance, it must be guided to its precise position by hand. Side walls will have to be swung around while they are being let down, a considerably more difficult procedure. The older sandbag system differs in several ways from the counterweight, aside from the fact that heavy canvas bags full of sand are used to balance the scenery. The lines are run up to the grid and back down individually, so that a full set of lines need not be used to fly a single small piece of scenery, as with the counterweight system. Some technicians prefer a combination of both systems, providing the greater convenience and safety of the counterweight method with the flexibility of the sandbags.

Even if a theater lacks provision for regularly flying scenery, it may be possible to fly a ceiling. If an entire box set is shifted by wagon, the ceiling need not be flown, but can be moved as an integral part of the set. For shifting by flying or by hand, however, the ceiling must first be raised to clear the flats. Occasionally, a series of beams resting on the upper edges of the flats are used instead of a ceiling. They too must be removed before the walls can be disassembled and shifted.

MANUAL SHIFTING

Seldom are all of the elements of a set flown. The method is best adapted to lighter structures, especially flats and drops, including the walls, ceiling, and skydrops. Heavier units such as platforms, ramps, stairs, and furniture are usually shifted by hand. For many sets it is perfectly practical to do all shifting by hand, and of course some theaters do not have adequate provision for flying and some horizontal method of shifting must be used.

The detailed plan of the shift will be worked out by the technical director in terms of the design of the specific sets, and may vary greatly from play to play. Usually a shift begins by removing from the flats any elements which would interfere with their being moved off stage—pictures hanging on the walls, pilasters attached with picture hooks-and-eyes, cornices or mopboards which run across the joints and which would keep the flats from being folded, and stiffeners fastened to the back. Meanwhile, furniture or platforms which would get in the way are moved to the front of the stage just behind the closed curtain. Lash lines at the corners of the set are unfastened, stage screws holding the stage braces in position are taken out, the braces removed, the walls folded and moved into the wings and stored by leaning them against one of the walls of the off-stage area. As soon as a path has been cleared, the furniture, platforms, and stairs are carried off stage and stacked or stored out of the way. Furniture for the following set is moved to center stage, the walls for the new set are brought in, braced, and lashed together, and the new stairs or platforms are set in place, door and window frames inserted, drapes and other decorative elements hung, and the furniture moved into position.

> No matter how tightly the screws are set in hinges, a little play will remain. When units such as platforms or flats are fastened together with loose-pin hinges, separated, and then must be rejoined, the leaves may not quite fit. A gentle tap on the projecting socket of each leaf, in opposite directions, will realign them, so that they can be refitted and the pins slipped into place.

THE SPEED OF SHIFTING

Usually a full shift is done during an intermission, so that at least ten minutes is available for it. It might seem that the process described would be more likely to require ten hours, and in fact watching the hectic and apparently chaotic frenzy of activity of a full shift is a somewhat unnerving experience. Fast shifting requires that sound procedures be followed. Violation of good practice can stretch a shift far beyond allowable limits; doing it right can shorten the time amazingly. One technical director reports a problem shift which ran twenty-three minutes at the technical rehearsal. After the rehearsal, the set crew was asked to stay on, the curtain was opened, and the shift replanned. Immediately the time was cut in half, and the third practice shift using the new plan was completed in just a few seconds over three minutes. Since a ten-minute intermission was available for the shift, the problem was declared solved, and the crew dismissed after a round of mutual congratulations.

That example illustrates perhaps the most important factor in fast shifting—the operation must be planned in detail and for maximum efficiency. The planning is the responsibility of the technical director, but the crew members need to be aware of some of the factors involved. Probably the greatest amount of time is lost in a slow shift by workers' unnecessarily waiting on each other. If one of a half dozen pictures hanging on the flats cannot be lifted off until a table standing below it is moved out of the way, the crew member assigned to strike the pictures may wait beside it until the furniture crew has moved the table—and it may be the last piece of furniture they strike. Instead, he should remove the other five pictures first, by which time the space may have been cleared so that he can reach the sixth. If a wall is made up of three flats, and each of the end flats must be folded against the center one for shifting, one of the stagehands may stand and wait until his partner completes folding his flat before he starts to move the final section.

In unusual circumstances some waiting may be necessary, but normally everyone involved in a shift should be actively working all of the time. The individual tasks will require different lengths of time, but if they all proceed simultaneously, the total length of the shift will be the time required for the longest task. If the different steps are done one at a time, the shift will be stretched to equal the total of all of the separate tasks. For that reason, the smaller the individual assignments and the larger the shift crew the faster the shift, so long as each one has space to work effectively. On the other hand, people who are not involved in the shift should be rigidly excluded from the stage or off-stage area. In particular, actors should be instructed to leave the stage the instant the curtain falls, unless they are taking part in the shift themselves. Even when the technical director is rehearsing the shift crew, he should stand well out of the way at the front of the stage.

All tools, ladders, lift poles, or other things needed for the shift should be collected off stage ahead of time, either before the performance begins or, if there is not enough space to store them during the performance, then while the last scene is being played, just before the fall of the curtain. Having to hold up a shift while a crew member races back to the shop to pick up a hammer or a pair of pliers might itself stretch the time unacceptably. Furthermore, the ladders or tools should be placed off stage as close as possible to where they will be used, and so that they can be moved into position when the curtain falls. Jockeying a ladder through the dark passage behind the wall, tripping over stage braces, can add disastrously to the length of the shift; it should be placed at the correct side of the stage in advance. The crew members themselves should take up their positions just before the end of the scene so that they can get to where they must begin work as quickly as possible. They should not be standing in the corners of the off-stage areas or lounging in chairs when the curtain closes. They should be waiting just out of sight near the entrances so that they can dash in and begin work without an instant's delay.

The technical director will have specified the sequence of the various steps in the shift; it must be followed precisely. Perhaps the underlying cause of the various delays sometimes encountered is the subconscious feeling on the part of some crew members that their own assignments are not important. There is such a bustle of activity going on around them, and their individual parts in it seem so minute, that they may feel the shift will somehow take care of itself, and that a little delay on their part will make no difference. In fact, a shift typically moves at satisfactory speed only if every worker holds himself to a high standard of efficiency. Certainly, every assignment is important.

WAGON SHIFTING

Some other methods of moving scenery horizontally may greatly simplify the shifting, although they require special architectural facilities, especially large off-stage areas, and so may not be possible in a particular theater.

Two of them provide for assembling entire sets on wagons, which must be as large as the entire acting area. The sets can then be shifted simply by pushing the wagon with the set used in the previous scene out of the way, and moving on the wagon already set up for the next scene. If a third set is to be used, the first can be struck and the third assembled on the same wagon while the second set is being used in performance.

Although the term *wagon* is used for this kind of structure, it is in fact a platform, as low as possible, supported on rigid casters. A hard surface is needed for it to roll on, the stage floor itself if it has not been permanently padded and covered with a floorcloth. If that has been done, 1 × 3 or 1 × 4 tracks can be laid for the casters to roll on, or the entire floor can be covered with sheets of heavy plywood (Figure 14.5).

In some theaters, the wagons are a permanent part of the stage, one placed at each side of the stage in the off-stage area, with the down-stage corner fastened to a pivot just behind the proscenium wall, so that the wagon can be swung back out of the way and the other moved into position. Since many plays require three sets, if there is enough space back stage a third wagon may be provided which can be pushed forward into playing position after both of the pivoted platforms have been swung back into the wings. The movement of the wagons can be powered by an electric motor, although more often they are pushed into position by the stagehands. The pivoted-platform arrangement is called a *jackknife stage,* because the movement of the platforms is similar to that of the blades fastened to opposite ends of the handle of a pocket knife.

FIGURE 14.5 Wagon stages.

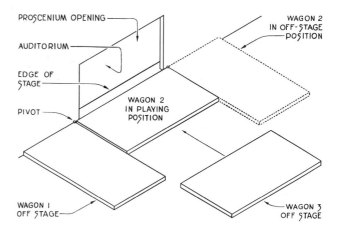

THE REVOLVING STAGE

Perhaps the use of a revolving stage should also be mentioned. The revolve may be simply a circular platform set on casters on the floor of the stage, fastened to a pivot in the center, and revolved by hand. More elaborately, the top may be level with the rest of the stage floor, and the circular section moved by electric power.

The revolving stage was once hailed as a definitive solution to the problems of shifting, and it may occasionally be useful for that purpose. Two or three sets can be fitted on it back to back, and shifted simply by turning it so that a different set becomes visible to the audience. However, the use of the revolve as a shifting device involves some difficult design problems. The shape of each set must be planned so that it will fit against the backs of the others, and considerable ingenuity is required to fill the space beyond the edge of the revolve. More often, the designer is likely to use the revolve for partial shifting or special effects, rather than as a major shifting device.

REVEALED SHIFTS

The discussion so far has assumed that scene shifts are to be hidden from the audience. For many productions the director and designer may decide to leave the front curtain open and carry out the shifts in full view. This method is least effective for sets which require massive shifting, for instance where an elaborate box set must be removed and replaced with another, or for naturalistic serious plays. Even with such plays, minor shifting can often be planned as part of the action of the play. If a lively cocktail party occurs in one scene of the play, and the next scene opens with the family coming down to breakfast the next morning, the actors playing maids or butlers can trot on and set the room to rights, with the lighting fading from night to morning as they exit to return in a moment bringing in the breakfast table, setting chairs around it, and laying out the silverware, dishes, coffee, toast, and bacon and eggs. Even though logically the brief moment between their exit with the party debris and their re-entrance with the breakfast things does not match the passage of entire night, their actions and the shift in lighting will have so clearly communicated the change in time to the audience that the viewers will accept it without difficulty.

For less realistic plays, even fairly major shifts can be made by the actors. If crew members are used instead, they can be costumed like servants, or (a little less effectively) clothed neutrally, perhaps in dark grey suits and dresses, which will not distract from the stage picture. It is essential that the shifts either be completely hidden or emphatically displayed; the worst possible effect is for the shift crew to sneak about the stage, unsuccessfully trying to hide what they are doing, and suggesting furtive embarrassment. Especially if the shifting is done by cast members, they should remain in character, and should move the furniture or turn the flats with verve and grace. Audiences love tricks and special effects; for them, they are part of the magic of the theater, and they enjoy seeing the feats of legerdemain by which the magic is created. Unless a play is very solemn or extremely naturalistic, open shifting may actually enhance the production, and may be chosen even when the mechanics of shifting do not require it.

Like so much of stagecraft, shifting is likely to be unnoticed when it goes well, but the sight of one platform still moving into place as the curtain opens, or of one stagehand darting past a window when he was not intended to be seen, will do much to create an impression of amateurishness. Smooth and efficient shifts, whether hidden or displayed, will contribute greatly to an effect of easy and skillful professionalism.

PART
III
SCENE-SHOP MANAGEMENT

15

Organizing
the Scene Shop

Some of the people who study stagecraft, either as apprentices in a college or community theater or as students in a formal course, may not continue to be active in backstage work. Almost certainly their appreciation and enjoyment of drama as members of the audience will be enhanced, and they may be able to make use of many of the techniques of construction and painting in other areas, in home decoration or in preparing displays or advertising structures in business. Most students do continue to work in the theater after their formal training is completed, and as their skill increases they are likely to move up to some level which involves the training or supervision of other workers, at least as crew chiefs, but often as high school teachers in charge of drama programs, as technical directors of community theaters, or as fully professional workers in colleges and universities or in the commercial theater. If they remain active only during their years at school, and certainly if they continue to work in the theater after graduation, some understanding of the problems and procedures of scene shop administration is essential to a mastery of the craft. Even if the crew member does not himself organize the scene shop space, make out purchase orders, or plan work schedules, understanding the reasons for the decisions that are made will help him work more efficiently, and increase the efficiency of others.

The preparation of scenery requires the use of five kinds of materials—lumber, fabrics, hardware, tools, and paint—and perhaps we should add a miscellaneous category in which such materials as papier-maché, plastics, rug pads, fiber glass, glues, and molding plaster can be grouped. In a few years the use of plastics may have become common enough to justify separating them into a category of their own. Not only must these materials be stored, but the space used for working with them should be organized carefully.

Work space for scenic construction is often inadequate—almost universally so for older theaters. If it is not organized carefully, construction will be slowed, work will become chaotic, and morale is likely to drop as tempers rise. Even under the ideal conditions provided by some of the recently built theaters, efficiency can be greatly increased by careful organization.

THE CONSTRUCTION PATH

In essence, scenery moves in a single direction along a line connecting the truck dock, where the raw materials are delivered, and the stage itself, where the finished scenery is to be used. As the materials move along this path they are subjected to an orderly sequence of operations which transform the raw material to the form in which the completed set is viewed by the audience. The first principle of sound spatial organization is that this movement should be constant and in the same direction, that materials not be carted along the line for construction, and then the structures moved back for painting, again forward for scene-shop assembly, backward for temporary storage, and finally forward again to be set up on the stage. If such an uneconomical pattern of movement is necessary—and too often it is—then the theater does not provide adequate facilities for stagecraft work. Even in that case, any increase in efficiency of plan is an improvement: semichaos is better than total chaos.

Unusual scenery may require unusual patterns of work; however, the standard sequence is followed such a large percentage of the time that the space should be organized to fit it, and deviations accepted as unforeseeable exceptions (Figure 15.1).

LUMBER STORAGE

The first step in building almost all scenery is to cut lumber and fasten it together into a basic structure. Lumber racks should consequently be placed at the beginning of the assembly line, preferably just inside the delivery dock, so that the lumber can be lifted off the dock and set directly on the shelves.

338

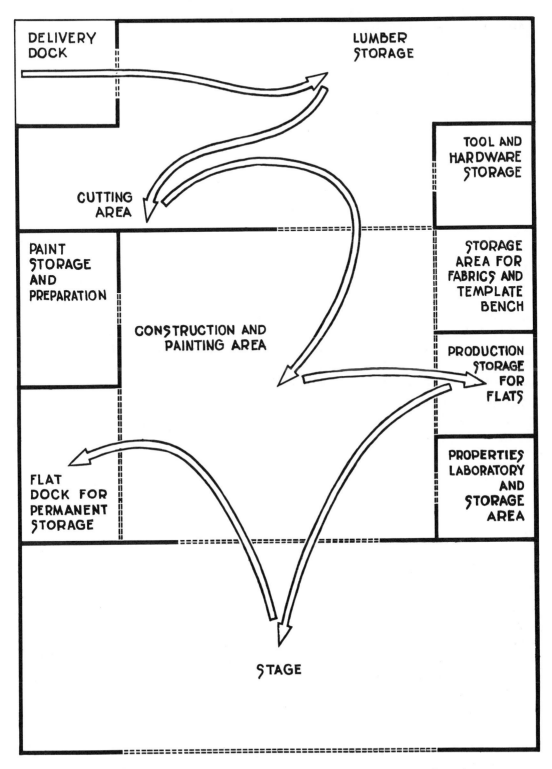

FIGURE 15.1 A schematic diagram of the areas needed for stagecraft work.
Arrows indicate the path of movement of materials during processing and use.

The racks should provide for the storage of five types of lumber: full lengths of 1 × 3, scrap 1 × 3, molding and stripping, 2 × 4s, and miscellaneous lumber; in addition, separate bins should be provided for full sheets of 3/4" (or 5/8") plywood and 1/4" plywood, and for scraps of the heavier plywood.

1 × 3s

By far the largest part of a year's lumber order will be of 1 × 3s the length of the standard flat (for most theaters, 12'-0"). Although the boards will stack compactly, a good deal of shelf space will be needed. If the shelves are made of full sheets of plywood, about three shelves should be provided, a foot apart.

If the lumber is to be loaded on the shelves from the side, they will have to be about a foot longer than the standard 1 × 3s, so that the boards will clear the corner legs. If the boards are pushed in from the end of the shelf unit, a single 4' × 8' sheet of plywood is satisfactory. The lumber is then shoved in so that the ends of the boards are even with one end of the shelves, and the boards stick out 4' beyond the far end of the shelves. At least 14' of clear space must be provided at the loading end so that the boards can be pulled all the way out when they are taken from storage.

SCRAP

Boards shorter than 12' (or whatever flat height is standard for the theater) are scrap, although of course many short lengths will be needed, and the shorter pieces are not worthless. Often scrap lumber is thrown on a shelf or in a pile on the floor. The result is that when a short board is needed the workmen must paw through the pile to find it, checking each likely board with a tape measure. Most often they will give up and cut from full boards, so that the pile of scrap steadily grows and the supply of boards usable for the stiles of flats is destroyed. Organizing the shorter lumber will prevent waste of the full-length boards, but also will promote efficiency and convenience in the use of the scrap.

A policy decision should be made identifying the length of the shortest boards which are to be saved. Boards shorter than stile length are used primarily for two purposes—the rails and toggles of flats, and legs for platforms; to those should be added a miscellaneous category for multiple uses which cannot be predicted. Rails and toggles will almost always be longer than a foot and a half. The shortest platform legs regularly needed will depend to some extent on the habits of the designer, but it is likely that a number of platforms 8″ or even 6″ high may be built. It is suggested that 12″ be set as the minimum length of board to be saved.

The scrap will be very much more usable if it is labeled and stacked by size. Labeling is best done by two workers, one measuring and the other marking. The length of each board should be printed on the end, and a felt pen with a moderately broad point is convenient for labeling. A worker who goes to the rack for twenty 6′-0″ boards should be able to pull out boards marked with that dimension with assurance that they will serve his purpose. If a board is split at the end, or contains a bad knot, the damaged section should be omitted in measuring, so that the dimension recorded identifies the length of sound lumber rather than the actual total length of the board. The boards need not be cut to the length marked. Almost always they will have to be specially cut when they are used, and cutting them to true length before storing them would be of little value. If the actual length of a board involves a fraction of an inch, the fraction should be omitted in marking it.

Sometimes boards will be found which have small splits running throughout, or which are badly knotted or warped. They may still be usable, but will be unsuited for some purposes such as flat frames; these defects should be noted by printing *S, K,* or *W* beside the dimension. Inch and foot marks can be omitted from the labeling to save time and space, with the two numbers separated by a hyphen; they should be printed well toward the left side of the end of the board, leaving space for abbreviations marking defects; even straight lumber may warp on the rack, so that it may be necessary to add a *W* at some later time. It is not necessary to mark full-length lumber, except that as defective boards are discovered it is helpful to note that fact.

The scrap should be stacked on the shelves by size, with the labeled ends toward the edges of the shelves, ideally with no two boards of different size in a single pile. Labeling and sorting are somewhat irksome, but a year's experience in using lumber handled this way will demonstrate how much it increases the speed and convenience of the work. A worker who needs thirty or forty boards of the same length for use as legs for platforms can go to the rack and pull them out without measuring, inspecting, or searching through a confused collection of scrap lumber. Once all scrap has been labeled and sorted, maintaining orderly shelves is a rather small job; scrap can be labeled as it accumulates and easily set in place on the shelves.

SHAPED LUMBER

Molding and stripping can be stored in a single bin, but it is more convenient to separate it into five or six groups—quarter round, cove molding, miscellaneous molding, 1 × 1s, miscellaneous stripping, and doweling. It is difficult to label these kinds of lumber, they are used less frequently than 1 × 3s, and the lengths needed are so variable that recording the dimensions is less helpful than with the standard lumber; if the pieces are simply separated by type they can be used with reasonable efficiency.

PLYWOOD

Most often plywood will be stocked in only two thicknesses, 1/4" and 3/4" (or 5/8", if it is used as an economy measure). It is much better to store the full sheets flat to minimize warping, but separate shelves should be provided for the two thicknesses. It is nearly impossible to pull out a sheet of 3/4" plywood when twenty or thirty sheets of 1/4" are laid on top of it.

Anything less than a full sheet of plywood is to be considered scrap. Large scraps may be stored on the same shelves as full sheets (for example, a 4' × 6' sheet, or a sheet from which a corner has been cut); smaller scraps should be stored in a separate bin. As has been indicated, it is not economical to save pieces of heavy plywood smaller than about 2' × 2' or 1' × 3'. Plywood scrap is likely to be of odd shapes, so that dimensioning is difficult, and may be dispensed with.

Pieces of 1/4" plywood smaller than 4' × 4' should be cut up into corner-blocks, which are stored in the area used for building flats. Larger scrap can be stored with the full-sized sheets, or can be thrown into the same bin as the 3/4" scraps. There are not likely to be many pieces, and it is easy to distinguish between the two thicknesses.

MISCELLANEOUS SHEET MATERIALS

Various manufactured materials are available in sheet form, having some of the characteristics of plywood, and often in the standard 4' × 8' size. Typically, they are made of a combination of wood chips or fibers mixed with glue and pressed into sheet form. Especially useful are cardboard sheets of varying thicknesses, sold under various trade names, the most familiar of which is upson board. Ordinary corrugated cardboard is also useful in the theater, and may be collected from discarded boxes or bought new in sheet form. They are available in various sizes, some of which are larger than standard plywood sheets. These materials cannot often be used as substitutes for plywood (they are likely to be too brittle for platform tops or corner-blocks), but they have characteristics of their own which make them occasionally valuable in building scenery, for example, greater flexibility than plywood, so that they can be used to cover curved surfaces.

Like plywood, they should be stored flat if possible. Since the sheets of corrugated cardboard require oversize shelves, it is usually more convenient to store them on edge.

THE CUTTING AREA

The second position along the line of operation is the cutting area. Most cutting will be done on a radial-arm saw, and although miscellaneous cutting may be done elsewhere, even on the stage itself, the major cutting area should be centered in the permanently located power saw. Usually when a board is cut it is placed on the saw with the waste to the right and the section needed to the left. For cutting stiles, therefore, there should be twelve feet of clear space to the left of the saw. Occasionally, it will be desirable to reverse the placement of a board, so that it is desirable to leave the same length of clear space at the right of the saw also. Even if it is seldom needed for cutting, the floor area can be used to stack piles of cut lumber or even partly assembled scenery. This is an especially convenient area for a large wastebasket, into which scraps too small to save can be thrown as they are cut, rather than allowing them to accumulate on the floor.

It is best to have permanent tables extending for the full twelve feet left of the saw blade, at the same height as the table which is part of the saw. At the least, sawhorses of that height should be available so that tables can be temporarily set up to support the lumber as it is being cut.

Other tables should be placed so that the lumber can be stacked quickly and conveniently as it is sawed. They will also be useful for miscellaneous purposes such as measuring and marking the scrap before returning it to the lumber racks. Very often, it is most economical to cut all the lumber for the entire set before construction begins. These tables can be used to store the cut boards, which can be conveniently picked up as needed and taken to the construction area.

THE CONSTRUCTION AREA

This is the fourth station in the work line (the third is discussed immediately below). Construction can be divided into two or three categories—flats, platforms (including ramps and stairs), and miscellaneous. The proportions of the different types of construction vary greatly from play to play; for example, one set may be made up almost entirely of flats, and may include no platforms at all. Another set may use no flats, but may require the construction of a full raked stage (a ramp covering the entire stage floor) as well as numerous other platforms. Consequently, the construction area should provide a large amount of open floor space, into which projects of varied type can be fitted.

Flats can be built directly on the floor, and often are, but it is much more convenient to use a template bench. This is a table 6' wide and as long as the standard flat height. The top is in the form of an open frame of 2 × 4s, arranged so as to support the rails, stiles, and toggles of a flat. Set into the top at the corners, and at the ends of the toggles, are permanent clinch plates. Running around the edge of the entire table is a lip formed by nailing 1 × 3 or 1 × 4 boards to the side, with their edges extending up about 3/4" above the top surface of the bench. The legs set it at convenient working height, about 3'.

The template bench must be sturdy, and must be made very accurately; the corners must be absolutely square. The lumber for a flat frame is laid in place against the edging lip, which serves as an automatic square, and fastened with corner-blocks and clout nails. Since the flats will be of varying widths, one stile is fastened first to the two rails, and then the structure slid across to the other edge to meet the second stile, which is nailed in place.

The template bench speeds up the work considerably, but it eats up a good deal of space when not in use, so that it is hardly practical if quarters are cramped. Even with adequate space, it should be equipped with lock casters so that it can be fastened firmly in place for use and then moved back into a corner out of the way to clear the space for other work after the flats have been finished.

An improved sawhorse design was described in chapter 3. A pair of these horses can be built in about an hour, a short enough time to justify making them as needed. However, it is better if an adequate number can be made and stored for permanent use; ten or twelve pairs of horses should be satisfactory.

TOOL AND HARDWARE STORAGE

The third area in the work line may be placed between the cutting and construction areas, or may open off the side of the construction space. This area is devoted to tool storage.

Tool maintenance is a constant problem in every scene shop. Without the most rigid system of checking there is a constant attrition in the supply of tools. Some may be stolen, others disappear innocently although just as permanently—a worker slips a tape measure into his pocket, discovers it only when he has got to his room, puts it up on a chest of drawers intending to return it to the scene shop the next time he goes to the theater—and then never remembers to do it.

Some theaters require workers to furnish their own tools, which are kept in individual padlocked chests. In other theaters, a supply of tools is assigned to each worker, and he is held responsible for returning them after each show or at the end of the year, with a replacement charge for each missing tool. In either case, the theater will have to supply certain tools such as nailpullers which are not used often enough to justify stocking one for each worker, and even with the more frequently used tools providing a full kit for each workman requires doubling or tripling the inventory.

In most theaters, the tools are used generally as needed, without being individually charged out. However, it is important that they be kept under lock and key between work sessions, and preferably keys should be restricted to supervisory workers, in a college theater to the technical director and his paid assistants. Most technical directors would permit the borrowing of tools by people other than the stagecraft crew (occasionally the technical director may need to borrow tools himself), but a careful record should be made of all tools taken from the theater area, and each borrower should be required to sign for them.

It should be established practice that all tools be returned to their proper storage places at the end of a work session, even if crisis work is being done under pressure. If a pair of pliers is tossed down in a corner or under a platform, it may take an hour or more of frantic search to find it when it is needed. The few minutes necessary to put tools back where they belong are repaid enormously in time saved in later work sessions.

Demanding that tools be properly stored, however, requires that adequate and clearly marked space be provided for them. In most scene shops, tools are hung on a board fastened to the wall, either a peg board or sheets of plywood into which good-sized finishing nails have been driven. The arrangement of the tools should be planned as efficiently as possible. Similar tools should be grouped together. Tools should be arranged according to frequency of use, with those most used closest to the door of the tool room, and those least used stored in the farthest area. After the arrangement has been worked out, the tools should be hung in place and traced on the backing board. If the surface is painted a light color, the outlining can be done with a felt pen. This will cut down the amount of time needed to identify where each tool goes when they are returned to storage.

Some tools cannot be hung easily, especially hand power tools such as drills, saber saws, and portable circular saws. A shelf should be built below the peg board on which these can be set. The best way to store screwdrivers is to make a narrow shelf from a 1 X 3 and drill a hole in it for each, larger than the shaft but smaller than the handle. The screwdrivers are then inserted until the handles rest on the surface of the wood, with the blade hanging below the shelf.

STORAGE AND WORK TRAYS

It is convenient to store hardware in the same area. Cleats, hinges, bolts, nails, screws, and a great miscellany of other types of harware must be stored, and efficiency is greatly promoted if they are fully separated, so that a worker who, for example, needs a dozen 5" bolts does not have to take time to search through and measure a container of bolts of mixed sizes.

The most convenient storage system is a series of shelves on which boxes can be set, one for each type of hardware. The boxes can be made by nailing four 1 × 3s or 1 × 4s together on edge to form a frame, and then fastening a sheet of 1/4" plywood to the bottom. They should be painted white and labeled on each of the four sides with a felt pen. The boxes should be square, so that no matter how they are set on the shelves they will fit. If some of the units to be stored are too large to go in a box of the standard size, special boxes of double or triple length can be made to accommodate them.

It is most effective to print a general identifying term first and then follow it with specific distinguishing information; when the boxes are set in alphabetical order, related types of hardware will thus be placed together. For example, the labels "Nails—Box," "Nails—Clout," "Nails—Common," and "Nails—Roofing" will ensure that all nails stand side by side on the shelves, rather than being scattered at different places, as they would be if the terms were reversed. The labels should give the workers all the information they would ordinarily need to decide which box to pull out.

The boxes can be used not only as storage bins but also as work trays. If it is likely that more than one workman will be using a particular type of hardware at the same time, enough boxes should be provided that each worker can have his own. This is especially likely to be true of clout nails, common nails, and screws. Harried workmen may be tempted to snatch up a handful of nails, toss them on the floor, and then when their project is finished neglect to pick them up and return them to the bin. If they can pull one of the storage boxes off the shelf and use it as a work tray without having to look for a special container, they are much less likely to waste nails or to leave them lying dangerously on the floor. Although it will probably not be possible to store the theater's full supply of such things as nails in the work trays, they can be regularly replenished from the larger containers.

Especially with nails, screws, and bolts, workers at the end of crisis sessions may not have time to sort out left-over hardware, and are likely to toss a handful into whatever storage box is nearest. This is especially probable during strikes. Individual boxes should be made for each of these types of materials, painted a distinctive color—perhaps red—and labeled "Nails—Unsorted," etc. Workers should then be instructed always to toss the hardware into these boxes, if they do not have time to sort it and return it to the correct containers. If even half a dozen screws of the wrong size are thrown into the regular box, it is necessary to inspect every screw in order to remove the ones which should be in another container, a laborious and unnecessary job. If instead they are put into the box labeled "unsorted," they can be checked and stored properly later with only a small expenditure of time.

With few exceptions, only a single size and type of screw is used in the scene shop. Many sizes of bolts are needed, of varying length and diameter. The most important of the two dimensions is the length, since they must be long enough to go through the combined thicknesses of the lumber being joined, which may vary from the thickness of two 1 X 1s (1½") up to the thickness of two, three, or even more 2 X 4s. Boxes for bolts should therefore be labeled first by length and then, if desired, by diameter. It is useful to store loose nuts and washers on the same shelf as the bolts, so they should be labeled "Bolts—Nuts" and "Bolts—Washers" to keep them at the same point in the alphabet.

> Washers tend to accumulate in the scene shop in a variety of sizes. A good deal of time can be wasted in searching through a storage tray of unsorted washers. They can be stored better by sorting them by size and running long bolts through them. The bolts can be filled with the washers and the nuts turned on to keep them from slipping off.

Besides washers, a miscellaneous collection of hardware shows up steadily in scene shops—odd-sized screws, enormous spikes, tiny brads, ornamental hinges, etc.—none of which were ever ordered, and the origin of which no one can explain. Even though such things will not be regularly used, they are too valuable to throw away, and they may provide easy solutions to special problems for which the materials regularly stocked are not suited, or they may be usable as substitutes when the regular supply of something unexpectedly runs out. Few theaters, for example, have enough hinges on hand, and if a set requires an unusually large number, some of the miscellaneous collection can be substituted where they will not be visible, for example in fastening a jack to the back of a flat.

In another instance, more foot-irons may be needed for a particular set than are available in stock, and it may be possible to substitute oversize hinges for some of them, fastening them to the stage floor with outsize screws taken from the odd-box. If a good supply of such materials shows up (for instance, a dozen or so identical large hinges), it may be desirable to assign a special storage box to them; usually they can be grouped generally and the boxes given such labels as "Hinges—Miscellaneous." It may be convenient to store a few tools in the boxes, such as staplers, which can then be set next to the supply of staples.

FABRIC STORAGE

Usually scenic structures require some application of fabrics. Flats must be canvassed, and platforms and stairs must be padded and covered with canvas. This work is likely to be done in the construction area, so that the fifth station on the assembly line consists of a canvas and padding storage area, which can be located in the tool room if there is sufficient space, in a corner of the construction area, or in an adjacent alcove or small room of its own.

Canvas is usually bought in a roll 6' wide. The most convenient way to store it is to run a pole through the center of the roll and set it in slots cut in heavy plywood supports fastened to the wall so that the roll is about six and a half feet above the floor.

Padding of plastic foam also may be bought in a roll of about the same width, but because of its greater bulk the rolls are likely to be much thicker than the rolls of canvas. Other forms of padding may be delivered folded rather than rolled.

Both canvas and padding are regularly salvaged after use, so that another type of storage must be provided for the pieces. Deep shelves, perhaps 3' × 4' or 6' are convenient. The materials can be folded and laid neatly on the shelves. Besides large sheets of canvas, strips wide enough for use as dutchmen are worth saving. Smaller scraps can be thrown out, but if a great deal of papier-maché work is done they are valuable for surface coating. For this purpose, very small pieces are useful, down to about an inch and a half by from four to six inches. The best way to store canvas for papier-maché is in a good-sized box.

A special type of cloth sold under the trade name *duvetyne* is frequently used in the theater. It is more likely to be stored in the costume shop, but it may also be used for some scenic purposes. It is sold in rolls, and can be stored most easily on a pole fastened to the wall, like the rolls of canvas. It is especially suited to surfacing papier-maché, so that even if it is used primarily for costumes rather than scenery, the costume crew should be asked to save their scraps, which can be periodically collected and stored in the scene shop. In that case it is better to provide two papier-maché bins, one for canvas and one for the softer duvetyne.

If the theater makes extensive use of plastics, a special storage room must be provided, along with the necessary cutting and shaping equipment. At present, most theaters probably store plastics in one end of the property laboratory. The division between scenery and props is a fine and somewhat artificial one. The work differs primarily in the size of the objects constructed, so that properties people often use stagecraft tools and work areas, and the set workers may occasionally make small units in the property laboratory. It is consequently desirable that the prop room be located close to the path along which scenery moves during construction, perhaps opening off the far corner of the construction area. Rather than considering this a division of the direct line of set work, however, it should probably be numbered area 5a.

THE PAINTING AREA

When units have been built and canvassed, they are ready to be painted. Ideally, a special area should be set aside for painting, but since it must be very large, more often it matches or overlaps the construction area. The use of the same space for both purposes causes minimal conflict, because usually painting is not begun until all construction has been finished.

Painting, especially of large drops or complete wall sections, is often done on the floor. A movable paint frame is a great convenience. Flats can be stood in it and raised or lowered so that the area to be painted is at the most convenient height. To use a rigid paint frame, a rolling multilevel platform must be provided, on which the painters can stand. However, probably more painting is done with flats lying on sawhorses than in any other position. In that case the new type of sawhorse described earlier is especially useful, since the supports can be stretched to any length desired, so as to hold even a very large wall.

PAINT STORAGE

However the painting is done, a paint storage and preparation area (station 6 in the work line) should be located as close as possible to the painting area. If traditional scene paint is used, a hot plate, electric paint pot, or more elaborate stove must be provided. For any type of paint, a large sink with both hot and cold water is needed. Here the paint will be mixed to the proper colors and diluted to brushing consistency. At the end of each session, the sink will be used for clean-up, not only of hands but also of brushes and buckets.

Two types of paint storage are needed, one for the full stock of paint, and the other for what is called production storage—where the paint to be used in the current set is kept during the week or so needed to apply it. Enough space should be provided for all of the paint needed for the set, including all colors. Usually it will be stored in open buckets, and since at least some of it will have been diluted, and since several mixes of each basic color may be necessary, a good deal of shelf space will be needed.

The full stock can be stored more compactly. The most convenient storage is provided by shelves just deep enough to take a single standard-sized container. Although this requires a great deal of shelving, at least three walls of the paint room can be lined with shelves, and no more floor space will be needed than for deeper shelves concentrated against a single wall. The paint should be arranged in the order in which the colors appear on the color wheel, separating the achromatic pigments (white, grey, and black) at the end of the series. Some painters prefer to pull brown out of the sequence, but since in fact it is a shade of orange, it seems more useful to shelve it with the orange section. A simple but often overlooked rule is that all cans of paint should be placed so that the labels are toward the front; having to turn a dozen cans around to identify their colors is irritating, and having them all legible at a glance makes it much easier to assess and use the stock. If the paint must be stored on deeper shelves, no container should be set behind another of a different color. A can of blue with two cans of green hidden behind it might easily lead the workers to assume that three cans of blue were available, an error which could prove disastrous when the supply of blue unexpectedly ran out in the middle of mixing a batch of paint.

In addition to storing the paint itself, space must be provided for brushes. Ordinary scenic brushes should be hung on nails with the handles up, so that the bristles will remain straight and water will not run down and collect at the base of the brush. If the brushes do not have holes to hang them by they should be drilled before the brushes are used. Long fine brushes with handles too small to be drilled should be laid on a shelf, which can be fastened over the sink, and need not be large.

Three additional rather bulky items must be stored: buckets and other containers, glue, and spraying equipment (if it is used). In addition, miscellaneous storage should be provided for small containers of odd types of paint, including spray paint, powdered metallic paint, shellac or varnish, and various oddments such as alcohol, detergent, scouring powder and scrub brushes, as well as candles for force-drying paint samples, paper for painting the samples on, pencils to record formulas, matches, felt pens and masking tape for labeling containers of mixed paint, and stirring sticks. Especially for doing detail work, it is often convenient to pour the paint into small containers. These should be collected and stored on the miscellaneous shelves.

PRODUCTION STORAGE FOR FLATS

As the flats are finished, they should be stored in a special area to await transportation to the stage. The facilities for production storage may consist of a formal flat dock. More often, the flats will be stood against the wall in one corner of the construction area. But even if the space is not visibly marked off, it must be carefully kept clear of furniture or other objects; a single flat out of place in the work area after it has been completed can eat up space, reduce efficiency, and even be accidentally damaged, and if the production storage area is kept open the workers are much more likely to stand their flats in it as they are finished. Platforms are less a problem because each one will probably be carried directly to the stage so that it can be used in rehearsal.

The seventh area in the production line is the stage itself, to which the scenery is transported for final assembly after it has been painted.

THE SCENE DOCK

Strike involves not only taking the scenery apart and processing it but also returning the salvageable sections to permanent storage, with one exception to the areas which have already been mentioned. The flats constitute the exception. They are placed in the permanent scene dock, where they will be stored until some of them are taken out for a later production.

The scene dock is usually constructed as an open frame of 2 × 4s six inches or a foot higher than the standard flat. It should be divided into six or seven sections, so that the flats can be grouped by width; a section is provided for each of the full-foot dimensions (1'-0", 2'-0", etc., up to 6'-0"), with an additional section for the 1'-6" flats. If it is the local policy not to build flats wider than 5'-0", the largest section can be omitted.

If the scene dock is built into a corner, the deepest section should be set against both walls; the vertical 2 × 4s at the front of the dock should be fastened out from the wall at a distance equal to the smaller of the two bins between which they stand. They will thus form a row 6'-0" at one end of the dock and 1'-0" at the other. As the flats are slipped into place, the front edges will match the dividing frames when the flats strike the wall behind the dock, and the flats can easily be inspected or pulled out one at a time without having to reach far past the front supports to get hold of flats which have been pushed back inside.

Obviously few existing theaters, especially older ones, will have been designed so that the spatial organization which has been described can be followed precisely, and it may not entirely fit the preferences or work habits of individual technical directors or set crews. Its pattern should be freely adjusted to local conditions and habits of work, but any effective arrangement must take into account the fundamental principle that the space should be arranged so that the work can be done in an orderly sequence, that the structures can be moved in a continuous path from scene shop to stage, and that work areas should be planned so that work need not be interrupted while scenery is being carried through.

16

Purchasing

Not only does careful organization promote efficiency of work, but it is essential for taking inventories as a guide for purchasing.[1] Ideally, all supplies needed for an entire season should be in stock when work is begun on the first play. Supplies always seem to run out at crisis moments, and the time spent in having to stop work, run to the store for a supply of nails or screws, and return to the scene shop may have to be replaced by working through early morning hours. Furthermore, many firms offer discounts for quantity orders, and over a few years a significant saving of money can be achieved by following a policy of buying by the year.

When one technical director joined the staff of a college theater in Michigan, he found that it was established policy to place two or three different lumber orders during the work on each show, and to order no more paint than was needed for the next production. On his first visit to the scene shop he discovered that the total supply of paint was something less than a gallon. The supplier from whom the paint was regularly purchased offered graduated discounts, ranging from no discount for small orders through ten, fifteen, and twenty percent discounts for larger orders. By instituting a policy of purchasing the entire year's supply of paint at the beginning of the season, the director was able to take advantage of the 20 percent discount, so that with exactly

---

1. Every theater should have a copy of *Simon's Directory of Theatrical Services and Information,* Package Publicity Service, Inc., New York, New York. Among other things, the directory gives the addresses of dealers in theatrical supplies, arranged geographically.

the same expenditure as had been customarily made, he was able to buy 25 percent more paint (the shift from 20 to 25 percent may be puzzling, but it is correct. The arithmetic is a little complicated).

When he resigned from the staff at the end of eight years, he left a full two years' supply of paint in stock which had not cost a penny more than had been spent under the previous hand-to-mouth purchasing practices. Establishing a policy of ordering an entire season's lumber did not produce such dramatic savings because the discounts offered were smaller, but the convenience of having a full stock on hand and not having to wait for emergency deliveries was a great advantage.

ESTIMATING LUMBER NEEDS

If designs for all of the plays to be performed during the following season are completed well before work must be started on the first play, the orders can be made with assurance. If, as more frequently happens, only the titles of the plays to be presented are available, a good deal of guessing must be done. A design may require quantities of unusual materials which would not normally be carried in stock—for instance, the designer might specify the construction of large areas of lattice work, for which stripping would have to be especially ordered, or he might make heavy use of doweling or cove molding as decoration for a set, requiring two or three times as much as the scene shop had on hand. But even in such cases, or where the technical director has simply guessed wrong with regard to the quantities needed, it is much easier to fill a few holes in the supplies by a special order than it is to adopt crisis and emergency purchasing as a standard procedure.

A quick examination of the scripts of the plays to be produced during the season will enable the technical director to estimate the number of sets which must be built during the year, as well as something about their type—how many exterior and interior sets will be needed, for example. Even though the designer may not follow the script specifications precisely, this information can be used as a guide in ordering.

BOX SETS

A simple formula has been worked out for estimating the amount of lumber needed for a fairly straightforward box set: W + 30' X H = linear footage of 1 X 3s needed, where

W = the width of the proscenium opening and H = the standard flat height. For a theater with a proscenium width of 32′ and 12′ flats the computation would then read:

$$32' + 30' \times 12 = 744'.$$

If the lumber is ordered by the board foot, this figure can be transformed into that unit by the standard formula.[2] If the lumber is ordered by the linear foot, a still simpler formula is usable. Omitting the foot marks, the width of the proscenium opening in feet is added to 30; the sum equals the number of boards of standard flat length needed for a simple box set, for the example given 32 + 30 = 62 boards needed, 1′ × 3′ × 12′.

PLATFORMS AND STAIRS

It is somewhat more difficult to guess how much material will be needed for platforms during a season, since their size and shape are more variable than those of flats, and since the number of platforms used by designers in setting the same plays may vary greatly. Assuming that the median size of platform is about 2′ × 4′ × 8′, each one would require approximately eleven 1 × 3s twelve feet long. If lumber must be ordered before set designs are available, the technical director can only guess how much platforming will be needed. If he suspects that the entire acting area of the stage will be covered with platforms for a particular show, he can estimate the framing lumber by the formula $W \times 6 = B$, where W = the width of the proscenium opening, and B = the number of 12′ long 1 × 3s needed.

Stairs can also vary in shape (curved or straight) and in all dimensions, but the following can be taken as close to average: width 3′-0″, risers 6″, treads 1′-0″. If heights of stairs that might be needed for a set can be estimated with any approach to accu-

---

2. The board foot is a somewhat fictional measurement based on the nominal rather than the real dimensions of the lumber, and using as its unit a section of lumber nominally 1″ thick, 12″ wide, and 12″ long. To convert linear to board feet, multiply the length (in feet) by the nominal thickness and width of the boards (in inches) and divide by 12; for a 1 × 3 × 12′ board, this computation would read 12 × 1 × 3 = 36 ÷ 12 = 3 board feet.

This formula is given for completeness. It is suggested that lumber be ordered instead by the board (350 boards 1 × 3 × 12′, for example), a measurement which is considerably more significant for planning scenic needs than the board foot. Although most books imply that lumber yards will quote prices only in terms of board feet, more than a third of a century spent in the theater has failed to uncover a single lumber yard employee who turned pale, staggered back, began to stammer, or even lifted his eyebrows in surprise when handed an order stated in linear feet or numbers of boards, and in fact when inquiries are made about prices, many lumber yards automatically state them in terms of linear feet. Dowelling, stripping, and molding, which cannot be handled by the board-foot formula, are always priced by the linear foot.

racy, so much the better. If not, a height of 3'-0" should be close to average. A flight of stairs with those dimensions will require eight 1 × 3 boards 12' long.

In estimating lumber needed for stairs, it is important to remember that access stairs must be provided off stage to enable actors to reach any platform which extends to the edge of the acting area. Probably the simplest way to handle this is to assume that every stair unit on stage will have to be matched by a hidden unit outside the acting area. In other words, the amount of lumber needed for stairs on stage is estimated, and then doubled. The resulting figure will usually be somewhat too large, but not enormously so.

CHECKING SUPPLIES ON HAND

Of course the amount of lumber which must actually be ordered depends on existing stocks, not only of raw lumber but also of finished scenery.

Checking should begin with the flats, either by referring to the flat inventory (discussed later) or by inspecting the actual flats in the dock. If the theater has a good supply of flats of standard dimensions and in good condition, it may be possible to build an entire box set with the flats already on hand; probably not more than two or three new flats will have to be built in any case. The amount of lumber tentatively set down for building flat frames can therefore be reduced in the light of the flats already on hand.

If platforms of standard size are also in storage, the lumber order can be further reduced to allow for them. Finally, the lumber storage area is checked. The full-length lumber is most significant here, and the boards should be counted and subtracted from the total order. Scrap lumber (shorter than standard flat height) cannot be assessed at its full length. Pieces shorter than 3' should be ignored, and the number of longer pieces counted or estimated. This figure should then be divided by 3, and the resulting number subtracted from the number of 12' boards to be ordered.

It should be obvious, as was indicated earlier, that this method of estimating lumber needs involves many uncertainties. Nevertheless, it is astonishing how close the resulting order often comes to the actual quantity of lumber used during a season. There are, however, two further factors which must be taken into account.

As the quality of lumber has deteriorated during the last fifteen years, a larger and larger percentage of the boards delivered have been warped or split so badly as to make them unsuited for the more precise scenic purposes, especially for use as flat stiles. Although such boards can often be used for diagonal braces and for internal supports of platforms and other purposes where they will be hidden from the audience, the stock of lumber must contain enough boards in good condition for use where defective boards will not do.

The other factor which must be considered is that the estimates suggested take into account only the major scenic structures, and a very large number of small miscellaneous scenic units will also have to be built—the frame for a bulletin board to hang on the wall of a set, a half dozen stools, a street vendor's cart and a gallows for *Three-penny Opera,* a dozen restaurant tables for *The Madwoman of Chaillot,* a dancing pole for *Indians.* To a large extent, such units can be built from scrap or from the less desirable boards, but some allowance must be made for them in the order.

The figure obtained by this process of estimating is therefore a minimum, and the actual order should be larger. Although the final figure will depend on the policies of the local scene shop (for example, how carefully scrap is used), it is suggested that the estimated quantity be increased by fifty percent as a minimum, doubled for a comfortable supply, and increased by 150 percent if the budget allows.

PLYWOOD

The plywood order should be placed at the same time, although not necessarily with the same lumber yard. Plywood prices vary greatly, and it is well worth an hour's telephoning to check prices with all the nearby lumber yards. One such survey produced a wide range of prices for 1/4" plywood, with a difference of $2.00 a sheet between the two lowest prices. Since the year's purchase was for 30 sheets, ordering from the cheapest supplier rather than the second cheapest resulted in a saving of $60.00, and of course the saving was still greater as compared with the more expensive sources.

The price of plywood depends on a number of factors, three of which are thickness, finish, and the kind of wood used for the surface layers. There is little choice with regard to thickness; only 1/4" plywood is usable for corner-blocks, and 3/4" plywood is by far the most desirable for platform floorings and stair treads. (Other thicknesses are available, and can sometimes be used in the theater, but for special purposes which make it impractical to carry them as part of the regular stock. For instance, 1/8" plywood is maximally flexible, and so may be especially ordered for covering a curved surface.) However, one technical director found that a special grade of 5/8" plywood was available locally at a much lower cost than the 3/4", so that it was adopted (with some regret) as standard for platform tops. The greater flexibility of the thinner plywood required that extra bracing be built into the platform supports, with some increase in the amount of lumber used and a small but significant increase in work time, but it was felt that the saving in cost of the plywood more than compensated for those increases. This choice might well be considered by theaters with a low budget, but generally the 3/4" plywood will be found more satisfactory.

Some plywood is supplied completely finished—smoothed and varnished, and ready to be installed in the home. Most plywood is more or less smoothed but not painted or varnished. Obviously, the more work done on the plywood the higher the cost, and the fully finished sheets are actually less desirable for the theater, since they will have to be repainted in any case and the factory finish may resist scene paint and make them unusable.

Unpainted plywood is usually available in one of two finishes—either planed so that it is smooth to the touch, or left somewhat rough. Quarter-inch plywood is most often used for corner-blocks, which are placed on the back of the flats out of sight of the audience; plywood used for stair treads and platform flooring is covered with padding and canvas, and so is also hidden from the audience. In both cases, the smoothness of finish is not of practical significance in the theater. If plywood of the same thickness is available in both finishes it is more economical to buy the rough.

Rough plywood is most likely to be stocked only in 5/8" or 3/4" thicknesses, intended to be used for making forms for pouring cement; this is much cheaper than smooth plywood of the same thickness, and is entirely practical for the theater.

Usually quarter-inch plywood is available only in smooth finish, but with various grades of surface layers distinguished in other ways. The type of wood used for the outside layers greatly affects the price, and since the plywood is either out of sight or covered with scene paint when it is used in the theater it is best practice to avoid the more expensive woods. In addition, the top layer may be solid and free of any defects. It may be pieced from two or three large sheets; defects such as knotholes may be tightly patched, or they may be left open. Each of these conditions constitutes a different grade, with a resulting difference in cost (they have been listed in descending order of price). Furthermore, the bottom layer of the plywood may also be of any of the different grades, and usually the grades of the top and bottom layers of the same sheet will differ. Such plywood is sometimes referred to as "good-one-side." In other lumber yards the different grades of surfacing are lettered, and the plywood might be called "A-C," the A indicating that one side has a top-grade surface, the C indicating that the other side is defective. C-C 1/4" ply would be cheapest for general scene-shop use, but is unlikely to be available, so that the A-C or good-one-side plywood is standard.

How many sheets of plywood should be stocked for a season is considerably more difficult to estimate than the amount of framing lumber needed. The use of 3/4" plywood may vary enormously from season to season in the same theater. For instance, if one show calls for a raked stage (a ramp covering the entire stage floor) a very large quantity would be needed, whereas a series of plays with interior sets might require minimal platforming and very little plywood. Obviously, the larger the stage the more area is likely to be used for platforms and stairs. Perhaps the simplest way to estimate for ordering is to buy enough plywood to cover the entire acting area of the stage. For a stage with a proscenium opening of 30' and an acting area with an approximate depth of 20, that would be 20 sheets.

Quarter-inch plywood is less readily salvageable, and a sheet is seldom used on stage without being cut into. However, even small scraps can be cut up into corner-blocks, so that most of the plywood can be used twice and some of it several times.

Flat designs vary, but a standard flat requires approximately 12 corner-blocks; a simple box set takes about 250. Seventy-two 10" corner-blocks can be cut from a single sheet of plywood, with some waste. The theater should have on hand between 200 and 300 corner-blocks at the beginning of the season. However, corner-blocks are hardly ever cut from new plywood. Instead, the scrap left over from each show is cut up as part of the strike or a day or two later, so that a continuing supply is maintained. The quarter-inch sheets are also used for a variety of other purposes, including building furniture, properties, pilasters, fireplace mantels, etc., and covering the visible sides of platforms. Probably a theater should have 20 or 30 sheets on hand at the beginning of the season.

MISCELLANEOUS LUMBER

Lumber of other types is also needed for scenery construction, including 2 × 4s, 1 × 1s, stripping, dowels and molding, especially quarter-round and 3/4" cove molding; some 1 × 2s and 1 × 4s may also be occasionally useful. It is difficult to estimate the need for these types of lumber, and they are probably best handled by special orders. Most scene shops will have at least small quantities of all of them on hand, and as more is ordered for particular shows it should be carefully salvaged and returned to stock after use in order to build up a supply. The 2 × 4s are most often used for constructing the frames for high platforms. The 1 × 4s are likely to be used for building outsized flats or as stiffening battens. The other types of lumber are most often used decoratively, and how much will be needed depends on the habits of the designer. Experience suggests that the cove molding is especially useful, and tends to be unduly neglected in most theaters. Some of the types mentioned are sold only in random lengths, particularly the molding, but they can readily be pieced. They are ordered by the total length needed, but on request most lumber yards will make an effort to see that most of the pieces delivered are close to the length which can be used most conveniently for the current stage set. The patterns in which molding is applied often call for some very short pieces, so that it is economical to salvage pieces even as short as three or four inches if they are in good condition.

CANVAS

Nearly all sets require some use of canvas, either to cover platform and stair padding or to canvas flats. The square-yard price of canvas is much greater if only part of a bolt is ordered, so it should always be purchased by the full bolt. The canvas comes in various widths, but the 6' (72") width is the most economical. About forty-two linear yards of canvas of that width are needed to cover the flats for a simple box set. Since most sets are built largely of flats taken from stock and already covered, it will not ordinarily be necessary to canvas such a large area during a single season. Nevertheless, canvas will be needed for covering platforms, and undoubtedly at least some new flats will be built and canvassed.

Drops can quickly deplete the canvas supply. Because most sets do not require drops, it is easy to overlook them in purchasing, but a single play (especially a musical comedy) may need a number of drops which will require as much as twice the amount of canvas usually stocked. Pieces of canvas shorter than the length needed for covering flats are scrap, and can be used in the scene shop only in small quantities. If at all possible, the canvas used to make drops should be cut in multiples of the height of standard flats (plus 6" to a foot). Thus, if strips are sewn together horizontally to form a drop 35' wide, they should be cut at least 37'-6"; and if the drop is made of vertical strips 18' high, they should instead be cut 25'. The excess can be handled by increasing the overall size of the drop, by using wider hems, or simply by letting it hang down behind the visible section. In this way after the show the drops can be taken apart and cut to lengths which can be used to canvas flats. If the canvas for drops must be scrapped after the show, it will add greatly to the cost. If it can be cut as recommended so that it is entirely reusable, the drops can be made at little or no extra expense.

A bolt contains approximately 100 linear yards of fabric; a half-bolt is the minimum safe amount to start a season. If the budget allows, a second bolt should be ordered at this point, but in any case must be ordered if the supply drops to a fourth of a bolt.

PAINT

The use of paint is subject to enormous variation from season to season. The set for one production of *Macbeth* completely exhausted the theater's supply of red paint. A couple of years later, a set was designed for *Come Blow Your Horn* in which the walls were painted a solid green. To a large extent, the use of color depends on the type of plays presented (comedies and musicals are likely to call for a considerably different color scheme than a series of classic tragedies), but even more on the taste and habits of the designer. Nevertheless, the paint must generally be ordered before designs for the season's shows are available, so that a good deal of guessing is involved.

The price of paint depends on the cost of the raw materials, plus the cost of the manufacturing processes necessary to produce the desired colors and combine the various ingredients in usable form. As a very general rule, intense colors tend to cost more than the duller, browner, and greyer colors. However, since dull colors cannot be made brighter by mixing, whereas the vivid colors can be easily greyed and dulled, at least some of the clear, intense colors must be stocked.

Fortunately, the color used in the greatest quantity—white—is one of the cheapest of the casein paints, and by far the cheapest of the dry pigments used for traditional scene paint (the next cheapest color costs six times as much). Most scene shops use so much white that it is best to order at least half as much white as the entire quantity of all other colors combined; if money is available, white might well be ordered in the same quantity as the total of the other pigments.

The use of black is somewhat more variable; some painters regularly use it to darken other colors, while others prefer to use complementaries. In any case, straight black will be needed for a variety of purposes, including hiding unsightly braces and painting the backs of particular flats to prevent backstage lights from showing through. Black should be ordered in a quantity equal to about a fourth or a third of the white.

At least a couple of buckets should be ordered of each of the near-primaries discussed in chapter 10—a warm and cool red, yellow, and blue. A single mix for each of the secondaries is adequate, as close to the center of the range as possible—central green, orange, and purple. These should be bought in considerable quantity, since they form the basis for most of the paint mixtures which will be prepared. The near-primaries are then used to adjust them, so that the purple can be moved toward the red end of the range by the addition of a little cool red, or toward the blue end by the addition of a little warm blue. Of the secondaries, experience suggests that green is likely to be needed in the largest quantity, orange second, and purple least.

Technically, the browns are dark oranges, which can be prepared by mixing black (or the complementary color, blue) with any of the colors in the entire orange range, from yellow yellow-orange through central orange and as far as red red-orange. The browns can also be lightened by the addition of white. Browns are easy to mix from the clearer colors; however, the so-called earth colors are manufactured from especially cheap ingredients, so that it is much more economical to buy them as browns rather than stocking the brighter colors and mixing to brown in the theater.

Although the brighter colors tend to dominate the stage picture, great quantities of brown are used for backgrounds, and also to represent natural objects such as tree trunks and wood paneling. It is easy to alter brown by adding quantities of other colors, so that a single central brown (made of central orange plus black) would serve. However, a lighter yellow brown is constantly needed, and should also be purchased; the color called *golden ochre* or *yellow ochre* is especially useful and, fortunately, cheap.

Many of the browns were originally made of clay (which is one reason they are called earth colors). It was discovered that the color could be altered by baking (or "burning") the clay; pairs of colors are still manufactured labeled "raw umber" and "burnt umber," "raw sienna" and "burnt sienna," etc. The burnt colors are richer than the raw, and are a better buy; even if the raw colors should be needed, they can easily be produced by mixing white and perhaps small quantities of other pigments with the burnt.

One further factor should be considered in choosing what paint to buy. Some colors alter sharply if diluted, for instance by the addition of white; other colors are so intense that they can be greatly extended without significant reduction in brightness. The best example is French orange, which is a very heavy, intense pigment, relatively expensive pound for pound, but so vivid that in actual use it is more economical than other similar colors with a lower unit cost.

Some pigments bleed, that is, they cannot be hidden by coats of paint applied over them. The persistence of bleeding may be astonishing. As an experiment, one painter applied twenty coats of white paint over a bleeding green, allowing the paint to dry thoroughly between coats. The initial green showed almost as vividly through the twentieth coat as through the first. Bleeding is a constant nuisance, and makes it especially difficult to correct errors, since they cannot be concealed by overpainting. It is impossible to predict exactly which colors may bleed, when ordering, since only two or three of the pigments supplied by a particular manufacturer will cause trouble, and the colors will vary from company to company; vivid purples and greens, especially the blue-greens, are the commonest offenders. When a bleeding color is discovered, a note should be made so that it will not be ordered again from the same manufacturer.

PAINT COVERAGE

The amount of paint needed to cover a particular area depends on such a variety of factors that most authors shudder and avoid mentioning the subject, and the rest explain that they can't estimate it. Yet, the technical director must decide how much of each color to order, so an attempt will be made here to suggest acceptable quantities, even though they can serve only as an inaccurate approximation. The number of square yards a gallon of paint will cover depends on factors such as the material painted (plywood, canvas, or papier-maché), on whether the canvas is loosely or tightly woven, on whether the surface has been previously painted or not, on the degree of contrast between the previous coat and the new paint, on whether the paint is brushed or sprayed, on the type of paint used (traditional, casein, or some other type), on the proportions of pigment, binder, and vehicle, on whether the paint is applied solid or blended, on how much overpainting is done, on the amount of detail work required, and even on who does the painting. It is no wonder that authors shrink from giving even tentative estimates.

Three buckets of paint are adequate for the base coat for an ordinary box set, assuming 2½ gallons to the bucket, or a total of 7 or 8 gallons of paint. Since casein paint can be safely diluted with at least one part of water to each two parts of the paint as supplied by the manufacturer, painting all the walls of a box set would require approximately 5 gallons of paint taken from stock.

Five gallons can then be used as a minimum quantity for each color, on the assumption that it might be necessary to use any of the colors as the basic coat for an entire set. The near-primaries will most often be used to alter other colors, so that they can safely be stocked in amounts of two or three gallons each. More of the greens is likely to be needed than for the other two secondaries, so that they should total at least 8 or 9 gallons; central green should be bought in the greatest quantity, perhaps 5 gallons, with two or three gallons of blue-green and a gallon or two of yellow-green. A still larger supply of browns will be needed, and since they are cheap they can be ordered generously. Two gallons of burnt umber, 9 gallons of burnt sienna, and 5 gallons of golden ochre should be adequate. At least 10 gallons of black should be stocked, and 20 of white—more if the budget allows.

This list assumes a great many things, all questionable. It is intended to suggest the needs of an average theater presenting four major plays a season, with perhaps a few additional laboratory or experimental plays which will require less scenery, the plays to be performed on a proscenium stage of average size (thrust or central stages usually require less scenery and consequently less paint).

At the end of the season, an examination of the paint stock will demonstrate that some colors have been entirely used up. These must be replaced by the paint order for the following season, and unless their use has been due to some peculiar kind of production which is not likely to be repeated, probably the order should be increased by 50 percent. Any paints not used within two seasons should be noted, and an effort made to use them up by including them in mixes where their colors can be incorporated into the formula; for instance, if a supply of primrose yellow somehow never seems to get used, it should be chosen as the base for preparing a light brown during the following season, or perhaps even a tint of green. A few seasons' experience will make it possible for the technical director to adjust his purchases to the pattern of paint use followed in his theater, and to maintain adequate supplies without overpurchasing or running out.

METALLIC PAINT

There is one final type of paint which was mentioned in an earlier chapter. It is the metallic paint sold as a fine powder. It is available in pound containers, although there is some economy in buying it in 3-pound or 5-pound lots. The pigment is actually pure metal, but ground so finely that it feels like talcum powder when it is rubbed between thumb and finger. It is not only the cheapest but the most brilliant form of metallic paint available, and although it is far more expensive than any of the other pigments, it is generally used only for small details, and a three-pound can will last for years. It is sold in various colors, including a vivid metallic blue, green, and red, as well as a somewhat dull silver and several shades of brilliant gold. The most useful of the colors is called pale gold, and probably should be the only one stocked; others can be especially ordered in small quantities if they are needed.

The metallic powder must be mixed with a binder and a vehicle before it can be used as paint. The best binders are gloss vinyl, bronzing liquid, or white shellac; clear varnish can be used, although it dulls the pigment noticeably. Recently especially colorless varnishes have been developed for craft use; they are sold in pints in art stores, and although they are quite expensive, they are effective for metallic paint and are used in such small quantities that they do not represent a great expenditure. Some of them are formulated for very fast drying, and may be dry to the touch after fifteen or twenty minutes. Ordinary white glue can also be used as a binder for the powder, diluted to brushing consistency with a little water. The resulting mixture is somewhat difficult to use, but not extremely so, and the ready availability of the glue may make it the preferred medium.

GLUE

Although casein paint does not require the addition of glue, the glue supply is usually stored in the paint room. It is most economical to buy white glue by the barrel, out of which containers of more convenient size can be filled. Probably most scene shops buy it in gallon bottles; for a season's supply, there should be about 12 gallons on hand. It is extremely uneconomical to buy the glue in containers smaller than a gallon.

BRUSHES

Along with his paint order, the technical director should replenish his stock of brushes. A good quality brush, properly treated, will last for years; a poor brush is an abomination, and will make the work difficult from the beginning. However, few tools or materials are so regularly abused in the scene shop as brushes. They are used to stir paint, they are laid aside full of paint or glue which when dry cannot be removed, and they may even, at hair-raising moments, be used as scrub brushes to clean out paint buckets or the sink. Consequently, the wisest course is to buy brushes at the middle of the price range, and try to train workers in how to care for them.

No painter should ever have to stand idle because all of the brushes are in use. There should be one brush for every member of the largest group of people who are likely to need to paint at the same time. The list below is based on the usual assumptions, and should be adjusted to local conditions.

Priming brushes—3 needed
> 7" wide, with bristles about 4" long.
> Laying-in brushes can also be used for priming; they are similar but smaller and lighter.

Laying-in brushes—8 needed
> 3" to 5" wide, with bristles 4" or 5" long.
> These are used for painting the base coat on flats, platforms, or the stage floor; 6 would be just barely adequate, 10 would be better than 8.

Fitches—6 needed
> Long-handled brushes with short bristles, from 1" to 3" wide.
> Used for blending, for painting foliage, and for applying miscellaneous decorative motifs of moderate size.

Liners—8 needed
> Long-handled brushes with bristles arranged in a flat rectangle from 1/4" to 1" wide.
> Used for painting lines or stripes.

Detail brushes—6 of the 1/4" size needed, 6 of the 1/2", and 4 of the 3/4"
> Have long pencil-like handles, and bristles that form a point when wet; measured at the widest part, the clumps of bristles vary from 1/4" to 1".

Stencil brushes—10 needed
> Have short, stiff bristles so that they can be pounded against a stencil, minimizing the tendency of the paint to seep under the edge. Ordinary brushes designed for applying polish to shoes make a cheap and effective substitute.

Graining brushes—at least 2 needed; 4 would be better
> Have bristles set in thin clusters so that streaks of paint are deposited. These can be bought ready made, although some painters prefer to take an ordinary laying-in brush and trim the tips of the bristles so as to form an irregular saw-toothed edge.

The quantities listed are judged as necessary for carrying on the painting efficiently. All numbers could be reduced, with some loss of work speed. The priming brushes are the most easily dispensable, and many scene shops do not stock them at all, but regularly use laying-in brushes as substitutes. Of the remaining brushes, the laying-in, graining, and detail brushes are the most important. For a new scene shop or one with a very low budget, these should be stocked first in adequate numbers, and the other types of brushes added as funds become available.

MISCELLANEOUS PRODUCTS

In discussing the organization of space, it was mentioned that the paint area must provide storage for a miscellaneous collection of materials and equipment. These shelves should also be checked and replenishments ordered at the same time as the paint. In particular, there should be at least two-thirds of a gallon of paint thinner. Although theoretically only water-base paint is used for scenery, varnishes and oil-based paints show up in a small but steady stream, and if the thinner is not available for cleaning brushes and containers, they will be ruined.

There should be some means of opening paint cans. Lid removers are often given away as advertising items by paint suppliers; a cheap screwdriver especially set aside for that purpose can be used, or even a discarded table knife. At least two should be stocked.

No paint room ever has enough stirring sticks. These also are supplied free by paint stores, but they may be reluctant to provide them in the quantity needed for the theater. Lath and miscellaneous thin wood, including even left-over plywood strips, can be cut to convenient lengths and stored in the paint room. The reason a large number are needed is that a different stick must be used for each color or mix, to prevent contamination. About twenty should be provided, with the stock replenished whenever it drops below ten. With casein paint, if the sticks are rinsed fairly clean and laid aside to dry, they can be used again, since once the paint has completely dried it will not redissolve.

Paint containers are also needed in considerable quantity. When new colors are mixed in preparation for painting a set, they can be stored in good-sized buckets, but smaller containers should be provided to hold the paint while it is being applied. Small plastic buckets can be purchased cheaply, and supplemented by collecting miscellaneous throw-away containers such as the large cans in which restaurants purchase fruit and vegetables (the campus cafeteria is a good source), and plastic milk bottles of various sizes (gallons for larger quantities of paint, quarts for detail work); the top half or third can be cut off with a knife. If the paint is mixed fairly thick, it will require fewer storage containers, and it can be thinned to brushing consistency in small quantities as needed. Plastic buckets are more satisfactory than those made of metal because they are easier to clean and will not rust.

A supply of scouring powder is convenient for cleaning the sink and paint buckets. It can be purchased most economically in industrial quantities. A scrub brush and a spatula or putty knife should also be provided for digging up dried paint.

TOOLS AND HARDWARE

The supply of tools and hardware must also be checked and supplemented as needed before the beginning of each season. As with painting, work should never be held up because not enough tools are available—no worker should have to stand and wait because all the hammers are in use.

In an established theater, only gaps in the supply of tools need be filled at the start of the season. Which tools are to be ordered can be determined by comparing the tools on hand with the number needed for fully efficient operation. Again, the list given is only suggestive; although it assumes average needs and conditions, it will have to be adjusted to the special circumstances and habits of work in the local theater.

Radial-arm saw—1 needed with at least two crosscut blades and one for ripping (if ripping is done infrequently, the crosscut blades can be used, and the special blade dispensed with).

Portable circular saws—at least 1; 2-3 would be better.

Saber saws—4 needed; 6 would be better; there should be a supply of 1 or 2 dozen replacement blades, plus 1 or 2 knife blades.

> Saber saws are available with a number of special features, such as fans to blow away the sawdust, lights that turn on automatically when the saw is used, and tilting bases. Each of these increases the cost. The tilting base is a defect; the saw is seldom or never used to cut at a slant in the scene shop, and the base may loosen and tilt accidentally during cutting. It is better to buy the simplest saw, without unnecessary gimmicks. The motors should provide at least 1/4 horsepower—more is preferable. Saber saws are frequently featured in sales at two or three dollars below the regular price; advertisements should be watched so that the supply can be bought at the cheaper price.

Heavy-duty electric drill, 3/8" chuck, with a full set of interchangeable drills—1 needed.

Crosscut hand saw—can be dispensed with; 1 preferable.

Brace and bit—1 needed, with a full set of interchangeable bits.

Tinsnips—1 needed.

Scissors—1 needed; 2 better.

Knives—10 needed, 15 better, with a supply of 100 blades.

> The type of knife which should be purchased has a removable blade set into a two-piece handle held together by a short bolt. These are sometimes called mat knives because of their use in cutting mats when framing pictures.

Wood rasp—1 needed.

> The modern type with a replaceable blade is preferable.

Pliers—1-2 pairs.

Adjustable **C**-*wrench*—1-4.

> Unless a great deal of bolting or pipe work is done in the scene shop, other wrenches can be borrowed from the light crew as needed.

C-*clamps*—1-3 dozen.

Rip hammer—15 needed.

Claw hammer—can be dispensed with; if desired, 5 can be supplied and the number of rip hammers reduced to 10.

Tack hammer—2 minimum, 4–6 better.

Crow-bars—1–2; up to 7 or 8 can be used during strike.

Screwdrivers—do not buy Phillips screwdrivers, with +-shaped points.
Ratchet—2 needed with blades which fit the slots in number 9 screws.
Plain—6 with blades which fit number 9 screws; 1 with a considerably larger blade and 1 with a considerably smaller blade.

Steel square (carpenter's square)—6 needed.

Try-square—2 needed, 3 or 4 better.

Pocket tapes—at least as long as standard flats, better if they are long enough to measure the diagonal of a flat 6' wide—15 needed, 20 preferred.

Fifty-foot tape—1 needed, 2 better.
Used primarily for laying out the ground plan of the scenery on the stage floor.

Yardsticks—5–10.
The type distributed free as advertisements by hardware stores are satisfactory.

Snap lines—2 needed.
These are metal containers with string wrapped inside. It is convenient to have an extra supply of string in case one of the lines is broken. There should be a supply of chalk in two colors; this will usually be sold along with the snap lines, although if traditional scene paint is used in the theater whiting and pigments of other colors can be substituted.

Nails[3]
Clout nails—1¼"—25 pounds.
Common—2" (6 penny)—50 pounds.
These cost a good deal more if they are bought in smaller quantities.
Common—4" (20 penny)—2 pounds.
Coated box nails—2"—50 pounds.
This will probably last more than one season, but they are more expensive in smaller quantities; the stock should be replenished when it falls below 15 pounds. Uncoated box nails should not be bought by mistake.

---

3. The lengths of nails are traditionally stated in terms of a medieval unit called the *penny*. The choice of lengths to buy, however, must be made in terms of inches. Nails are either intended to extend all the way through a joint and far enough beyond so that the point can be clinched, in which case the length should equal the combined thickness of the pieces of lumber plus at least 1/4", or they should be slightly shorter than the total thickness of the lumber, so that the points will not stick through dangerously, that is, approximately 1/4" less than the lumber thickness. Since common nails are most often used to join two pieces of nominal 1" lumber (actually 3/4" + 3/4"), the 2" nail is suggested as the basic size, to be stocked in the greatest quantity. Nails of other sizes can be bought in small quantities for special projects, as they are needed.

Odd nails (clout nails and roofing nails, for example) are usually sized in inches. If the technical director prefers, he can use the penny system of dimensioning, although long experience has failed to uncover a supplier who seemed in the least surprised, disapproving, or reluctant to sell nails ordered by the inch.

Double-headed nails—1½" if available; otherwise buy the shortest size longer than 1½"—1 pound.

Round-headed roofing nails—10 pounds.

Square-headed roofing nails—2 pounds.

> The round-headed nails are prefereable for fastening easily torn materials such as cardboard because they are less conspicuous; the square-headed nails are useful as ornaments, especially on furniture.

1/2" headless brads—2 pounds.

> Used to fasten cove molding.

1" headless brads—2 pounds.

> Used to fasten quarter-round.

Carpet tacks—1/2" or 3/4"—3-5 pounds.

Spring-powered staplers—6 to 10 needed.

Staples—5,000 needed.

> Note: nearly all staplers are designed so that they can be used only with staples sold by the same manufacturer; if the wrong staples are used, the staplers will jam and perhaps be damaged. It is much better to buy only one brand of staplers, and staples from the same manufacturer, so that there is no chance of the wrong combination's being used.

Screws—5 gross (720 screws).

> Number 9 flat head wood screws; do not buy screws with Phillips heads by mistake; they have crossed slots in the form of +.

Bolts

Round head stove bolts—1/4" × 3"—3 dozen.

Carriage bolts—3/8" × 5"—2 dozen.

Carriage bolts—3/8" × 7"—1 dozen.

Washers (sized by the diameter of the hole).

1/4"—2 pounds.

3/8"—2 pounds.

Clinch plates—6.

Stovepipe wire—100 yards.

Electric glue guns—1-2 needed.

Supply of glue for the guns—2-3 dozen sticks.

Loose-pin back-flap hinges—2" × 4½"—3-6 dozen (no scene shop ever has enough).

> The hinges are dimensioned opened out flat; each leaf is approximately 2" square; the smaller size, with 1½" leaves, are less generally usable. Hinges of identical dimensions bought from different companies may vary minutely, but still too much to enable halves of the different hinges to be fitted together; it is better to buy them only from a single supplier.

Strap fasteners

Flat **L**s—12.

Bent **L**s—12.

S-hooks—2-3 dozen.

> Different types of products are identified as **S**-hooks; these are made of strap metal bent into a squarish **S** shape, and are used primarily to fasten stiffening battens to the backs of flats; **S**-hooks made of bent wire should not be bought by mistake.

Cleats.

> Brace cleats—15 to 20 needed (1 for each stage brace).

>> Brace cleats are of two types, identical except that one is cut from a flat sheet of metal and the other has the strip of metal beyond the large hole pushed up to form a hump, making it somewhat easier to fit the hook of the stage brace into the hole; either type is acceptable, but the humped are preferable.

> Stop cleats—6-12 needed (brace cleats can be used as a substitute).

> Lash eyes—4-6 needed (but a hole drilled in the top corner-block will do as well).

> Lash cleats—20-30 needed (various substitutes are available, although none is quite as convenient as the lash cleats themselves; a supply of tie-off cleats can also be purchased, although the lash cleats will do about as well).

Picture hooks-and-eyes—12 to 24 sets.

Hinged foot-irons—6-10 needed.

> Rigid foot-irons are less generally usable.

Turnbuckles—2-6.

Stage braces—15-20 needed.

> Either all-metal or hardwood braces with metal fittings are acceptable.

Stage screws—15-25 needed.

Rimlocks and knobs for doors—4-6 needed.

> These are seldom used any more outside the theater, but they are standard on stage, since doors in scenery are usually too thin to use the more familiar locks set into a socket cut in the door thickness.

Magnetic door fasteners—6-12 needed.

Wooden drawer pulls—12 needed.

Pencils—either carpenters' pencils (10 needed) or ordinary number 2 lead pencils—4 dozen needed.

Pencil sharpener—1 needed in the scene shop; preferably also one in the paint mixing area.

Felt pens—6 needed; the refillable type are the most economical.

Chalk (ordinary blackboard chalk)—50-100 pieces.

Masking tape—2 dozen rolls, 3/4" wide.

Luminous tape—2 rolls.

> Used for marking the edges of off-stage steps so that they can be seen in the dark.

Cotton sash cord, 1/4" (number 8)—50-100 yards.

> This is used for lashing flats together, but also as decoration for furniture, picture frames, paneling, etc.

Safety goggles—1 minimum, 2–4 better.

Filter masks—1 minimum, 2 needed, 4 better.

First-aid kit—1 needed.

    The more fully equipped industrial type is preferred.

It is not intended that this list of tools, equipment, and supplies provide for every possible scenic need. However, if the items are ordered even in the smallest quantities where a range is indicated, it should be possible to build a season's sets with only occasional supplementary purchases to meet unusual needs.

MISCELLANEOUS FOUND MATERIALS

Various odd structures and materials tend to show up in scene shops, often of mysterious and untraceable provenance; in particular abandoned furniture appears frequently. Before it is thrown out it should be checked to see if any of it is salvageable. Often a sizable supply of matched hinges can be retrieved, a number of wood or metal drawer pulls, and even metal braces. During a period when screws were in short supply, one technical director removed all the screws from an abandoned piano, in such quantity that the scene shop was able to run for almost two full seasons without having to buy more. Unusual sizes of screws, nails, bolts, or other materials are occasionally purchased for some special need. Rather than discarding the few which are left over, they should be stored in the miscellaneous boxes; even a few unusually large screws may solve a construction problem at some later time which would otherwise require a special trip to the nearest hardware store, with the loss of an hour or two of work time.

FREE AND LOW-COST MATERIALS

One source of scenic materials which is generally neglected is products peculiar to the area where the particular theater is located. Too often it is assumed that only standard materials are usable for scenery and that if they are not stocked in local stores they must be ordered from professional theatrical supply houses. But each area has its own pattern of materials and products; even the most readily available types of wood will vary. The local resources should be explored with an open mind, to see what can be used in the scene shop. At the expenditure of a small amount of time and a good deal of ingenuity, the technical director will often be able to uncover materials which will significantly extend his resources, which may reduce work time, and some of which are almost certain to reduce costs. Far from being amateurish, the imaginative exploitation of local resources is the mark of sound artistry—and of course it fits in with the current movement of recycling. A few examples will be given, from theaters in three different states, but an ingenious technical director will be able to find many more in his own area.

A day spent in visiting all the local lumber yards resulted in the discovery of a special type of plywood manufactured in Korea of oriental woods, incidentally beautiful, but for the scene shop important because it was so much cheaper than all other types of plywood that it was being cut up for one-time use by a manufacturer as a padding for shipping ice cream containers. The director bought a large supply for use in his home because of its appearance, and a still larger supply for use in the theater because of its low cost.

Paper factories in Wisconsin use a particular kind of fabric known as papermill felt, although it is not actually felt but a very heavy, closely-woven napped material, about six feet wide and cut to very long lengths. When the nap begins to wear, the material is discarded, and the manufacturers were glad to give it free to local theaters. It was ideal for platform padding and miscellaneous purposes, and in fact was used to pad the entire stage floor in one theater.

A factory in Michigan discarded enormous quantities of cardboard boxes, which were flattened, tied with metal straps, and sent to the dump. Permission was granted the local theater to collect as much of the cardboard as was needed, and it was available in such quantity that even after a truck had been fully loaded the pile seemed hardly to have been reduced at all. This source was used for eight years, at no cost except for having to drive a college truck to the factory and load it up.

At another college a large number of small sturdy cardboard boxes were discarded by the library. Several hundred of them were carried into the scene shop to use as work trays for screws and small nails—except that the light, properties, and costume crews discovered them and carted two-thirds of the supply away to store buttons, thread, pins, and other small objects. By calling on local rug stores in North Carolina, one director was able to find unlimited supplies of the cardboard rug centers around which the rugs are rolled when delivered. Since they were regularly burned at the store, they were obtained free, and transported to the theater in the back of a station wagon or small truck, where they were used as bases for pillars, to make roof tiles, and for miscellaneous other purposes. In many areas of the south, tobacco is delivered to the factories in bags made of a loosely woven burlap called tobacco cloth. It can be obtained in any quantity at very little cost, and was used by one theater to cover the stage floor for one play, and in other ways where its particular texture was desired.

Many other products have been imaginatively utilized in scene shops—the large cans in which restaurants buy fruit and vegetables, which make excellent paint containers, and which can also be used decoratively when both ends are removed; sawdust, which can be mixed with glue and whiting to make a modeling compound; plastic sheeting, which can be used to protect floors when flats are being spattered, and which can be cut and twisted to form decorative motifs; foam plastic used for packing fragile articles; even egg cartons have been used effectively. One technical director with an unusually large collection of small quantities of odd nails, screw-eyes, bolts, etc., asked his married students to save baby-food bottles to store them in. He discovered that the bottles were also useful for storing small paint samples as guides for further mixing if supplies of paint ran out during work on a set.

One high school director in Illinois, working with a near zero budget, needed to paint pillars for one set a slightly creamy off-white. He discovered that the mimeograph paper used at the school was exactly the color he wanted, and that large quantities of it were being discarded. The paper was salvaged, and pasted on the pillars with the un-printed side out.

Wire coathangers can be easily collected in almost any quantity, and the wire is just stiff enough to hold its shape and yet readily bendable. It is excellent for making chandelier frames, and can be used for a variety of other purposes, as armatures for papier-maché units, as pins for hinges, to make ornamental chains, for screen door hooks, to form frames for dipping into liquid plastic, etc.

Most of these materials can be obtained free. Others may be had in exchange for mentioning the donor in the list of acknowledgments on the play programs. At most, any charge is likely to be nominal. It is false economy to try to use materials which require so much time to rework them that the work load is significantly increased, but when they can genuinely contribute to the efficiency of the work and the effectiveness of the scenery, it is a mark of practicality and artistry to exploit them as fully as possible.

INVENTORIES

All purchasing is greatly facilitated by the maintenance of careful inventories. Record-keeping should not be allowed to get in the way of the work, but typically too scanty records are kept rather than too full. Within a week after every strike, paint, lumber, canvas, and tool stocks should be checked and the inventories revised to show the current supplies. Not every spoonful of paint need be accounted for, or every single board; rather, practical estimates should be recorded. Generally, a can of paint from a third to two-thirds full should be recorded as half a can; scrap lumber shorter than 3 or 4' should be disregarded, and the quantity of the longer scrap estimated. The most significant figure is that showing the number of full-length pieces of 1 X 3 on hand in good condition, for use as flat stiles; these should probably be counted. In checking the plywood, only full sheets need be recorded.

Special attention should be paid to the tools most likely to disappear, especially tape measures. Materials which are used up should be checked, for instance masking tape, pencils, staples, and glue cylinders for the glue gun. Although presumably such materials will have been stocked in sufficient quantities for the entire season, unusual patterns of use may have depleted them, and if so they should be replenished before work begins on the next show.

FLAT AND PLATFORM INVENTORIES

More elaborate inventories should be maintained of scenic units, particularly flats and platforms. A separate sheet should be prepared for each flat as it is built, and should include the date it was built and a sketch of the flat, giving its dimensions (Figure 16.1).

FIGURE 16.1 A flat inventory sheet.

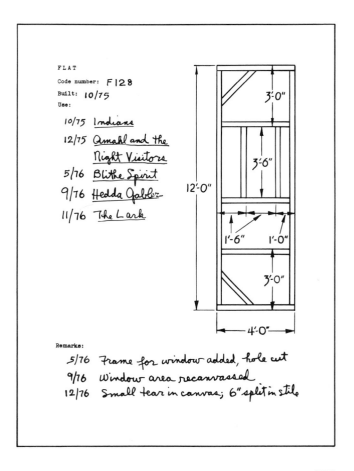

FLAT

Code number: F128
Built: 10/75
Use:

10/75 Indians
12/75 Amahl and the
      Night Visitors
5/76 Blithe Spirit
9/76 Hedda Gabler
11/76 The Lark

3'-0"
3'-6"
12'-0"
1'-6" 1'-0"
3'-0"
4'-0"

Remarks:
5/76 Frame for window added, hole cut
9/76 Window area recanvassed
12/76 Small tear in canvas; 6" split in stile

If the flat has an opening or any other peculiarity, it should also be drawn, dimensioned, and if necessary described. Each time a flat is used, the date and name of the play should be recorded, and whenever a flat is altered in any way the alteration should be indicated. If flats are not repaired as part of strike, any needed repairs should be described on the inventory sheet, including a splitting stile or a hole in the canvas. These records should be kept carefully up to date.

Similar records should be made of platform and step units (Figure 16.2). Their dimensions should be indicated, the date built, the plays they are used for, any peculiarities (such as a socket cut in one corner of the top to receive a pole), and any repairs which might be needed should be carried out during strike or noted on the inventory sheet. Platforms should be identified as rigid or folding, and the type of folding platform indicated by a description or a sketch. Step units and ramps should be recorded in the same way.

The flat and platform inventories are useful for the construction crew, since they will prevent a unit's being built new when a matching one is available in stock. They are equally important for the designer, who can plan the scenery so as to incorporate as

FIGURE 16.2 A platform inventory sheet.

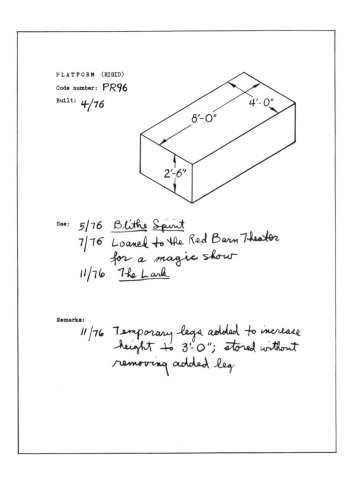

PLATFORM (RIGID)

Code number: PR96

Built: 4/76

8'-0"   4'-0"   2'-6"

Use: 5/76 Blithe Spirit
7/76 Loaned to the Red Barn Theater for a magic show
11/76 The Lark

Remarks:
11/76 Temporary legs added to increase height to 3'-0"; stored without removing added leg

many existing elements as possible, with a saving of time and material costs. For one production of Shaw's *Misalliance,* the designer was asked to plan a set which could be built with no expenditure except for paint. Although his design incorporated several platforms of different heights, and door openings also varied in height, he was able to plan it entirely from units already in stock; a few platforms had to be cut down in height, but only one door opening had to be altered. Preparing such a design would have been impossible without adequate inventories. Certainly, no designer can be expected to struggle through a pile of platforms to determine the dimensions of the bottom one at the back of the stack. Instead, he will design without reference to them, often with a resulting sizable increase in construction time. As with most scene shop procedures, an orderly and systematic handling of the work saves time, money, and irritation, even though taking inventories and keeping records may occasionally seem less valuable or productive than other activities.

17

Scheduling the Work

All theater work tends to be done under the pressure of tight schedules. Many factors must be taken into account in deciding when plays are to open, including in the professional theater the availability of theaters, in educational and community theaters the scheduling of other local events which might compete for audiences, and in the college theater the dates of vacations, of final examinations, and of other campus performances. Summer theaters often open a new show each week, so that at best stagecraft work must be done at top speed. And even if a comfortable period is allowed for production work, unforeseeable emergencies can produce crises—including a flu epidemic, an industry strike which delays the shipment of essential materials, and, in the case of one North Carolina theater, the collapse of the roof during a torrential rainstorm. But to glory in crises, to create them intentionally or through negligence, to brag about spending overtime in order to get set work done is an indication of the grossest kind of amateurism. One of the clearest and soundest marks of professionalism is that no foreseeable and avoidable emergency is allowed to happen.

The commonest cause for a construction crisis is that the technical director fails to notice that the work is behind schedule until it has fallen far behind. With only four or five days left, he suddenly realizes that two weeks' work must somehow be done. In an efficiently run scene shop, the director should assess the work completed at the end of each day, and should determine whether the crew is exactly on schedule, ahead of schedule, or behind schedule. If the work is behind schedule, the problem can then be attacked and solved while it is of manageable size, and while there is still some cushion of time which can be used for catching up. So important is this that the daily check at the end of each work session should be an invariable procedure, carried out with unfailing care, but with extra care when the pressure of work increases.

WORK ESTIMATES

Checking depends on a detailed analysis of the work required for the set, and a careful estimate of the time needed. This analysis and estimate must be completed before the crew work begins, and is one of the technical director's most important responsibilities.

The work estimate can be made only on the basis of the designer's drawings. Except in some unavoidable emergency, it is the responsibility of the designer to deliver his entire set of finished drawings to the technical director well in advance of the time when construction work must start—a minimum of three days ahead. Where a genuine emergency has prevented the preparation of the drawings, any technical director and all the crew members can be confidently expected to stretch themselves to help solve the problem, but no workman can properly be asked or expected to engage in crisis work to compensate for the director's indecisiveness or the designer's negligence, and the responsibility for handling crises due to those factors belongs entirely to the staff members who are at fault.

Even in a justifiable emergency, the technical director cannot make his work estimates without an accurate ground plan and perspective drawing of the set, supplemented by a detailed conference with the designer. The discussion in this chapter, however, will assume normal conditions—the delivery of the full set of working drawings to the technical director at least half a week before construction work must start.

CONSTRUCTION REQUIREMENTS

The technical director should first study the ground plan and perspective drawing or painting of the set to get its general pattern clearly in mind. His further analysis can be conveniently divided into three sections—construction, painting, and assembly. The construction can also be divided into three types of projects—flats, platforms (including stairs and ramps), and miscellaneous. The miscellaneous category will include such things as furniture, doors and door frames, decorative architectural units such as arches, pillars, and pilasters, and such otherwise unclassifiable projects as constructing chandeliers and magic effects for *Blithe Spirit,* the barrels for *Rosencrantz and Guildenstern Are Dead,* and the revolving bed for *A Flea in Her Ear.*

FLAT CONSTRUCTION

The designer can be expected to have identified which flats can be taken from stock, and which must be built new, as well as any alterations which must be made in the stock flats. Examining the flat inventory sheets will indicate whether repairs are needed in the stock flats. At this point, the technical director should prepare a scratch list of the flat construction which must be done. This can be done most conveniently by using code letters for the flats. If the designer has not indicated them, they should be added to the drawings. This list will be broken into two parts—the flats which must be built new, and those which can be taken from stock. The stock flats will also be divided into two groups, those which can be used without alteration, and those which must be repaired or reworked.

PLATFORM CONSTRUCTION

The technical director then turns to the platforms and prepares similar lists, again using code letters, and showing which platforms must be built new, which can be taken from stock and used unaltered, and which of the stock platforms must be repaired or re-built. Since the side surfacing of platforms is often removed before they are stored, it will almost always be necessary to resurface the areas which will be visible to the audience in the new set. This is a fast and simple job, and may be disregarded in estimating the work, in which case these platforms will be listed with the group which can be used unaltered; or, if preferred, this can be considered a rebuilding project, and they can be included in the third group. Ramps and step units should be treated in the same way, and separate lists prepared for them, divided into the same categories.

MISCELLANEOUS CONSTRUCTION

It will be more difficult to prepare the miscellaneous list, because each project may have to be described individually. Of course, if several identical units are to be built (for instance, five pilasters), they can be listed as a single item.

PAINTING

The painting requirements of the set are then analyzed similarly, and again it is usually most convenient to group the work in three areas—flats, platforms (and ramps and stairs), and miscellaneous. If the stage floor will be painted as part of the set, it can be included in the miscellaneous listing, or placed in a category of its own.

ASSEMBLY

Finally, the work of assembly should be evaluated. The work required to fasten up a simple box set can be taken as a kind of basic measure, and only a supplementary list prepared indicating unusual or special problems or projects. In addition, the complexity of the ground plan should be evaluated, particularly how difficult it will be to mark it on the floor of the stage.

TIME ESTIMATES

The result of this analysis is a series of lists on which are included all of the different work projects which must be completed by the stagecraft crew. The technical director's next task is to estimate how many work-hours each project will require.

This estimate is of course difficult to make accurately. Especially in a college or community theater, the crew members can be expected to display at least four and perhaps five different levels of skill, and consequently to work at varying speeds. Some of the people will be working on their first play; others will have had moderate experience; still others will have served as crew members for several plays, and a final small group (usually the paid assistants) will be thoroughly familiar with stagecraft work, and capable of training the new people. If the technical director himself takes part in the construction, rather than serving simply as a supervisor, he presumably supplies a fifth and fully professional level of skill. The work estimates must be somehow fitted to this range of ability, and should of course represent neither the length of time the novice workers would require for the different jobs, nor the speed at which the technical director himself could turn out the work. Probably the best method of arriving at a figure is to estimate how long it would take the more experienced workers (those who have extensive experience in set building, including the supervisory staff but excluding the technical director), and then multiply the figure by two.

The estimates should be stated in work-hours, so that if it is concluded that a two-person team could finish a project in one 3-hour work session, it should be recorded as a six-hour job. If the two-person team is assumed to be experienced, the assessment should be doubled to represent the probable average production speed for the entire crew, and the project marked as a twelve-hour job.

Although it is most convenient to state the estimates in work-hours, it may be easier to make them in terms of a normal work session, which in most theaters would constitute a 3-hour evening period. Some jobs can be done most efficiently by a single worker (for instance, building and decorating a picture frame). Others go more than twice as fast if two people work together as a team (for instance, canvassing a flat, which two people can do in considerably less than half the time that would be required for one person alone); other jobs can most efficiently be done by a larger crew. The technical director should decide on the number of workers which would be most efficient for a particular project, estimate how long it will take his fully experienced workers to complete the project, in terms of a normal evening or afternoon work session, translate that into hours, multiply by the number of workers assumed, and double to represent the average time required for the project, on the assumption that some of the workers will be inexperienced and hence less productive.

As a very inexact guide, a few estimates will be given for typical projects. Two moderately experienced workers ought to be able to cut, assemble, and canvas two flats during a 3-hour evening session (fully skilled workmen of course can turn out many more than this). Probably it will require a 2-person team a full evening to build a simple 4' × 8' platform. Even a relatively complicated table should take two workers no more than an evening. A more elaborate piece of furniture, such as an armchair or a bookcase, will probably require an evening and a half or two evenings for two workers. An ordinary worker can hinge and dutchman two flats together in an hour. Painting an average-sized flat (4' × 12') with a priming coat or a base coat should take one person not more than a half hour. Spattering one of the three walls of a box set with one color should take about an hour. In others words, two workers can spatter an entire box set with two colors in one evening.

Painting a simple repeated pattern over an entire flat, for example, drybrushing stone shapes, should require about an hour and a half. Graining a 4' flat to represent wood should require about 20 minutes (after the base coat has been painted). A painter should be able to lay in a ½" wide stripe at about the rate of 30 to 50 feet an hour. Blending takes much more time, and so variably that it is impossible to estimate it, but blending a detailed pattern such as a wallpaper design would require something like four or five times as long as laying on the base coat.

Copying the ground plan on the floor of the stage takes much longer than it apparently should, although sets vary enormously in the time needed, primarily because some require a much greater number of measurements than others. The time runs up because a sizable crew is needed. The work can hardly be done with fewer than three people (two to hold the tape and one to mark), but five or six people can do it more conveniently. Probably six to ten work-hours should usually be allowed for this job.

The time required for painting the stage floor also varies greatly; if a detailed tile design is to be applied, it will take many work-hours; if the floor is simply painted solid, and rugs laid over large areas, the painting can go very quickly. The range is something like three or four hours for straight painting up to ten or twelve for more detailed painting.

Assembling a set requires a crew of at least six workers. A simple box set can probably be fastened together by a half dozen workers in a couple of hours (that is, 12 work-hours). If platforms and stairs must be moved into position, if ceiling beams are used, and if the set is heavily decorated, it could easily require 36 to 40 work-hours. Often a full Saturday is set aside for this work, and the entire stagecraft crew takes part.

It is hoped that these estimates will be of assistance, especially for a construction worker who is just beginning service as a technical director. Growing experience will make his planning increasingly accurate, but even at first a careful assessment and scheduling of the work needed for a particular show will be invaluable to him, and will go far toward preventing the development of surprising emergencies, and toward creating an atmosphere of well planned, businesslike procedures which are absolutely essential if the construction work is to proceed in an orderly fashion, if it is to be done on time, and if the members of the stagecraft crew are to retain their sanity and to remain on speaking terms with each other.

When the number of work hours needed for all the projects has been arrived at, the figures should be totaled. This then represents the number of man-hours which must be spent in building, painting, and assembling the set.

DAILY ESTIMATES

The technical director has some slight control over when work is started. The completion date is not subject to his control, but is set by the director of the play. One rehearsal will have been reserved about a week before opening night, and identified as the "technical rehearsal." The work of all crews must have been finished by the time rehearsal is scheduled to begin on that evening. However, much of the work of the light crew can be done only after the set has been assembled on stage, so that the deadline for the stagecraft crew is at least a couple of days earlier.

Checking with a calendar, the technical director then determines the number of work days available for building the set. It is better to omit weekends. Not only is it unreasonable to ask crew members to work for a month or six weeks without a break, but it is essential that the weekends be left as a cushion so that if difficulties develop some extra time is available for handling them. The total number of work-hours needed to complete the set is then divided by the number of work days. The resulting figure indicates the number of hours of work which must be completed each day if the work is to be done on schedule.

The student is likely to ask at this point, "But what if I estimated wrong?" Oddly, it makes very little practical difference. Suppose that a wildly exaggerated error had been made—that each project had been estimated as requiring twice as much time as it actually will (or half as much time). At the end of the first week (if six weeks are available for the work), one-sixth of the total work must have been completed, and checking the work actually done with the preliminary estimates will indicate clearly whether a sixth or more or less has been finished, whether the work hours have been estimated accurately or not. Erratic errors in both directions, with some projects greatly overestimated and others greatly underestimated, can obscure the assessment of progress, but usually not disastrously. The only way in which a real crisis could be produced by an error in estimating is if the projects carried out in the first half of the work period were uniformly overestimated, and the projects carried out in the last half were uniformly underestimated. In that case, the daily checks would incorrectly show the work well on schedule during the first three weeks, when actually it was running behind—but that kind of neat reversed error in estimating is almost inconceivable.

CHECKING WORK PROGRESS

At the end of the first day's work, all of the projects which have been completed are marked off the list; for projects on which a significant amount of work has been done, but which are not finished, the proportion of the work done should be estimated, and recorded as a percentage of the preliminary estimate of the time required for the project (the actual time spent on the work should be ignored). The work-hours given on the preliminary list for the projects finished and for parts of projects begun, should be totaled. If the figure is the same as the daily work load required to complete the set, the work is proceeding exactly on schedule. If the completed figure is smaller, the work is behind schedule, and if it is larger, the work is ahead of schedule.

A slight deviation from schedule is of little significance: if the original estimate indicated that 16 hours of work must be done each day, and the estimates for the work completed the first day total only 15 or 15½ hours, the work can be considered to be proceeding satisfactorily. Not only does the staff tend to work more efficiently as they hit their stride, but until a clear pattern has been established there is little cause for alarm. If, however, the work completed falls short by a half hour a day for a full week, that should be taken as an indication that a real problem exists, and a vigorous attempt should be made to find the cause and correct it. If 30 work days are available, and the work done each day falls short by a half hour, at the end of the period it will be 15 work-hours behind schedule, and it is far better to catch up as soon as the slipping is clearly demonstrated.

EMERGENCY PROCEDURES

If the crew, working normally, fails to keep up with the schedule, obviously the work program must be revised by substituting abnormal procedures. The most obvious corrective measures are increasing the number of workers, inserting extraordinary work sessions into the schedule, or increasing the length of the regular sessions. Unfortunately, none of those adjustments is likely to be very effective. The most interested and skillful workers are probably already members of the crew, and additional workmen must be recruited from an inexperienced peripheral group who may be less strongly motivated and who are almost certain to require extensive supervision, so that they increase production minimally if at all.

Longer hours or added sessions will increase production only temporarily. If an unforeseeable emergency has arisen, such as a key worker's being taken to the hospital, theater workers can be counted on to leap into the situation and cheerfully push up hours and production, but even then the extra effort can hardly be sustained longer than a week. Other responsibilities which have been postponed for the crisis work will become pressing and have to be attended to, but even if the crew can be kept at work, fatigue will begin to cut productivity. Probably two weeks is the absolute longest that stretching work time can be used to increase production, and one week is a more practical limit, short of the direst and clearest emergency.

Nevertheless, there are half a dozen other ways in which the work can be speeded up. All scene shop administration should be based on careful planning. The first step in handling a crisis is to restudy the plans in detail, looking closely for ways in which they can be revised to save time. Too often a technical director's instinct is to do the opposite—to toss his plans aside, snatch up a hammer, and begin work himself. But even though restudying his plans may seem to delay production, it will often do more to speed the work of the entire crew than anything else he could do.

THE SIZE OF WORK CREWS

One item which should be carefully checked is the number of crew members who are working together on each project. For every work assignment there is a particular size of crew which will complete it in the fewest man-hours. Let us suppose that one person is using a snap line to lay out a grid on a sheet of plywood, preparatory to copying a design to be cut out. Two people working together could lay out the grid in about a third of the time; on the other hand, three people would require nearly as much time as two. Building small pieces of furniture, making decorative structures out of papier-maché, cutting plywood for corner-blocks or stair treads can usually be done most efficiently by one person. Building and assembling large platforms and stair units may often be done fastest by a sizable crew, and it might well be that the construction of a full raked stage would require the fewest work-hours if the entire stagecraft staff worked on it simultaneously.

With plenty of time, the workers can be left free to arrange themselves as they please. When productivity must be stepped up, however, the technical director should carefully reassess the most efficient crew size for each project and then adjust the organization of the workers to match it, pulling an extra person off one job and increasing the number of workers for other jobs.

FRAGMENTING ASSIGNMENTS

The first time a worker carries out a project requires much longer than repetitions of the same task. If he builds a series of identical leg supports for a platform, the first of which requires an hour and a half, the second is likely to take only an hour, and he may be able to complete the third in as little as half an hour. After that, there is not likely to be much further reduction.

That fact can be used to produce a very great saving in work-hours. The work projects should be divided into their smallest practical components, and each worker's assignment made so that he can repeat a single small task rather than switching from one larger project to another and different one. For example, if six identical platforms are to be built, they will require the fewest work-hours if one person makes all of the sides, another all of the ends, a third all of the center supports, and a fourth cuts all of the tops.

Similarly, in painting a floral wallpaper design on flats, the work will go most quickly if all of the stems are painted by the same worker or workers, all of the leaves by another, and all of the flowers by a third.

This is especially true with beginning workers, since each must be especially taught the skills or techniques necessary for his assignment, and the smaller the assignment the more quickly the training can be done. As an example, the walls of the set for one production of *The Lion in Winter* were painted to represent shaped blocks of stone. The work was done by students who had never served on a set crew before. The process was divided into seven steps:

1 — painting the base coat
2 — drawing the mortar lines
3 — applying the shadow for each stone
4 — applying the highlight for each stone
5 — painting the mortar lines
6 — spattering dark
7 — spattering light.

Each step was carried out by a different worker or pair of workers, who were trained only in their particular task, for example, the correct pattern for drybrushing the shadows. The work was done to an uncomfortably tight schedule, and it was estimated that the work-hours required for painting the flats were cut about in half by this fragmentary method.

THE AVOIDANCE OF DELAY

Another vital factor in maintaining production is to make sure that work is constantly available for each crew member, so that he need not stand and wait. A staggering amount of time can be lost if a percentage of the workers are regularly kept idle. One otherwise excellent supervisor, a graduate student, never kept more than three-fourths of his staff supplied with assignments; whenever he was supervising a group of four workers, one or another was always required to wait. For every hundred man-hours available, twenty-five were thus wasted, and the total by the end of a month often made the difference between all-night crisis work and the comfortable production of scenery.

At best there will be occasional moments when some work will have to be stopped. It may be necessary for painters to wait for the last flat to be base-coated before the area can be cleared for spattering; if the theater owns only two nail pullers and both are in use a worker may have to wait a few moments until one is free. But seeing that there is a project available for every worker at every moment is so important that the supervisory staff should be instructed to stop their own work instantly whenever they see a crew member apparently without an assignment, and volunteer their help in finding him one.

This is not to suggest that an impression of pressure or tension be created, or that workers be made to feel they are being driven relentlessly. In fact, frequent coffee breaks should be not only allowed but strongly encouraged—they contribute to efficiency, rather than reducing it. But having work contantly available is more likely to raise morale than to lower it. Few things are more irritating than having to stand idle when there is work to be done, and if workers did not want to produce the scenery they would not have joined the crew.

In restudying his plans, the technical director should especially look for jobs which can be worked at for short intervals, so that if a workman's assigned project must be briefly interrupted he can turn to the other task until tools or work space are again available. One production for *The Importance of Being Earnest* required the cutting of some hundreds of cardboard strips for constructing lattice work. Once the strips had been marked, the sheets of cardboard were laid aside on a work table, so that during even a brief period of enforced idleness a worker could turn to them and cut one or two. Not only was the job made less irksome by being done a little at a time, but having it constantly available meant that no crew member had to wait impatiently until he could resume work.

THE MARGIN OF ERROR

It is pleasant to do work neatly and carefully, but unnecessary precision can waste a great deal of time. All theater work involves a margin of permissible error, which may vary greatly from project to project; it may be as small as a minute fraction of an inch, or as large as several feet. For example, if a board cut for use as one leg of a platform is 1/8" too long it is possible that the platform will teeter when the actors walk across it; in this case the allowable margin of error might be as small as 1/16". On the other hand, if a board is needed to nail to the back legs of two 8' platforms to hold them together, and it is placed so that it is invisible to the audience, it is quite possible that any board as short as 2' or as long as 15' might be acceptable; in that case, the margin of error would be 13'.

Time is saved if the workers take advantage of the margin of allowable error. When one set was being assembled on stage, a worker was asked to go to the lumber rack and bring back a board about 6' long. He took a partner with him (thus doubling the number of man-hours needed for the task), and both were gone for something like twenty minutes. When they finally showed up and were asked what had taken them so much time, they replied that none of the boards they looked at was longer than 5'-9", and they finally had to dig up a long board and cut it down to exactly 6'. The crucial error here is in the substitution of the word "exactly" for the word "about," resulting in an unnecessary reduction of the margin of error and a significant increase in work time at a moment when every second was precious.

The same principle is applicable to every aspect of set work. If one crew member is painting the stem of a flower for a wallpaper design, and a second crew member then paints a flower two inches in diameter over the end of the stem, it is a waste of time for the stem to be painted with great precision up to the edge of the flower; the two-inch margin of error should be used, and the stems swept up into the area. Since hundreds or even thousands of motifs may have to be painted on a set, a few seconds saved on each can make a significant difference in how fast the work is completed.

The most effective workers will assess margins of error themselves, and take advantage of them to speed up the work when necessary, but ordinary workers cannot be expected to. The technical director should carefully identify how much leeway is available, and whenever time can be saved by making use of it, instruct the crew members to do so.

METHODS OF WORK

In the precrisis tours of inspection, the technical director will probably have concentrated primarily on the quality of work being done. If it must be speeded up, he should revisit each team of workers and watch especially for the use of unnecessarily slow techniques. A worker who is using a steel square as a guide for cutting cardboard strips with a mat knife may place the square so that the short end hangs out in the air, creating an imbalance which must be resisted with muscle power. He may lay the square so that he must cut along the edge closest to him; he may have difficulty keeping the square from shifting as he cuts; and he may be pressing too hard with the knife. All of those methods reduce accuracy and increase the amount of time needed to cut each strip. Instead, the square should be turned so that it rests entirely on the cardboard, the cut should be made against the far side of the metal strip, if the square shifts the workman should hold one end tight with his knee and the other with one hand, and the cardboard should be cut with light fast passes of the knife rather than a few heavy ones.

A builder who keeps interrupting his work to trot back to the tool room for a few nails should be instructed to bring out a full work tray. If two workers share the same tape, each one stopping work while the other measures, they should be sent to get another. If a true straight-edge 8' long is used to draw a line across the length of a sheet of plywood, only the two guide points at the ends of the sheet should be marked. It is a waste of time to measure auxiliary guide points every two feet. A painter who is stretching out far past the center of a flat to do precision painting should be instructed to walk around to the other side.

These are only a few examples. Brief inspection of the work being done on each project should reveal any inefficient methods which are being used, and the workers should be instructed in the faster techniques. In almost every case they will also be less awkward. It is not unusual for a few simple suggestions to double the per-hour output of a worker, and a general tightening up of procedures might well increase the productivity of the set crew as a whole by fifty percent.

SCENE SHOP MAINTENANCE

There is some temptation as work pressure rises to relax policies for maintaining order in the scene shop. If anything, the workers should be abnormally careful to observe practices which will promote work efficiency. Even though it may seem like an interruption of their work, tools must be scrupulously returned to their proper places, work trays put back, and the work space cleared in readiness for the next session. Perhaps working fifteen minutes longer would make it possible to fasten the last leg on a platform support, but if it means that the work area must be left in chaos or that tools not be properly stored, the next work period may be delayed by a half hour or an hour, with a loss in productivity outweighing the momentary gain.

POSTPONING WORK

On the other hand, work which does not genuinely contribute to the play should be postponed if possible. If a pile of scrap lumber in the corner of the scene shop will not get in the way of the workers, in a crisis it is better to let it lie. It can be sorted, labeled, and stored after the immediate task of getting the set done has been completed. If a box of bolts has been misshelved, it is better to leave it where it is—if they will not be needed for the current show. If the supply of chalk is down to one midget piece, it is uneconomical to interrupt the work even for five minutes to replenish the supply, unless it will be needed for the current set.

Normally, of course, it is best for maintenance, storage, and replenishment of supplies to be carried on steadily, but for crises abnormal policies should be substituted, and any job that can be delayed without reducing the efficiency of the work on the set being built should be let go. Distressing as this may be to anyone with orderly tastes, it is preferable to having to make a curtain speech before each performance to explain to the audience why the wallpaper pattern just somehow never got finished on one flat, or why some other task necessary to the production did not get done.

THE SEQUENCE OF WORK

In addition to checking on the amount of work done each day, the technical director must plan the order in which the projects are worked on. To a considerable extent, the sequence of work is inevitable and obvious; a flat must be built before it is painted. However, the needs of the director and actors must also be taken into account.

MARKING THE STAGE

The set crew is usually asked to mark the ground plan of the set on the floor of the stage before the first rehearsal. This marking need not be quite as accurate as that used for actually assembling the scenery. Probably if key points are marked within three or four inches of their true position it will be accurate enough for rehearsal. Since the actors will walk across the marks for at least two weeks, chalk lines will rub off. Instead, 3/4" masking tape should be used to indicate the positions of the flats, platforms, and other scenic elements, including the placement of the furniture. This task is therefore the first one undertaken by the set crew. The key points should be marked with chalk, and then the full lines laid in with the tape.

PRECUTTING

If any sizable amount of new construction is involved in preparing a set, it is likely that a number of the board lengths will have to be cut in quantity. It is much faster to cut all boards of the same length at the same time, using methods described in chapter 3. Only the first board must be measured; it is nailed temporarily to the saw table, and the other boards cut by aligning their left ends with the far end of the first board. Since it takes an appreciable amount of time to measure and mark a board and then line it up accurately with the saw blade, this method speeds up the work significantly. For the *Tempest* set which has been mentioned earlier, several board lengths had to be cut in quantities of more than a hundred. The extreme example was 3'-11 3/8"; 441 boards were needed of that length. Simply to mark that many boards would have taken a full evening. Cutting them all at the same time, using the first one as a guide, made it possible to complete the cutting in considerably less time than it would have taken just to measure them individually. A further advantage of precutting all the lumber is that accurate cutting is extremely important if the platforms and stairs are to stand firmly, and if the different units of scenery are to fit together properly. Furthermore, cutting accurately requires some skill. If it were done by beginning workmen, as would be the case if each person cut the lumber for his own project, a good deal of supervision would have to be provided. It is much more efficient to assign all of the cutting for the set to the more experienced members of the staff.

Precutting requires that a list be prepared showing the lengths of all boards needed for the set. If the designer has included cutting lists on his drawings, they can be copied and organized in a single list. Otherwise, the list will have to be prepared by recording the various board lengths and counting the number of each needed, on the basis of the designer's working drawings. This should be done unit by unit. In particular, care should be taken to multiply by the number of units needed. For instance, if supports for stairs are mirror images, the designer may draw only one, and add a note indicating that another must also be built, reversed. The board count must then be multiplied by two; or, if five identical platforms are needed, he will draw only one, so that the number of boards of each length must be multiplied by five.

When all of the boards of various dimensions have been recorded, a master list should be prepared. If more than one size of lumber is used, a separate list should be made for each (1 × 3s, 1 × 4s, 2 × 4s, etc.) (Figure 17.1). Within each list, the dimensions should be given in descending order. Cutting the longest first will prevent all the longer boards' being cut up into the shorter lengths. In addition, it will probably be possible to cut many of the shorter boards from scrap left from cutting the longer ones, so that the scrap can be used up immediately and need not be measured, marked, and returned to the lumber racks.

As each group of boards of a particular length are cut, they should be neatly stacked on the floor or a bench. It will be easier for the workers to find the boards they need if the stacks are arranged in order by size. The length of each board should be marked as it is cut. A great deal of time will be lost if the workers must measure a series of boards in order to find the lengths they need. The marking is somewhat irksome, and someone is sure to suggest that only the top board in each pile need be dimensioned, but that is the first board that will be picked up when construction begins. Instead, each one must be labeled. The marking should be done in chalk or pencil, about in the center of one face. Grease pencil must not be used, since it will resist painting, and a felt pen mark is difficult to cover. The foot and inch symbols can be omitted, but a hyphen should be placed between the two numbers; although the writing can be done very quickly, it should be legible. A dimension which cannot be read is useless, and an ambiguous one which was misread by the workers could cause considerable trouble if the board was used in a structure requiring a board of a different length.

The cutting proceeds most efficiently if it is done by two people. One worker sets each new board up on the table, removes it after it has been cut, marks it, and sets it aside. The other worker aligns each board with the guide which has been nailed to the saw table, cuts it, and pushes the waste piece aside on to the floor.

CUTTING LIST FOR <u>THE IMAGINARY INVALID</u>

<u>1 x 3</u>

12'-0"	cut 3
10'-0" − 1W	2
9'-6" − 1W	2
8'-10"	4
8'-0"	4
8'-0" − 2W	4
7'-11¾" − 1W	4
5'-2"	6
4'-8½"	2
½ of (8'-0" − 3W)	16
3'-8"	4
3'-10" − 2W	4
2'-10½"	10
2'-11¼" − 1W	20
2'-9"	4
2'-3¾"	1
2'-0"	4
1'-11½"	1
1'-10½"	4
1'-9¾"	6
1'-9"	32
1'-8¼"	14
1'-7½"	16
1'-6½"	1
1'-6"	44
1'-5¾"	64
1'-5¼"	13
1'-5"	24
1'-4¾"	18
1'-4½"	10

1'-9" − 2W	4
1'-2¾"	17
1'-2½"	1
1'-5¼" − 1W	12
½ of (2'-10½" − 3W)	4
1'-0"	7
1'-5¼" − 2W	8
11¼"	12
10"	1
9"	11
8"	4
7½"	14
7¼"	6
6¼"	10
5½"	1
5¼"	8

<u>1 x 2</u>

1'-5"	8
2'-10¼"	2

<u>1 x 1</u>

12'-0"	7
1'-0"	14
Width of a 1 x 3	24

<u>1/4" Plywood</u>

8" x 7'-11¾"	4
8" x 3'-6"	2
8" x 3'-4½"	2
7¾" x 8'-0"	2

<u>1/2" Plywood</u>

2'-0" x 8'-0"	3
2'-0" x 2'-6"	1
1'-0" x 8'-0"	9
1'-0" x 6'-0"	5
1'-0" x 4'-0"	1
1'-0" x 3'-0"	3

<u>3/4" Plywood</u>

2'-0" x 3'-0"	2
1'-5" x 3'-0"	4
1'-5" x 1'-10½"	4
1'-¾" x 2'-0"	2
1'-0" x 2'-0"	2
9" x (1'-6" + width of a 1 x 3)	7
6" x 8'-0"	4
6" x 4'-4"	2
5¼" x 4'-9"	1
5¼" x 5'-2"	1
5" x 4'-4½"	1
1½" x the width of a 1 x 3	24

The following items are omitted from the cutting list:

corner-blocks

cove molding

pieces of plywood with curved edges

diagonal braces

lumber for furniture.

FIGURE 17.1   A cutting list.

A few pieces can be cut more efficiently during construction, especially diagonal braces which must be specially fitted to the frame of the flat or platform. Whether plywood is precut or not depends on the sizes and shapes of the pieces needed. There is some satisfaction in having all possible lumber precut, but since most plywood must be cut with a saber saw or a portable circular saw, little or no time is saved. Of course, a full supply of corner-blocks should already be on the shelves, and if the stock has run short, it should be replenished as part of the preliminary cutting, using the radial-arm saw.

THE ORDER OF CONSTRUCTION

The actors' need for scenery during rehearsal varies for the different types of scenic elements. Substitute furniture is nearly always used during rehearsal, with a table representing a sideboard, and three or four chairs set side by side as a substitute for a sofa. So long as the position of the flats is marked on the floor, with the door openings indicated, the actors can practice their paths of movement effectively. The scenic units which they need most are those which provide different levels of support. An actor can remind himself that he will eventually be stepping up on a low platform, if the outline is marked on the stage floor, but it is difficult for him to practice walking up a flight of stairs unless they are actually present, and if a high platform is included in the set which some actors will stand on and other actors will walk under, rehearsal is almost impossible unless the platform is provided. Even a low ramp requires actors to make use of their muscles in an unusual way, which is difficult to rehearse on the stage floor. And from the director's standpoint, any differences in height of the areas on which the actors will stand and walk significantly affect their visual relationships and the stage picture as a whole.

For those reasons, platforms, ramps, and stairs should be provided for the cast at the earliest possible moment. They should be the first units built, and they should be delivered to the stage as soon as they are braced and usable. Often it is more convenient to delay finishing the platforms until late in the construction process (padding, canvassing, covering the side surfaces), but so long as the actors can use them, that will not interfere with rehearsal. It may be possible to assemble substitute platforms taken from stock for the first half-week of rehearsals, even if they are not exactly the right size. They should be the correct height if at all possible, but if the floor area is larger than the platforms which will actually be used, the excess can be extended off stage, and the dimensions of the final platforms marked with masking tape. Often it will be possible to place substitute step units next to the platforms so that the actors can rehearse with them, even if they are of different width than those which will be built for the show. This is especially true for off-stage access stairs.

Any scenic units which are important to the action of the play should be built next. For example, in *Hedda Gabler* the actress playing the title role must burn a manuscript in a stove, which should be provided as early as possible in the rehearsal period. The barrels out of which actors must climb in *Rosencrantz and Guildenstern Are Dead* should also be scheduled for early construction, so that the actors can have them to practice with.

Once the special rehearsal needs have been met, the remaining work can be scheduled at the convenience of the set crew. Usually flats are built, repaired, hinged together, and dutchmanned as the next major step in construction. Miscellaneous jobs, such as furniture construction, architectural decorative elements, and any large properties which have been assigned to the set crew are built last.

PAINTING

Painting begins only after the construction work has been finished. Both construction and painting require a good deal of work space, and trying to do both at once is likely to create interference. In addition, some of the same colors of paint may be used for very different scenic elements, and there is a saving of both time and paint if all of the colors are mixed at the same time, with the added advantage that it is easier to see the relationships among the various colors, and so to ensure a consistent color scheme. Following this sequence of work rigidly would result in some loss of time. If more workers are available than are needed for flat construction, the extra ones should be given projects even though the theoretical list indicates that they would be started only after the flat work had been completed.

THE WORK LIST

The technical director's analysis of the set work for the production should be combined in a master list, carefully typed, and posted on a bulletin board in the scene shop before the start of the first work session (Figure 17.2). The individual projects should be listed in the order in which they are to be done, the time estimate for each indicated, and a space provided for writing in the names of the workers to whom each project is assigned. These names should be recorded on the list as soon as the assignment is made, so that two workers will not unnecessarily build duplicates of the same

WORK LIST FOR <u>THE IMAGINARY INVALID</u>

The number of workers suggested for each project is given in brackets; the figures
at the right are estimates of the number of man-hours required for the projects.

Precutting .... Work hours: 26	Pillars: Painting [4-6] 17	Steps [2] 6
Cutting 1" lumber [2] 6		Small 2
Cutting plywood [2-10] 20		Large 4
	Base coat 2	Furniture: Desk [2] 7½
	Graining 1	
	Molding 14	Cut lumber 2
	Door frames [2] 9	Assemble 4
		Paint 1½
Flats: Preliminary work [3] 9	Build 5	Furniture: Desk chair [2] 7
	Add molding 1	
Pull from scene dock 3	Paint base coat & spatter ... 1	Cut lumber 2½
Repair as needed 4	Paint molding 2	Assemble 3
Build & canvas 2 headers 2	Doors [2-4] 13½	Paint 1½
Flats: Hinge & dutchman [6-8] 35		Furniture: Arm chair [2] 12½
	Build 4	Cut lumber 3
	Add molding 4	Assemble 5
	Paint base coat & spatter ... 1	Paint 1½
Mix paint [2-3] 8	Paint molding 4	Upholster 3
	Cornice [12] 36	Furniture: Sofa [2] 21
		Cut lumber 4
Flats: Paint [6-8] 15		Assemble 4
		Add papier-maché 4
		Glue on ornamental rope 2
		Paint 2
Base coat 6	Cut plywood 6	Upholster 5
Spatter 3	Assemble plywood & frame 8	Transport scenery to the theater
Wallpaper pattern 6	Add facing 4	[full crew] 30
Nail molding on flats [2] 4	Paint base coat & spatter ... 3	Assemble scenery on stage [full
	Glue on ornamental rope 6	crew] 35
Thickness for arch [2] 5	Paint decoration 8	
	Ceiling [4] 9½	Total hours estimated 338
Assemble 4		Work begins ..... Monday, September 29
Paint 1	Assemble 6	Number of work days (including
Pillars: Construction [4] 25	Dutchman cracks 1½	Saturday, November 8, but ex-
	Paint base coat & spatter ... 2	cluding all other Saturdays &
Make braces 3	Platforms [4] 6	Sundays) 31
Assemble flats & braces 6		Number of man-hours of work
Bases and capitals:		which must be completed each
Fasten on 1" lumber 4	Small 2	work day 11
Add molding 6	Large 4	
Add fluting 6		

FIGURE 17.2   A work list and sign-up sheet.

unit of scenery because neither is aware that the other is working on it. The total number of work-hours needed for the set should be indicated at the bottom of the list, as well as the amount of work which must be completed each day. As projects are finished, they should be marked off the list and the total changed to indicate the work remaining. The deadline for completion of the entire set should also be stated.

Occasionally, the preparation of these plans and schedules may seem like irksome busywork. It is not, and even if several hours are required to do it well, days of work may be saved and unnecessary crises prevented.

SCENE-SHOP MAINTENANCE

The pressure of stagecraft work varies throughout the season. Construction begins about six weeks before a play is scheduled to open, and the quantity and intensity of the work typically rise slowly, with a sharp spurt during the last week before the technical rehearsal. The run of the show provides a lull, interrupted by strike, which may be followed by a week or two before work is started on the next show.

Ideally, the work should proceed at a calm and uniform pace, but such an ideal is seldom achieved. Nevertheless, everything possible should be done to reduce the pressure during the peak periods. Work which can be postponed without interfering with the construction or damaging the equipment should be scheduled for the slack periods, for example sorting hardware, labeling and storing scrap lumber, and repairing tools.

The run of the show should be used for putting the scene shop back in order, provided the crew is still sane and has not physically collapsed. Even with efficient workers, a good deal of maintenance must be done after strike, including a general inspection of the entire area and a correction of any errors in storage, as well as at least an informal inventory inspection, so that any missing tools or materials in short supply can be replaced or replenished.

All of this must inevitably be done. If, as is common, it is let go until after work is started on the next show, it must be done under the worst conditions, and as an interruption of the new construction. Scheduling maintenance for the slack periods not only relieves pressure at other times, but helps establish a general policy of businesslike efficiency, and facilitates the work for the next production.

18

Supervising the Staff

In the educational theater, the technical director may be most vividly aware of the necessity of getting the current set built and assembled. Yet, his responsibility for training the workers is at least as important, and it can be argued that it is more important. The theater work is a part of the educational program as a whole. Most often the technical director is officially a part of the teaching staff, and even for workers not enrolled in his stagecraft course the basic raison d'etre of the program is to contribute to the students' educational growth.

New workers display varying degrees of skill and experience. Some may have worked on scenery for high school or community theater plays, some may be accomplished carpenters or painters, others may have had no related experiences. These differences are not as great as they might seem, however. The techniques used in the theater are so different from those used in other types of carpentry and painting that nontheatrical experience may even be a slight handicap—some skills will have to be unlearned before the theatrical methods can be mastered. Certainly, many new workers are likely to be entirely unfamiliar with scene shop procedures.

PRELIMINARY TRAINING

Such people are likely to feel extremely hesitant and uncertain; they need to be assured that they will be given all of the assistance they need, and that lack of experience is only a minute handicap, if it is any at all. As a preliminary to work, each one should be given a tour of the work areas, and the different processes involved in constructing scenery should be explained, preferably illustrated by pulling out flats and other units as examples of the work. If some crew members are already engaged in projects, they can be used as examples of the type of work which is done.

SELECTING A PROJECT

The new staff member should then be taken back to the cutting room and the designer's drawings for the current set displayed and discussed. The perspective drawing or painting should be examined first, and then the ground plan. Next the working drawings should be discussed, project by project. The worker should be assisted in selecting a project for himself, and although his preference should be given precedence, an effort should be made to find one of the easier assignments.

The apprentice system is usually followed in the educational or community theater, with the more experienced workers training and assisting the new crew members. Unless the inexperienced worker has a strong preference for a one-person project, it is much better if he can work with a small group of the more skilled workmen, so that he can have help immediately available whenever he needs it, without having to stop and find a supervisor each time a question arises. Before he joins the group, the drawings for his particular project should be studied in detail, the order of work described, and any special difficulties pointed out.

ASSISTANCE FOR NEW WORKERS

New crew members vary greatly in their contribution to the work. Some require so much supervision and assistance that the group actually functions more slowly than if they were not involved; others, after brief initial training may contribute almost as much as the fully experienced crew members. Probably on the average, the time spent in training new people is approximately balanced by the amount of work they do—they neither delay nor speed up the work. However, the training is a vitally important part of the program. They can be expected to make a significant contribution to the work for later shows, and since the most experienced workers are graduated at the end of each school year, the continuance of the program requires that new workers be added each season.

Workers should be given all of the assistance they need or want, but they should not feel that they are under constant or belligerent surveillance. Especially at the start of his first project, the technical director or a member of his supervisory staff should stay with the new worker, giving any necessary instructions, and observing until it is apparent that he can function effectively on his own. After that, the supervisor should walk by every half hour or so to check on how the work is progressing. One member of the supervisory staff should be precisely identified for the beginner as the person to approach for assistance (preferably the most experienced person who will be working on the same project), and the other supervisors should be pointed out as also available for help at any time.

Whenever the work of a new crew member is checked, he should be given a report. If the work is progressing well, he should be told so, and if he has handled any particularly difficult or tricky detail effectively, that should be pointed out. On the other hand, if errors are discovered they should be explained to him, and the method for correcting them described. If necessary the supervisor should demonstrate by doing some of the work himself, explaining the reason for using one technique rather than another. The ideal impression should be that reported by one novice worker, who said, "The technical director didn't watch me all the time, but whenever I needed help, he was available."

The supervisors need not expect almost total ignorance from beginners, but they should be prepared for it. No one is born knowing how to build scenery. The methods, techniques, and skills must be learned, and although long experience may make the work automatic, the supervisory staff, including the technical director himself, were also once novices. Ignorance in fact is the least troublesome and most easily corrected of handicaps (some others are much more serious). If a crew member does not know the difference between a lash cleat and a brace cleat, cannot identify a foot-iron, does not know that corner-blocks are sized by the short sides of the triangle rather than the hypotenuse, has not learned how to spatter—all of these and the thousands of similar items of information can be taught him.

It may be more surprising to find that students have not mastered more ordinary skills, such as driving nails and screws. For example, sometimes workers are unaware of the fact that the shaft of the screwdriver must be directly in line with the screw, and especially if the screw has been set slightly crooked, may hold the screwdriver at right angles to the surface of the board rather than in line with the screw, so that the blade keeps slipping out of the slot. Other workers will attempt to pull a nail out of a board with the claws of the hammer at right angles to the edge, so that the head of the hammer is pressed against the air instead of firmly against the surface of the board. When gaps of information appear, or inefficient techniques are observed, the supervisors should provide the information, describe and demonstrate the correct methods—and explain why they are better.

MORALE IN THE SCENE SHOP

New workers are likely to feel extremely uncertain of themselves and their ability to do the work, and apprehensive of their treatment. Few things are more destructive of efficiency than an atmosphere of censoriousness and tension. Not only will the immediate work be hampered, but crew members will avoid asking for help when it is needed, so that mistakes will have to be corrected after the fact, rather than having been prevented, and the workers are likely to avoid taking part in future productions, and so be lost to the program. Every worker should be assured, not so much directly as by the continuing treatment he receives, that any honest question will be answered respectfully, that supervision will be carried on only so long as it is actually needed, that assistance is readily available whenever he wants it, and that work well done will be recognized and appreciated, and that he will be given credit for it. It is at least as important to point out work well done as it is to prevent or correct errors.

On the other hand, the maintenance of an atmosphere of fatuous euphoria, unrelated to the work actually being done, makes no contribution to the educational goals of the program, and does not increase either the quality or quantity of the product. Certainly there are many types of behavior which should not be tolerated, and which should lead to firm and vivid censure. A worker who displays carelessness, who interferes with the work of others, who does not bother to pick up spilled nails or return his tools to storage at the end of a work session, who tosses supplies into the wrong containers, who ignores established scene shop policies, particularly with regard to safety, who is unconcerned about meeting established standards for the quality of his work, who does significantly less than his reasonable best—such a worker should have his behavior described for him in graphic and picturesque terms, preferably with dramatic gestures and a somewhat elevated tone of voice. A technical director who feels impatience with someone who is doing close to his best work should also feel ashamed of himself. To express his impatience would be inexcusable; but coddling a careless and negligent worker by patting him on the head and making soothing coos of undeserved approval can only damage the efficiency of the scene shop, and is likely to lead the worker, quite correctly, to question the intelligence of his supervisor.

There are of course limits to the ability of every worker, and occasionally crew members may simply be unable to carry out some of the tasks necessary to building scenery. Such limitations may be intellectual or emotional, but they are likely to be most obvious in the case of people with physical handicaps. Every effort should be made to provide them with assignments within their ability. One technical director cites the example of a very pleasant and capable young woman who had to wear leg braces because of childhood polio. Although she could not climb ladders or carry heavy weights, she was able to do almost every other kind of scene shop work, and made a valuable member of the crew. In another theater, a young man with a back injury who walked with canes asked if he might take part in the set work. There was some difficulty in adjusting tasks to his physical limitations, which required that nearly all of his work be done sitting down, but with a little searching jobs were found for him. For one play, he built a number of complexly designed and ornamented stools, not only very skillfully but with evident enjoyment. As a matter of fact, physically handicapped crew members will often work better than others, provided the work can be done within their limitations.

MAINTAINING INTEREST

Most scene shop work involves drudgery, often the repetition of a single task four or five or even hundreds of times. However, the crew members' enthusiasm and interest in the work may transform it into an enjoyable experience. One technical director reports many such instances in his experience. In one theater, a student had been assigned a difficult and complicated project which the director assumed would be irritatingly uninteresting. When the work had been half completed, he decided that he would finish it himself out of sympathy, but on arriving at the scene shop he found a note prominently taped to the structure which read: "Please don't let anyone else work on this; I want to finish it myself!" It is not surprising that the student later enrolled in graduate school to prepare himself for a career as a technical director.

In another theater, two fellows and a girl were assigned as their first set project to make one of five twelve-foot ornamental trees for a set, a tedious and irksome task. When the work was completed and approved by the technical director, he suggested that they might prefer some more interesting project for their next assignment, leaving the other trees to other workers; instead, they asked as a special favor that they be allowed to build all of them themselves, a project which they completed so well that the director of the theater asked that the trees be preserved as part of the permanent scenic stock.

Much of the interest in such work, especially for new staff members, comes from the discovery that they can do well things they did not know they could do at all—one of life's most gratifying experiences. Nevertheless, every effort should be made to spread the especially repetitious and uninteresting assignments among the crew so that no one has to do more than his share.

SCENE SHOP POLICIES

Every scene shop should have a series of clear-cut and emphatically announced policies, preferably posted conspicuously on the wall, and explained to each new crew member.

400

Every rule must clearly pay its way by contributing to the pleasantness, safety, or efficiency of the work; if there is doubt about the necessity of a particular policy, it should be omitted. But the kind of person who loves rules for their own sake, who feels most comfortable when everyone is thoroughly trussed up in yards of red tape, is unlikely to choose the theater as a profession; scene shops are more likely to err in having too few formal policies rather than too many.

SAFETY

A fundamental and overriding rule should be that all work must be done safely. Workers should be instructed that if they are in doubt about whether an operation is safe or not, they should not do it. It is better for the work not to be finished than for someone to be injured. This rule should take precedence over all other considerations. At best every scene shop involves some hazards, and they should be avoided not simply sensibly but fanatically; workers who violate this rule should be reprimanded with emphatic force, and if they continue to violate it, they should be barred from the theater. Leaving boards on the floor with nails point up, stretching out far past a ladder instead of moving it to a safe position, holding a board close to the saw blade while cutting it—these and any other dangerous practices should be stopped instantly.

> Before starting to work in the scene shop, every worker should have a series of antitetanus shots. Even a single shot provides some protection, but a full series is required for immunity; booster shots are needed at intervals. This is good advice for everyone, but especially for scene shop workers, for whom cuts, scratches, and splinters are fairly common, and stepping on a nail not unknown.

A fully outfitted first-aid kit should be part of the scene shop equipment; it should be stored in a conspicuous and easily accessible place and should be pointed out to every worker during his introductory tour of the area. If there is no telephone in the scene shop itself, the location of the nearest phone should be typed in duplicate, and one copy taped to the lid of the first aid kit and the other on the wall just above where it is kept. A card should be fastened beside the phone giving the number of the nearest clinic, and the number of a hospital to call for ambulance service. Of course, it is hoped that true emergencies will not arise, and in a well run shop there is a good chance that they never will, but if help must be summoned it should not be necessary to take even a few extra seconds to look through the phone book for the number to call.

In a conversation with the distinguished set designer, Mr. Jo Mielziner, he reported a freak accident in which a stagecraft worker was seriously injured while using a circular power saw. The scene shop was lit by fluorescent fixtures which emit light in flashes rather than continuously, as do incandescent lamps. Although the individual flashes are too brief to be seen by the eye, they happened to be synchronized with the speed of the saw blade, so that it seemed not to be moving, and since noisy work was being done in the shop the worker was unable to hear the sound of the saw, and was cut by a blade which he believed to be standing still. Although this was an unusual accident, it would be safer to follow Mr. Mielziner's advice and use only incandescent lights in the scene shop.

STORAGE

Maintenance of materials and tools in good order has already been stressed. Workmen should be instructed to return all equipment to its proper place at the end of each work session. Having to hunt for a stapler left carelessly under a platform on stage can easily eat up a full hour better spent in productive work; putting it away would require only a few seconds. This rule is most likely to be violated at moments of stress, when work has fallen behind schedule, but it is exactly at those times that the policy is most important.

NEATNESS

Neatness and cleanliness should be the rule in the scene shop; they contribute greatly to the pleasantness of the work, and make at least a small contribution to efficiency. All scraps should be put in containers, preferably as they accumulate but at least at the end of every work session. Finished projects should be stored out of the way, units in progress moved to clear the work space, and the entire area swept. At moments of extreme crisis, when even an extra half hour is not available for cleaning, it may occasionally be acceptable to leave a moderate mess for another day, but the regular procedure should be always to quit work early enough to straighten and clean the shop.

402

MISUSE OF EQUIPMENT

Workers should be discouraged from putting small tools in their pockets, especially tapes. Without any intention of theft, it is too easy to forget them when leaving the theater and too difficult to remember to bring them back. They should be trained to use tools and materials so as to avoid damage or waste.

USE OF PAINT

It should be emphasized that special mixes of paint must not be used for other than their intended purposes without the permission of the technical director. Similarly, small quantities of special mixes should not be discarded until after the last performance of the play—they may be needed for touching up the scenery if it should get damaged.

Napoleon is said to have pulled a noblewoman aside to make way for a worker carrying a heavy load, with the remark, "Respect the burden, madam." A fundamental principle of theater etiquette is that anyone who is working takes precedence over anyone who is not. Visitors, casual observers, or even supervisors, including the director and technical director, are expected to keep out of the way of crew members while they are working, and, for example, must move back to make room for a flat or platform to be carried past—the workers need not walk around them or wait for them to finish their conversation. Of course, if nonworkers are not aware that they are in the way, a warning call should be given, but it is they who must step aside, not the workmen.

Most workers can be safely presumed to have a good supply of common sense. The policies adopted should cover real needs, but they should be minimal, and the supervisor can rely on the workers' sound judgment to supplement them.

THE PERSONALITIES OF WORKERS

Good stagecraft workers display a particular pattern of personal, intellectual, and emotional characteristics; ineffectiveness may be due to a variety of causes. One experienced technical director reports his astonishment at the discovery of how complex the factors are which are involved in set work. He said, "When I first started building scenery, I assumed it was a relatively impersonal activity, in which people might differ in the degree of muscular control and strength, but which would not involve emotional or intellectual factors in any great degree. I found differently during my first season, and have had my error demonstrated over and over again throughout the following years."

Building scenery is a highly specialized activity, and personal characteristics affect it enormously. And of all the factors, muscular control and strength are among the least significant. Even in lifting weights, as one technical director has put it, "You lift with your mind at least as much as with your muscles."

INTELLECTUAL PATTERNS

Intellectual habits are of great significance. Most scenic work involves the application of established techniques, which can be learned. But almost all sets present some problems which cannot be solved by textbook methods, but which must be analyzed individually, and for which innovative solutions must be found. An effective worker must display two characteristics which are not contradictory but which supplement each other. He must have a capacity for learning a large number of standard methods, and at the same time must be able to approach unusual problems imaginatively. A worker who is impatient with established methods will waste enormous amounts of time inventing new solutions to problems which have already been solved; and one who cannot do independent analysis and original thinking will be unable to handle the new situations which arise during every show.

Even applying standard techniques requires constant observation, analysis, and decision. A worker who memorizes established methods in their simplest form and applies them without thought will often be wrong. Scene-shop decisions must be purposeful. Even with familiar methods, there are nearly always several ways to do something, and the worker must choose the one which best serves the immediate purpose —which provides the proper support, which conserves materials, which produces the intended visual effect. A worker who habitually fails to observe, to analyze his materials and methods, and to draw sound conclusions will often build unacceptably.

ENCOURAGING INDEPENDENCE

Even normal workers, without special emotional problems or odd intellectual attitudes, are likely to display an initial overdependence on the assistance of others, because of the uncertainty produced by the strangeness of the scene shop and their unfamiliarity with the work. Demonstrating to them the importance of analytical and creative thinking in their work is at least as important as giving them specific instructions or information about established techniques. If time allows, the alternative methods available for solving the present problem should be discussed with them, and the full process of observation, analysis, and decision displayed with regard to the difficulty which has led them to ask for help. The importance of sound thinking should be emphasized, perhaps by direct statement but certainly by demonstration, and they should be encouraged to think for themselves as actively and soundly as they can.

One young woman spent thousands of hours in the scene shop, working superbly, in fact at a level of effectiveness unsurpassed by any other worker in the experience of the technical director. Curiously, she frequently (about once a week) remarked that she was not interested in the theater, and did not intend to continue working in it after graduation. Nevertheless, she worked not only during the regular semesters, but also during one Christmas vacation, and even came back for a few days' work during the summer after she had transferred to another college. On the last day she announced, "This is it; I'm never going to work in the theater again." The technical director, who had been increasingly puzzled by her devotion to the program in spite of her announced lack of interest in the theater, decided he must ask for an explanation before she disappeared forever into the humdrum activities of ordinary life. She said, "I visited the scene shop first out of curiosity—I wanted to see what was going on here. When I walked in, one person was working alone, and I stayed to help. But I kept on working because this is the only place, outside my home, where my judgment is really valued."

Few people who have been actively involved in the theater can actually leave it entirely behind. She not only changed her career plans and became a speech correctionist, but she married a technical director. But the decisive factor was that her judgment was in fact superb, and that she had been encouraged to use it in theater work.

Not all crew members are able to think quite so soundly or freely, but analytical and creative thinking are the most vital elements in stagecraft. It is not muscular skill which distinguishes between an outstanding worker and a mediocre or poor worker—it is thinking. Just as effective lifting depends as much on mind as muscle, so if nails bend, boards split, platforms collapse, it is because the workmen have made the wrong decisions. It is possible, of course, for the supervisory staff to do all the thinking for the workers (now put the next nail there; you should use a halved joint instead of a lap joint for that corner; better check the squareness once more, because the boards may have shifted when you drove that last nail; we'd better clear a path before you pick up that platform and start to walk off with it)—but to do that would require providing a supervisor for each worker, and production would drop rather than rise. In a short-term crisis it may be necessary to make firm, unexplained decisions for the workers, but for the long stretch nothing contributes more to the quantity and quality of set work than training the crew members in sound decision making, and encouraging them to do it.

IDENTIFYING ERRORS

Many beginners, even those who will later become effective workers, get into difficulties because they do not check on themselves closely enough. The projects may seem simpler than they really are, and the workers are likely to assume unjustifiably that they can remember a series of dimensions correctly, that they know how boards are to be arranged for joining, that they can easily distinguish between the top and bottom of a row of flats. One experienced technical director has said, only half facetiously, "The only real superiority I have over ordinary crew members is that I expect to make mistakes, and they expect not to." It takes only a few seconds to glance back at a working drawing during construction and verify that the leg really should be nailed on top of the crosspiece rather than the reverse, or that the board should actually be 7'-8" long instead of 8'-7", but one error caused by a failure to check can require an hour or more to correct. In fact, one of the distinguishing marks of a skilled worker is that he refers constantly to his working drawings during construction, rather than analyzing them once and then laying them aside.

AVOIDANCE OF DECISION

Emotional patterns greatly affect scene shop work. One brilliant worker volunteered the fact that he had been physically punished as a child for making decisions ("Who do you think you are—you got a mind of your own?"). As a result, he had come to associate fear with situations in which even the smallest decisions were required, so much so that he could not make such simple choices as where to best drive nails, but had to have assistance at every moment. That is an extreme case, of course, and yet many people have a fundamental emotional pattern which leads them to avoid making independent judgments, and to rely always on the opinions of others.

EMOTIONAL CONSERVATISM

Other people have a strong preference for the repetition of familiar patterns. There are two ways to cut cardboard with a razor blade. One method is slow and inaccurate, and quickly makes the finger sore; the other method is faster, more accurate, and can be used for at least three or four hours without injuring the finger. One technical director reports that he has explained and demonstrated the preferred method to at least half a dozen workers who acknowledged its superiority but who chose to continue with the less effective technique simply because it was more familiar. This attitude, which might be described as emotional conservatism, the preference for the familiar as opposed to the new, overriding any practical considerations, is of course a severe handicap for stagecraft workers.

THE IDEAL WORKER

Set work requires alertness, the habit of observation, analysis, and decision, and flexibility in the application of familiar techniques and in the solution of new problems. It requires the ability to be self-directing, to work independently without constant supervision, to work well under direction, to supervise others, and at the same time to work cooperatively as a member of a group with shared purposes. It will be seen that this pattern of characteristics is generally admirable, and good stagecraft workers as a group are very fine people indeed.

The rewards of set work are many. New workers discover that they have unsuspected skills, and they have the pleasure of steadily acquiring new ones. Both individual achievement and the sharing of work are part of the experience. The atmosphere is generally both relaxed and bustling, and often involves at least short periods during which the crew pushes ahead with intensity. The finished scenery in performance always surprises the workers by looking a great deal more attractive and effective than they had expected while they were building it in the scene shop, and their justifiable pride in achievement makes even the occasional crises pleasant to remember.

Aside from all of these things is the pleasure of the work itself, the odor of the resin in the lumber, the gratification at seeing formless materials take meaningful and attractive shape under the hand, and of course the camaraderie which almost without exception characterizes a well-run scene shop, and which may turn the workers into theater enthusiasts for life. It is understandable that the chairman of one college department should have said, "I hate to have my students start working in the theater, because in most cases I never see them again."

Index

The page numbers of illustrations are given in italics.